Read to

3/1

MILESTONES IN WESTERN CIVILIZATION:
SELECTED READINGS

Volume I: Ancient Greece Through the Middle Ages

edited with introductions by
JOAN MICKELSON-GAUGHAN

The Scarecrow Press, Inc.
Metuchen, N.J., & London
1990

British Library Cataloguing-in-Publication data available

Library of Congress Cataloging-in-Publication Data

Milestones in Western Civilization : selected readings / edited with introductions by Joan Mickelson-Gaughan.
    p.   cm.
  Contents: v. 1. Ancient Greece through the Middle Ages.
  ISBN 0-8108-2188-5 (alk. paper)
  1. Civilization, Occidental--History--Sources. I. Mickelson-Gaughan, Joan, 1940-
CB245.M496 1990
909'.09821--dc20   90-46171

Copyright © 1990 by Joan Mickelson-Gaughan
Manufactured in the United States of America
Printed on acid-free paper

In Memory of Ellen Lee, My Friend.

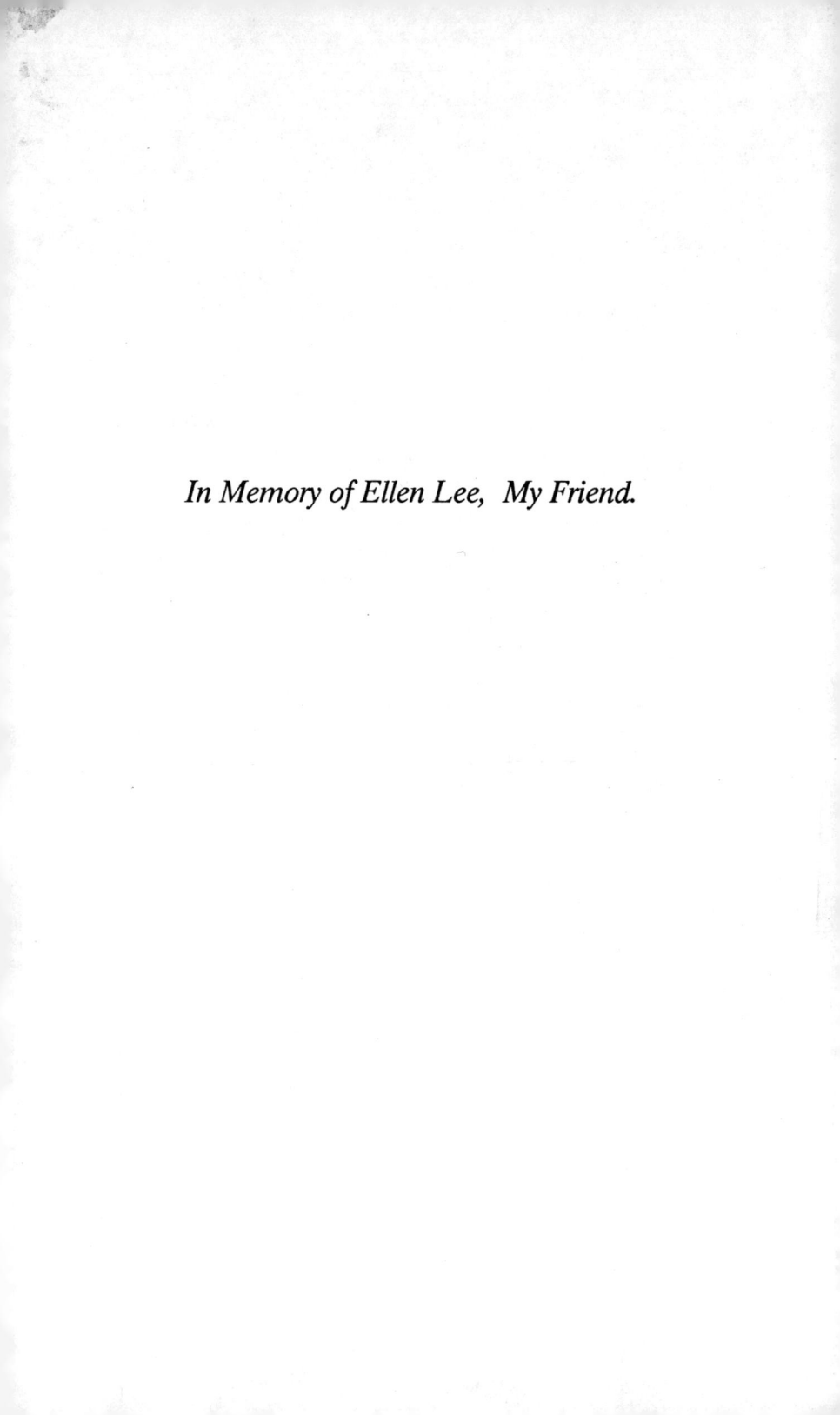

TABLE OF CONTENTS

I. The Formation of Greece 1

    Homer from The Iliad 12
    Homer from The Odyssey 19
    Plutarch on The Customs of the
        Lacedaemonians 24
    Herodotus from The Histories 27
    Thucydides from History of the
        Peloponnesian War 35

II. Greek Philosophy and Art 42

    Plato from The Republic 52
    Aristotle from The Nicomachean Ethics 59
    Sappho, Lyrics 66
    Sophocles from Antigone 69
    Aristophanes from Lysistrata 80

III. The Hellenistic Age 88

    Plutarch on Alexander The Great 95
    Theocritus, "The Desperate Lover" 98

IV. The Roman Republic. 509-27 B.C. 102

    From the Twelve Tables 114
    Livy from History of Rome 121
    Plutarch on Cato the Elder 127
    Julius Caesar from The Civil War 132
    Catullus, Poems 137
    Cicero from On Moral Duties 140

V. The Roman Empire. 27 B.C.-476 A.D. 145

Cicero from The Laws 156
Virgil from The Aeneid 160
Virgil, Eclogue IV 165
Horace, Ode 168
Ovid from The Art of Love 171
Petronius from Satyricon 177
Marcus Aurelius Antoninus
   from Meditations 181

VI. Early Christianity 185

From the Sermon on the Mount 193
Saint Paul from First Letter to the
   Corinthians 194
The Edict of Milan 197
Theodosius I's Edict on Catholic and
   Heretic 200
Saint Jerome's Dream 201
Tertullian on "Women's Dress" 204
From Rule of Saint Benedict 207
Saint Augustine from The Confessions 213
Saint Augustine from City of God 218
Gregory I's Instruction to
   Augustine, 601 A.D. 221

VII. Early Middle Ages 224

Tacitus from Germania 231
The Trial By Ordeal 235
Gregory of Tours, from History of the
   Franks 239
From the Quran 243
Donation of Pepin, 756 246
Boethius from Consolation of
   Philosophy 248
Saint Bede from A History of the
   English Church and People 256
From Beowulf 259

VIII. Charlemagne ... 263

Einhard from Life of Charlemagne ... 269
From a Capitulary of Charlemagne ... 274
The Strassbourg Oaths, 842 ... 279
Treaty of Verdun ... 282
The Norsemen Invade Europe ... 283

IX. Medieval Society ... 285

Feudal Charter, 1110 ... 296
Survey of Dues from Hurstbourne Priory ... 300
Articles of the Spurriers Guild of London ... 302
Decrees of the Hanseatic
  League, 1260-1264 ... 306
William Fitz-Stephen, Description of
  Medieval London, 1173 ... 308

X. The Development of Medieval States ... 312

From the Domesday Book ... 322
From Magna Carta, 1215 ... 325
Election of Hugh Capet, 987 ... 333
Philip Augustus Acquires Vermandois ... 336
Jean de Joinville on Louis IX ... 339
Salimbene on "The Follies of
  Frederick II" ... 342

XI. Reform and Revival Within the Church ... 346

From the 1059 Reform Decrees ... 354
Dictatus Papae, 1075 ... 358
The Deposition of Gregory VII
  by Henry IV, 1076 ... 362
Concordat of Worms, 1122 ... 365
Pope Urban II Calls the First
  Crusade, 1095 ... 368
Innocent III on Papal Authority, 1198 ... 373
St. Francis of Assisi, Prayer ... 375

XII. The Schools and Scholasticism 376

    Frederick Barbarossa Protects
        Students, 1158 383
    Student Songs 385
    St. Anselm Proves the Existence of God 388
    Abelard from Sic et Non 390
    Thomas Aquinas from the Summa
        Theologica 393

XIII. Medieval Culture 399

    Dante Alighieri from the
        Divine Comedy 406
    From the Romance of the Rose 414
    Troubadour Lyrics 417
    Geoffrey Chaucer from
        Canterbury Tales 420
    "Cuckoo's Song" 424
    Dies Irae (Day of Wrath) 426
    Miracles of the Virgin 429

GENERAL INTRODUCTION

History, besides being exciting, is challenging. We are all locked into a tiny corner of the universe, a tiny slice of time. We are finite. We cannot see very far ahead. Despite our best efforts, we may only very dimly get a sense of where we are going as individuals, as a nation, as a part of the human community. But we can know the past. In fact, we can know it rather well and we are the only creatures on this planet who can. And the present and the future, so history teaches us, contain the past. Thus, though our vision is limited, it does not have to be witless. The passion, the frenzy, the glitter, the grief, the love, the hate of the moment need not cause us to lose our bearings. Our personal experiences are not unique. Someone, in fact, lots of people, have been here before. Through the words of people whose hearts, minds and deeds have shaped our own lives, I invite the reader to be in the past, to confront directly the men and women who lived before us in order to understand men and women --- us --- living through similar trials and triumphs now.

This collection of primary documents is intended for use in college level humanities and European history courses. The readings have been arranged chronologically in three volumes: <u>Ancient Greece through the Middle Ages</u> (Volume One), <u>The Renaissance to Waterloo</u> (Volume Two) and <u>1815 to the Present</u> (Volume Three). There are bound to be criticisms of the documents I have chosen to include. In general, they have been selected with three criteria in mind: (1) the intrinsic historical value of the document, (2) the extent to which the document reflects the values and attitudes of the era in which it was written, and (3) its inherent readability, <u>viz.</u>, would a college freshman be able to read it with understanding and enjoyment. Each reading is preceded by a little biographical sketch intended to place the reading and its author in their proper historical setting. Each reading is also followed by a set of study questions designed to *guide the reading and to <u>start</u> analysis. It is expected that the perceptive student will be led down many more avenues of speculation than the few provided here.*

The introductory essays preceding each chapter are meant to place the documents in their appropriate historical niche. They are deliberately sketchy. Hence, the bibliographies that follow them are meant to be seriously pursued. Obviously, however, the original readings themselves are preeminent sources and the student is strongly urged to read further in them. A single small crumb is so much less satisfying than the whole meal.

Throughout all three volumes of this work, I have used the generic "Man/Mankind" (and similar terminology) rather than the gender-neutral "person/ humankind." I find it more pleasing stylistically but, more importantly, it allows for consistency with the documents themselves.

I don't think I shall ever be able to adequately thank the generous, warm and patient people who have helped me produce these volumes. Debra Shillington in the College's Word Processing Center seemed to make this the only project she had to work on. She not only word-processed the text but often edited, corrected and suggested stylistic changes that I had either missed or didn't know about. Jacqueline Menté, also in the Word Processing Center, has borne, along with Debra, an unconscionable work load cheerfully and with an abiding grace that leaves me in awe. I have been blessed with a most competent and tolerant staff. I am grateful, too, to the publishers, cited in the text, who have so kindly granted me permission to use excerpts from their sources.

Over the years in which this has been in progress many, many students have offered suggestions, have caught editorial --- and sometimes, to my complete delight --- historical errors. Ultimately it has been these students who have determined what documents were worth keeping and which ones were not. It was also a group of students in 1987 who gave the work its name.

I owe much to Ellen Lee who was my student and friend and who began the word processing part of this project back in the days when the technology was much less sophisticated than it is now. Her death was a personal and a professional loss.

Above all, my thanks to my family --- to my beloved husband Jack, who endured the clutter in the house, and encouraged and cared for me and didn't let go of me when I got tired and exasperated. One's marriage vows take on new beauty when one's best friend and most helpful critic is also one's spouse. My thanks also to my sweet daughter Allison. Because of her, the Sappho poem, "Mother Love" is included here. To her big brother Morgan, I owe a special debt. His curiosity, sensitivity and lively enthusiasm has been a consistent delight and challenge. And finally, my thanks also to Dan Hilson, a very special and wise young man.

                Joan Mickelson-Gaughan
           Washtenaw Community College
                  Ann Arbor, Michigan

PREFACE TO VOLUME I

There are certain characteristics which are unique to Western Civilization --- an affirmation of the intrinsic worth of the individual, of rationalism and justice and a conscious pursuit of excellence. Nowhere in the ancient world can these characteristics be found so completely as in Greece; hence, this volume begins with the Greeks.

To find the roots of ancient Greek culture one would probably have to go to the island of Thera in the southern Aegean Sea, the center of what is called Cycladic civilization. Thera, as well as dozens of other islands in that region, circled or "cycled" the island of Delos where the shrine of Apollo, the sun god was located. That made sense. All of us can see that the sun moves across the sky in a day. Without the sun, everything is dark, hard to see and understand. Apollo illumined everything and the sun made life itself possible; hence, a civilization circling around the sun-god, the god of wisdom made perfect sense. Archaeologists and historians know precious little about Cycladic culture but we can guess that it contained two elements which remained central to later Greek culture as well. First, because they were islands they were almost forced to engage in trade. The sea would have been an avenue for contact not a barrier. Thus, a commercial, a middle class was inevitable and important politically as well as economically. Secondly, it would have been almost impossible for despotic, absolutist political systems to evolve simply because if someone did not like the conditions in which he lived he could simply get on his ship and leave. Later, Greeks would have kings but at no time would they have much real power.

About 2000 or so B.C., the center of Aegean civilization shifted to the island of Crete. Again, an island, forced to engage in commerce, fostered a healthy middle class. Because trade was so important, a system of writing (in order to keep accounts) was developed. Crete also had a nobility and a monarchy. Because the king was called a "Minos," his subjects called themselves "Minoans." The capital of Crete, the city of Knossos, contained a palace whose walls were adorned with exquisite frescoes which reveal a royal interest in ordinary things --- men fishing, women weaving, children playing ball. They also show evidence of a bull-leaping contest, associated with religion, wherein young men and girls, oiled and naked, engaged in a graceful little dance and, when an enraged bull was let into the arena, they would somersault onto its back. That trick obviously required not only physical strength but dexterity, precise timing and a great deal of mental acuity. In other words, Minoan gods and goddesses were pleased, not when men were passive, not when they merely offered some sacrifices, but when they acted fully as men, with all their physical and mental powers at their peak. Later generations would define this as "humanism." Significantly, no great temples or monumental statues of gods and goddesses have been found on Crete. What has been found are little shrines where men would have had to stand upright, fully as men, to address their deities.

What happened to Minoan civilization we can only guess at. Apparently an earthquake, followed by a tidal wave, devastated Knossos and the island about 1750 or so B.C. The natural catastrophe was followed by an invasion from the Peloponnesian peninsula, from a people called the Myceneans. They destroyed much but they also built fortresses, cities and colonies. And they had the good sense to preserve whatever they could of Minoan culture. One of the cities built by these vigorous folk was Ilium, the "Troy" of Homer.

The cities and states founded by the Myceneans fought each other chronically. In reading Greek history, one is struck by the fact that when the Greeks are not fighting invaders they are fighting each other. By the late thirteenth century, B.C., they had perhaps bled each other in interminable warfare so that they were then all vulnerable to invasion from a people along the lower Danube called the Dorians. Apparently the Dorians had no manners whatsoever --- no _idea_ of government (the local chief was in charge), no writing, no system of law, no monetary system and, above all, no sense that courtesy and gentleness and kindness are somehow better than force and brutality. The Dorians first invaded and then settled in Greece and then amalgamated with the local population. The result was that, what came to be called the Hellenes, or Greeks (the latter term is Latin) were, like Americans, a racial mix.

By about 800 B.C., something of settled life had emerged. Great nobles were defending the people in their immediate localities from fortified citadels in return for tribute. There was no real peace, no absence of conflict --- the absence of conflict was a luxury few Greeks would ever know until the Romans imposed it upon them. But out of this period, two remarkable things emerged which were to leave a permanent imprint on Western civilization --- the polis or city-state and the epics of Homer.

THE FORMATION OF GREECE

The shaping of a characteristically Greek and thus Western mind begins with the poet Homer about 800 B.C. Who Homer was and whether he was blind as legend has it, have been debated by scholars, but his name is associated with the two greatest epics in Western literature --- *The Iliad* and *The Odyssey*. The two stories revolve around the Trojan War which had occurred about 1250 B.C. They had evolved out of a rich oral tradition that had long circulated in the Aegean and in the wider Mediterranean world.

The Iliad and *The Odyssey* coincided with a period of peace and stability following a time of invasion and anarchy which the Greeks thereafter called the "dark ages." Peace led to an increase in population and wealth but that in turn brought new problems. The soil of Greece is too thin and sandy to support much of an agrarian population. The Greeks handled this by seeking new homes elsewhere in the Mediterranean. From about 750 to 550 B.C., Greek colonies blossomed on the southern coasts of France, Spain and Italy, in Sicily, Egypt, around the shores of the Black, Ionian and northern Aegean Seas and along the North African coast. What happened to Greece was a cosmopolitan, Orientalizing tendency very evident in the art of the period. Equally important, however, was the Hellenizing of the Mediterranean world to which Rome would later fall heir.

The work of colonizing was undertaken by that most characteristic of Greek institutions, the polis, or city-state. The polis had begun to emerge before Homer. It had grown up around a fortified hill called an "acropolis." The acropolis was crowned with a temple dedicated to the polis' patron deity and would always be the heart of any polis. Any Greek would have taken for granted Aristotle's comment that "Man is a political animal." Greek architecture, sculpture, drama and even *philosophy were rooted in the polis. The Greek simply could not conceive of civilized human life except within the context of the polis.*

Not all poleis had the same kind of government but they did go through similar patterns of evolution. In Homer's day, most poleis had kings whose meager powers were checked by the heads of powerful aristocratic clans. Aristocratic governments prevailed until a commercial class arose. Then, the merchants demanded a voice in the making of laws. This stage was often accompanied by a good bit of violence but the result was usually an oligarchy --- government by a few nobles and merchants. Because the getting of wealth does not depend on birth, the next stage was often but not always a democracy. At any stage, however, a tyranny could emerge. A tyrant was simply someone who seized power illegally. Greek tyrants, far from being Hitlers or Stalins, were often benevolent men who enriched and strengthened their states. Nonetheless, by the end of the fifth century, most Greeks were wary of tyranny and had taken steps to avoid it.

Sparta

The two states which eventually came to dominate Greece were Sparta and Athens. Sparta, located in the Peloponnesian peninsula, was originally a coalition of five towns. Those neighbors who refused to join the coalition were forced into subjugation as "perioeci" --- the "dwellers around" who would be free but voteless. Sparta became the military camp of Greece but not by accident. Her peculiar development may be traced in large part to conflicts in the eighth and seventh centuries with her neighbor to the west, Messenia. In two wars, the Messenians were annihilated. Every man, woman and child not slain was turned into a helot or state-owned slave.

The Messenian wars left an indelible imprint on the Spartan state and character. First, a boxlike formation called a "phalanx" had been the key to defeating the Messenians but the strength of the phalanx depended on each man standing his ground to the death, if necessary. The Spartans would devise a government that would keep that phalanx secure. At the same time, the prolonged wars were wearying. Sparta would always be prepared for war but would enter it reluctantly.

The Messenian wars had also necessitated the use of non-nobles as warriors. These "hoplites" demanded greater political rights --- and got them. The result was the creation of an oligarchic government. According to Spartan tradition, her constitution was given her by a half-legendary ninth-century lawgiver named Lycurgus who in his turn had gotten it from the god Apollo. There would thus be an understandable reluctance to change it. The constitution provided for two kings but real power lay in the hands of five "ephors" representing Sparta's five villages. The ephors were elected by the citizen assembly, or "ecclesia." They received or rejected embassies, supervised the kings, and presided over the ecclesia. The ephors, the kings and twenty-eight nobles at least sixty years old made up the "gerousia." The gerousia drafted bills which the ecclesia then either approved or rejected. If they were approved, the bills became law.

Sparta operated as a communism. Rancour over who had what could open up the phalanx so no one owned anything. Everything, every person, belonged to the state. Children belonged not to their parents but to the state and were trained by it. Until the age of seven, boys and girls were together in something like an Israeli kibbutz. Then the sexes were separated but both underwent a rigorous physical training. At the age of twenty-four, the men became front-line soldiers but they were not full citizens, eligible to sit in the ecclesia, until they reached the age of thirty. All his life, a Spartan was expected to be constantly in training, fit for combat. He was expected to come home either with his shield --- victorious --- or on it --- dead. Retreat or defeat was not in the cards.

While most other Greeks would not have wanted to live in Sparta, they did admire her for three reasons. First, they all admired balance and harmony, and the Spartan oligarchy represented a perfect blend of the three kinds of government available to men --- monarchy, aristocracy (but a true aristocracy of the best and wisest) in the gerousia and democracy in the ecclesia. Secondly, all Greeks spoke of patriotism and most of them lived it. But the greatest strength of the polis was also its greatest weakness --- it gave wide play to the individual's will and ambitions, often at the expense of the polis. In Sparta, that could not happen. The individual's will, his body, his entire soul belonged to Sparta. Wealth, luxury, personal fame might appeal to another Greek, but not to a Spartan. Third, all Greeks were reared on The Iliad and The Odyssey but only in Sparta could one find nothing but Homeric heroes.

Athens

Athens was a coalition of four tribes that eventually came to dominate Attica. There were the two figurehead kings and an aristocracy governing through a nine-man council called an Areopagus. The noble heads of the four clans who controlled the Areopagus quarreled with each other quite regularly. In 621, a period of particularly bloody civil war ended when the Areopagus elected an aristocrat named Draco as archon, or chairman. In order to curb further violence, Draco codified Athenian custom into a code of written law. It was not "fair". It recognized social and economic inequities and included such harsh penalties as physical mutilation and death for relatively minor crimes. Despite its flaws, however, Draco's code was a human document and thus, unlike Lycurgus' code, could be changed to fit changing human needs.

Draco's code left untouched several economic inequities that continued to fester. In 594, an aristocrat named Solon who had gained the respect of the newly emerging merchant class, was elected archon. Solon was convinced that law ought to rest on justice, viz., it was not the tool of any one group, or really even of the majority. In order to achieve justice, Solon abolished the death penalty for all crimes except homicide, thus inviting back many craftsmen and merchants who had fled to escape Draco's code. He cancelled enslavement for debt and existing mortgages and allowed even the poorest to sit on the ecclesia. He also organized all Athenians into four economic groups which cut across the four tribal lines. Representatives from these four groups then sat on a Council of 400 which had a voice in the election of magistrates. He ordered all fathers to teach their sons a trade and urged the cultivation of olives and grapes instead of grain in an attempt to alleviate rural poverty. At his urging too, the clay soil of Attica was put to the manufacture of pottery which would compete with the wares of Corinth on Aegean and then Mediterranean markets. Then, having bound everyone by oath to uphold his reforms, Solon left Athens.

The Formation of Greece 5

His reforms brought greater participation in the polis to more people but did not end conflict entirely. In 561, Peisistratus, taking advantage of disputes, seized power illegally and established a tyranny. It was the "little man" --- the peasant, miner and herdsman --- who had benefitted least from Solon's reforms and it was these that Peisistratus sought to help. He redistributed land (against the opposition of both the noble and the wealthier middle classes) and abolished sharecropping. His enemies drove him into exile but then, faced with a possible revolution from his supporters, they were forced to allow him to return in 546. Silver mining had begun in Attica shortly before his first tyranny but in the absence of legislation on their behalf, the miners were cruelly exploited. Peisistratus guaranteed a high minimum wage which encouraged laborers from other parts of Greece to come to Athens allowing for the further expansion of the mining industry. A new silver coin, the owl (so-called because it had Athena's image on one side and her symbol, the owl, on the other), was minted. It was so stable that it soon became the standard currency not only of the Aegean world but of Mediterranean trade as well. Peisistratus was able to cut taxes by half and still had enough money to lavishly adorn Athens with lovely temples, aqueducts and exquisite sculpture. In 534, when Thespis introduced an actor to carry on a dialogue with the chorus in the annual Dionysian festival, Greek drama was born. By drawing the lower classes fully into the economic and thus the political life of Athens, Peisistratus had laid the foundation for democracy. He died in 527 and his sons, Hippias and Hipparchus, also promoted the economic and intellectual flowering begun by their father. Following Hipparchus' murder in 514, however, Hippias became suspicious and harsh and even sought an alliance with Persia. He was exiled and in 510 Cleisthenes was elected archon.

Cleisthenes divided Athenians into ten new tribes based not on blood but on geography. Each tribe was then divided into eighteen demes which cut across three groups --- the coastal, urban, and inland farming and mining interests. Thus, it was impossible for any one clan or economic group to dominate tribe politics. A new Council of 500, the "boule," was formed consisting of fifty men elected from each tribe by lot. The boule drafted legislation, supervised the magistrates and controlled diplomacy and finance. The ecclesia, containing all male citizens, voted on the boule's proposals and passed capital sentences. The

HOMERIC GREECE

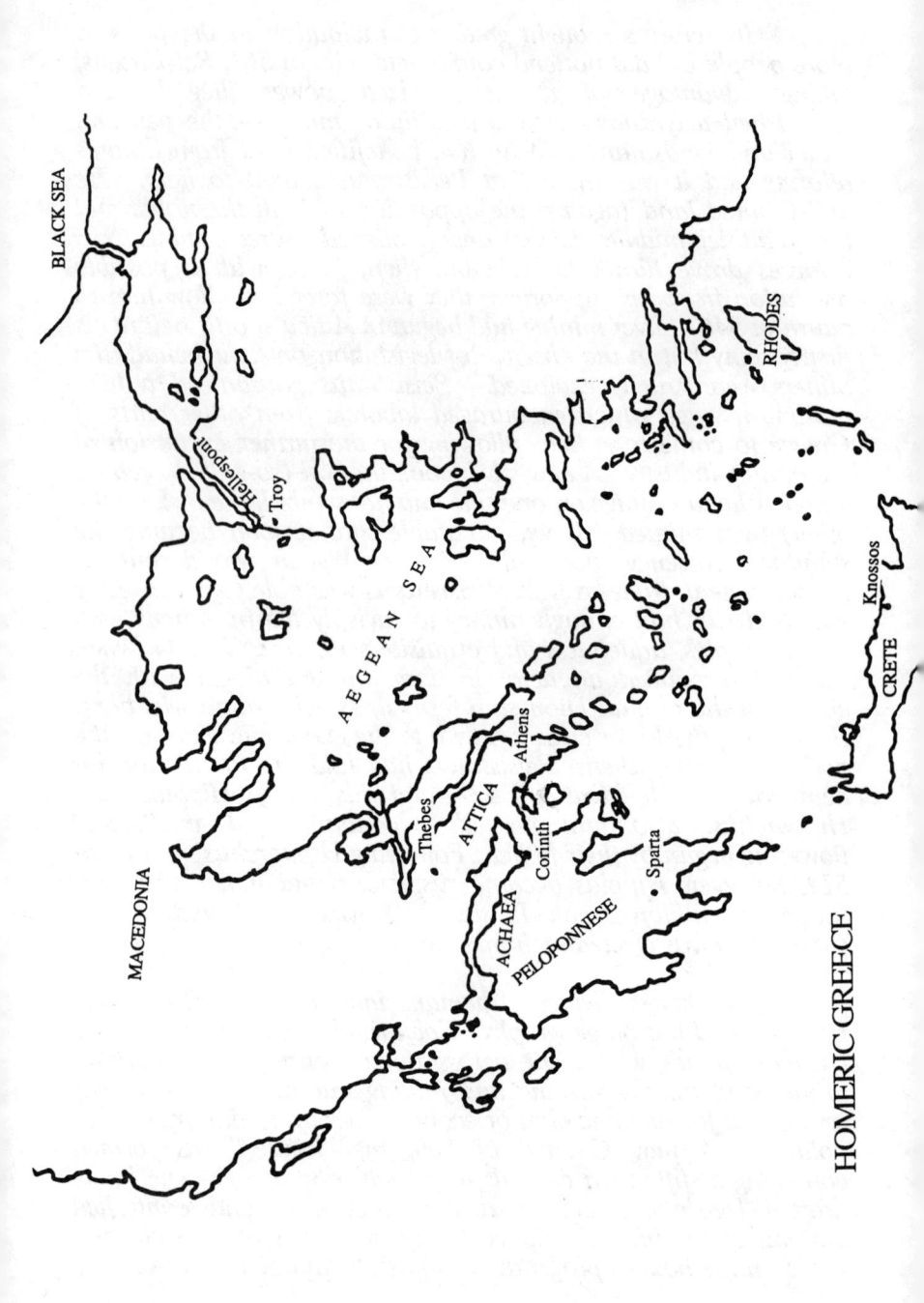

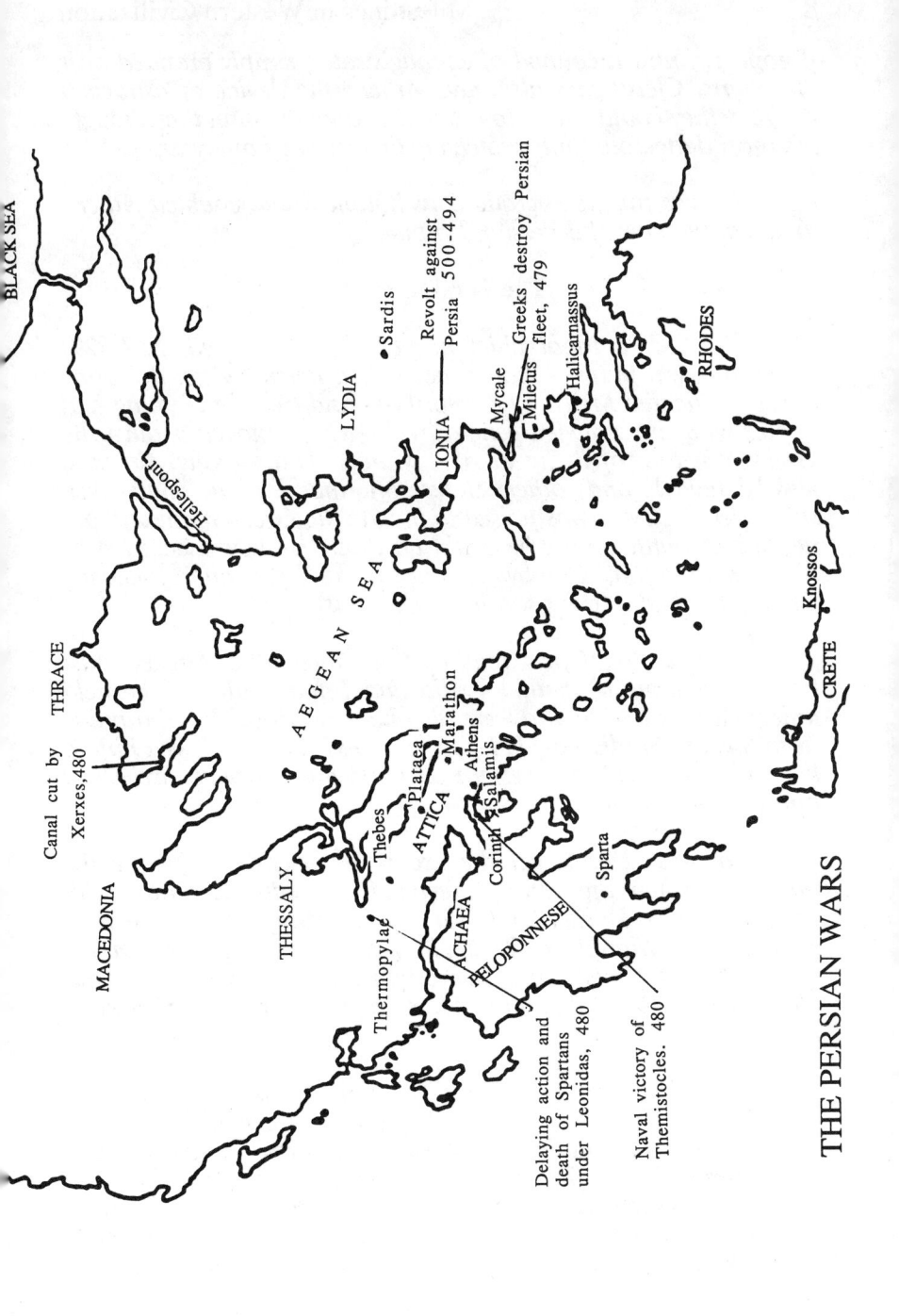

THE PERSIAN WARS

Areopagus, now a council of ex-magistrates, simply presided over the courts. Cleisthenes also gave Athens the device of ostracism whereby they could vote into a ten-year exile the man they thought the most dangerous, thus protecting themselves from tyranny.

It was this democratic constitution which enabled Athens to defeat the powerful Persian Empire.

The Persian Wars

In 557, a tribal chief named Cyrus (reigned, 557-529) came to power in an obscure place called Persia. After defeating the sophisticated Medes to his north --- and treating the king and nobles with unparalleled generosity --- Cyrus moved against the Greek kingdom of Lydia in Asia Minor. Lydia's king, Croesus, was defeated and other states on the Ionian coast also surrendered. Cyrus was poised to invade the Greek mainland but he died in battle before he could do that. He was succeeded by his unstable son, Cambyses, who took Egypt and, following Cambyses' death, by his son-in-law, Darius.

Darius, like Cyrus, realized that either all of Greece must be held or none of it, that Lydia and Ionia could not be held unless Athens and Sparta were also held. A Royal Road running from Susa to Sardis with 111 post stations along it allowed him to keep in touch with his western outposts but it would also allow him to move troops.

In 499, Darius got the excuse he needed to invade the mainland when the Ionians revolted and burned Sardis with Athenian help. Darius landed a gigantic army at a place near Athens called Marathon. There, he was soundly defeated. In one of the most decisive battles in western history, Darius lost about 6400 men to 192 Athenian dead. Cleisthenes' reforms had done their work.

In 486, Darius died leaving his throne and his dream of conquering Greece to his son, Xerxes (reigned, 486-465). Confronted with a massive invasion, Sparta and Athens decided to cooperate for the first and only time in their histories and even then the alliance was fragile. Athens would control all naval operations; Sparta, those on land. Sparta's king, Leonidas, hoped to block Xerxes' advance into central and southern Greece at a

The Formation of Greece

narrow mountain pass called Thermopylae. Betrayed by a Greek traitor, Leonidas and 300 of his picked Spartans tried to hold the pass until, in the finest Spartan tradition, all had perished. So, however, had nearly 3000 Persians.

The way to the rest of Greece now lay open to Xerxes. He invaded Attica and burned Athens, evacuated earlier by order of the naval commander, Themistocles. Then, in the narrow waters between Salamis and the mainland, in the dead of night, Themistocles torched most of the huge Persian fleet. The next spring a Persian army was defeated at Plataea in Boetia. To finish matters, an amphibious battle at Cape Mycale off the Ionian coast cost Xerxes another army and the rest of his navy. He died before he could launch another invasion.

The Peloponnesian War

The defeat of Persia left the leadership of Greece to Athens. Sparta, true to form, withdrew. A Delian League was formed (its treasury was on the island of Delos) initially as a defense against Persia. Athens presided over the rebuilding of the fleet but she shortly began to view secession from the League as rebellion and to coerce neutral states to join. The voluntary contribution became a forced tribute and the owl and Athenian garrisons were imposed on her allies. The Delian League, in short, became the instrument of empire.

The greatest empire builder was Pericles (494-429) who came to power in 461. His aim was to make Athens supreme in Greece and to thoroughly break Persia's power. And he had ready support at home. He had inaugurated welfare-state legislation and, by providing compensation for jury service, had made those bodies open to the poor. A vigorous building program, supported with Delian funds, had allowed Pericles' friend, the sculptor, Phidias, to adorn the Parthenon. This was also the age of the playwrights Sophocles, Eurpides and the historian Thucydides, and Socrates was beginning to annoy his fellow citizens with his interminable questions. Pericles was presiding over Athens' Golden Age.

Then the empire crumbled. Athens was defeated when she intervened in an Egyptian revolt against Persia and at about the same time Boetia rebelled against her. In 433, she sided with

Corcyra against Corinth, one of Sparta's allies, and the next year, Athens and Corinth collided again over the Corinthian colony of Potidaea. Athens won but Sparta, now thoroughly alarmed, finally and reluctantly declared war.

The Peloponnesian Wars (431-404) began when a Spartan ally, Thebes, attacked Plataea. In 430, a devastating plague broke out in Athens which claimed Pericles among its victims. His death brought a new breed of politicians to the fore ---men of great personal ambition who were often rash and headstrong. A peace, concluded in 421, brought only a cold war and in 416, Athens brutally compelled the surrender of the neutral island of Melos. The architect of this was a spoiled, irreverent aristocrat named Alcibiades who, though he thought democracy a great joke, was the darling of Athenian democrats. He persuaded the Athenians to invade Syracuse in Sicily but the undertaking was scrapped when Alcibiades was accused of sacrilege and ordered to return. Instead of doing so, he went to Sparta, seduced the queen and advised his hosts on how to deal with Athens. In 414, the Athenians besieged Syracuse and were horribly defeated the following year.

The Sicilian disaster renewed hostilities in Greece itself. Sparta's declaration of war in 413 was accompanied by revolt throughout the Delian empire. A Spartan fleet built and equipped by Persia and commanded by the brilliant Lysander destroyed the Athenian fleet. She was then starved into submission and capitulated in 404. Her empire and her democracy were then dismantled, her fortifications destroyed, about 1500 Athenians, including Alcibiades, were slaughtered and Thirty Tyrants were installed to govern her.

The last act is thoroughly unhappy. The Peloponnesian Wars had exhausted all of Greece and had demonstrated that no one state was able to impose hegemony on all of Greece. But the struggle nonetheless continued. A Theban-Athenian alliance threw out the Thirty Tyrants less than a year after they were installed and democracy was restored. It was this radical democracy which would sentence Socrates to death five years later. Spartan arrogance and imperial ambition, as it turned out, matched Athens'. Even with Persian help, though, Sparta was defeated by a Theban general, Epaminondas, in 371. That battle left Thebes the most powerful state in Greece but she was no

The Formation of Greece

more able to dominate her neighbors than Athens and Sparta had been, and a stalemate maintained. Then, in 338, a combined Athenian-Theban force was defeated at Charonea by Philip II, king of the hitherto insignificant kingdom of Macedonia on Greece's northern border. It was Philip and his son, Alexander, who would impose upon Greece that unity which she had been unable to give herself. In the process, the polis which had already become exhausted, would be put to the grave.

Yet it was the polis which had given the West its ideals of freedom, of human dignity and the foundations of its science and philosophy. The drama and art of the polis would inspire generations ever after in its humanism --- its conviction of the essential worth of the individual human being.

Suggested Readings

1. Bowra, C. M., *The Greek Experience* (London: Weidenfeld and Nicolson, 1957). One of the better introductions to Greek civilization.

2. _____, *Periclean Athens* (New York: Dial Press, 1971). An excellent account of the Golden Age of Athens.

3. Fine, John, *The Ancient Greeks* (Cambridge, Mass: Belknap Press of Harvard University Press, 1983). A new study of Greek history.

4. Finley, M. I., *The Ancient Greeks* (London: Chatto and Windus, 1964). One of the more popular accounts of Greek civilization.

5. Hooper, Finley, *Greek Realities* (New York: Scribners, 1967,). A warm portrayal of Greek society and culture.

6. Kitto, H. D. F., *The Greeks* (Baltimore: Penguin Books, 1957). An excellent and readable survey of Greek life and ideas.

HOMER from THE ILIAD

The Iliad is about the war at Ilium --- Troy. This is how the war started.

Once, all of the gods and goddesses were invited to celebrate the wedding of Peleus and Thetis except Eris, goddess of discord. Enraged, Eris tossed a golden apple among the guests, bearing the inscription, "To the fairest". Hera, the wife of Zeus, and Zeus' two daughters, Athena and Aphrodite, all claimed the apple. Zeus, unwilling to mediate the dispute, sent the three goddesses to Paris, son of Troy's King Priam, to decide. All three tried to bribe Paris. Hera offered him power, Athena offered him wisdom and Aphrodite offered him the most beautiful woman in the world. Paris awarded the apple to Aphrodite, thus making Athena and Hera his --- and Troy's --- implacable enemies.

Under Aphrodite's protection, Paris sailed to Sparta where he was treated hospitably by King Menelaus. Then, aided by Aphrodite, Paris persuaded Menelaus' wife, Helen, the loveliest of women, to elope with him and they sailed off to Troy. This was the cause of the Trojan War.

Menelaus called upon his brother, Agamemnon, and all the other chieftains in Achaea to help him win back his wife. Odysseus, King of Ithaca, wise old Nestor, King of Pylos, Diomede, the courageous and not very bright Ajax all responded to the call. Agamemnon was the commander-in-chief but the greatest of the Achaean heroes was Achilles, son of Thetis and Peleus. Arrayed against them in Troy were Aeneas, Deiphobus and Glaucon but the most formidable was Priam's son, Hector. The war lasted for ten years. It is in the tenth year that *The Iliad* opens.

Agamemnon and Achilles have just made a daring raid on the Trojan camp and have returned with lots of loot including two girls. Chryseis, daughter of Chryses, a priest of Apollo, is given to

The Formation of Greece

Agamemnon but Chryses comes to Agamemnon's tent to beg for the return of his daughter. Agamemnon angrily refuses and Chryses begs Apollo for revenge. Apollo strikes the Achaeans with a plague. A council is called and the Achaeans urge Agamemnon to return Chryseis to her father. Agamemnon agrees to do so but only if Achilles will surrender his girl, Briseis, to him. Achilles is furious but finally has to submit. But then, he withdraws into his tent and refuses to take any further part in the war.

Without Achilles the Achaeans are driven from the field and are forced to retreat to their ships. And now instead of besieging Troy, they are themselves besieged. An embassy from Agamemnon offering an apology and even the return of Briseis is angrily rejected by Achilles. Finally, Achilles' best friend, Patroclus, comes to his tent and asks for Achilles' armor, which had been made by the god Hephaestus. Achilles gives it to him along with his own troops, the Myrmidons. He also warns Patroclus not to press the Trojans without him. The Trojans, seeing Patroclus leading the Myrmidons and wearing Achilles' armor, flee in dismay. Hector, however, turns and does battle with Patroclus and slays him. There is a tremendous fight for the body of Patroclus. Hector gets the armor but the Achaeans finally get the body and bear it back to their camp.

When word of Patroclus' death is brought to Achilles, he grieves so greatly that his friends fear for his sanity. He now must fight Hector to avenge his friend's death. Hephaestus makes a new suit of armor for him and he goes out to battle Hector. He chases Hector three times around Troy's walls; then Hector, knowing he is doomed, faces him. This is the description of perhaps the most famous single hand-to-hand combat in all of western literature.

By such words and guile Athena led [Hector] on. And when they came close to one another in their onset, great Hector of the glancing helmet first addressed Achilles: "No longer, son of Peleus, will I flee you, as before I fled thrice around the great city of Priam, nor could I bear to abide your on slaught. But now my spirit bids me stand and face you. I would take you or be taken. Come, let us look to the gods, for they will be the best witnesses and guardians of covenants. For I will not mutilate you horribly if Zeus gives me to endure to victory and I take away your life. But when I have stripped you of your glorious armor, Achilles, I will give back your corpse to the Achaeans. And do you do the same."

Swift-footed Achilles looked at him scornfully and said: "Hector, it is not to me that you, the unforgivable, may talk of covenants. As between lions and men there are no faithful oaths nor do wolves and lambs have a harmonious spirit but ever devise evil for one another, so it is not possible for me and you to be friends, nor shall there be oaths between us until one of us sate with his blood the warrior Ares with the bull's-hide shield. Remember all your skill, for now indeed must you be a spearman and a valiant warrior. There is no more escape for you, and Pallas Athena shall at once subdue you by my spear. Now you shall pay back all at once for the woes of my companions, whom you slew as you raged with your spear."

So speaking, he drew back his long-shadowed spear and cast it, but glorious Hector was watching out and dodged it, for he ducked as he saw it, and the bronze spear flew above him and fixed itself in the earth, but Pallas Athena picked it up and gave it back to Achilles unseen by Hector, shepherd of the people. And Hector said to Peleus' blameless son: "You missed; not even yet, godlike Achilles, have you known my doom from Zeus. You thought so, but you were glib-tongued and wily of words, that hearing you I might forget my strength and valor. You shall not plunge your spear into my back as I run away, but drive it through my chest as I rush straight for you, if God grant you that. Now then, dodge my spear of bronze; would that you would take it all in your flesh. The war would be lighter for the Trojans with you slain, for you are their greatest trouble."

So speaking, he drew back his long-shadowed spear and cast it, and struck the shield of Peleus' son in the center, nor did he miss, but the spear rebounded far from the shield. Angry was Hector that his sharp spear had sped from his hand in vain, and he stood confounded, nor had he any other spear of ash. He called in a loud voice to Deiphobus of the white shield and asked him for a long spear, but he was nowhere near him. Then Hector knew in his heart, and said: "The gods

The Formation of Greece

have really called me to my death, for I thought brave Deiphobus was here, but he is within the wall and Athena has deceived me. Now evil death is near to me, no longer far away, and there is no deliverance. Such must long ago have been the pleasure of Zeus and Zeus' son, the unerring one, who formerly protected me with zeal. Now my fate has found me out. Let me not perish tamely or without glory, but having done some great deed for the ears of generations who are yet to be."

So speaking, he drew the sharp sword that hung great and mighty at his side, and he crouched and darted like a high-soaring eagle that swoops earthward through dark clouds to seize a tender lamb or cowering hare. So Hector darted, brandishing his sharp sword. Achilles rushed forward, and his heart was filled with a wild fury. He held his fair and subtly fashioned shield before his breast and his helmet nodded with its shining, four-ridged crest, and around it waved the fair golden plumes which Hephaestus had set thick upon it. As the evening star moves among the other stars in the darkness of the night--it is the fairest star that stands in heaven-- such was the radiance from the sharp spear point which Achilles brandished in his right hand with evil purpose against godlike Hector as he looked at his fair flesh, to see where it would be most yielding. All the rest of Hector's flesh was covered by the fair bronze armor he had taken when he slew mighty Patroclus, but it showed through where the collarbones separate the neck from the shoulder, the hollow of the throat, where life's destruction is swiftest. There godlike Achilles struck him with his spear as he rushed forward, and the point pierced straight through his soft neck. But the bronze-weighted ash did not sever his windpipe, so that he might speak to him and answer him with words. He fell in the dust, and godlike Achilles boasted: "Hector, you thought to be safe in despoiling Patroclus and took no heed of me, who was far away, fool that you were. I, his far mightier comrade, was left behind, far off by the hollow ships, I who have loosed your knees. You the dogs and birds shall rend shamefully, but him the Achaeans shall give burial."

Weakly, Hector of the glancing helmet said to him: "I beg you by your life, by your knees and by your parents, do not let the dogs of the Achaeans devour me beside the ships but accept ample bronze and gold, the gifts my father and my queenly mother will give to you, and give my body back home, that the Trojans and the Trojans' wives may give to me in death the meed of fire."

Swift-footed Achilles looked at him scornfully and said: "Dog, beseech me neither by my knees nor by my parents. Would that my angry heart would let me cut off your raw flesh and eat it, for what you have done to me. There is none who could ward the dogs off from your head, not though they bring ten and twenty times your ransom and weigh it out here and promise yet more besides; not even though Dardanian Priam should bid them buy you for your weight in gold, not even so shall your queenly mother lay you in your bed and weep for you she bore herself, but the dogs and birds shall devour you entirely.

Then, as he died, Hector of the glancing helmet said to him: "Well do I know you as I look upon you; there was no hope that I could move you, for surely your heart is iron in your breast. Take care now lest I be cause of anger of the gods against you on that day when Paris and Phoebus Apollo shall slay you for all your valor at the Scaean gates."

As he said this, the end of death enwrapped him. His soul fled from his limbs and passed into the house of Death, bewailing its fate and forsaking manliness and youth. Even when he had died, godlike Achilles said to him: "Die, and my fate I will accept whenever Zeus and the other immortal gods desire to fulfill it."

He spoke, and dragged the bronze spear from the body and set it down apart. He stripped the bloody armor from Hector's shoulders, and the rest of the sons of the Achaeans ran about him and gazed at Hector's stature and surpassing beauty, nor did any stand beside him without giving him a wound. And thus would one speak, glancing at his neighbor: "Hector is much softer to touch than when he burned the ships with blazing fire."

So one would say, and deal him a wound as he stood beside him. But when swift-footed, godlike Achilles had stripped him, he stood among the Achaeans and spoke winged words: "My friends, leaders and counselors of the Argives, since the gods have given to death this man who did much harm, more than all the others, come, let us make trial with our arms about the city, that we may know what purpose the Trojans have, whether they will leave the citadel now this man has fallen, or wish to remain even though Hector lives no more. But why did my soul say this to me? Beside the ships, an unwept, unburied corpse, lies Patroclus. Him I will not forget so long as I am among the living and my knees can move. And even if in Death's house they forget the dead, even there will I remember my dear comrade. Come now, youth of the Achaeans, let us sing a paean of victory as we go to the hollow ships, taking this body. We have won great glory; we have slain godlike Hector, to whom the Trojans prayed throughout the city as to a god."

He spoke, and devised foul treatment for godlike Hector. The tendons of both feet he pierced behind from heel to ankle and threaded them with ox-hide thongs and tied them to his chariot and allowed the head to drag. He mounted the chariot, held aloft the glorious armor, and lashed the horses to a gallop, and not unwillingly the pair flew off. A cloud of dust rose from the dragging Hector; his dark hair spread about, and all in the dust lay his head that was so fair before; but now Zeus gave him to his enemies to mutilate in his own native land.

Alston Hurd Chase and William G. Perry, Jr., trans., *Homer: The Iliad* (New York: Bantam Books, Inc., 1950), 340-343.

Study Questions

1. *Is the fight fair? What kind of extra help does Achilles get? Are the gods fair? Explain.*

2. *How is Hector killed? On what grounds does he beg Achilles to deal gently with his body? How does Achilles answer him?*

3. How is Hector's body treated by the Achaeans after he has been slain?

4. How does Achilles treat Hector's body?

5. What peculiarity do you notice about the way in which Hector and Achilles address each other?

6. How does the language in this passage differ from what you read in a newspaper article?

HOMER from THE ODYSSEY

It was not the death of Hector which caused the fall of Troy. Achilles too was treacherously slain by Paris but even that was not the end. The city finally was taken by a ruse concocted by the wily Odysseus. At his suggestion, the Achaeans pretended to abandon the siege as if in despair at Achilles' death and most of the fleet withdrew out of sight behind a neighboring island. Then they made a huge wooden horse which they hoped the Trojans would view as a victory trophy and take within their city. Concealed inside the horse were armed Achaeans, including Odysseus.

The trick worked. Despite the warning of the priest Laocoon to "beware Greeks bearing gifts," the Trojans dragged the horse into Troy, dismantled the garrison and celebrated. That night, Odysseus and his men left the horse and opened the gates of the city to their fellow Greeks who had by now returned. The city was torched and its inhabitants, overcome with sleep and feasting, were slain or taken captives. Helen was reconciled with Menelaus. Agamemnon returned home to be murdered by his wife and her lover.

The Odyssey is the story of Odysseus' journey to his home on the island of Ithaca. Unlike The Iliad which is a single story, The Odyssey is a set of stories strung together by the figure of the wandering hero. The main story is Odysseus' journey and the recovery of his home and queen from the clutches of evil suitors. But interlaced with that are stories of the Sirens whose lovely melody lures sailors to their deaths, the bewitching Circe who turns visitors to her island into animals, the horrible rocks Scylla and Charybis, and the one-eyed, man-eating Cyclops who is blinded by Odysseus.

It is as he is leaving Circe's island that he journeys into Hades, the land of the dead. This excerpt is from that encounter.

"As we two stood talking together of our sorrows in this mournful way, other ghosts came up: Achilles and Patroclus, and Antilochos, the man without stain and without reproach, and Aias, who was most handsome and noble of all next to the admirable Achilles. The ghost of Achilles knew me, and said in plain words:

"Here is Prince Odysseus who never fails! O you foolhardy man! Your ingenious brain will never do better than this. How did you dare to come down to Hades, where dwell the dead without sense or feeling, phantoms of mortals whose weary days are done?"

"I answered him, 'My lord Achilles Peleides, our chief and our champion before Troy! I came to ask Teiresias if he had any advice or help for me on my way to my rugged island home. For I have not yet set foot in my own country, since trouble has ever been my lot. But you, Achilles, are most blessed of all men who ever were or will be. When you lived, we honoured you like the gods; and now you are a potentate in this world of the dead. Then do not deplore your death, Achilles.'

"He answered at once, 'Don't bepraise death to me, Odysseus. I would rather be plowman to a yeoman farmer on a small holding than lord Paramount in the kingdom of the dead.'

* * * * * * *

Odysseus returns to Ithaca to find his home filled with suitors who have been badgering his wife, Penelope. With his son, Telemachus, and a faithful servant, Odysseus slays the suitors, but he is not fully home until his wife receives him.

They little knew what had happened. Within that house Eurynome bathed Odysseus and rubbed him down and gave him good clothes. Then he seemed another man, taller and

The Formation of Greece

stronger than before, and splendid from head to foot by grace of Athena; his head covered with a thick curly crop like the thick clustering petals of the hyacinth. He was a noble and brilliant figure; you might think of some perfect work of art made by one who is inspired by the divine artists, Hephaistos and Pallas Athena, brilliant with gold over silver. He came out of the bathroom looking more like a god than a man, and returned to his former seat facing his wife. Then he said to her:

"Strange woman! The inscrutable will of God has made your heart unfeeling beyond mortal women. No other wife could endure to keep her husband at a distance, when he just returned after twenty years of dreadful perils. Very well. Come, Nanny, lay me a bed and I will sleep alone. She has a heart of steel, it is clear."

His clever wife replied:

"Strange man, I am not proud, or contemptuous, or offended, but I know what manner of man you were when you sailed away from Ithaca. Come, Eurycleia, make the bed outside the room which he built himself; put the fine bedstead outside, and lay out the rugs and blankets and fleeces."

This was a little trap for her husband. He burst into a rage:

"Wife, that has cut me to the heart! Who has moved my bed? That would be a difficult job for the best workman, unless God himself should come down and move it. It would be easy for God, but no man could easily prize it up, not the strongest man living! There is a great secret in that bed. I made it myself, and no one else touched it. There was a strong young olive tree in full leaf growing in an enclosure, the trunk as thick as a pillar. Round this I built our bridal chamber; I did the whole thing myself, laid the stones and built a good roof over it, jointed the doors and fitted them in their places. After that I cut off the branches and trimmed the trunk from the root up, smoothed it carefully with the adze and made it straight to the line. This tree I made the bedpost. That was the beginning of my bed; I bored holes through it, and fitted the other posts about it, and inlaid the framework with gold and silver and ivory, and I ran through it leather straps coloured purple. Now I have told you my secret. And I don't know if it is still there, wife, or if someone has cut the olive at the root and moved my bed!"

She was conquered, she could hold out no longer when Odysseus told the secret she knew so well. She burst into tears and ran straight to him, throwing her arms about his neck. She kissed his head, and cried:

"Don't be cross with me, my husband, you were always a most understanding man! The gods brought affliction upon us because they grudged us the joy of being young and growing old together! Don't be angry, don't be hurt because I did not take you in my arms as soon as I saw you! My heart has been frozen all this time with a fear that some one would come and deceive me with a false tale; there are so many impostors! But now you have told me the secret of our bed, that settles it. No one else has seen it, only you and I, and my maid Actoris, the one my father gave me when I came to you, who used to keep the door of our room. You have convinced your hard-hearted wife!"

W. H. D. Rouse, *Odyssey* (Copyright (c) 1937, 1965 by John C. G. Rouse. Reprinted by arrangement with NAL Penguin Inc., New York, New York), 133-134, 256-257.

Study Questions

1. What does Achilles think of Hades? How is this view of the afterlife likely to affect Greek thought about this life? About the gods and Man's relationship to them?

2. How does Penelope test Odysseus? Why do you think she does so? How does Odysseus react?

3. *Odysseus is always referred to as "clever," "witty," "wise." What does this incident reveal about the relationship between Odysseus and Penelope?*

4. *What qualities do the Greeks admire? What "virtues" might they find a little useless?*

PLUTARCH on
THE CUSTOMS OF THE LACEDAEMONIANS

Plutarch, a native of Chaeronea was born about 50 A.D. He is best known for his parallel Lives of Noble Greeks and Romans *but he also wrote a number of other works, including the* Moralia *in which he discourses on a number of subjects such as the training of children, the cure for anger, the virtues of women, and many other subjects. One of these essays is on the habits of the Spartans. The first excerpt refers to the "syssition", the common dining hall of the Spartans; the second is an observation on Spartan intellectual life.*

---

1. It was a singular instance of the wisdom of this nation, in that they took the greatest care they could, by an early sober education, to instill into their youth the principles of virtue and good manners, that so, by a constant succession of prudent and valiant men, they might the better provide for the honor and security of their state, and lay in the minds of every one a solid and good foundation of love and friendship, of prudence and knowledge, of temperance and frugality, of courage and resolution. And therefore their great lawgiver thought it necessary for the ends of government to institute several distinct societies and conventions of the people; amongst which was that of their solemn and public living together at one table, where their custom was to admit their youth into the conversation of their wise and elderly men, that so by daily eating and drinking with them they might insensibly, as it were, be trained up to a right knowledge of themselves, to a just submission to their superiors, and to the learning of whatever might conduce to the reputation of their laws and the interest of their country. For here they were taught all the wholesome rules of discipline, and daily instructed how to demean themselves from the example and practice of their

great ones; and though they did not at this public meeting confine themselves to set and grave discourses concerning the civil government, but allowed themselves a larger freedom, by mingling sometimes with their politics the easy and familiar entertainments of mirth and satire, yet this was ever done with the greatest modesty and discretion, not so much to expose the person of any one, as to reprove the fault he had committed. Whatever was transacted at these stated and common feasts was to be locked up in every one's breast with the greatest silence and secrecy, insomuch as the eldest among them at these assemblies, pointing to the door, acquainted him who entered the room that nothing of what was done or spoken there was to be talked of afterwards.

4. They never applied their minds to any kind of learning, further than what was necessary for use and service; nature indeed having made them more fit for the purposes of war than for the improvements of knowledge. And therefore for speculative sciences and philosophic studies, they looked upon them as foreign to their business and unserviceable to their ends of living, and for this reason they would not tolerate them amongst them, nor suffer the professors of them to live within their government. They banished them from their cities, as they did all sorts of strangers, esteeming them as things that did debase the true worth and excellency of virtue, which they made to consist only in manly actions and generous exercises, and not in vain disputations and empty notions. So that the whole of what their youth was instructed in was to learn obedience to the laws and injunctions of their governors, to endure with patience the greatest labors, and where they could not conquer, to die valiantly in the field. For this reason likewise it was, that all mechanic arts and trades, all vain and insignificant employments, such as regarded only curiosity or pleasure, were strictly prohibited them, as things that would make them degenerate into idleness and covetousness, would render them vain and effeminate, useless to themselves, and unserviceable to the state; and on this account it was that they would never suffer any scenes or interludes, whether of comedy or tragedy, to be set up among them, lest there should be any encouragement given to speak or act any thing that might savor

of contempt or contumely against their laws and government, it being customary for the stage to assume an indecent liberty of taxing the one with faults and the other with imperfections.

A. H. Clough and William W. Goodwin, eds., *Plutarch's Essays and Miscellanies*, 5 vols. (New York: The Colonial Company, Limited, 1905), I, 82-83, 85-86.

Study Questions

1. What is the purpose of allowing Spartan youth to eat with older men?

2. Why won't science and philosophy develop in Sparta? How are such people dealt with? Why do you think Sparta does this and other poleis, Athens, for instance, do not?

HERODOTUS from THE HISTORIES

Herodotus (c. 485 - c. 424 B.C.) was the first to deliberately use prose as an artistic medium. Equally important, however, he was the first to study the past scientifically.

Men have been keeping records and telling stories of their deeds ever since they were able to stand upright. What Herodotus did --- and the reason we call him the "father of history" --- was to ask why things happened. As he says at the beginning of The Histories,

I hope to do two things: to preserve the memory of the past. . . .; secondly, and more particularly, to show how the two races [*the Persians and Greeks*] came into conflict.

Herodotus chronicles the rise of the Persian Empire from the time of Cyrus against the background of Sparta and Athens. In the process, he describes the customs of all sorts of people who fell under Persian rule. And the broadness of his scope is matched only by his thoroughness. He loved to travel. From his home, Halicarnassus on the southern coast of Asia Minor, Herodotus travelled widely --- to Egypt, Palestine, Mesopotamia, northern Africa and southern Russia. He was curious, intelligent and he genuinely liked people whether they were Greeks or not. He relied on chronicles written in Greek, inscriptions and oral testimony. Where his sources are contradictory, he will give all the versions he has and then indicate which version he prefers and why, but he will leave the reader to make his own choice. Thus, a chronicle of the "big events" is interlaced with detail, popular beliefs and the customs of ordinary people.

Running through The Histories *is his idea that the wars between Persia and Greece were not merely a battle of armies but a clash of values. Herodotus was convinced that history was cyclical, that Fate or Destiny shapes events generally but individuals do bring their glory --- and their ruin --- upon themselves. Men, or nations, by remaining faithful to their gods, their ideals, achieve greatness. Sooner or later, however, men inevitably forget that it is the gods, not merely his own efforts, which have given them glory. They commit the fatal sin of "hubris" or spiritual pride and then Destiny, or God, decrees the fall.*

Herodotus is entertaining, easy and fun to read. His style is graceful and never stuffy. The following excerpt is his version of the famous battle of Thermopylae.

The 300 men whom Leonidas brought on this occasion to Thermopylae were chosen by himself; they were all men in middle life and all fathers of living sons. He also took with him the Thebans I mentioned, under the command of Leontiades, the son of Eurymachus. The reason why he made a special point of taking troops from Thebes, and from Thebes only, was that the Thebans were strongly suspected of Persian sympathies, so he called upon them to play their part in the war in order to see if they would answer the call, or openly refuse to join the confederacy. They did send troops, but their secret sympathy was nevertheless with the enemy. Leonidas and his 300 were sent by Sparta in advance of the main army, in order that the sight of them might encourage the other confederates to fight and prevent them from going over to the enemy as they were quite capable of doing if they knew that Sparta was hanging back, the intention was, when the Carneia was over (for it was that festival which prevented the Spartans from taking the field in the ordinary way) to leave a garrison in the city and join the confederate army with all the troops at their disposal. The other allied states proposed to act similarly; for the Olympic festival happened to fall just at this same period. None of them ever expected the battle at Thermopylae to be decided so soon --- which was the reason why they sent only advance parties there.

* * * * * * *

How to deal with the situation Xerxes had no idea; but while he was still wondering what his next move should be, a man from Malis got himself admitted to his presence. This was

Ephialtes, the son of Eurydemus, and he had come, in hope of a rich reward, to tell the king about the track which led over the hills to Thermopylae --- and the information he gave was to prove the death of the Greeks who held the pass.

Later on, Ephialtes, in fear of the Spartans, fled to Thessaly, and during his exile there a price was put upon his head as an assembly of the Amphictyons at Pylae. Sometime afterwards he returned to Anticyra, where he was killed by Athenades of Trachis. In point of fact, Athenades killed him not for his treachery but for another reason, which I will explain further on; but the Spartans honoured him none the less on that account. According to another story, which I do not at all believe, it was Onetes, the son of Phanagoras, a native of Carystus, and Corydallus of Anticyra who spoke to Xerxes and showed the Persians the way round by the mountain track; but one may judge which account is the true one, first by the fact that the Amphictyons, who must surely have known everything about it, set a price not upon Onetes and Corydallus but upon Ephialtes of Trachis, and, secondly, by the fact that there is no doubt that the accusation of treachery was the reason for Ephialtes' flight. Certainly Onetes, even though he was not a native of Malis, might have known about the track, if he had spent much time in the neighbourhood --- but it was Ephialtes, and no one else, who showed the Persians the way, and I leave his name on record as the guilty one.

Xerxes found Ephialtes' offer most satisfactory. He was delighted with it, and promptly gave orders to Hydarnes[1] to carry out the movement with the troops under his command. They left camp about the time the lamps are lit.

The track was originally discovered by the Malians of the neighbourhood; they afterwards used it to help the Thessalians, taking them over it to attack Phocis at the time when the Phocians were protected from invasion by the wall which they had built across the pass. That was a long time ago, and no good ever came of it since. The track begins at the

---

[1] The leader of the famous Immortals, the crack troops of the Persian army.

Asopus, the stream which flows through the narrow gorge, and, running along the ridge of the mountain --- which, like the track itself, is called Anopaea --- ends at Alpenus, the first Locrian settlement as one comes from Malis, near the rock known as Black-Buttocks' Stone and the seats of the Cercopes. Just here is the narrowest part of the pass.

This, then, was the mountain track which the Persians took, after crossing Asopus. They marched throughout the night, with the mountains of Aeta on their right had and those of Trachis on their left. By early dawn they were at the summit of the ridge, near the spot where the Phocians, as I mentioned before, stood on guard with a thousand men, to watch the track and protect their country. The Phocians were ready enough to undertake this service, and had, indeed, volunteered for it to Leonidas, knowing that the pass at Thermopylae was held as I have already described.

The ascent of the Persians had been concealed by the oakwoods which cover this part of the mountain range, and it was only when they reached the top that the Phocians became aware of their approach; for there was not a breath of wind, and the marching feet made a loud swishing and rustling in the fallen leaves. Leaping to their feet, the Phocians were in the act of arming themselves when the enemy was upon them. The Persians were surprised at the sight of troops preparing to resist; they had not expected any opposition --- yet here was a body of men barring their way. Hydarnes asked Ephialtes who they were, for his first uncomfortable thought was that they might be Spartans; but on learning the truth he prepared to engage them. The Persians' arrows flew thick and fast, and the Phocians, supposing themselves to be the main object of the attack, hurriedly withdrew to the highest point of the mountain, where they made ready to face destruction. The Persians, however, with Ephialtes and Hydarnes paid no further attention to them, but passed on along the descending track with all possible speed.

The Greeks at Thermopylae had their first warning of the death that was coming with the dawn from the seer Megistias, who read their doom in the victims of sacrifice; deserters, too, had begun to come in during the night with news of the Persian movement to take them in the rear, and, just as

The Formation of Greece

day was breaking, the look-out men had come running from the hills. At once a conference was held, and opinions were divided, some urging that they must on no account abandon their post, others taking the opposite view. The result was that the army split: some dispersed, the men returning to their various homes, and others made ready to stand by Leonidas.

There is another account which says that Leonidas himself dismissed a part of his force, to spare their lives, but thought it unbecoming for the Spartans under his command to desert the post which they had originally come to guard. I myself am inclined to think that he dismissed them when he realized that they had no heart for the fight and were unwilling to take their share of the danger; at the same time honour forbade that he himself should go. And indeed by remaining at his post he left a great name behind him, and Sparta did not lose her prosperity, as might otherwise have happened; for right at the outset of the war the Spartans had been told by the oracle, when they asked for advice, that either their city must be laid waste by the foreigner or one of their kings be killed. The prophecy was in hexameter verse and ran as follows:

> Hear your fate, O dwellers in Sparta of the wide spaces;
> Either your famed, great town must be sacked by Perseus' sons.
> Or, if that be not, the whole land of Lacedaemon
> Shall mourn the death of a king of the house of Heracles.[2]
> For not the strength of lions or of bulls shall hold him,
> Strength against strength; for he has the power of Zeus,
> And will not be checked till one of these two he has consumed.

I believe it was the thought of this oracle, combined with his wish to lay up for the Spartans a treasure of fame in which no other city should share, that made Leonidas dismiss those troops; I do not think that they deserted, or went off without orders, because of a difference of opinion. Moreover, I am strongly supported in this view by the case of Megistias, the seer from Acarnania who foretold the coming doom by his

---

[2]Leonidas claimed descent from Heracles.

inspection of the sacrificial victims: this man --- he was said to be descended from Melampus --- was with the army, and quite plainly received orders from Leonidas to quit Thermopylae, to save him from sharing the army's fate. But he refused to go, sending away instead an only son of his, who was serving with the forces.

Thus it was that the confederate troops, by Leonidas' orders, abandoned their posts and left the pass, all except the Thespians and the Thebans who remained with the Spartans. The Thebans were detained by Leonidas as hostages very much against their will --- unlike the loyal Thespians, who refused to desert Leonidas and his men, but stayed, and died with them. They were under the command of Demophilus the son of Diadromes.

In the morning Xerxes poured a libation to the rising sun, and then waited till about the time of the filling of the market-place, when he began to move forward. This was according to Ephialtes' instructions, for the way down from the ridge is much shorter and more direct than the long and circuitous ascent. As the Persian army advanced to the assault, the Greeks under Leonidas, knowing that the fight would be their last, pressed forward into the wider part of the pass much further than they had done before; in the previous days' fighting they had been holding the wall and making sorties from behind it into the narrow neck, but now they left the confined space and battle was joined on more open ground. Many of the invaders fell; behind them the company commanders plied their whips, driving the men remorselessly on. Many fell into the sea and were drowned, and still more were trampled to death by their friends. No one could count the number of the dead. The Greeks, who knew that the enemy were on their way round by the mountain track and that death was inevitable, fought with reckless desperation, exerting every ounce of strength that was in them against the invader. By this time most of their spears were broken, and they were killing Persians with their swords.

In the course of that fight Leonidas fell, having fought like a man indeed. Many distinguished Spartans were killed at his side --- their names, like the names of all the three hundred,

I have made myself acquainted with, because they deserve to be remembered. Amongst the Persian dead, too, were many men of high distinction --- for instance, two brothers of Xerxes, Habrocomes and Hyperanthes, both of them sons of Darius by Artanes' daughter Phratagune.

There was a bitter struggle over the body of Leonidas; four times the Greeks drove the enemy off, and at last by their valour succeeded in dragging it away. So it went on, until the fresh troops with Ephialtes were close at hand; and then, when the Greeks knew that they had come, the character of the fighting changed. They withdrew again into the narrow neck of the pass, behind the walls, and took up a position in a single compact body --- all except the Thebans --- on a little hill at the entrance to the pass, where the stone lion in memory of Leonidas stands today. Here they resisted to the last, with their swords, if they had them, and, if not, with their hands and teeth, until the Persians, coming on from the front over the ruins of the wall and closing in from behind, finally overwhelmed them.

Of all the Spartans and Thespians who fought so valiantly on that day, the most signal proof of courage was given by the Spartan Dieneces. It is said that before the battle he was told by a native of Trachis that, when the Persians shot their arrows, there were so many of them that they hid the sun. Dieneces, however, quite unmoved by the thought of the terrible strength of the Persian army, merely remarked: "This is pleasant news that the stranger from Trachis brings us: for if the Persians hide the sun, we shall have our battle in the shade." He is said to have left on record other sayings, too, of a similar kind, by which he will be remembered. After Dieneces the greatest distinction was won by the two Spartan brothers, Alpheus and Maron, the sons of Orsiphantus; and of the Thespians the man to gain the highest glory was a certain Dithyrambus, the son of Harmatides.

The dead were buried where they fell, and with them the men who had been killed before those dismissed by Leonidas left the pass.

Over them is this inscription, in honour of the whole force:

Four thousand here from Pelops' land Against three million once did stand.

The Spartans have a special epitaph; it runs:

Go tell the Spartans, you who read: We took their orders, and are dead.

For the seer Megistias there is the following:

I was Megistias once, who died. When the Mede passed Spercheius' tide. I knew death near, yet would not save Myself, but share the Spartans' grave.

<u>Herodotus: The Histories</u>, translated by Aubrey de Selincourt and revised by A. R. Burn (Penguin Classics, 1954, 1972), copyright (c) the Estate of Aubrey de Selincourt, 1954, revisions copyright (c) A. R. Burn, 1972 (Baltimore: Penguin Books, 1954), 486, 489-494.

Study Questions

1. Who commands the Greek forces at Thermopylae? Why had this man made a special point of taking along middle-aged Spartans and Thebans?

2. Who is Ephialtes? How does Herodotus deal with the varying accounts of Ephialtes' death?

3. Who was guarding Thermopylae? Who is Megistias? What was the prophecy concerning Sparta and Leonidas?

4. What was discussed at the conference held by the Greeks as the Persians advanced? What are the various accounts of what happened? Which account does Herodotus himself trust?

5. Why did Leonidas detain the Thebans?

6. Who was Dieneces?

THUCYDIDES from
HISTORY OF THE PELOPONNESIAN WAR

Thucydides (c. 460 - c. 400) belonged to a leading Athenian family, was elected general in 424, and stationed in Thrace where he failed to prevent the capture of Amphipolis by the Spartans. For this, he was exiled. He returned in the dismal year 404, but apparently died not too many years after that.

Exile gave Thucydides the chance to travel, to interview people, but we know very little of what he actually did. In fact, we know very little of his personal life at all. Exile apparently acted upon him much as it later would affect Dante and Machiavelli, that is, a consummate passion for politics would continue to fill their lives, but unlike the two Florentines, Thucydides seems to have felt little if any bitterness for his native state. Rather, exile seems to have given him the perspective of a cool-headed observer of the war.

Thucydides, like Herodotus, saw history scientifically. Like the older man, he was careful to weigh his sources against one another. But Thucydides gave little weight to Destiny. For him, human events were caused by power blocs acting and reacting upon one another. Athens was a democratic, naval, commercial power. Arrayed against her was Sparta, oligarchic, military, agrarian. Those are the two major blocs, but within Athens itself Thucydides saw the wisely-led democracy of Pericles against the corrupt, self-seeking characters who followed. Thus, besides being an historian, Thucydides is also our first political scientist.

This excerpt, the Melian dialogue, shows the other side of democracy. Thucydides, in exile, was not an eyewitness to these events. His sources were oral witnesses and his own sense of what most probably was said.

ATHENIANS -- "For ourselves, we shall not trouble you with specious pretences -- either of how we have a right to our empire because we overthrew the Mede [Darius and Xerxes], or are now attacking you because of wrong that you have done us -- and make a long speech which would not be believed; and in return we hope that you, instead of thinking to influence us by saying that you did not join the Lacedaemonians, although their colonists, or that you have done us no wrong, will aim at what is feasible, holding in view the real sentiments of us both; since you know as well as we do that right, as the world goes is only in question between equals in power, while the strong do what they can and the weak suffer what they must."

MELIANS -- "As we think, at any rate, it is expedient -- we speak as we are obliged, since you enjoin us to let right alone and talk only of interest -- that you should not destroy what is our common protection, the privilege of being allowed in danger to invoke what is fair and right, and even to profit by arguments not strictly valid if they can be got to pass current. And you are as much interested in this as any, as your fall would be a signal for the heaviest vengeance and an example for the world to meditate upon."

ATHENIANS -- "The end of our empire, if end it should, does not frighten us: a rival empire like Lacedaemon, even if Lacedaemon was our real antagonist, is not so terrible to the vanquished as subjects who by themselves attack and overpower their rulers. This, however, is a risk that we are content to take. We will now proceed to show you that we are come here in the interest of our empire, and that we shall say what we are now going to say, for the preservation of your country; as we would fain exercise that empire over you without trouble, and see you preserved for the good of us both."

MELIANS -- "And how, pray, could it turn out as good for us to serve as for you to rule?"

ATHENIANS -- "Because you would have the advantage of submitting before suffering the worst, and we should gain by not destroying you."

MELIANS -- "So that you would not consent to our being neutral, friends instead of enemies, but allies of neither side."

ATHENIANS -- "No; for your hostility cannot so much hurt us as your friendship will be an argument to our subjects of our weakness, and your enmity of our power."

MELIANS -- "Is that your subjects' idea of equity, to put those who have nothing to do with you in the same category with people that are most of them your own colonists, and some conquered rebels?"

ATHENIANS -- "As far as right goes, they think one has as much of it as the other, and that if any maintain their independence it is because they are strong, and that if we do not molest them it is because we are afraid; so that besides extending our empire we should gain in security by your subjection; the fact that you are islanders and weaker than others rendering it all the more important that you should not succeed in baffling the masters of the sea."

MELIANS -- "But do you consider that there is no security in the policy which we indicate? For here again if you debar us from talking about justice and invite us to obey your interest, we also must explain ours, and try to persuade you, if the two happen to coincide. How can you avoid making enemies of all existing neutrals who shall look at our case and conclude from it that one day or another you will attack them? And what is this but to make greater the enemies you have already, and to force others to become so who would otherwise have never thought of it?"

ATHENIANS -- "Why, the fact is that continentals generally give us but little alarm; the liberty which they enjoy will long prevent their taking precautions against us; it is rather islanders like yourselves, outside our empire, and subjects smarting under the yoke, who would be the most likely to take a rash step and lead themselves and us into obvious danger."

MELIANS -- "Well then, if you risk so much to retain your empire, and your subjects to get rid of it, it were surely great baseness and cowardice in us who are still free not to try everything that can be tried, before submitting to your yoke."

ATHENIANS-- "Not if you are well advised, the contest not being an equal one, with honour as the prize and shame as the penalty, but a question of self-preservation and of not resisting those who are far stronger than you are."

MELIANS -- "But we know that the fortune of war is sometimes more impartial than the disproportion of numbers might lead one to suppose; to submit is to give ourselves over to despair, while action still preserves for us a hope that we may stand erect."

ATHENIANS -- "Hope, danger's comforter, may be indulged in by those who have abundant resources, if not without loss at all events without ruin; but its nature is to be extravagant, and those who go so far as to put their all upon the venture see it in its true colours only when they are ruined; but so long as the discovery would enable them to guard against it, it is never found wanting. Let not this be the case with you, who are weak and hang on a single turn of the scale; nor be like the vulgar, who, abandoning such security as human means may still afford, when visible hopes fail them in extremity, turn to invisible, to prophecies and oracles, and other such inventions that delude men with hopes to their destruction."

MELIANS -- "You may be sure that we are as well aware as you of the difficulty of contending against your power and fortune, unless the terms be equal. But we trust that the gods may grant us fortune as good as yours, since we are just men fighting against unjust, and that what we want in power will be made up by the alliance of the Lacedaemonians, who are bound, if only for very shame, to come to the aid of their kindred. Our confidence, therefore, after all is not so utterly irrational."

ATHENIANS -- "When you speak of the favour of the gods, we may as fairly hope for that as yourselves; neither our pretension nor our conduct being in any way contrary to what

The Formation of Greece

men believe of the gods, or practise among themselves. Of the gods we believe, and of men we know, that by a necessary law of their nature they rule wherever they can. And it is not as if we were the first to make this law, or to act upon it when made: we found it existing before us and shall leave it to exist for ever after us; all we do is to make use of it, knowing that you and everybody else, having the same power as we have, would do the same as we do. Thus, as far as the gods are concerned, we have no fear and no reason to fear that we shall be at a disadvantage. But when we come to your notion about the Lacedaemonians, which leads you to believe that shame will make them help you, here we bless your simplicity but do not envy your folly. The Lacedaemonians, when their own interests or the country's laws are in question, are the worthiest men alive; of their conduct towards others much might be said, but no clearer idea of it could be given than by shortly saying that of all the men we know they are most conspicuous in considering what is agreeable honourable, and what is expedient just. Such a way of thinking does not promise much for the safety which you now unreasonably count upon."

MELIANS -- "But it is for this very reason that we now trust to their respect for expediency to prevent them from betraying the Melians, their colonists, and thereby losing the confidence of their friends in Hellas and helping their enemies."

ATHENIANS -- "Then you do not adopt the view that expediency goes with security, while justice and honour cannot be followed without danger; and danger the Lacedaemonians generally court as little as possible."

MELIANS -- "But we believe that they would be more likely to face even danger for our sake, and with more confidence than for others, as our nearness to Peloponnese makes it easier, for them to act, and our common blood insures our fidelity."

ATHENIANS -- "Yes, but what an intending ally trusts to, is not the good-will of those who ask his aid, but a decided superiority of power for action; and the Lacedaemonians look to this even more than others. At least, such is their distrust of their home resources that it is only with numerous allies that they attack a neighbour; now is it likely that while we are masters of the sea they will cross over to an island?"

MELIANS -- "But they would have others to send. The Cretan sea is a wide one, and it is more difficult for those who command it to intercept others, than for those who wish to elude them to do so safely. And should the Lacedaemonians miscarry in this, they would fall upon your land, and upon those left of your allies whom Brasidas did not reach; and instead of places which are not yours, you will have to fight for your own country and your own confederacy."

ATHENIANS -- "Some diversion of the kind you speak of you may one day experience, only to learn, as others have done, that the Athenians never once yet withdrew from a siege for fear of any. But we are struck by the fact, that after saying you would consult for the safety of your country, in all this discussion you have mentioned nothing which men might trust in and think to be saved by. Your strongest arguments depend upon hope and the future, and your actual resources are too scanty, as compared with those arrayed against you, for you to come out victorious. You will therefore show great blindness of judgment, unless, after allowing us to retire, you can find some counsel more prudent than this. You will surely not be caught by the idea of disgrace, which in dangers that are disgraceful, and at the same time too plain to be mistaken, proves so fatal to mankind since in too many cases the very men that have their eyes perfectly open to what they are rushing into, let the thing called disgrace, by the mere influence of a seductive name, lead them on to a point at which they become so enslaved by the phrase in fact to fall wilfully into hopeless disaster, and incur disgrace more disgraceful as the companion of error, than when it comes as a result of misfortune. This, if you are well advised, you will guard against; and you will not think it dishonourable to submit to the greatest city in Hellas, when it makes you the moderate offer of becoming its tributary ally, without ceasing to enjoy the country that belongs to you; nor when you have the choice given you between war and security, will you be blinded as to choose the worse. And it is certain that those who do not yield to their equals, who keep terms with their superiors, and are moderate towards their inferiors, on the whole succeed best. Think over the matter, therefore, after our withdrawal, and reflect once and again that it is for your country that you are consulting, that you have not more than one, and that upon this one deliberation depends its prosperity or ruin."

John H. Finley, Jr., trans., *The Complete Writings of Thucydides* (New York: Modern Library, Random House, 1951), 331-336.

Study Questions

1. *Why have the Athenians come to Melos? Why won't the Athenians discuss a just policy?*

2. *Why can't Athens permit Melos to remain neutral?*

3. *How do the Melians argue against submitting to Athens? How do the Athenians respond?*

4. *When the Melians argue that the gods will favor them because they are just men fighting unjust men, how do the Athenians answer? What seems to be their attitude toward the gods? What is their attitude toward the Spartans? Why don't they think the Spartans will help the Melians?*

5. *The Melians should fear disgrace and what, according to the Athenians, could cause them disgrace?*

6. *In the end, how has imperialism affected Athens' democracy?*

GREEK PHILOSOPHY AND ART

It was the Greeks who developed philosophy. In so doing, they laid the foundations for the way in which the Western mind approaches almost any problem. The two Greek words, "philo" and "sophia" meant a love of knowing all things. Thus, what to us are separate disciplines of biology, medicine, ethics, politics, mathematics, music, physics and so on, were not to the Greeks. All knowledge initially fell under a single umbrella.

Greek philosophy began about the mid-sixth century at a school in the polis of Miletus in the district of Ionia in Asia Minor. A school was no formal body but rather a number of thinkers who, in general, asked the same kinds of questions and expected the same kinds of answers. What distinguished the Milesian school was that they expected to find the answers to questions about Nature embedded within Nature itself. Thus, they separated the study of Nature from religion. And they were the first to do so. Always before --- in Babylon, Egypt, Persia --- the study of Nature had been inseparable from the gods who had created and ruled Nature. The Milesians were not denying the existence of the gods at all. They were merely denying that Nature **was** god and, therefore, beyond human comprehension.

They were materialists. They believed that all of Nature consisted of four basic elements --- earth, air, fire and water. Where they differed was on the basic underlying stuff from which the elements derived. The earliest of them, Thales (c. 624-548) was convinced that it was water. He was wrong, of course, but he had reached that conclusion by observing the silting up along river beds and marshy areas and, using observation --- as any modern scientist would --- he concluded that the earth rested upon water.

The second of the Milesians was the restless, energetic Anaximander. He was interested in geography, drew accurate maps and concluded that the world was round. Anaximander

Greek Philosophy and Art 43

was convinced that all matter came from a "Boundless", something infinite but nonetheless still matter, indestructible and unchangeable.

The third, Anaximenes, thought the underlying stuff was air. He was also convinced that the entire cosmos was governed by order, laws which could be understood by the rational mind. Thus, there was nothing in the universe that could not be known by human reason.

The Milesians, however, left one fundamental question unanswered, even unasked. Regardless of what the underlying stuff was in Nature, what made it all cohere in an orderly way? Why, in a tree, for instance, do the elements of which it is made appear day in and day out, season after season as tree? What keeps the elements from flying apart? It was Pythagoras who picked up that problem and answered it with the notion of Form. The imposition of mathematical proportions and geometric relationships upon matter give a thing its being --- its realness. The key to understanding Reality then has to be not merely observation but the use of logic to determine Form. By moving away from the absolute materialism of the Milesians and introducing Form, the Pythagoreans brought the study of ethics into philosophy. Since it is Form --- or Soul --- rather than Matter which underlies all being, it becomes important to understand that part of Man which transcends the physical body, namely the Soul.

Another problem confronting the philosophers was change. Is change part of Reality, of Being, or does it merely act upon Being? Heraclitus insisted that everything moves, that all Being is necessarily in a state of flux --- or it ceases to be. But Parmenides insisted that change was only in the appearance of things. The essence of Being remains unchanged. And Democritus believed that all Nature was composed of invisible little atoms and all Being was simply a result of their combinations. It was these disagreements that gave rise to two basic problems. First, how do we ever know that what we say about any thing is true? Second, does it matter? Of what use is such knowledge anyway to conducting one's life?

In the fifth century, philosophical speculation began to split. The inquiry into the physical world culminated in the work of Hippocrates, the "father of medicine." Meanwhile, the stress of the Persian and Peloponnesian Wars, especially in Athens, turned philosophy there toward political and moral questions.

Hippocrates of Cos (469-399) insisted that disease was a natural affliction, not something sent by the gods. Thus, it could be cured by natural means. He thought that since the body is natural, it too must be composed of the four elements, or humors --- yellow and black bile, phlegm and blood. Disease is caused by the imbalance of the humors and to cure it one must simply restore the balance. The fact that he was wrong is beside the point. It was his approach that makes him so revolutionary. He also insisted on treating the patient rather than merely the disease, hence, the importance of keeping case histories. He also would treat symptoms. It really does not matter how one came to start bleeding, for instance. The doctor's job is to staunch the flow. He also thought the best cure for disease was not to get it in the first place. Thus, he insisted on preventive medicine --- a balanced diet and plenty of fresh air, sunlight, exercise and rest.

The stress of war in fifth century Athens raised difficult moral questions. Democracy seemed to have been vindicated by her victories in the Persian Wars, especially her brilliant single-handed defeat of Darius at Marathon. But the Delian imperialism and then the unclear issues and downright failures of the Peloponnesian Wars threw democracy itself into question. Was it really the best kind of government available to men? If not, what would be better? What, anyway, was government supposed to do, to be? As a human institution wrought by men, for men, a good government would presumably be the creation of good men. And what was the good man, the good life?

In the early fifth century, people called Sophists were extremely popular in Athens. They taught logic, grammar, rhetoric --- all for rather substantial fees --- in order to train their students for skillful debate in the ecclesia. They attacked traditional religious beliefs and practices, arguing that good, truth, justice are not absolute principles at all but simply matters of personal opinion. Nothing is absolute. Morality, even the laws and constitution of the state are relative --- related directly to the individual's need of them. One man's idea of truth or justice is as worthy and valid as any other's. That fitted Athenian democracy admirably where one man's vote in the ecclesia weighed no more

Greek Philosophy and Art

nor no less than any other's. The Sophists insisted on majority rule. The minority, precisely because it was the minority, had no claim in public policy.

Socrates (469-399) had two problems with Sophism. First, he was afraid that by attacking religious principles the Sophists were, in fact, undermining the foundations of the state itself. Second, he was also convinced that the Sophists were dead wrong. Socrates was certain that Truth, Justice, Beauty and Good were not mere matters of opinion at all, but absolute, eternal and immutable. By constantly examining and trying to define ever more clearly our ideas of such things, we may come to a closer understanding of what they are by seeing more clearly what they are not. Socrates used a method called the "dialetic" or dialogue to draw his students into an examination of their beliefs because, as he said, "An unexamined life is not worth living". He made his contemporaries uncomfortable and in 399, he was tried by a jury on the two charges of corrupting the young and introducing new gods. The jury found him guilty and sentenced him to death. By law, the death sentence was carried out by the condemned himself, so about two months after his trial, Socrates calmly, almost joyfully, swallowed a cup of hemlock believing that the death of his body would simply free his soul to pursue the Good as it really is, without the bother of mere appearances.

Socrates' pupil, Plato (428-347), popularized and recorded Socrates' teachings in a number of written dialogues. Like his gentle teacher, Plato believed that Idea alone was real and the highest idea of all was Good. Visible, tangible things are only copies of eternal, pre-existing Forms, or ideas. Matter is a source of error, irrational and unknowable. What we understand through reason, Idea, is true and unchanging. Further, being rational beings, we cannot help but desire that which is true and thus, what is good. To desire less, is simply not to be fully human. Once we know the Good, we cannot help but choose it. Virtue then follows from knowledge and to chose evil --- what is not good --- is simply the result of ignorance.

To transmit knowledge of the Good, he established his Academy. One of his pupils was Aristotle (384-322). Aristotle, like Plato, was convinced of the reality of Forms but he parted from Plato in insisting that Being was both Form and Matter. In order to understand reality rightly, Aristotle insisted on using both observation and a strict kind of logic called a "syllogism". There was nothing that did not interest Aristotle, that he did not carefully examine --- botany, zoology, ethics, metaphysics, motion, politics. Aristotle also took up the Milesian investigation of the cosmos and concluded that the earth was the unmoving center of a spherical and eternal universe brought into being and sustained by an Uncaused Cause, a Prime Mover, Itself uncreated Being which causes all being.

The Art of the Classical Age

As the polis was central to Greek philosophy, so was it to the art of the fifth century. Well before Aristotle said anything about a golden mean, the Greeks had concluded that balance, order, harmony were the prerequisites of the good life and thus of the good state. There is a certain wistfulness in that when one remembers that the Peloponnesian Wars, plague, defeat and Athens' own internal turmoil must have made order and harmony seem an almost impossible ideal.

Athenian architecture and sculpture, however, reveal the power of that longing. The most perfect piece of fifth-century building is the Parthenon, the temple to Athena designed by Phidias. No building so exquisitely evokes the Greek control of logic, optics, math and geometry and their love of beauty, of the human. The Greeks never built in anything but a post and lintel style upon which they would place a low pitched roof. The only variation would be in the adornment, or lack of it, on the columns. The simplest style, the Doric, rested flat on the floor or ground, had a smooth surface and a simple, squared-off top or "capital". It was the Doric style which Phidias used in the Parthenon. A slightly more elaborate style, the Ionic, placed the column on a rounded or squared-off base, had a scrolled capital and up to 24 volutes on the column's surface.

In sculpture, the aim was to portray not the real, which is often chaotic and irrational, but the ideal. The sculptor would portray Man, perfectly proportioned, calm, controlled. One sculptor, Polyclitus, even wrote a book, The Canon, on how to mold the perfect, mathematically correct nude male figure. Myron's Discus Thrower illustrates the principles of The Canon.

Greek Philosophy and Art

Greek literature evolved partly from Homer's two epics. Professional singers would travel from place to place, chanting all or parts of The Iliad and The Odyssey. They might also chant elegies, long, formal, declamatory recitations of lofty subjects such as Justice, Honor, or a Homeric theme. By the sixth century, a shorter, more personal and private "lyric" (because it was sung to the accompaniment of a lyre)[1] had also become popular. And in the late sixth century, still another genre, drama, began to evolve.

Athenian drama, like the other arts, grew out of the polis. It began in the festivals honoring Dionysus, god of wine, spring and song. Each year the Athenians would go in a formal procession to the acropolis and there present their gifts while a chorus chanted a praise, or "dithyramb," in Dionysus' honor. During the tyranny of Peisistratus, the honor of organizing and running these festivals was often given to Thespis. Rather often, Thespis would pull one person out of the chorus and make him carry on a chanted dialogue with the chorus. It was only a small step to take another person and then another, and so on. The playwright Aeschylus would do this in the next generation. The chorus would recede but it would never disappear. Nor did the religious content of drama. During the festival, a goat, "tragos," was sacrificed, hence tragedy, which would examine the relationship between Man and the gods and by extension, the polis. Athenian drama, then, while it was decidedly entertaining, was like an American editorial page, a forum where questions of interest to the polis were presented and examined. In the fifth century, the plays would be presented in trilogies, or sets of three, revolving around a single theme or character. Subsidized always by the state, they were presented in the outdoor theatre of Dionysus at the foot of the acropolis by actors who wore masks to designate their different roles.

The first of the three great Athenian tragedians was Aeschylus (525-456). The most patriotic of the three, Aeschylus was also the first to dramatically explore the agony of individuals caught in a fate they had nothing to do with creating. His only

---

[1] Besides the lyre, the Greeks also played a kithara which was a larger, seven-stringed lyre, an aulos which was a double-reed instrument resembling an oboe, flutes and drums.

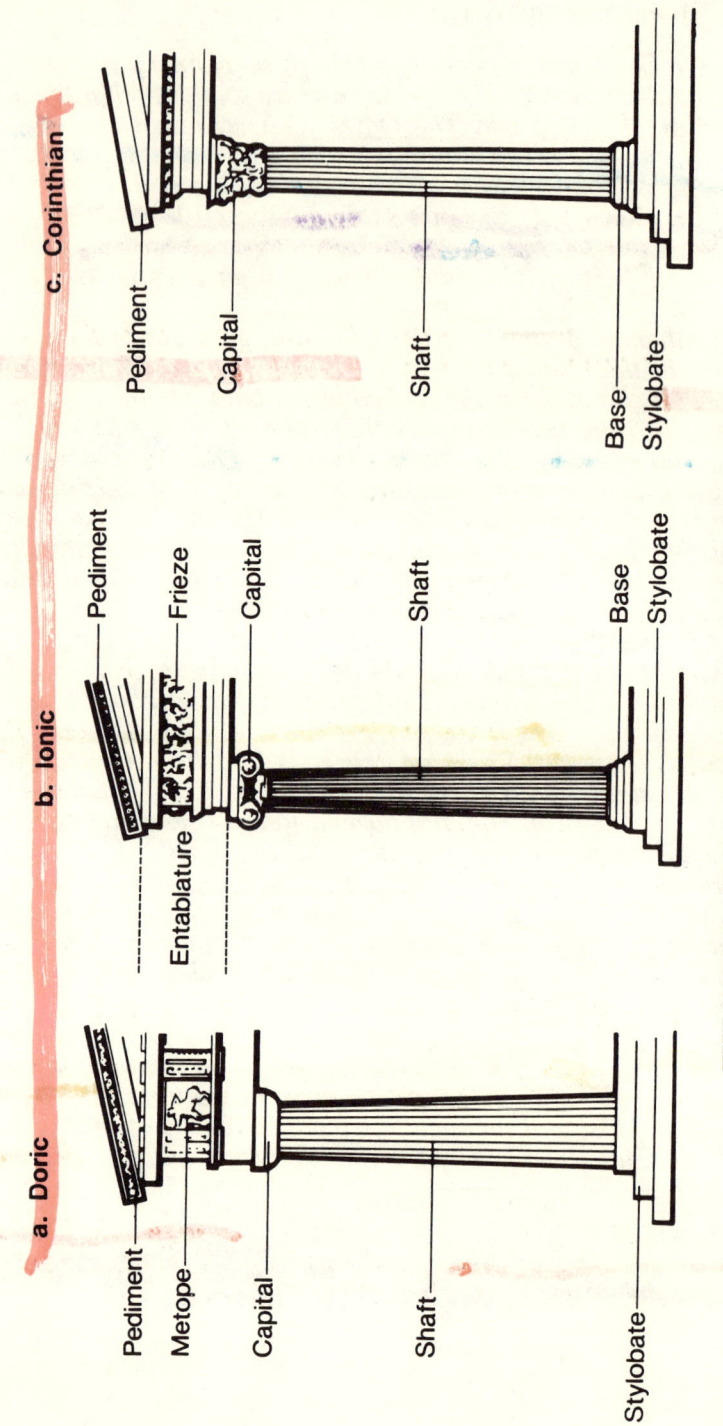

THE THREE ORDERS OF GREEK ARCHITECTURE

a. Doric
- Pediment
- Metope
- Capital
- Shaft
- Stylobate

b. Ionic
- Pediment
- Frieze
- Capital
- Entablature
- Shaft
- Base
- Stylobate

c. Corinthian
- Pediment
- Capital
- Shaft
- Base
- Stylobate

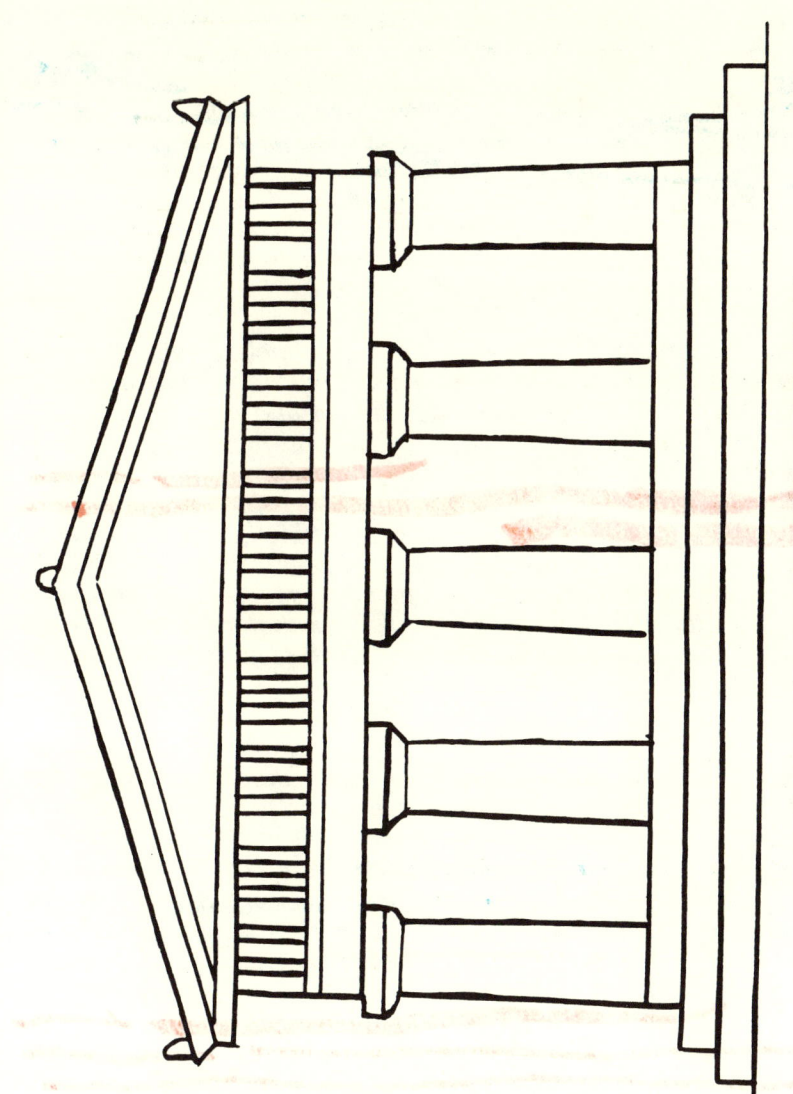

FACADE OF A GREEK TEMPLE

fully surviving trilogy is the Orestaia. In the first play, Agamemnon, that hero returns from the Trojan War and is murdered by his wife, Clytemnestra and her lover. In the second play, The Libation Bearers, Agamemnon's son, Orestes, at Apollo's urging, murders his mother in vengeance for his father's death. In the third play, The Eumenides, the Furies pursue Orestes to punish him for the murder of his mother. Orestes finally appeals to Athena who convenes a jury of Athenian citizens to decide his guilt or innocence. She invites the Furies in to preside over its deliberations now, not as the Furies, but as the nine Worthies. The jury splits evenly and Athena intervenes again on the side of compassion. The play ends with a prayer that discord will always be settled with reason, justice and compassion.

The second of the tragedians, Sophocles (496-406), also examined the relationship between the individual and the state. Like Aeschylus' heroes, Sophocles' heroes and heroines are often caught in fates not of their own making and their choice is either to submit to that fate or rebel. His Oedipus, for instance, try as he might to avoid killing his father and marrying his mother, is simply doomed to do so. Yet by committing hubris, by trying to avoid that awful destiny, he inevitably does bring it on himself. Sophocles' point is that human happiness is to be found in simply accepting the will of the gods however grim that might be, for even when they seem capricious and cruel, ultimately they are just and benevolent.

The last of the three, Euripedes (480-406), was more concerned with the passions of the individual than his relationship with either the gods or the polis. He had no time for the old patriotic jargon and Homeric grandeur. In a moving play, The Trojan Women, the main characters are not the Hectors and the Agamemnons but the widows, the survivors who are left with the desolation and sorrow caused by the heroic butchery of war. And war has no glory for such as these, only grief.

The comic writer Aristophanes (445-386) loved to lampoon the foibles of Athens' leading citizens. He wrote satire which took a sharp scalpel to the prejudices and idiocies not only of the Athenians but all of us. In The Clouds, his target was Socrates but in The Birds, he leveled his wit at democracy itself. By the end of the play, all of the characters in a city have followed

Greek Philosophy and Art

a fellow with a very good scam and are up in the trees, wearing feathers, chirping and behaving just like birds.

There was yet another genre of literature that appeared in that remarkable fifth century, history. It has been said that all of intellectual history is simply a footnote to Plato and Aristotle. It is also true that Herodotus and Thucydides, whom we met in the preceding chapter, taught us how to think about the past.

Suggested Readings

1. Baldry, H. C., *The Greek Tragic Theatre* (New York: Norton, 1971). An excellent introduction to Greek drama.

2. Copleston, Frederick, *A History of Philosophy*, Vol. I (Westminster, Maryland: Newman Press, 1962). For the student seriously interested in further study of Greek philosophy, this volume is essential.

3. Guthrie, W. K. C., *The Greek Philosophers from Thales to Aristotle* (London: Methuen & Co., Ltd., 1950). A short, readable survey of Greek philosophy.

4. Lawrence, A. W., *Greek Architecture*, 4th. ed., (New York: Penguin, 1983). A fairly readable introduction to the subject.

PLATO from THE REPUBLIC

The concerns of Plato (c. 428 - 347 B.C.) were the same as those of his teacher, Socrates --- to know the Good, to apply it to the polis and to transmit knowledge of the Good through teaching --- and he founded his Academy in Athens to do just that. The Academy was the first institution of higher learning and would last until 529 A.D. In order to know the Good, Plato worked out his doctrine of ideas. Idea, for Plato, was not someone's opinion but rather something that exists independently of men's minds, eternal and unchanging. A particular chair, for instance, is only a reflection of the idea, chair. I might destroy the particular chair but I cannot destroy the idea chair. Similarly, when I draw a circle, I have simply a representation of Circle which exists quite apart from my picture. Two and two will always equal four whether I am talking about groups of books, men or continents.

The highest Idea or Form is Good, and Man must try to know what Good is. In order to do that, they must clear their minds of prejudices and assumptions through careful examination of opinions. Out of that process can gradually emerge the idea of Good and once we know the Good, then we cannot help but choose it and thus become good.

Plato's political theory followed from this. Only when men are good can the state be good. But knowing the Good requires not only great natural gifts but also hard work of both mind and body. Not everyone then is equally capable or willing to attain the Good. The rulers of the just state ought, however, to be only those who have most fully realized the Good. It would not do for everyone to participate equally in the running of the polis since the aim of the state is not commanding obedience but securing Justice, the Good. The just state would be run then by a philosopher-king. In the famous allegory of the Cave, given below, Plato describes the emergence of this philosopher-king. It

Greek Philosophy and Art

is clear that Plato's aim is not merely the wise rule of the state but also of the individual. It is not only the foolish citizen but also the foolish man who would wish to remain chained to the cave of the physical world.

The Republic is in the form of a dialogue. You will find this again in Cicero and Boethius. It became a favorite method of expository writing for both classical and medieval writers.

Imagine mankind as dwelling in an underground cave with a long entrance open to the light across the whole width of the cave; in this they have been from childhood, with necks and legs fettered, so they have to stay where they are. They cannot move their heads round because of the fetters, and they can only look forward, but light comes to them from fire burning behind them higher up at a distance. Between the fire and the prisoners is a road above their level, and along it imagine a low wall has been built, as puppet showmen have screens in front of their people over which they work their puppets."

"I see," he said.

"See, then, bearers carrying along this wall all sorts of articles which they hold projecting above the wall, statues of men and other living things, made of stone or wood and all kinds of stuff, some of the bearers speaking and some silent, as you might expect."

"What a remarkable image," he said, "and what remarkable prisoners!"

"Just like ourselves," I said. "For, first of all, tell me this: What do you think such people would have seen of themselves and each other except their shadows, which the fire cast on the opposite wall of the cave?"

"I don't see how they could see anything else," said he, "if they were compelled to keep their heads unmoving all their lives!"

"Very well, what of the things being carried along? Would not this be the same?"

"Of course it would."

"Suppose the prisoners were able to talk together, don't you think that when they named the shadows which they saw passing they would believe they were naming things?"

"Necessarily."

"Then if their prison had an echo from the opposite wall, whenever one of the passing bearers uttered a sound, would they not suppose that the passing shadow must be making the sound? Don't you think so?"

"Indeed I do," he said.

"If so," said I, "such persons would certainly believe that there were no realities except those shadows of handmade things."

"So it must be," said he.

"Now consider," said I, "what their release would be like, and their cure from these fetters and their folly; let us imagine whether it might naturally be something like this. One might be released, and compelled suddenly to stand up and turn his neck round, and to walk and look towards the firelight; all this would hurt him, and he would be too much dazzled to see distinctly those things whose shadows he had seen before. What do you think he would say, if someone told him that what he saw before was foolery, but now he saw more rightly, being a bit nearer reality and turned towards what was a little more real? What if he were shown each of the passing things, and compelled by questions to answer what each one was? Don't you think he would be puzzled, and believe what he saw before was more true than what was shown to him now?"

"Far more," he said.

"Then suppose he were compelled to look towards the real light, it would hurt his eyes, and he would escape by turning them away to the things which he was able to look at, and these he would believe to be clearer than what was being shown to him."

"Just so," said he.

"Suppose, now," said I, "that someone should drag him thence by force, up the rough ascent, the steep way up, and never stop until he could drag him out into the light of the sun, would he not be distressed and furious at being dragged; and when he came into the light, the brilliance would fill his eyes and he would not be able to see even one of the things now called real?"

"That he would not," said he, "all of a sudden."

"He would have to get used to it, surely, I think, if he is to see the things above. First he would most easily look at shadows, after that images of mankind and the rest in water, lastly the things themselves. After this he would find it easier to survey by night the heavens themselves and all that is in them, gazing at the light of the stars and moon, rather than by day the sun and the sun's light."

"Of course."

"Last of all, I suppose, the sun; he could look on the sun itself by itself in its own place, and see what it is like, not reflections of it in water or as it appears in some alien setting."

"Necessarily," said he.

"And only after all this he might reason about it, how this is he who provides seasons and years, and is set over all there is in the visible region, and he is in a manner the cause of all things which they saw."

"Yes, it is clear," said he, "that after all that, he would come to this last."

"Very good. Let him be reminded of his first habitation, and what was wisdom in that place, and of his fellow-prisoners there; don't you think he would bless himself for the change, and pity them?"

"Yes, indeed."

"And if there were honors and praises among them and prizes for the one who saw the passing things most sharply and remembered best which of them used to come before and which after and which together, and from these was best able to prophesy accordingly what was going to come --- do you believe he would set his desire on that, and envy those who were honoured men or potentates among them? Would he not feel as Homer says, and heartily desire rather to be serf of some landless man on earth and to endure anything in the world, rather than to opine as they did and to live in that way?"

"Yes indeed," said he, "he would rather accept anything than live like that."

"Then again," I said, "just consider; if such a one should go down again and sit on his old seat, would he not get his eyes full of darkness coming in suddenly out of the sun?"

"Very much so," said he.

"And if he should have to compete with those who had been always prisoners, by laying down the law about those shadows while he was blinking before his eyes were settled down --- and it would take a good long time to get used to things --- wouldn't they all laugh at him and say he had spoiled his eyesight by going up there, and it was not worth-while so much so to release them and take them up, if they could somehow lay hands on him and kill him?"

"That they would!" said he.

"Then we must apply this image, my dear Glaucon," said I, "to all we have been saying. The world of our sight is like the habitation in prison, the firelight there to the sunlight here, the ascent and the view of the upper world is the rising of the soul into the world of mind; put it so and you will not be far from my own surmise, since that is what you want to hear; but God knows if it is really true. At least, what appears to me is, that in the world of the known, last of all, is the idea of the good, and with what toil to be seen! And seen, this must be inferred to be the cause of all right and beautiful things for all, which gives birth to light and the king of light in the world of sight, and, in the world of mind, herself the queen produces truth and reason; and she must be seen by one who is to act with reason publicly or privately."

"I believe as you do," he said, "in so far as I am able."

"Then believe also, as I do," said I, "and do not be surprised, that those who come thither are not willing to have part in the affairs of men, but their souls ever strive to remain above; for that surely may be expected if our parable fits the case."

"Quite so," he said.

"Well then," said I, "do you think it surprising if one leaving divine contemplations and passing to the evils of men is awkward and appears to be a great fool, while he is still blinking --- not yet accustomed to the darkness around him, but compelled to struggle in law courts or elsewhere about shadows of justice, or the images which make the shadows, and to quarrel about notions of justice in those who have never seen justice itself?"

"Not surprising at all," said he.

"But any man of sense," I said, "would remember that the eyes are doubly confused from two different causes, both in passing from light to darkness and from darkness to light; and believing that the same things happen with regard to the soul also, whenever he sees a soul confused and unable to discern anything he would not just laugh carelessly; he would examine whether it had come out of a more brilliant life, and if it were darkened by the strangeness; or whether it had come out of greater ignorance into a more brilliant light, and if it were dazzled with the brighter illumination. Then only would he congratulate the one soul upon its happy experience and way of life, and pity the other but if he must laugh, his laugh would be a less downright laugh than his laughter at the soul which came out of the light above."

W. H. D. Rouse, *Great Dialogues of Plato* (Copyright (c) 1956, 1984 by John C. G. Rouse. Reprinted by arrangement with NAL Penguin Inc., New York, New York), 312-316.

Study Questions

1. What is the condition of the prisoners in the cave? Where does light come from? What do they think of the images on the wall?

2. What happens to the one who is released? What is his initial reaction to seeing things in the sunlight?

3. How would his fellow prisoners treat him when he returned to the cave?

4. Explain the allegory in terms of our perceptions of reality. What political application does the story have?

ARISTOTLE from THE NICOMACHEAN ETHICS

Plato insisted that there is a Reality beyond our immediate senses and that only the Good is worth seeking. Aristotle (384 - 322 B.C.) taught us how to classify nature and to order our thinking about it through logic. The essential difference between the two is that, while Plato insisted that matter was meaningless and reality was only in the realm of Idea, Aristotle thought that reality was both matter and Form or Idea. In order to understand reality fully, then, we have to use not only reason but the evidence also of our senses. We must look at the characteristics of a thing and decide which are part of its essential being and which are not. In studying and classifying animals, for instance, we may be struck by the brownness of a cow and by the fact that it gives milk. But the brownness and the quality of giving milk also belong to goats. Thus, while our inquiry may begin with what is immediately sensible, it must order that data carefully.

Aristotle was born in the little town of Stagira; hence he is sometimes called the "Stagirite." His father was court physician to the father of Philip of Macedon and Aristotle's early interest in the biological sciences no doubt came from his father. At the age of seventeen, he was sent to Athens where he was closely associated with Plato's Academy for twenty years until the death of Plato. In 343, Philip invited Aristotle to be the tutor to his son, Alexander. He probably only stayed in Macedonia a little less than three years and took no active part in Alexander's subsequent career. He returned to Stagira and then again to Athens where, for about twelve years, he devoted himself to organizing the Lyceum, a program dedicated to pursuing an investigation into just about every branch of inquiry. Here, what we call the experimental method was developed. After Alexander's death in 323, he was in danger of meeting the fate of Socrates so he left, as he said, lest the Athenians sin twice against philosophy. He died in Euboea of chronic acute indigestion brought on by overwork.

Like Plato, Aristotle was interested in ethics and politics. For Aristotle, however, the key was always moderation, the "golden mean" between two extremes. Thus, virtue was the mean between two extremes. But there are different kinds of virtue as there are different kinds of motion and of poetry. The point is always to classify things properly and avoid violating the rules of logic. There are different kinds of states too but the ideal state would be a mean between monarchy on the one hand and democracy on the other, a middle-class polity neither too large nor too small, neither too close to the sea nor too distant and governed by a middle class.

The excerpt here is from his discussion of virtue.

Let us again return to the good we are seeking, and ask what it can be. It seems different in different actions and arts; it is different in medicine, in strategy, and in the other arts likewise. What then is the good of each? Surely that for whose sake everything else is done. In medicine this is health, in strategy victory, in architecture a house, in any other sphere something else, and in every action and pursuit the end; for it is for the sake of this that all men do whatever else they do. Therefore, if there is an end for all that we do, this will be the good achievable by action, and if there are more than one, these will be the goods achievable by action.

So the argument has by a different course reached the same point; but we must try to state this even more clearly. Since there are evidently more than one end, and we choose some of these (e.g., wealth, flutes and in general instruments) for the sake of something else, clearly not all ends are final ends; but the chief good is evidently something final. Therefore, if there is only one final end, this will be what we are seeking, and if there are more than one, the most final of these will be what we are seeking. Now we call that which is in itself worthy of pursuit more final than that which is worthy of pursuit for the sake of something else, and that which is never desirable for the sake of something else more final than the things that are desirable both in themselves and for the sake of that other thing, and therefore we call final without qualification that which is always desirable in itself and never for the sake of something else.

Now such a thing happiness, above all else, is held to be; for this we choose always for itself and never for the sake of something else, but honour, pleasure, reason and every virtue we choose each of them, but we choose them also for the sake of happiness, judging that by means of them we shall be happy. Happiness, on the other hand, no one chooses for the sake of these, nor, in general, for anything other than itself.

* * * * * * *

For this reason also the question is asked, whether happiness is to be acquired by learning or by habituation or some other sort of training, or comes in virtue of some divine providence or again by chance. Now if there is any gift of the gods to men, it is reasonable that happiness should be god-given, and most surely god-given of all human things inasmuch as it is the best. But this question would perhaps be more appropriate to another inquiry; happiness seems, however, even if it is not god-sent but comes as a result of virtue and some process of learning or training, to be among the most god-like things; for that which is the prize and end of virtue seems to be the best thing in the world, and something godlike and blessed.

* * * * * * *

It is natural, then, that we call neither ox nor horse nor any other of the animals happy; for none of them is capable of sharing in such activity. For this reason also a boy is not happy; for he is not yet capable of such acts, owing to his age; and boys who are called happy are being congratulated by reason of the hopes we have for them. For there is required, as we said, not only complete virtue but also a complete life, since many changes occur in life, and all manner of chances, and the most prosperous may fall into great misfortunes in old age, as is told of Priam in the Trojan Cycle; and one who has experienced such chances and has ended wretchedly no one calls happy.

* * * * * * *

The question might be asked, what we mean by saying that we must become just by doing just acts, and temperate by doing temperate acts; for if men do just and temperate acts, they are already just and temperate, exactly as, if they do what is in accordance with the laws of grammar and of music, they are grammarians and musicians.

Or is this not true even of the arts? It is possible to do something that is in accordance with the laws of grammar, either by chance or at the suggestion of another. A man will be a grammarian, then, only when he has both done something grammatical and done it grammatically; and this means doing it in accordance with the grammatical knowledge in himself.

Again, the case of the arts and that of the virtues are not similar; for the products of the arts have their goodness in themselves, so that it is enough that they should have a certain character, but if the acts that are in accordance with the virtues have themselves a certain character it does not follow that they are done justly or temperately. The agent also must be in a certain condition when he does them; in the first place he must have knowledge, secondly he must choose the acts, and choose them for their own sakes, and thirdly his action must proceed from a firm and unchangeable character. These are not reckoned in as conditions of the possession of the arts, except the bare knowledge; but as a condition of the possession of the virtues knowledge has little or no weight, while the other conditions count not for a little but for everything, i.e., the very conditions which result from often doing just and temperate acts.

Actions, then, are called just and temperate when they are such as the just or the temperate man would do; but it is not the man who does these that is just and temperate, but the man who also does them as just and temperate men do them. It is well said, then, that it is by doing just acts that the just man is produced, and by doing temperate acts the temperate man; without doing these no one would have even a prospect of becoming good.

VIRTUE IS UNCHANGING

But most people do not do these, but take refuge in theory and think they are being philosophers and will become good in this way, behaving somewhat like patients who listen attentively to their doctors, but do none of the things they are ordered to do. As the latter will not be made well in body by such a course of treatment, the former will not be made well in soul by such a course in philosophy.

* * * * * * *

How this is to happen we have stated already, but it will be made plain also by the following consideration of the specific nature of virtue. In everything that is continuous and divisible it is possible to take more, less, or an equal amount, and that either in terms of the thing itself or relatively to us; and the equal is an intermediate between excess and defect. By the intermediate in the object I mean that which is equidistant from each of the extremes, which is one and the same for all men; by the intermediate relatively to us that which is neither too much nor too little --- and this is not one, nor the same for all. For instance, if ten is many and two is few, six is the intermediate, taken in terms of the object; for it exceeds and is exceeded by an equal amount; this is intermediate according to arithmetical proportion. But the intermediate relatively to us is not to be taken so; if ten pounds are too much for a particular person to eat and two too little, it does not follow that the trainer will order six pounds; for this also is perhaps too much for the person who is to take it, or too little --- too little for Milo, too much for the beginner in athletic exercises. The same is true of running and wrestling. Thus a master of any art avoids excess and defect, but seeks the intermediate and chooses this --- the intermediate not in the object but relatively to us.

If it is thus, then, that every art does its work well --- by looking to the intermediate and judging its works by this standard (so that we often say of good works of art that it is not possible either to take away or to add anything, implying that excess and defect destroy the goodness of works of art, while the mean preserves it; and good artists, as we say, look to this in their work), and if, further, virtue is more exact and better than any art, as nature also is, then virtue must have the quality of aiming at the intermediate. I mean moral virtue; for it is this that is concerned with passions and actions, and in these there is excess, defect and the intermediate. For instance, both fear and confidence and appetite and anger and pity and in general pleasure and pain may be felt both too much and too little, and in both cases not well; but to feel them at the right times, with reference to the right objects, towards the right people, with the right motive, and in the right way, is what is both intermediate and best, and this is characteristic of virtue. Similarly with regard to actions also there is excess, defect and the intermediate. Now virtue is concerned with passions and actions, in which excess is a form of failure, and so is defect, while the intermediate is praised and is a form of success; and being praised and being successful are both characteristics of virtue. Therefore virtue is a kind of mean, since, as we have seen, it aims at what is intermediate.

* * * * * * *

We must, however, not only make this general statement, but also apply it to the individual facts. For among statements about conduct those which are general apply more widely, but those which are particular are more genuine, since conduct has to do with individual cases, and our statements must harmonize with the facts in these cases. We may take these cases from our table. With regard to feelings of fear and confidence courage is the mean; of the people who exceed, he who exceeds in fearlessness has no name (many of the states have no name), while the man who exceeds in confidence is rash, and he who exceeds in fear and falls short in confidence is a coward. With regard to pleasures and pains --- not all of them, and not so much with regard to the pains --- the mean is tem perance, the excess self-indulgence. Persons deficient with regard to the pleasures are not often found; hence such persons also have received no name. But let us call them 'insensible'.

With regard to giving and taking of money the mean is liberality, the excess and the defect prodigality and meanness. In these actions people exceed and fall short in contrary ways; the prodigal exceeds in spending and falls short in taking, while the mean man exceeds in taking and falling short in spending. (At present we are giving a mere outline or summary, and are satisfied with this; later these states will be more exactly determined.) With regard to money there are also other dispositions --- a mean, magnificence (for the magnificent man differs from the liberal man; the former deals with large sums, and latter with small ones), an excess, tastelessness and vulgarity, and a deficiency, niggardliness; these differ from the states opposed to liberality, and the mode of their difference will be stated later.

Richard McKeon, ed., "Nicomachean Ethics," in *The Basic Works of Aristotle* (New York: Random House, 1941. Reprinted by permission of Oxford University Press), 941-942, 945-946, 955-956, 956-958, 959-960.

Study Questions

1. *How does the aim of a doctor differ from that of a general? Are goods always alike? What is the final end for all men?*

2. *How is happiness achieved?*

3. *Why can't an animal be happy? Why can't a boy? How old does a person have to be in order to be called happy?*

4. *What three qualities must an act possess in order to be called virtuous?*

5. *How does a man become virtuous? How does this differ from Plato's view of virtue?*

6. *Is virtue always the same for all men at all times?*

SAPPHO, LYRICS

<u>Sappho was born in the mid-seventh century B.C. on the island of Lesbos,</u> but political troubles eventually caused her to go to Sicily where she died.

Only fragments of her works have survived. In ancient times, there were nine books of her works, most or all of which were housed in the library at Alexandria, but they had disappeared from general knowledge by the Christian era. By the late second and early third centuries, however, some of them were in circulation again and they attracted the hostility of Christians.

In the eleventh century, both the Byzantine and Roman churches banned her works and they gradually disappeared again. It was not until about the beginning of this century that fragments began again to surface. The following are part of that treasure.

Peer of the Gods

Peer of the Gods I deem him near thee sitting
Who heareth thy low words and lovely laughter, flitting
Soft from thy sweet mouth through the languid hours
Like bees among flowers.

How at the thought my heart is set aflutter!
For when I see thee nothing can I utter,
Rare be the moments, all too swiftly fleeting,
And gracious thy greeting.

Breaketh my tongue down; fire runneth sparkling
Under my skin; eyes strangely are darkling;
Sounds in my ears ring; sweat, to ague leading,
My body is beading.

Duller than dead grass when the summer waneth
Saffron my cheeks grow; not a tint remaineth
Relic of rose joy --- corpse of all gladness
I seem in my madness

But I must dare all: let my love ungifted
Please through my muteness.
Pity hath uplifted
Poor folk to high place; so in queenly fashion
Lend thy compassion.

* * * * * * *

Mother Love

(On Her Daughter Cleis)
Daughter I have with beauty's dower,
Graceful in form as a golden flower;
Darling Cleis, whose deep eyes shine
Reflecting the love that lies in mine;
And not for Lydia's land in fee
Would I trade that trust which she holds in me.

* * * * * * *

Love Sickness

I loved thee once --- dost thou delight to know?
I loved thee, At this, once long, long ago,
When, still in blossoming maidenhood, I smiled
On thee, then but a little graceless child.
Later, when to the noon of life I came,
For thee, abloom in turn, I grew aflame.
Mayhap thou wilt the recollection greet
With pluming pride; to me 'tis bitter sweet
I was the prey of Passion --- tigerish thing
That tore my breast, and left me quivering
With pain's wild ecstasy, while thou didst spurn
My mute appeal, and to another turn.
Thou hatedst me, and still my hate, yet know,
At this, I loved thee once --- but long ago.

* * * * * * *

My skin became as yellow as though in boxwood dyed;
My hairs fell out, and all my frame wasted to skin and bone.
Was there a wizard in the town whose arts
I had not tried?
A magic haunt unvisited, or cave of sibyl lone?
For not a lightsome thing it was, and swift
the days did glide.
Bethink thee of my love, O Moon, and whence its heat hath grown!

Marion Mills Miller and David Moore Robinson, trans., *The Songs of Sappho* (New York: Frank-Maurice, Inc., 1925), 94, 119, 98.

Study Questions

1. *Describe the meter and rhyme scheme.*

2. *What sort of things are Sappho's subjects here?*

3. *Compare these songs with modern love songs.*

SOPHOCLES from ANTIGONE

The life of Sophocles (496 - 406 B.C.) spanned Athens' Golden Age. He was 16 when Athens defeated Xerxes at Salamis, saw the heyday of the Athenian empire, was part of the artistic and intellectual flowering under Pericles, and died two years before Athens' dismal defeat by Sparta. Sophocles was handsome, wealthy, proficient in dancing and playing the lyre, and his plays were popular. He won more prizes than any of his rivals and retained his powers until the end of his life. His <u>Oedipus at Colonus</u> was written when he was about 90 years old. He wrote 120 plays and his tetralogies won 24 "firsts", <u>viz</u>., 96 of his plays were victorious. Only seven have survived intact, however.

Yet for all his success, Sophocles was profoundly sensitive to human suffering. Like Aeschylus, Sophocles used familiar myths and dramatic techniques but he was less certain than Aeschylus of the overall benevolence of Fate and thus of the polis.

In modern American eyes, Antigone may seem like the noble heroine defying the cruel tyrant. But Creon is no tyrant. He blusters a lot but Antigone, while indeed noble, almost begs for martyrdom in going far beyond the token strewing of dust upon Polynices' corpse which is all that was required. In judging between the two, the Athenian audience would probably have been as sympathetic to one as to the other.

After Oedipus discovers that he has murdered his father and married his mother in the play <u>Oedipus the King</u>, he blinds himself and leaves the government of Thebes in the hands of his two sons, Polynices and Eteocles. Their war against each other had been treated by Aeschuylus in <u>Seven Against Thebes</u>. The brothers kill each other and their uncle, Creon, now regent, orders that Polynices' body, because he died attacking his city, will be left unburied and dishonored. Further, anyone who does bury him *will be treated as a traitor and die by stoning. Antigone, caught in a conflict of loyalties, to her dead brother and to the State, decides to defy Creon's edict. It is daybreak. She calls her sister out from the palace.*

ANTIGONE   My darling sister Ismene, we have had
    A fine inheritance from Oedipus.
    God has gone through the whole range of sufferings
    And piled them all on us,--grief upon grief,
    Humiliation upon humiliation.
    And now this latest thing that our dictator
    Has just decreed . . . you heard of it? Or perhaps
    You haven't noticed our enemies at work.

ISMENE   No news, either good or bad, has come
    To me, Antigone: nothing since the day
    We were bereaved of our two brothers. No,
    Since the withdrawal of the Argive army
    Last night, I've heard nothing about our loved ones
    To make me glad or sad.

ANTIGONE   I thought as much.
    That's why I brought you out, outside the gate,
    So we could have a talk here undisturbed.

ISMENE   You've something on your mind. What is it then?

ANTIGONE   Only that our friend Creon has decided
    To discriminate between our brothers' corpses.
    Eteocles he buried with full honors
    To light his way to hell in a blaze of glory.
    But poor dear Polynices,--his remains
    Are not allowed a decent burial.
    He must be left unmourned, without a grave,
    A happy hunting ground for birds
    To peck for tidbits. This ukase[edict] applies
    To you,--and me of course. What's more, friend Creon
    Is on his way here now to supervise
    Its circulation in person. And don't imagine
    He isn't serious,--the penalty
    For disobedience is to be stoned to death.

So, there you have it. You're of noble blood.
Soon you must show your mettle,--if you've any.

ISMENE   Oh my fire-eating sister, what am I
Supposed to do about it, if this is the case?

ANTIGONE   Just think it over--if you'll give a hand . . . .

ISMENE   In doing what? What do you have in mind?

ANTIGONE   Just helping me do something for the corpse.

ISMENE   You don't intend to bury him? It's forbidden.

ANTIGONE   He is my brother, and yours. My mind's made up. You please yourself.

ISMENE   But Creon has forbidden . . . .

ANTIGONE   What Creon says is quite irrelevant.
He is my brother. I will bury him.

* * * * * * *

Despite Antigone's arguments, Ismene refuses to be led into the enterprise and finally walks away from her sister calling Antigone, "fool, wonderful fool, and loyal friend." Antigone buries the corpse of Polynices, is discovered and brought before Creon and charged with her crime.

CREON   (to GUARD) All right, clear off. Consider yourself lucky.
To be absolved of guilt.
(to ANTIGONE) Now tell me, briefly,--I don't want a speech
You knew about my edict which forbade this?

ANTIGONE   Of course I knew. You made it plain enough.

CREON   You took it on yourself to disobey?

ANTIGONE   Sorry, who made this edict? Was it God?
Isn't a man's right to burial decreed
By divine justice? I don't consider your
Pronouncements so important that they can
Just . . . overrule the unwritten laws of heaven.
You are a man, remember.
These divine laws are not just temporary measures.
They stand forever. I would have to face
Them when I die. And I will die, without
Your troubling to arrange it. So, what matter
If I must die before my time? I'd welcome
An early death, living as I do now.
What I can't stand is passively submitting
To my own brother's body being unburied.
I dare say you think I'm being silly.
Perhaps you're not so very wise yourself.

CHORUS   She's difficult, just like her father was.
She doesn't realize when to give in.

CREON   I know these rigid temperaments. They're the first
To break. The hardest-tempered steel
Will shatter at a blow. The highest-mettled
Horses are broken in with a small bit.
That's what is needed, discipline. This girl
Knew damned well she was kicking over the traces,
Breaking the law. And now when she has done it,
She boasts about it, positively gloats,
If she gets away with this behavior,
Call me a woman and call her a man.
I don't care if she is my sister's daughter.
I don't care if she's closer to me than all
My family. She and her sister won't get off.
I'll execute them.
Oh yes, her as well.
She's in it too. Go get her. She's inside.
I saw her in there muttering, half-balmy.
It is her conscience. She can't hide her guilt.
At least she doesn't try to justify it.

ANTIGONE   Won't my death be enough? Do you want more?

CREON   No, that will do, as far as I'm concerned.

ANTIGONE   Then why not do it now? Our wills conflict
　　Head-on. No chance of reconciliation.
　　I can't think of a finer reason for dying,--
　　Guilty of having buried my own brother.
　　These men are on my side. But they daren't say so.

* * * * * * *

　　　　Ismene is brought in and confesses to equal guilt in the crime. Antigone protests that she is innocent but Creon condemns them both. In the next episode, Haemon, Creon's son and Antigone's fiance, confronts his father.

HAEMON   I am your son. So while your policies
　　Are just, you have my full obedience.
　　I certainly wouldn't consider any marriage
　　As important as the right leadership by you.

CREON   Good, good. Your heart is in the right place. Nothing
　　Should come before your loyalty to your father.
　　Why else do fathers pray for well-behaved sons?
　　They do things together. Work together against
　　Their common enemy. Vie with each
　　Other in being good friends their friends.
　　As for the man who brings up useless sons,
　　He's got himself a load of trouble,--all
　　His enemies laugh at them, a bad team.
　　Never get carried away by a woman, son.
　　Sex isn't everything. If she's a bitch,
　　You'll feel a coldness as she lies beside you.
　　Can there be anything worse than giving your love
　　To a bitch that doesn't deserve it? No, reject her,
　　And let her go and find a husband in hell.
　　Now that I've caught her flagrantly disobeying
　　When everybody else has toed the line,
　　The eyes of the nation are on me. I must stay
　　True to my principles. I must execute her.
　　I don't give a damn for all her talk

About family ties. If I allow
My own relations to get out of control,
That gives the cue to everybody else.
People who are loyal members of their families
Will be good citizens too. But if a person
Sets himself up above the law and tries
To tell his rulers what they ought to do,--
You can't expect me to approve of that.
Once a man has authority, he must be obeyed,--
In big things and in small, in every act,
Whether just or not so just. I tell you this,
The well-disciplined man is good
At giving orders and at taking them too.
In war, in a crisis, he's the sort of man
You like to have beside you. On the other hand,
There's nothing so disastrous as anarchy.
Anarchy means an ill-disciplined army,
A rabble that will break into a panic rout.
What follows? Plundered cities, homeless people.
A disciplined army loses few men;
Discipline pulls them through to victory.
We can't go about kowtowing to women.
If I must lose my throne, let it be a man
That takes it from me. I can't have people saying
My will has been defeated by a woman.

CHORUS   I think your observations very just,
     In general . . . though perhaps I'm old and silly.

HAEMON   Father, don't you agree,--
     Of all God's gifts, good sense is far the best.
     I'm sure I'd be the last person to deny
     That what you said is true. Yet there may be
     A lot of justice in the opposite view.
     I've one advantage over you,--I know
     Before you what the people think about you,
     Especially criticism. You're so held in awe
     That people dare not say things to your face.
     But I am able to hear their secret talk.
     The people feel sorry for Antigone.
     They say it isn't equitable she must die
     A horrible death for such a noble action.

They say that she in fact deserves special
Honor for refusing to allow
The body of her brother to be left
Unburied for dogs and birds to pull to pieces.
That is their secret opinion, and it's gaining ground.
Of course I want your rule to be a success.
There's nothing more important to me than that.
Such feeling is mutual, between father and son,--
One's glad to see the other doing well.
Don't be too single-minded, then. Don't think
You have a complete monopoly of the truth.
Isn't it true that people who refuse
To see any other point of view but theirs
Often get shown up and discredited?
However acute one is, there's no disgrace
In being able to learn, being flexible.
In winter, when the streams turn into torrents,
You can see the trees that try to resist the water
Get rooted out and killed. But those that bend
A little, manage to survive the flood.
In a gale at sea if you cram on full sail,
You'll soon have the waves breaking aboard
And bowling over all the furniture.
Why not relax and change your mind for once?
Perhaps at my age I should not express
An opinion, but I would like to say this:--
Not everyone can be right on every issue,
But the next best thing is to take notice of
And learn from the judicious thoughts of others.

****

    The argument becomes more heated until Haemon finally commends Creon to "other friends to condone your madness." Creon then decides to release Ismene and, rather than publicly stone Antigone, he will instead bury her alive in a rock-hewn vault. Antigone, now alone with the Chorus, allows her own pain to be revealed.

ANTIGONE   I shall go to sleep like Niobe.
   I know her story well. On Mount Sipylus

The rock grew, like ivy, round her and weighed her down.
And now the rain and snow
Make tears that run across her stony face.

CHORUS   There's no comparison. For she was born
Of divine parentage. You would be lucky
To share the fate of mythical heroines.

ANTIGONE   Are you getting at me? Wait till I'm dead.
I'm going to die, -- do I merit no respect?
O my city, O my friends, rich householders,
O river Dirce, with the sacred grove
Of Thebes the Charioteer, I call you all
To witness that I die with nobody
To shed a tear for me, the victim
Of an unjust law. Who'd like to go with me
To an eerie heap of stones, a tomb that is no tomb,
A no-man's land between the living and the dead?

CHORUS   You tried to do the right thing by your brother.
You stepped boldly towards the altar of Justice,
But somehow stumbled. I fear you must suffer
For your father's sins.

ANTIGONE   Don't speak of it again. It's only too well known,--
My father's fate. To think how much
Our family was admired, in generations past.
Then came successive strokes of doom. My mother's
Marriage to her son, the union
From which I came, to end like this.
My brother, dishonored, drags me down with him.
And so I go to join my stricken family in hell.

* * * * * * *

Antigone is sealed in the tomb and the blind prophet, Teiresias, pleads with Creon to release her. Creon still refuses and Teiresias foretells doom on his house. After re-considering with the Chorus, Creon finally relents and decides to free Antigone. It is too late. Teiresias' prophecy is dreadfully fulfilled.

EURYDICE *[Creon's wife]* As I was going out, I heard you talking.
I was opening the door when I heard it,
Some more bad news about my children. I fainted,
But my maids held me up. Tell me about it.
I am quite used to suffering.

MESSENGER I'll tell you everything, my dear mistress.
I was there, you know. No sense in glossing things over
You've got to hear it sometime.
I went with my master, your husband, to the place
Where Polynices' corpse was exposed,
Cruelly torn by dogs. We said prayers
Placating Hecate and Pluto; then we washed
The body to purify it, gathered branches
Of olive, and cremated him or what
Was left of him. We piled him up a mound
Of his mother-earth; then went to get
Antigone. While we were on the way,
Somebody heard a sound of crying coming
From the stone chamber. He went up to Creon
And told him of it. Creon hurried on.
As we got near, the sound was all around us,--
Impossible to tell whose it was.
But Creon, in a voice breaking with grief,
Said, "Dare I prophesy? These yards of ground
Will prove the bitterest journey of my life.
It's faint, but it's my son's voice. Hurry, men,
Get round the tomb, pull back the stones, and look
Inside. Is it Haemon's voice, or do the gods
Delude me?" At the far end of the tomb
We saw Antigone hanging by the neck
In a noose of linen. He was hugging her
And talking bitterly of their marriage and
His father's action. Creon saw him and
Cried out and ran in, shouting, "Oh my son,
What is this? What possessed you? Why are you trying
To kill yourself? Come out now, please, I beg you."
His son made no reply, just looked at him
Savagely with a look of deep contempt.
Then he suddenly drew his sword, evaded Creon,

Held it out, and plunged the blade into his ribs.
He collapsed against Antigone's arms which were
Still warm, and hugged her. Then his blood came coughing,
And covered all her white cheeks with scarlet.
So now he lies, one corpse upon another;
And thus their marriage is consummated,--in hell.
It only goes to show good sense is best,
When all this tragedy comes from one rash action.

CHORUS   What a strange thing. Eurydice has gone,
Without saying a word.

MESSENGER   It is surprising.
I dare say she's too well-bred to go
Showing her grief in public. I expect
She's gone to have a good cry inside.

CHORUS   Perhaps. Noisy grief is a bad thing.
But this extraordinary silence is ominous.

MESSENGER   You're right. Let's go in then,
and find out.
She may have had her mind on something rash.

CHORUS   Who's coming? Creon with
The body of his son.
If truth be told, he is
Himself the murderer.

CREON   Wrong! How could I have been so wrong?
And these deaths I caused--you have seen them--
In my own family by my stubbornness.
Oh my son, so young, to die so young,
And all because of me!

CHORUS   It's a bit late to find out you were wrong.

CREON   I know that. God has taken his revenge,
Leapt on my head and beaten me
And trampled on the only joy I had.
And all the years that I have labored--wasted.

SERVANT   My lord, what you see before your eyes,--
   It isn't all. You'd better come inside.

CREON   What fresh disaster could I suffer now?

SERVANT   Your wife, the mother of this corpse is dead.
   Only a moment ago, she stabbed herself.

* * * * * * *

CREON   Lead me away, a wreck, a useless wreck.
   I'll keep out of the way. I killed them both.
   Everything has crumbled. I feel
   A huge weight on my head.

CHORUS   Who wants happiness? The main
   Requirement is to be sensible.
   This means not rebelling against
   God's law, for that is arrogance.
   The greater your arrogance, the heavier God's revenge.
   All old men have learned to be sensible;
   But their juniors will not take the lesson as proved.

Michael Townsend, trans., *Sophocles: Antigone* (Scranton, Pennsylvania: Chandler Publishing Company, 1962), 3-4, 12-13, 16-18, 21, 27-29, 30.

Study Questions

1.   Would you have released Antigone? Why or why not?

2.   How do you think the Athenian audience reacted?

ARISTOPHANES from LYSISTRATA

Aristophanes (c. 445 - 386 B.C.) has been called a good hater. The targets of his lacerating wit were some of the best people that Athens, or the western world, has ever seen. In <u>The Clouds</u> he satirized Socrates; in <u>The Frogs</u>, Aeschuylus and Euripedes are ridiculed as they quarrel for the tragic prize among the dead; in <u>The Acharnians</u> he attacks the war-party in Athens; and in <u>The Knights</u> he levels his scalpel at Creon, an Athenian demagogue. There is a possibility that an Athenian had not really "made it big" unless he had been lampooned by Aristophanes.

In the <u>Lysistrata</u>, the Athenian heroine of that name hits on a scheme for ending the Peloponnesian War. She calls a meeting of the women from Sparta and Athens and several other states. They are late for the meeting. Lysistrata proposes that the women of both sides should withhold their sexual favors from their husbands until they agree to a truce. She induces them to take the following oath.

Repeat after me:

LYSISTRATA
I will withhold all rights of access or entrance

KLEONIKE *[Her neighbor and friend]*
I will withhold all right of access or entrance

LYSISTRATA
From every husband, lover, or casual acquaintance

KLEONIKE
from every husband, lover, or casual acquaintance

LYSISTRATA
Who moves in my direction in erection. ---Go on.

KLEONIKE
who moves in my direction in erection. Ohhhhh!
---Lysistrata, my knees are shaky. Maybe I'd better . . .

LYSISTRATA
I will create, imperforate in cloistered chastity,

KLEONIKE
I will create, imperforate in cloistered chastity,

LYSISTRATA
A newer, more glamorous, supremely seductive me

KLEONIKE
a newer, more glamorous, supremely seductive me

LYSISTRATA
And fire my husband's desire with my molten allure--

KLEONIKE
and fire my husband's desire with my molten allure--

LYSISTRATA
But remain, to his panting advances, icily pure.

KLEONIKE
but remain, to his panting advances, icily pure.

LYSISTRATA
If he should force me to share the connubial couch,

KLEONIKE
If he should force me to share the connubial couch,

LYSISTRATA
I refuse to return his stroke with the teeniest twitch.

KLEONIKE
I refuse to return his stroke with the teeniest twitch.

LYSISTRATA
I will not lift my slippers to touch the thatch

KLEONIKE
I will not lift my slippers to touch the thatch

LYSISTRATA
Or submit sloping prone in a hangdog crouch.

KLEONIKE
or submit sloping prone in a hangdog crouch.

LYSISTRATA
    If I this oath maintain,
    may I drink this glorious wine.

KLEONIKE
    If I this oath maintain,
    may I drink this glorious wine.

LYSISTRATA
    But if I slip or falter,
let me drink water.

KLEONIKE
    But if I slip or falter,
let me drink water.

LYSISTRATA
---And now the General Pledge of Assent:

WOMEN
    A-men! Lysistrata
Good. I'll dedicate the oblation.
[She drinks deeply.]

KLEONIKE
    Not too much, darling. You know how anxious we are to become allies and friends.

* * * * * * *

The men are distraught but Lysistrata's plan begins to falter when the women themselves weaken.

KORYPHAIOS[2] OF WOMEN
[Mock-tragic.]

Mistress, queen of this our subtle scheme, why burst you from the hall with brangled brow?

LYSISTRATA
Oh, wickedness of woman! The female mind does sap my soul and set my wits a-totter.

KORYPHAIOS OF WOMEN
What drear accents are these?

LYSISTRATA
 The merest truth.

KORYPHAIOS OF WOMEN
Be nothing loath to tell the tale to friends.

LYSISTRATA
'Twere shame to utter, pain to hold unsaid.

KORYPHAIOS OF WOMEN
Hide not from me affliction which we share.

LYSISTRATA
In briefest compass,

[Dropping the paratragedy.]
we want to get laid.

KORYPHAIOS OF WOMEN
 By Zeus!

---

[2]Chorus

LYSISTRATA
No, no, not HIM!
   Well, that's the way things are. I've lost my grip on the girls--they're mad for men!
But sly--they slip out in droves.
   A minute ago, I caught one scooping out the little hole that breaks through just below Pan's grotto. One had jerry-rigged some block-and-tackle business and was wriggling away on a rope.

   Another just flat deserted.
   Last night I spied one mounting a sparrow, all set to take off for the nearest bawdy house. I hauled her back by the hair. And excuses, pretexts for overnight
passes? I've heard them all.
   Here comes one. Watch.
[To the First Woman, as she runs out of the Acropolis.]

---You, there! What's your hurry?

FIRST WOMAN
   I have to get home. I've got all this lovely Milesian wool in the house, and the moths will simply batter it to bits!

LYSISTRATA
   I'll bet. Get back inside.

FIRST WOMAN
   I swear I'll hurry right back! ---Just time enough to spread it out on the couch?

LYSISTRATA
Your wool will stay unspread. And you'll stay here.

FIRST WOMAN
No I have to let my piecework rot?

LYSISTRATA
   Possibly. *[The Second Woman runs on.]*

SECOND WOMAN
Oh dear, oh goodness, what shall I do--my flax!
I left and forgot to peel it!

LYSISTRATA
    Another one. She suffers from unpeeled flax.
    ---Get back inside!

SECOND WOMAN
I'll be right back. I just have to pluck the fibers.

LYSISTRATA
No. No plucking. You start it, and everyone else will want to go and do their plucking, too.

[The Third Woman, swelling conspicuously, hurries on, praying loudly.]

THIRD WOMAN
O Goddess of Childbirth, grant that I not deliver until I get me from out this sacred precinct!

LYSISTRATA
What sort of nonsense is this?

THIRD WOMAN
    Today I am--
a miracle!
Let me go home for a midwife,
please!
I may not make it!

LYSISTRATA
[Restraining her.]
    You can do better than that. *[Tapping the woman's stomach and receiving a metallic clang.]*
What's this? It's hard.

THIRD WOMAN
    I'm going to have a boy.

LYSISTRATA
    Not unless he's made of bronze. Let's see. *[She throws open the Third Woman's cloak, exposing a huge bronze helmet.]*

Of all the brazen...You've stolen the helmet from Athene's statue! Pregnant, indeed!

THIRD WOMAN
    I am so pregnant!

LYSISTRATA
Then why the helmet?

THIRD WOMAN
    I thought my time might come while I was still on forbidden ground. If it did,
I could climb inside Athene's helmet and have
my baby there.
The pigeons do it all the time.

LYSISTRATA
Nothing but excuses!

[Taking the helmet.]

    This is your baby. I'm afraid you'll have to stay until we give it a name.

THIRD WOMAN
But the Acropolis is awful. I can't even sleep! I saw the snake that guards the temple.

LYSISTRATA
    That snake's a fabrication.

THIRD WOMAN
I don't care what kind it is--I'm scared! *[The other women, who have emerged from the citadel, crowd around.]*

KLEONIKE
And those goddamned holy owls! All night long, tu-wit, tu-wu---they're hooting me into my grave!

LYSISTRATA
Darlings, let's call a halt to this hocuspocus.
You miss your men--now isn't that the trouble?

[Shamefaced nods from the group.]

Don't you think they miss you just as much? I can assure you, their nights are every bit as hard as yours. So be good girls; endure! Persist a few days more, and Victory is ours. It's fated: a current prophecy declares that the men will go down to defeat before us, provided that we maintain a United Front.

* * * * * * *

A truce is finally reached when the men get drunk and sign a treaty.

Douglass Parker, trans., <u>Four Comedies by Aristophanes</u> (Ann Arbor: University of Michigan Press, 1969), 22-23, 51-54.

Study Questions

1. *What (who) is Aristophanes satirizing in the play?*

2. *This play has become a favorite of modern feminists. Do you think the Athenian audience regarded it in the same way? Explain.*

THE HELLENISTIC AGE

To his contemporaries, Alexander the Great was a god. More secular generations since then have given him scarcely any less stature. Without question, he is one of history's handful of giants.

Alexander's father, Philip II of Macedon (reigned 359-336 B.C.), however, was a man of no mean stature himself. Philip turned his poor, backward state into the most formidable power in Greece by a combination of courage, relentless energy and shrewdness, qualities he would bequeath to his son.

Philip's first task, and perhaps his most difficult, was to turn the fiercely independent and proud chieftains of his mountainous realm into a united and formidable force, loyal to him. Having done that, he then turned to his ever-quarrelling southern neighbors. His superior army was soon poised at Thebes who pleaded with Athens for help. In usual Greek fashion, the Athenians were perfectly willing to leave Thebes to her fate, until the brilliant orator, Demosthenes, in a series of bitterly invective speeches called "philippics", warned his fellow-citizens against Philip. Athens then joined with Thebes to defeat Philip but were themselves defeated by him at the battle of Charonea in 338. Philip's next target was the Peloponnese but before he could fully accomplish that, he was stabbed to death in 336.

Between Alexander and his father there had never been any great love. Yet Alexander inherited his father's genius and Philip's dream of leading a united Greece against Persia. In 334, at the age of twenty-two, Alexander began to carry out that dream but it was to be more than a conquest, for Alexander's vision went far beyond his father's. Alexander, the student of Aristotle, included poets, scientists, philosophers, musicians, artisans and even an historian on his staff. In the next three years he won brilliant victories at the Granicus River, Issus and Gaugamela against Persian forces ineptly commanded by the king, Darius III.

The Hellenistic Age

The victory at Gaugamela opened the heart of Persia itself to Alexander. In 331, in pursuit of Darius, he entered the exquisite capital of Persepolis and burned it, he said, in retribution for Xerxes' burning of Athens a century and a half earlier. Still pursuing Darius, Alexander then marched north, raided the royal treasury at Susa and finally caught up with Darius at Rey, just south of modern Teheran. He found a corpse. Darius' own generals had murdered him.

That did not end it. For Alexander, the march had perhaps not ever been a matter of conquest so much as one of discovery. He moved northeastward into Sogdiana and then into northern India, where in a battle on the Hyphasis River in 326, he met the Indian king Porrhus' army mounted on elephants. After defeating Porrhus, he moved quickly to make peace with his erstwhile foe as he had in all his conquests. All along he had adopted the customs and manners, sometimes even the dress of those he had just conquered. He also had a habit of giving rank and office to those who had ability, whether they were Greeks, Egyptians, Persians or whatever to the consternation of many of his Greek followers who thought they should get preference. There had been talk of mutiny long before but when, after the battle at the Hyphasis, it appeared that Alexander would follow his usual pattern and appoint Indians to preferential positions, his men simply rebelled and Alexander was forced to turn back. He followed the southern rim of Persia and reached Babylon in 323. There, he died at the ripe old age of thirty-two.

He left behind at least seventy new cities, many named Alexandria, thus scattering Greek magistracies, settlers and Greek culture all over the East. Moreover, he had been eager to enlist the aid and talents of non-Greeks. The result was the fusion of Hellenic and Oriental cultures into something that was both and neither --- the Hellenistic --- a cultural unity upon which Rome would merely impose a political unity in a short while.

Alexander's political legacy was a bit of chaos. When asked on his deathbed who should succeed him, Alexander replied, "Let the best man rule." His generals buried him with a good bit of pomp and then fell to fighting among themselves to determine the "best man." Ultimately, Alexander's close boyhood friend, Ptolemy, acquired Egypt, and Seleucus received much of Asia Minor and Persia. The Seleucids, however, would lose their

Persian holdings when a new dynasty, the Parthians, successfully rebelled against them about a generation after Alexander's death. Lysimachus and Antigonus fought over Greece and Macedonia and eventually the Antigonids achieved dominance.

Although all of these monarchies fought each other chronically, they bore some common characteristics. Most importantly, the tiny, homogenous polis was supplanted by sprawling, multi-racial kingdoms. The personal involvement and sense of deep loyalty generated by the polis simply evaporated in the large, impersonal state. The city became simply an industrial and commercial center. It had libraries, theatres and offered all kinds of cultural, economic and educational opportunities. It was an exciting place. In the bazaars one could find exotic goods and people and strange customs and dress from the Indus to the Nile. One heard a bewildering variety of languages but a common language for business, diplomacy and scholarship soon emerged. This was koine, a mixture of Greek and Oriental borrowings. It was <u>koine</u> that St. Paul would use to communicate to his new converts.

The opening of the East meant wider career opportunities for Greeks. Talented, ambitious men could sell their military, naval and administrative skills to Hellenistic kings. And the kings, in their turn, were quite willing to employ men whose service rested, not on any patriotism but on the regular delivery of a paycheck. There was something of a self-serving opportunism and egotism in this. Very simply a man would serve the king who could offer the best pay.

Alexander's conquests also brought the East into the economic orbit of the Greek world and in turn opened the West to the goods, customs, habits and geography of the East. The gold and silver bullion of Persia financed the building of roads, harbors and new cities. The kings used the same Attic standard so most money had the same value, and since Greek commercial law and methods of transacting business were used, trade thrived. It was in the ports and bazaars that the greatest intermingling occurred. Obviously, it was not merely goods but ideas that were also being exchanged.

The Hellenistic Age

Hellenistic Science and Philosophy

As in government, so too in the cultural life of the Hellenistic world Greeks were dominant. In science, especially, there were exciting developments. It is crucial to remember that the study of the physical world had long before been separated from the study of ethics, metaphysics and politics. The Hellenistic Age made significant contributions in both areas.

One of the giants of the period was Aristarchus of Samos (310-230) who, although he was educated at Aristotle's Academy, broke with the master's conception of the universe. Rather than an earth-centered universe Aristarchus believed in a heliocentric or sun-centered universe in which the earth and planets revolve around the sun. He also thought the stars and sun are much bigger than they appear and that they are much farther away than previously thought. Not too many people thought Aristarchus was right. First, the evidence of our senses seems to contradict him and he had no telescope. Second, he was at odds with Aristotle and Aristotle's irrefutable logic is very difficult to argue with. Still Aristarchus' theory was picked up here and there in the ancient world and handed down to the Middle Ages. Thus, it was not an entirely new or unheard of idea when Nicolaus Copernicus picked it up in the sixteenth century.

There were other important advances. Euclid (c. 300?) gave us *The Elements of Geometry* and Archimedes (287-212) gave us the screw and pulley. His grasp of the idea of the lever enabled him to construct siege engines, catapults and artillery that struck terror into Roman hearts. He also founded the science of hydrostatics when he discovered that a solid displaces its own weight when placed into a liquid.

There was also Eratosthenes who thought the world was a sphere and calculated its circumference. He was off by only about 185 miles. He made a world map and was also sure one could get to India by sailing west, an idea tested by Columbus and then proven by Magellan.

* * * * * * *

Hellenistic philosophy was derived directly from the thought of the fifth century Athenians. The moral relativism of the Sophists found expression as Cynicism which taught that, if there were any absolutes, Man could never know them. The best thing is to abandon social conventions and live simply according to Nature with as few luxuries as possible. The most colorful of the Cynics was Diogenes of Sinope (412-323) who went about the world with a lamp in search of an honest man.

The idealism of the Socratics came though in Epicureanism and Stoicism. Epicurus (340-270) who founded his school in Athens about 306, believed that the fundamental aim of all human conduct is to pursue pleasure and avoid pain. By pleasure, however, he meant not a mindless hedonism but that serenity of mind which comes only through knowledge. The chief obstacle to serenity is anxiety, particularly anxiety about death and fear of the gods. But this anxiety too can be removed through understanding.

The founder of Stoicism was Zeno (335-263) from Cyprus, who came to Athens and met his followers in a colonnaded arcade there called a "stoa," hence, the name of the philosophy. The Stoics believed in a natural order which is Reason. Since all men possess the "divine spark" of Reason, they are all brothers. There is then no difference between Greek and non-Greek, rich and poor, slave and freemen. All men belong to a commonwealth ruled by the law of Nature which is Good. Thus, the Stoics gave a kind of philosophical underpinning to the heterogeneous yet culturally united Hellenistic world. Because Nature is orderly and rational and therefore good, thought Zeno, there is nothing mysterious nor accidental about it. Wars, personal misfortune, pleasure, fame, grief all have a purpose, and the individual's best job then is to understand as much as possible and accept it all. Each of us has a role, a place in Nature and, as rational beings, we must not shirk our duties either within the Natural Order or to our fellow man. To resist Nature is both futile and evil. Stoicism was soon to be enthusiastically picked up by the Romans. It would not only provide a philosophical basis on which Rome could rule her empire but would also pave the way for Rome's acceptance of Christianity.

Hellenistic Art

Greek contact with other peoples resulted in artistic works that were often monumental and extremely sensuous. Greek

The Hellenistic Age

humanism was still paramount but now instead of moderation, balance, and rational control, the arts often focused on the emotional, the extreme. In architecture, kings and wealthy officials wanted buildings that were grand and impressive. And they got them --- great complexes like the one in Pergamum filled with palaces, temples and theatres. The post and lintel design still held but, instead of the simple Doric and Ionic columns, the more elaborate Corinthian column now appeared. It had a fancier, raised base and a bell-shaped capital adorned with leaves, flowers and various other tracery.

In sculpture, the favorite theme was still the human body. But rather than the ideal Man, the Hellenistic sculptor liked to depict all kinds of human activity. Old people and children became favorite subjects, that is, people at one extreme or the other of life, not the "golden mean" of young manhood. One of the most charming pieces is of a little boy and his pet goose. They were interested in exploring the entire range of human emotion. The famous <u>Laocoon</u> shows the old Trojan priest, Laocoon, and his two sons being squeezed to death by huge serpents after he has warned the Trojans not to bring the Wooden Horse into the city. The pain and agony on their faces, their writhing, twisted bodies cannot leave the viewer unmoved.

As sculpture overflowed with violence and intense emotion, so too did drama. With the polis now no longer in existence, drama lost its political and therefore much of its moral content. Where Hellenic tragedy had examined the relationship between Man and the gods and had been restrained and fairly quiet (most of the violence took place off-stage), Hellenistic tragedy was filled with on-stage violence, murky, intricate plots, sorcery, omens and ghosts. That same appeal to the emotions appears in comedy as well which now became slapstick. Menander of Athens was a favorite. His plays are full of mistaken identities, cuckholded husbands, misers, braggarts, sweet young lovers and boisterous drunks. Shakespeare, Molière and Congreve would be influenced by Menanderian characters and plots and even Mozart's delightful Figaro has roots in Menander.

The center of Hellenistic learning was Alexandria. The first Ptolemy ordered the creation of a museum and libraries there and for centuries, poets, philosophers, scientists and artists would be lured there. Eventually there was an astronomical observatory, *a zoo, a botanical garden and an anatomical institute. Something close to 700,000 scrolls were housed there. Callimachus (305-240) catalogued the library and wrote hymns and epigrams. He flourished about the same time as Theocritus (310-250) who is famous for his pastoral poetry. He loved the bustle of the city, its crowds and gossip, yet his pastorals praising flowers and the simple life in the country are some of the sweetest works to come out of the age.*

Suggested Readings

1. Bonnard, Andre, <u>Greek Civilization</u>, translated by R. C. Knight, Vol. III (London: G. Allen and Unwin, 1961). Contains chapters on the classical and Hellenistic periods.

2. Bury, J. B., et al., <u>The Hellenistic Age</u> (Cambridge, England: University Press, 1925). First published in 1923, this classic contains essays by leading scholars.

3. Grant, Michael, <u>From Alexander to Cleopatra</u> (London: Weidenfeld and Nicolson, 1982). A recent survey of various phases of Hellenistic culture.

4. Hamilton, J. R., <u>Alexander the Great</u> (London: Hutchinson, 1973). Perhaps the best biography of Alexander.

5. Lloyd, G. E. R., <u>Greek Science After Aristotle</u> (London: Chatto & Windus, 1973). Perhaps the best survey of Hellenistic science.

6. Rostovtzeff, M., <u>The Social and Economic History of the Hellenistic World</u>, 3 Vols. (Oxford: Clarendon Press, 1941). An indispensable work for really understanding the period.

7. Tarn, W. W. and Griffith, G. T., <u>Hellenistic Civilization</u>, 3rd ed., (London: E. Arnold, 1952). A good survey of Hellenistic civilization.

PLUTARCH on ALEXANDER THE GREAT

We have already met Plutarch in his description of the manners of the Spartans (see Chapter 1). This excerpt also is taken from the <u>Moralia</u>. You will notice here Plutarch on the side of history that movies are made of. It is not Aristotle nor Plato nor Zeno nor the playwrights who matter so much as the hero who spreads the knowledge of them, the giant who makes the network news.

You will say therefore that Alexander was too rash and daringly inconsiderate, with such a slender support to rush upon so vast an opposition. By no means: for who was ever better fitted than he for splendid enterprises, with all the choicest and most excelling precepts of magnaminity, consideration, wisdom, and virtuous fortitude, with which a philosophical education largely supplied him for his expedition? So that we may properly affirm that he invaded Persia with greater assistance from Aristotle than from his father Philip. As for those who write how Alexander was wont to say that the Iliad and Odyssey had always followed him in his wars, in honor to Homer I believe them. Nevertheless, if any one affirm that the Iliad and Odyssey were admitted of his train merely as the recreation of his wearied thoughts or pastime of his leisure hours, but that philosophical learning, and commentaries concerning contempt of fear, fortitude, temperance, and nobleness of spirit, were the real cabinet provision which he carried along for his personal use, we contemn their assertion. For he was not a person that ever wrote concerning arguments or syllogisms; none of those who observed walks in the Lyceum, or held disputes in the Academy; for they who thus circumscribe philosophy believe it to consist in discoursing, not in action.

On the other side, take a view of Alexander's discipline, and you shall see how he taught the Hyrcanians the conveniency of wedlock, introduced husbandry among the Arachosians, persuaded the Sogdians to preserve and cherish --- not to kill --- their aged parents; the Persians to reverence and honor --- not to marry --- their mothers. Most admirable philosophy! Which induced the Indians to worship the Grecian Deities, and wrought upon the Scythians to bury their deceased friends, not to feed upon their carcasses. We admire the power of Carneades's eloquence, for forcing the Carthaginian Clitomachus, called Asdrubal before, to embrace the Grecian customs. No less we wonder at the prevailing reason of Zeno, by whom the Babylonian Diogenes was charmed into the love of philosophy. Yet no sooner had Alexander subdued Asia, than Homer became an author in high esteem, and the Persian, Susian, and Gedrosian youth sang the tragedies of Euripides and Sophocles. Among the Athenians, Socrates, introducing foreign Deities, was condemned to death at the prosecution of his accusers. But Alexander engaged both Bactria and Caucasus to worship the Grecian Gods, which they had never known before. Lastly, Plato, though he proposed but one single form of a commonwealth, could never persuade any people to make use of it, by reason of the austerity of his government. But Alexander, building above seventy cities among the barbarous nations, and as it were sowing the Grecian customs and constitutions all over Asia, quite weaned them from their former wild and savage manner of living. The laws of Plato here and there a single person may peradventure study, but myriads of people have made and still make use of Alexander's. And they whom Alexander vanquished were more greatly blessed than they who fled his conquests. For these had none to deliver them from their ancient state of misery; the others the victor compelled to better fortune. True therefore was that expression of Themistocles, when he was a fugitive from his native country, and the king entertained him with sumptuous presents, assigning him three stipendiary cities to supply his table, one with bread, a second with wine, a third with all manner of costly viands; Ah! young men, said he, had we not been undone, we had surely been undone. It may, however, be more justly averred of those whom Alexander subdued, had they not been vanquished, they had never been civilized. Egypt had not vaunted her Alexandria, nor Mesopotamia her Seleucia; Sogdiana had not gloried in her

The Hellenistic Age

Propthasia, nor the Indians boasted their Bucephalia, nor Caucasus its neighboring Grecian city; by the founding of all which barbarism was extinguished and custom changed the worse into better.

If then philosophers assume to themselves their highest applause for cultivating the most fierce and rugged conditions of men, certainly Alexander is to be acknowledged the chiefest of philosophers, who changed the wild and brutish customs of so many various nations, reducing them to order and government.

A. H. Clough and William F. Goodwin, eds., *Plutarch's Essays and Miscellanies*, 5 vols., (New York: The Colonial Company, Limited, 1905), I, 478-481.

Study Questions

1. *How many cities has Alexander founded? Name the principal cities of the Hellenistic world.*

2. *What civilizing traits has he taught the Sogdians, the Hyrcanians, the Persians, Scythians and Indians?*

3. *Of what value to Alexander were Homer, Philip and Aristotle?*

4. *Why is Alexander greater than all the philosophers of Greece?*

5. *Explain Themistocles' remark, "... had we not been undone, we had surely been undone". Is it possible to justify imperialsim?*

THEOCRITUS, "THE DESPERATE LOVER"

Theocritus (310 - 250 B.C.) was a native of Syracuse in Sicily. He visited Cos and Alexandria, the center of Hellenistic learning. He wrote charming, rustic poems about rural life in Sicily that later influenced the Roman poet Virgil. He also wrote this kind of poem.

I'll sing to Amaryllis while my goats,
Tended by Tityrus, browse along the hill.
O Tityrus, my belov'd one, feed my goats,
And lead them to the spring, and oh, beware
The horns of yonder tawny Libyan buck!

Fair Amaryllis, why no more wilt thou call to me:
'Darling, darling,' and peep from thy bower?
    Am I loathed by thee?

When thou see'st me anear, is my nose too
    flat, or my chin too long?
Girl, thou wilt drive me to hang myself for
    this cruel wrong.

Lo! here, from the tree thou bad'st me gather
    them, half a score
Of apples I bring, and to-morrow I'll bring
    thee as many more.

Ah, look on my grievous woe! Would that I now
    might turn
Into yon humming bee, and win to thy shy
    retreat.
Lightly thridding the ivy that clings and the
    sheltering fern!

Now know I Love and his might most sore. A lioness' teat

He sucked, and was reared by his dam in an oakwood's deep
    recess.
He drives his dart to the bone; I am smouldering
    in his heat.

Dark-browed girl of the lovely glance, thou
    daintiness,
Fold thy goatherd to thee that so I may kiss
    thee, dear;
For 'e'en in an empty kiss is a sweet delight
    fulness.'

Thou wilt make me rend in shreds the coronal I
    bring here,
Of ivy and fragrant parsley and roses wreathed, for thee.
What shall I do, alas, poor wretch! Wilt thou
    not give ear!

I shall doff my cloak and leap from yon head
    land into the sea,
Where Olpis the fisherman watches for tunny
    down in the bay;
And if I be drowned - ah well- my death will
    be joy to thee.

* * * * * * *

This bitter thing did I learn as I mused upon
    thee one day;
For a poppy-petal I smote as it lay on my
    elbow smooth,
And the love-in-absence gave no crack, but
    withered away.

Groio the sieve-divineress told me erewhile
    the truth,
She who would gather the hay by my side as I
    mowed on the lea:
For all of my heart is thine, but thou reck'st
    not of me, poor youth.

A white she-goat with her twins have I been
    keeping for thee:
But Erithacis begs for them oft - the girl
    with the dusky brow.
And I will give them to her, for thou but
    playest with me.

My right eye quivers - shall I see her now?
Here by this pine I'll throw me down and sing;
Perchance she'll cast on me a pitying look,
For sure she is not made of adamant.

Hippomenes yearned a maid to wed;
Apples he took and ran.
Love's wave went o'er Atalanta's head
When she beheld the man.

Melampus the prophet drove the neat
From Othrys to Pylos town,
    And Alphesiboea's mother sweet
In Bias' arms lay down.

Adonis, upon the mountain-side,
So maddened with love's unrest Love's goddess, that e'en in
    death he'll bide
        For ever on her breast.

        Happy Endymion is, I trow,
        Who sleepeth and waketh not,
And ye profane, ye shall never know Iasion's happy lot.

My head aches, but thou carest not; I'll sing
No more, but here will lay me down and die;
And wolves shall batten on my flesh. May that
Be sweet to thee as honey in the mouth!

James Henry Hallard, trans., *The Idylls of Theocritus*, 3rd ed., (London: Rivington's, 1913), 17-19.

Study Questions

1. *How does the style of this poem differ from the Homeric epics or the drama of the fifth century?*

2. *Who is Amaryllis? What has she done to the "I" of the poem?*

3. *Who are Tityrus and Groio?*

4. *How does this resemble (or differ from) the poetry of Sappho?*

ROMAN REPUBLIC. 509 - 27 B.C.

According to the historian Livy, Mars, the god of war, sired twin sons, Romulus and Remus. The boys were raised by a she-wolf and about 753 B.C. they founded Rome on three of her famous seven hills. When Remus, jealous of his brother's settlement on the Palotine Hill, ridiculed it by jumping over its unfinished wall, Romulus slew him and vowed that so would anyone die who would dare leap over his wall. The settlement which would bear Romulus' name, however, very shortly fell under the influence of a people about whom very little is known, the Etruscans. As a loose confederacy of city-states, they had established control over much of northern and central Italy by the mid-eighth century. They drained the swamps and deliberately laid the city out on a spoked-wheel design. The Etruscans also gave Rome her alphabet (in its turn a borrowing from the Greeks), the toga, public games such as chariot races and gladiator contests, a number of guilds including ceramics, coppersmiths, metalworkers and most importantly perhaps, contact with the wider Mediterranean world. The Forum, graced by public buildings and temples, became the center of the city. Etruscan art showed a love of nature. That, combined with the Greek love of humanism, filtered through Rome, would become the two major themes in Western art.

The Etruscans also gave Rome a line of kings who ruled Rome with the advice and consent of a Senate, a body of patricians, or nobles. Apparently the arrangement worked admirably until in 509 B.C., the king, Tarquin the Proud, was overthrown and murdered.

Tarquin's overthrow inaugurated a revolution, but an extremely conservative one. One hunts in vain for a Roman political theorist such as a Plato, a Locke, or a Jefferson. The Romans were practical. What worked they used; what didn't work, they got rid of. Thus, the constitution drafted in 509 retained the Senate as the law-making body because it worked,

Roman Republic. 509 - 27 B.C.

but the monarchy, which hadn't, was replaced by an intentionally weak executive in the hands of two consuls, elected for one-year terms. The consuls commanded the army, acted as judges and initiated legislation. Realizing that strong leadership is required in times of crisis, the constitution allowed the Senate to name a dictator for the duration of the emergency, at the end of which he would be required to step down. The Senate controlled public finances and foreign policy and senators were either appointed for life terms by the consuls or were ex-magistrates.

Among the other public offices was a "praetor" or chief legal official, a "quaestor" who assessed, collected and disbursed revenue, and an "aedile" who was in charge of public works such as roads, bridges and aqueducts. There was also a "pontifex maximus" in charge of religious matters, seeing to it that religious rites were observed, temples kept in repair, foreign cults licensed --- and some of the more outrageous ones outlawed. The most powerful of these officials was the censor. As the name suggests, his job was two-fold. He took the census, counted people and their property for voting purposes and he also censored dangerous or immoral speeches, broadsides and other writings.

Voting for these offices was in the "comitia centuriata" but it was done in such a way as to exclude plebians, or non-nobles from any of these offices. It was this state of affairs which led to the Struggle of the Orders, a struggle of the plebians for full political equality.

The first step in the Struggle was taken in 471 when the Senate allowed the creation of a Plebian Assembly and the office of tribune. The Plebian Assembly had no legal power but the Senate learned quickly to listen to the voice of the people. The tribune was a liaison between the Assembly and the Senate and protected the plebians against arbitrary patrician magistrates. The tribune had to be a plebian and this office, the repository of the people's trust, came to be one of the most honored in Rome.

The second step came a mere twenty years later in 451, when the Senate ordered that Roman law be codified and engraved on twelve bronze tablets and placed in the Forum. The Twelve Tables made law the possession of all Romans, not merely of the priests or the Senate.

The third step came a century later. A law was passed requiring that one of the two consuls elected each year be a plebian and in 351, a plebian was elected censor. With that, no office was now in fact closed to plebians.

The last step in the Struggle was really frosting on the cake. In 287, the Hortensian Law allowed the Plebian Assembly to veto legislation passed by the Senate and gave resolutions it passed the force of law. In fact, then, no bill could become law without the consent of both the Senate and the Assembly.

At any stage in the Struggle, class warfare or anarchy could have erupted. It didn't. Roman tenacity and willingness to stick with a problem until a practical solution was worked out had resulted in full equality of citizenship and, at least theoretically, had made the highest office available to plebian and patrician alike. The Senate's concessions, however, had been due to more than just magnanimity and good sense. Almost from its earliest days, the Republic was at war. The plebians could threaten to withhold their military service, their taxes and their labor if concessions weren't forthcoming.

The Romans did not always win these wars but in fighting them they developed the attitudes and techniques that gradually made them the most formidable power in the peninsula. The Roman legion itself, resembling the Greek phalanx but more mobile and flexible, became almost invincible because by law only Romans who owned property were enrolled in the army. Each man then had something dear to fight for. Each man knew that his companions, like himself, would fight to the death --- either the enemy's or his own. Desertion from one's post was punished by a disgrace worse than death. Also, bred into each Roman soul was *pietas*, a single-minded devotion to the family and the family's gods --- and Rome was simply the family writ large. The head of the family was the *pater familias*, the eldest male, whose authority was absolute. He could disown a son, kill an adulterous wife and arbitrarily arrange the marriages of his children. The Roman never was very good at being self-centered then. It was at home that he learned to put the family, the Roman family, before his own individual good. And it was there that he learned the discipline and patriotism (derived from *pater* = father) that would enable his legions to conquer and rule the Western world.

Roman Republic. 509 - 27 B.C.

The conquest of Latium was accomplished by the end of the fifth century. Then, in the early fourth century, a new people, the Celts, or "Gauls" as the Romans called them, swept down from the north and in 390 sacked Rome and levied a heavy tribute. In their sweep, the Gauls had also destroyed much of what remained of the Etruscan empire. After the Gauls had taken their gold and returned to their home beyond the Alps, the Romans rebuilt their city, conquered Etruria and then turned southward and defeated the Samnites to gain possession of the Campania and southern Italy.

Rome's greatest legacies to the West have been in law and administration and at this early stage when her empire included not quite the whole Italian peninsula, that genius is evident. Again, she never developed any theory or policy of empire. She simply met each situation as she found it. Thus, there was a network of treaties and alliances. With many of their older Italian allies, the Romans shared full citizenship. In other cases, they granted citizenship but without the right to vote or hold office. They paid taxes and served in the army but were left free to run their own local affairs. That willingness to extend the benefits of citizenship and with it access to Rome's courts and the benefits of the protection of Rome's legions made Roman rule more often welcome than not. Practical as always, Rome early realized that sharing with her former enemies the benefits of her own system ultimately strengthened and enriched the Roman state itself.

By the early third century, only the Greek states in the Italian toe and heel eluded Rome. Alarmed by the Roman steamroller, in 282, the Greek city of Tarentum asked for help from the Antigonid king, Pyrrhus, one of the best generals of his day. In the ensuing war with the Romans, Pyrrhus technically won but his losses were so great that he was forced to withdraw leaving the Greek south to Rome.

That "Pyrrhic" victory put Rome across the narrow strait from the island of Sicily. Sicily was a colony of the powerful Carthaginian empire. Perhaps conflict between the two "super powers" was inevitable. In any case, in 264, they came to blows over the city of Messana which commands the strait. This ushered in the first of three Punic Wars, so-called from the language spoken at Carthage. The First Punic War (264-241) *forced Rome to fight on the seas for the first time. With typical flexibility and resolve, and with help from Naples, Rome put together a navy and defeated Carthage.*

The peace treaty in 241, however, brought no peace. Convinced that peace with Rome was impossible, Carthage moved to consolidate and expand the foothold which she had earlier established in Spain. In 22l, under a brilliant young commander named Hannibal, Carthaginian troops lay siege to the city of Saguntum. The Romans declared that Hannibal had attacked a friendly city and the Second Punic War began. In 218, in an epic march, Hannibal crossed the Alps into northern Italy and embarked on a policy of terror designed to draw Rome's allies away from her. It was here that Rome's generosity paid off. Some of the newer conquests deserted her but older allies such as Latium, Etruria and Samnium held firm despite Hannibal's ravages. Rome's darkest, and one of her finest hours, came at the battle of Cannae in 216, when nearly 60,000 Romans were slaughtered. The survivors buried their dead, declared a short period of mourning and strode right back into battle. With one Roman army chasing him in Italy, another lodged in Spain and still a third attacking Syracuse in Sicily, Hannibal was unable to capitalize on Cannae. Finally in 207, Spain was wrested from his grasp and in 204, a Roman fleet landed at Carthage itself, thus forcing Hannibal to return to defend his own homeland. In 202, Scipio Africanus defeated Hannibal at the battle of Zama, near Carthage. Hannibal himself escaped and found refuge at the Antigonid court where he was later poisoned.

The Third Punic War was almost entirely the work of Cato the Elder, a plebian who had risen to some of Rome's highest offices. Regardless of what the Senate was debating, Cato would end every speech with the words, "Carthage must be destroyed". His reasoning was that so long as Carthage even existed at all, yet another Hannibal might threaten Rome. He got his way. The Third Punic War, savage and unjust and no doubt unnecessary, ended in 146 when Carthage was annihilated.

By 146, not only the western Mediterranean, but also the east, lay in Roman hands. The perennial conflicts among the Hellenistic kings had allowed Roman diplomacy combined with her legions to bring much of the area under her control.

Roman Republic. 509 - 27 B.C.

Apart from the acquisition of territories, however, the Punic Wars had an enormous impact on Rome's political life. The new territories needed administrators, garrisons, courts and tax collectors. Also, great generals who had commanded large bodies of troops for a long time were enormously popular. Would the state be able to control them? Moreover, Rome's Italian allies had borne much of the brunt of the fighting but they reaped few of the rewards and they now agitated for full citizen ship. Most dangerous of all, however, was the growing body of indigent citizens crowding into the city. The Second Punic War, especially, had left the Roman countryside in a shambles. The prolonged fighting had drawn many men away from their farms and the families had often been unable to keep them under full cultivation. Veterans returned to ruined fields and vineyards, broken and/or rusted equipment, wrecked buildings, wasted herds and flocks. They could either try to rebuild, a daunting prospect, or they could sell their holdings to those who had made money on war and were willing to buy their farms. Many elected the latter course realizing that big profits, in fact any profit, could not be made on small farms. Nor did they remain as renters. The wealthy landowners who held large "latifundia" (landed estates) sometimes hired free labor but they preferred to use slaves who could not demand a share of the profits. The small landholder would thus often migrate to the cities, especially to Rome. But there both unskilled and even skilled labor were in the hands of slaves or small shopkeepers who simply could not absorb a large labor force. Thus, the veteran who had recently fought for his country now found himself without land, without work, without hope and living in an unsanitary, crowded, shabby slum with neither fire nor police protection. The situation was explosive. Though veterans, by selling their land, they were now ineligible for military service. But they were willing to follow anyone who held out a helping hand.

A patrician named Tiberius Gracchus did just that. He was elected tribune in 133 and then proposed that the large latifundia be broken up so that no single holding would be larger than 312 acres. The excess land would then be made available in plots to be sold to the poor. The money to compensate the former owners and also to create a fund from which the poor could borrow money to buy this land would come from the revenues of the newly acquired province of Pergamum. The scheme naturally enraged the wealthy latifundia owners but it also alarmed them.

In the first place, Tiberius put his plan before the Plebian Assembly without consulting the Senate which, if it wasn't illegal, was at least undiplomatic. Worse, however, Tiberius obviously had the wildly enthusiastic support of the poor. Given the unsettled state of things, it looked like Tiberius could become Rome's de facto ruler. So one night a group of senators simply slaughtered Tiberius in cold blood. It was the first time, and unhappily not the last, that Romans would settle a political dispute among themselves by violence. Nonetheless, Tiberius' bill did become law.

Ten years later Tiberius' younger brother, Gaius, also took up the problem of the urban poor. Elected tribune in 123, Gaius proposed making grain available to the poor at less than half the market price. He also proposed granting citizenship to Rome's Italian allies. Again, it was not so much the proposals themselves as the massive following Gaius had which generated the alarmed hostility of the Senate. In 121, fearing for his life, he armed his supporters. The Senate ordered the consul to restore order and he did so by killing Gaius and 3,000 of his followers. Again, attempts to reform had met with bloodshed. The deaths of the Gracchi were also the end of any attempt to solve the problem of the urban poor through legal, constitutional methods.

In 112, Jugurtha, the ruler of the client state of Numidia, rebelled against Rome. The war which followed went badly for Rome until 107 when a plebian general named Marius became consul. A courageous and ambitious man, Marius took the unprecedented step of enrolling the landless poor in his legions. Thus, he created an army of professionals, not a force of drafted conscripts. And in 106, he handily defeated Jugurtha. The next year when war broke out in the north, that same army again won and Marius was awarded the consul ship consecutively, and thus illegally, in the years 104-100. There was another small glitch. In order to encourage enlistments, Marius had promised land to his veterans after the war and naturally the poor and landless had flocked to him. The Senate, however, in 101, refused to authorize his proposal, thus dooming the Republic. Henceforth, it would be to military magnates like Marius that men would look to further their interests and protect them, not the state.

In the Social War (91-88), Marius came into conflict with the patrician Sulla. The Social War resulted from the Senate's

Roman Republic. 509 - 27 B.C.

registration of Gaius Gracchus' plan to award full citizenship to Rome's Italian allies. It was a bitter war --- and avoidable --- and resulted in the grant of citizenship anyway in 88. In that year, Sulla gained the consulship but in the final stages of the Social War, Sulla was deposed. He immediately marched on Rome and restored a modicum of order. Then he marched against Mithridates, the king of Pontus who had become a bleeding thorn on Rome's eastern flank against Persia. While he was gone, violence erupted again in Rome as Marius butchered his way into the city and launched a reign of terror. Even though Marius died peacefully in 86, his supporters held Rome until 82 when Sulla returned and butchered the Marians and then proclaimed himself dictator. Sulla then weakened the tribunate, the office from which the Gracchi had moved. He also packed the Senate with his own supporters, increased the number of provincial magistrates, abdicated in 79 and then died, like Marius, in bed the next year.

Sulla's protégé and political heir was Pompey who had won the support of southern Italian merchants by clearing out a nest of pirates who had preyed on Mediterranean shipping for years. In a third war against Mithridates, Pompey defeated him. But, with typical Roman thoroughness, Pompey realized that the rebellions Mithridates had sparked in Rome's eastern provinces had caught fire only because of Rome's own administrative mismanagement and abuses such as tax farming. Pompey simply cleaned house believing that good government is also cheap and efficient government.

Meanwhile a millionaire named Crassus had also risen to prominence. By quashing a slave rebellion led by Spartacus in 73, he won the support of the wealthy landowners. In the year 60, Pompey and Crassus joined forces with Julius Caesar to form an alliance known as the First Triumvirate. Lacking Senate approval, the Triumvirate was illegal, a small technicality by now. By the arrangement, Caesar got the West where he had already made a name for himself by a successful campaign in Spain. The East understandably went to Pompey.

Crassus died in 53 and in 49, war broke out between Caesar and Pompey who was backed by most of the Senate. The civil war raged from Spain to Greece. Finally, at Pharsalus, Pompey was defeated. He was shortly killed but Caesar granted a *general amnesty to Pompey's supporters. The Senate then granted him the office of dictator and with that authority Caesar then set about healing Rome's wounds. He opened up the newly-conquered lands in Gaul and also in Spain and North Africa to Roman settlement in order, partly, to accommodate veterans and the poor, but also to enhance the Romanization of the Western empire. He reformed the courts and provincial administrations. He also extended citizenship to many of the provincials who had supported him and reformed the calendar.*

Then in March 44, a group of senators led by Brutus and Cassius assassinated Caesar because they feared that he wanted to be a king. In the turmoil which followed, a Second Triumvirate was formed which included the general Lepidus who had been Pompey's successor in the East, Marc Antony who had been Caesar's secretary, and a relative unknown, Caesar's nephew and heir, the young Octavian. The Senate did ratify this Triumvirate because it was formed ostensibly to track down Caesar's assassins and bring them to justice. This was done when the conspirators were defeated at Philippi in 42 B.C. The Second Triumvirate, too, fell apart when Octavian found Antony plotting with the Egyptian queen, Cleopatra, to control the Roman world. In a naval battle in the Bay of Actium, Antony's forces were defeated and he and Cleopatra committed suicide. Lepidus had been forced into obscurity and again a Caesar ruled Rome. After receiving his triumph, Octavian was awarded the title of princeps and then Augustus. It would be this man who would end the century of civil war and inaugurate the Pax Romana and a new era of Rome's history. Bearing now only the facade of Republican institutions, Augustus would construct, in fact, an autocracy that could effectively rule what Rome had now become --- no longer the little city-state on the Tiber but a Rome that had become a world.

Culture in the Late Republic

The turmoil of the Republic's death throes saw the emergence of some of Rome's finest art and thought. Perhaps the "noblest Roman of them all" was not Brutus, as Shakespeare had it, but Cicero. In fact, generations since have referred to the last century of the Republic as the Age of Cicero. A brilliant orator and stylist, Cicero was dedicated to republicanism but he thought of the republic as a "res publica", a public thing, belonging not to

Roman Republic. 509 - 27 B.C.

this or that general or interest group, but to the whole community, past and future, as well as present. He remained passionately dedicated to that ideal even as the Republic collapsed in ruins about him.

One of the more troubling aspects of Rome's expansion had been how to deal with the sophisticated, urban culture of the Hellenistic world. There was a tendency to look down upon it as degraded, effeminate, hopelessly indecent and corrupt. Yet as libraries and works of art came to Rome, citizens realized, too, the value of Greek science and philosophy and developed a taste for Greek arts and literature. Among the status symbols for the wealthy Roman were Greek tutors for his children or even a stay at one of the schools in Athens itself. Statues done in imitation of Greek styles adorned his garden.

The comic playwright Plautus (254-184) wrote plays with Greek characters in Greek settings but with enough drunken soldiers, boisterous womanizers, baudies, gluttons and sweet young lovers to attract sellout crowds in Rome. Terence (190-159) was a little more polished than Plautus and, influenced by Menander, his style was more graceful. He also attracted smaller audiences.

In philosophy, the Romans borrowed Epicureanism and Stoicism as if they had invented them. The Epicurean, Lucretius (94-55), living in the midst of the conflict between Marius and Sulla, understandably longed for tranquility. His <u>On the Nature of Things</u>, argues for a purely materialistic concept of nature and scoffs at traditional religion as superstition. The Roman, however, was usually more attracted to Stoicism simply because the Stoic insistence on duty and a universal, rational order squared nicely with the empire Rome had become.

In sculpture, there was little enthusiasm for the overdone, emotional poses of the Hellenistic artist. Roman sculpture tended to be more realistic and restrained. Thus, in depicting the human form, the artist usually gives us authentic portraits of his subjects. In another way, too, the Romans broke from Greece. The Greek had never been terribly interested in the physical world beyond Man. The Roman was, and carefully detailed carvings of flowers, sheaves of grain, birds and other animals survive on bowls, cups, sarcophagi, jewelry, columns and even shields and armor.

In architecture, too, the Romans were innovators. The invention of concrete allowed them to create first the arch and then the barrel vault and dome. They could then create impressive public buildings of great majesty and dignity.

Ironically, the greatest outpouring of artistic and intellectual activity came in the turmoil of the Republic's last century --- as it had in Athens.

Suggested Readings

1. Boren, H. C., *Roman Society* (New York: Twayne Publishers, 1977). A highly readable social, economic and cultural history of both the Republic and the Empire.

2. _____, *The Gracchi* (New York: Twayne Publishers, 1968). Treats the work of the two brothers and their effect on the fortunes of the Republic.

3. Brunt, P. A., *Social Conflicts in the Roman Republic* (New York: Norton, 1971). The discontents of both urban and rural poor and the struggles of the propertied classes and their effects on Rome's political life are studied here.

4. Errington, R. M., *The Dawn of Empire: Rome's Rise to World Power* (Ithaca, New York: Cornell University Press, 1972). Shows Rome acquiring empire only with a good bit of reluctance.

5. Grant, Michael, *A History of Rome* (London: Weidenfeld and Nicolson, 1978). Recent and good survey of both the Republic and the Empire.

6. Gruen, E., *The Last Generation of the Roman Republic* (Berkeley: University of California Press, 1974). Studies the last days of the Republic from Sulla to Caesar.

Roman Republic. 509 - 27 B.C.

7. Pallottino, M., *The Etruscans* (Bloomington, Indiana: Indiana University Press, 1975). A fairly recent account of Rome's founders.

8. Scullard, H. H., *From the Gracchi to Nero* 2nd ed., (London: Methuen, 1963). A readable and competent account of the death of the Republic and the rise of the Empire.

9. Syme, R., *The Roman Revolution* (Oxford: Clarendon Press, 1952). This classic covering the late Republic should not be overlooked.

FROM the TWELVE TABLES

Published and mounted on twelve bronze tablets in the Forum about 451 B.C., the Tables are a model of conservative common sense in which a careful attempt has been made to balance the rights of the individual against the legitimate needs of the community. You will notice, however, that there are inequities in punishments and slavery is assumed. Differences in social position, property, etc., would have made the Roman scorn the idea that "all men are equal" and his law recognized that. Nonetheless, Table XI was repealed by a law in 445 which did allow plebians and patricians to marry each other.

The Twelve Tables were not a statement of ideals or principles. Rather, they expressed law as it already existed. You will note that the style is curt, imperative and simple.

Table IV. - Patria Potestas.

1. Monstrous or deformed offspring may be put to death[1].
2. The father shall, during his whole life, have absolute power over his legitimate children. He may imprison the son, or scourge him, or keep him working in the fields in fetters, or put him to death, even if the son held the highest offices of state, and were celebrated for his public services. He may also sell the son.
3. But if the father sell the son a third time, the son shall be free from his father.
4. A child born within ten months of the death of the mother's husband shall be held legitimate.

---

[1] Dion, 2, 15 says the law of Romulus required that such offspring should first be shown to five neighbors, and that these should approve of the course proposed.

Roman Republic. 509 - 27 B.C.

Table V. - Inheritance and Tutelage.

1. All women shall be under the authority of a guardian; but the vestal virgins are free from tutelage.
2. The mancipable things belonging to a woman that is under the tutelage of her agnates are not subject to usucapion, unless she herself deliver possession of them with the authority of her tutor.
3. The provisions of the will of a pater familias concerning his property and the tutelage of his family, shall be law.
4. If a man cannot control his actions, or is prodigal, his person and his property shall be under the power of his agnates, and, in default of these, his *gentiles* . . . . if he has no curator.
5. If a freedman die intestate, and without *usus heres*, his patron shall succeed.

Table VI. - Ownership and Possession.

1. If a wife . . . wishes to avoid subjection to the hand of her husband by usucapion, she shall absent herself for a space of three nights in each year from his house, and thus break the usus of each year.
2. No length of possession by an alien can vest in him a title to property as against a Roman citizen.
3. If a man finds that his timber has been used by another in building a house, or for the support of vines, he shall not remove it.
4. But he shall have a right of action against the other for double its value.

Table VII. - Real Property Law.

1. A clear space of two feet and a half shall be left around every house. (That is to say, every two houses must stand at least five feet apart.)

* * * * * * *

3. A space of five feet between adjoining lands shall not be liable to usucapion.
4. For the settlement of disputes as to boundaries, three arbiters shall be appointed.

5. The breadth of road over which there is right of way is eight feet in the straight, and sixteen feet at the bends.
6. The neighbouring proprietors shall make the road passable; but if it be impassable, one may drive one's beast or vehicle across the land wherever one chooses.
7. If one's property is threatened with damage from rain-water that has been artificially diverted from its natural channels, the owner may bring an action *aquae pluviae arcendae*, and exact compensation for any damage his property may sustain.
8. The branches of trees that overshadow adjoining land shall be lopped to a height of fifteen feet from the ground.
9. Fruit that falls from one's trees upon a neighbour's land may be collected by the owner of the tree.

Table VII. - Torts.

1. Whoever shall publish a libel --- that is to say, shall write verses imputing crime or immorality to anyone --- shall be beaten to death with clubs.
2. If a man break another's limb, and do not compromise the injury, he shall be liable to retaliation.
3. For breaking a bone of a freeman, the penalty shall be 300 as[s]es; of a slave, 150 as[s]es.
4. For personal injury or affront, 25 as[s]es.
5. Accidental damage must be compensated.
6. A quadruped that has done damage on a neighbour's land, shall be given up to the aggrieved party, unless the owner of it make compensation.
7. He that pastures his animals on a neighbour's land is liable to an action.
8. A man shall not remove his neighbour's crops to another field by incantations, nor conjure away his corn.
9. For a person of the age of puberty to depasture or cut down a neighbour's crop by stealth in the night, shall be a capital crime, the culprit to be devoted to Ceres and hanged; but if the culprit be under the age of puberty, he shall be scourged at the discretion of the magistrate, and be condemned to pay double the value of the damage done.

Roman Republic. 509 - 27 B.C.

10. If a man wilfully set fire to a house, or to a stack of corn set up near a house, he shall be bound, scourged, and burned alive; if the fire rose through accident, that is, through negligence, he shall make compensation, and, if too poor, he shall undergo a moderate punishment.
11. If a man wrongfully fell his neighbours trees, he shall pay a penalty of 25 as[s]es in respect of each tree.
12. A person committing theft in the night may lawfully be killed.
13. But in the day-time a thief may not be killed, unless he defend himself with a weapon.
14. If theft be committed in the day-time, and if the thief be taken in the fact, and do not defend himself with a weapon, then, if a freeman, he shall be scourged and adjudged as a bondsman to the person robbed; if a slave, he shall be scourged and hurled from the Tarpeian rock. A boy under puberty shall be scourged at the discretion of the praetor, and made to compensate for the theft.
15. A person that searches for stolen property on the premises of another, without the latter's consent, shall search naked, wearing nothing but a girdle, and holding a plate in his hands; and if any stolen property is thus discovered, the person in possession of it shall be held as a thief taken in the fact. When stolen property is searched for by consent in the presence of witnesses (without the girdle and plate), and found in a person's possession, the owner can recover by action of _furti concepti_ against the person on whose premises it is found, and the latter can recover by action _furti oblati_ against the person who brought it on his pre mises, three times the value of the thing stolen.
16. For theft not discovered in commission, the penalty is double the value of the property stolen.
17. Title to property in stolen goods cannot be acquired by prescription.
18. A usurer exacting higher interest than the legal rate of ten per cent per annum is liable to fourfold damages.
21. A patron that wrongs his client shall be devoted to the infernal gods.

22. If any one that has consented to be a witness, or has acted as scale-bearer (in mancipation), refuses to give his evidence, he shall be infamous and incapable of giving evidence, or of having evidence given on his behalf.
23. False witnesses shall be hurled from the Tarpeian rock.
24. If one kill another accidentally, he shall atone for the deed by providing a ram to be sacrificed in place of him.
25. For practicing incantations or administering poisonous drugs, the penalty shall be death.
26. Seditious gatherings in the city during the night are forbidden.
27. Associations (or clubs) may adopt whatever rules they please, provided such rules be not inconsistent with public law.

Table IX. - Public Law.

1. No laws shall be proposed affecting individuals only.
2. The assembly of the centuries alone may pass laws affecting the caput of a citizen.
3. A judex or arbiter, appointed by a magistrate to decide a case, if guilty of accepting a bribe, shall be punished with death.
4. Provisions relating to the quaestors (or court appointed for the investigation of cases) of homicide. --- There shall be a right of appeal from every decision of a judex (judicium), and from every penal sentence (poena).
5. Whoever stirs up an enemy against the state, or betrays a citizen to an enemy, shall be punished capitally.
6. No one shall be put to death, except after formal trial and sentence.

Table X. - Sacred Law.

1. A dead body shall not be buried or burnt within the city.
2. More than this shall not be done. The wood of the funeral pile shall not be smoothed with the axe.

Roman Republic. 509 - 27 B.C.

3. Not more than three mourners wearing ricinia,[2] one wearing a small tunic of purple, and ten flute-players may attend the funeral.
4. Women shall not tear their cheeks, nor indulge in wailing.
5. The bones of a dead person shall not be preserved for later burial, unless he died in battle or in a foreign country.
6. Regulations regarding [prohibiting] unction, drinking [banquets], expensive libations (of wine perfumed with myrrh), chaplets, and incense boxes.
7. But if the deceased has gained a chaplet, by the achievements either of himself or of his slaves or his horses, he or his parents may wear such, in virtue of his honour and valour [while the corpse is lying within the house or is being borne to the sepulchre].
8. No person shall have more than one funeral, or more than one bier.
9. Gold shall not be burned or buried with the dead, except such gold as the teeth have been fastened with.
10. A funeral pile or sepulchre for burning a corpse shall not be erected within sixty feet of another man's house, except with his consent.
11. Neither a sepulchre for burning nor its vestibule can be acquired by usucapion.

Table XI. - Supplementary

1. Patricians shall not intermarry with plebians.

William A. Hunter, *A Systematic and Historical Exposition of Roman Law*, 2nd ed. (London: William Maxwell & Son, 1885), 18-22.

---

[2] The ricinium was a small square sheet of woollen cloth, doubled and wrapped over the head and shoulders; a mourning dress assumed more especially by females.

Study Questions

1. Describe the power of a Roman father.

2. How was libel treated?

3. Explain the possible reasons behind Table VII, #6 and #7.

4. How was arson, deliberate and accidental, treated?

5. Why do you suppose the Romans felt it necessary to enact the provisions of Table X? Why would anyone be given more than one funeral (#8)?

6. There may have been reasons other than mere class snobbery for Table XI. Can you think of any?

7. List as many principles from the Twelve Tables as you can which have survived in Western legal practice.

LIVY from HISTORY OF ROME

Titus Livius (Livy) (64 or 59 B.C. - 17 A.D.) was born in Padua and, something unusual in a Roman, he never aimed for a public career. His whole life was devoted to writing his History of Rome *from its foundation by the Trojan hero, Aeneas, to 9 B.C. The work reached 142 volumes of which only 35 are still extant. He came into contact with Augustus but probably was not a close friend, possibly because, according to a later historian, Tacitus, Livy may have been a supporter of Pompey, the enemy of Augustus' uncle, Julius Caesar.*

History was not a recreation for him but his entire career. Like Thucydides, he thought history could be explained in terms of individuals and that the lessons of the past could be applied to the present. In fact, in the Preface he says that the present state of Rome is the direct consequence of the failure of the moral character of the Romans. He tended to view the past as a kind of Golden Age, but there was a sense of pride, too, in the achievements of Augustus, a sense that Rome's past had culminated in the present age.

The excerpt below tells the story of Cincinnatus. One of Rome's earliest enemies was the Aequi who had just surrounded a Roman army under Minucius. The Senate has decided unanimously to give the dictatorship to Cincinnatus.

Now I would solicit the particular attention of those numerous people who imagine that money is everything in this world, and that rank and ability are inseparable from wealth: let them observe that Cincinnatus, the one man in whom Rome reposed all her hope of survival, was at that moment working a little three-acre farm (now known as the Quinctian meadows) west of the Tiber, just opposite the spot where the shipyards are today. A mission from the city found him at work on his land --- digging a ditch, maybe, or ploughing. Greetings were exchanged, and he was asked --- with a prayer for God's blessing on himself and his country --- to put on his toga and hear the Senate's instructions. This naturally surprised him, and, asking if all were well, he told his wife Racilia to run to their cottage and fetch his toga. The toga was brought, and wiping the grimy sweat from his hands and face he put it on; at once the envoys from the city saluted him, with congratulations, as Dictator, invited him to enter Rome, and informed him of the terrible danger of Minucius's army. A state vessel was waiting for him on the river, and on the city bank he was welcomed by his three sons who had come to meet him, then by other kinsmen and friends, and finally by nearly the whole body of senators. Closely attended by all these people and preceded by his lictors he was then escorted to his residence through streets lined with great crowds of common folk who, be it said, were by no means so pleased to see the new Dictator, as they thought his power excessive and dreaded the way in which he was likely to use it.

Next day, after a quiet night in which nothing was done beyond keeping careful watch, the Dictator was in the Forum before dawn. He appointed as his Master of Horse a patrician named Lucius Tarquitius --- a man who had the reputation of being the best soldier in Rome, in spite of the fact that he was too poor to keep a horse and had served, in consequence, as an infantryman. Accompanied by Tarquitius, the Dictator then appeared before the assembled people, to issue his instructions: legal business was to be suspended, all shops closed and no private business of any kind transacted; all men of military age were to parade before sunset in the Campus Martius with their equipment, each man bringing with him a five days' bread ratio and twelve stakes. All men over military age were to prepare the food for their younger neighbors, who would employ themselves meanwhile in looking over their equipment and collecting their stakes.

The Dictator's orders were promptly executed: stakes were hunted out by the soldiers and taken from wherever they were found, nobody objecting to their removal; every man presented himself punctually. Then column of march was formed, all prepared, should need arise for instant action, and

Roman Republic. 509 - 27 B.C. 123

moved off with Cincinnatus at the head of the infantry and Tarquitius in command of the mounted troops.

In each division, infantry and calvary, could be heard such words of command or encouragement as the occasion demanded: the men were urged to step out, reminded of the need for haste, in order to reach the scene of action that night, pressed to remember that a Roman army with its commander had already been three days under siege; no one could tell what the next day or the next night might bring, and events of tremendous import often hung upon a single moment of time. The men themselves, too, to show their spirit and gratify their officers, exhorted each other to every effort, shouting to the standard-bearer to move faster and to their companions to follow him.

At midnight the army reached Algidus and halted not far from the enemy's position. The Dictator rode round it on his horse, to inform himself, so far as he could in the darkness, of the extent and lay-out of their camp, and then ordered his officers to instruct their men to pile their baggage in a selected spot and return to their ranks with only their weapons and the stakes which each was carrying. Then, in the same formation as on the march from Rome --- a long column, that is --- he so maneuvered them as to form a complete ring round the enemy's position. Their orders then were to raise the war-cry on a given signal, and then to begin digging, each man at the spot where he stood, and to fix his stakes, so as to form a continuous trench and palisade. The signal soon came and the work began. The shout which rose from the Romans' throats told the enemy that they were surrounded, and carried beyond their lines into the beleaguered camp of Minucius, bringing alarm to the one and joy to the other. Minucius's men knew it was the voice of friends; with satisfaction and relief they told each other that help had come, and their sentries and outposts began to assume the offensive. Minucius himself, aware that instant action was vital, urged that the welcome cry meant not only that their friends had come but that they were already engaged, and had almost certainly started an assault on the outer ring of the enemy's position. So he ordered his men to draw their swords and follow him.

It was still dark when the fight began, and the relieving troops of Cincinnatus knew by the war-cry of their beleaguered friends that they, too, were in action at last.

The Aequians were preparing to resist the work of circumvallation, when Minucius started his offensive. To prevent his troops from forcing a way right through their lines, they were compelled to turn inward to face them, thus withdrawing their attention from the troops of the Dictator, who were, in consequence, left free to continue all night the construction of their trench and palisade. The battle with Minucius lasted till dawn; by that time the circumvallation was completed, and Minucius's men were beginning to get the upper hand. For the Aequians the moment was critical: the Dictator's troops, their work finished, promptly began an assault on the outer defenses, thus forcing the Aequians to fight on a second front while still heavily engaged on the first. Caught as it were between the two fires, they soon gave up the struggle and begged both Cincinnatus and Minucius not to proceed to a general massacre but to disarm them and let them go with their lives. Minucius referred them to the Dictator, who accepted their surrender, but on humiliating terms: their commander Gracchus, with other leading men, was to be brought before him in chains; the town of Corbio was to be evacuated; the Aequian soldiers were to be allowed to go with their lives, but, to force a final confession of absolute defeat, they were to pass 'under the yoke'. A 'yoke' was made from three spears, two fixed upright in the ground and the third tied across them, and the Aequian soldiers were made to pass under it.

As the Aequians had been stripped before their dismissal, their camp, when it fell into the Dictator's hand, was found to contain much valuable property. All this Cincinnatus turned over to his own men exclusively; Minucius's men, and Minucius himself, got nothing. 'You', the Dictator remarked severely, 'shall have no share of the plunder taken from an enemy who nearly took you.' Then, turning to Minucius, he added: 'Until, Lucius Minucius, you learn to behave like a consul and commander, you will act as my lieutenant and take your instructions from me.'

Roman Republic. 509 - 27 B.C. 125

Minucius resigned the consulship and remained with his troops as second in command; his men were quick to appreciate the military qualities of the Dictator, and gave him implicit obedience; they forgot their disgrace in the memory of the service he had done them, and voted him a gold circlet of a pound in weight, and when he left them, saluted him as their protector.

In Rome the Senate was convened by Quintus Fabius the City Prefect, and a decree was passed inviting Cincinnatus to enter in triumph with his troops. The chariot he rode in was preceded by the enemy commanders and the military standards, and followed by his army loaded with its spoils. We read in accounts of this great day that there was not a house in Rome but had a table spread with food before its door, for the entertainment of the soldiers who regaled themselves as they followed the triumphal chariot, singing and joking as befitted the occasion, like men out to enjoy themselves. The same day Mamilius of Tusculum by universal consent was granted Roman citizenship.

Only the impending trial of Volscius for perjury prevented Cincinnatus from resigning immediately. The tribunes who were thoroughly in awe of him made no attempt to interfere with the proceedings, and Volscius was found guilty and went into exile at Lanuvium. Cincinnatus finally resigned after holding office for fifteen days, having originally accepted it for a period of six months.

Livy: The Early History of Rome, translated by Aubrey de Selincourt (Penguin Classics, 1960, 1971), copyright (c) the Estate of Aubrey de Selincourt, 1960, Books I-IV (Baltimore: Penguin Books, 1960), 213-216.

Study Questions

1. What was Cincinnatus doing when he was told he had been named dictator?

2. *Why did he have to put on his toga before he could hear the mission's announcement?*

3. *How did the common folks react to his being named dictator?*

4. *Who did Cincinnatus name as his Master of Horse? Why?*

5. *What were his instructions to the people of Rome?*

6. *What formation did Cincinnatus keep the army in? Why?*

7. *What time did the battle start? Why, do you think? How did Minucius react?*

8. *What predicament had Cincinnatus put the Aequians in?*

9. *How did Cincinnatus treat the Aequians after he had defeated them? What did he do with their property?*

10. *How did he treat Minucius?*

11. *What did the Senate grant Cincinnatus?*

12. *Why didn't Cincinnatus resign immediately? How long was he dictator?*

13. *What moral lesson is Livy deriving from this story?*

PLUTARCH on CATO THE ELDER

The best loved of Plutarch's works has been the parallel <u>Lives of Noble Greeks and Romans</u> from which this selection is taken. In the strictest sense, Plutarch is not an historian. He developed no theory of why things happen the way they do. He was not a profound thinker. He believed that history was made by great men; hence, his <u>Lives</u>. And he was a moralist. The flaws in a great man, he thought, destroy not only him but contribute to the ruin of the state as well. Like Herodotus, he genuinely liked people but he especially liked noble, great and good people. He possessed an amiable humanity, polished style and an intelligent urbanity. Above all, he loved a good story and the <u>Lives</u> are filled with anecdotes that illumine not only the subject but his age as well. Thus, he is probably the easiest introduction for the general reader into the world of antiquity.

Cato himself represents the Roman of the "good old days," the stern, self-disciplined, totally upright man who could be counted on to put duty to Rome before any personal considerations. In the second century B.C., Rome was not only faced with the problem of Carthage but the fundamental moral problem of how to deal with the Hellenistic east. Cato had no problem --- he simply rejected what he regarded as the frivolity and softness of the east. Plutarch tells us that he once ran for the office of censor on a platform that pledged a complete moral purge of Rome. He would cut out all "luxury and voluptousness" because Rome was in need of not the gentlest but the roughest of physicians. He got elected and then carried out his campaign promise.

The following selection is Plutarch's description of Cato and the account of how he persuaded the Senate to declare the Third Punic War against Carthage.

127

He gained, in early life, a good habit of body by working with his own hands, and living temperately, and serving in war; and seemed to have an equal proportion both of health and strength. And he exerted and practised his eloquence through all the neighborhood and little villages; thinking it as requisite as a second body, and an all but necessary organ to one who looks forward to something above a mere humble and inactive life. He would never refuse to be counsel for those who needed him, and was, indeed, early reckoned a good lawyer, and, ere long, a capable orator.

Hence his solidity and depth of character showed itself gradually, more and more to those with whom he was concerned, and claimed, as it were, employment in great affairs, and places of public command. Nor did he merely abstain from taking fees for his counsel and pleading, but did not even seem to put any high price on the honor which proceeded from such kind of combats, seeming much more desirous to signalize himself in the camp and in real fights; and while yet but a youth, had his breast covered with scars he had received from the enemy; being (as he himself says) but seventeen years old, when he made his first campaign; in the time when Hannibal, in the height of his success, was burning and pillaging all Italy. In engagements he would strike boldly, without flinching, stand firm to his ground, fix a bold countenance upon his enemies, and with a harsh threatening voice accost them, justly thinking himself and telling others, that such a rugged kind of behavior sometimes terrifies the enemy more than the sword itself. In his marches, he bore his own arms on foot, whilst one servant only followed, to carry the provisions for his table, with whom he is said never to have been angry or hasty, whilst he made ready his dinner or supper, but would, for the most part, when he was free from military duty, assist and help him himself to dress it. When he was with the army, he used to drink only water; unless, perhaps, when extremely thirsty, he might mingle it with a little vinegar; or if he found his strength fail him, take a little wine.

Roman Republic. 509 - 27 B.C.

* * * * * * *

For now the state, unable to keep its purity by reason of its greatness, and having so many affairs, and people from all parts under its government, was fain to admit many mixed customs, and new examples of living. With reason, therefore, everybody admired Cato, when they saw others sink under labors, and grow effeminate by pleasures; and yet beheld him unconquered by either, and that not only when he was young and desirous of honor, but also when old and greyheaded, after a consulship and triumph; like some famous victor in the games, persevering in his exercise and maintaining his character to the very last. He himself says, that he never wore a suit of clothes which cost more than a hundred drachmas; and that, when he was general and consul, he drank the same wine which his workmen did; and that the meat or fish which was bought in the market for his dinner, did not cost above thirty asses. All which was for the sake of the commonwealth, that so his body might be the hardier for the war. Having a piece of embroidered Babylonian tapestry left him, he sold it; because none of his farm-houses were so much as plastered. Nor did he ever buy a slave for above fifteen hundred drachmas; as he did not seek for effeminate and handsome ones, but able, sturdy workmen, horse-keepers and cow-herds: and these he thought ought to be sold again, when they grew old, and no useless servants fed in a house. In short, he reckoned nothing a good bargain, which was superfluous; but whatever it was, though sold for a farthing, he would think it a great price, if you had no need of it; and was for the purchase of lands for sowing and feeding, rather than grounds for sweeping and watering.

* * * * * * *

Finding Carthage, not (as the Romans thought) low and in an ill condition, but well manned, full of riches and all sorts of arms and ammunition, and perceiving the Carthaginians carry it high, he conceived that it was not a time for the Romans to adjust affairs between them and Masinissa; but rather that they themselves would fall into danger, unless they should find means to check this rapid new growth of Rome's ancient irreconcilable enemy. Therefore, returning quickly to Rome, he acquainted the senate, that the former defeats and blows given to the Carthaginians, had not so much diminished their strength, as it had abated their imprudence and folly; that they were not become weaker, but more experienced in war, and did only skirmish with the Numidians, to exercise themselves the better to cope with the Romans: that the peace and league they had made was but a kind of suspension of war which awaited a fairer opportunity to break out again.

More, they say that, shaking his gown, he took occasion to let drop some African figs before the senate. And on their admiring the size and beauty of them, he presently added, that the place that bore them was but three days' sail from Rome. Nay, he never after this gave his opinion, but at the end he would be sure to come out with this sentence, "ALSO, CARTHAGE, METHINKS, OUGHT UTTERLY TO BE DESTROYED." But Publius Scipio Nasica would always declare his opinion to the contrary, in these words, "It seems requisite to me that Carthage should still stand." For seeing his countrymen to be grown wanton and insolent, and the people made, by their prosperity, obstinate and disobedient to the senate, and drawing the whole city, whither they would, after them, he would have had the fear of Carthage to serve as a bite to hold in the contumacy of the multitude; and he looked upon the Carthaginians as too weak to overcome the Romans, and too great to be depised by them. On the other side, it seemed a perilous thing to Cato, that a city which had been always great, and was now grown sober and wise, by reason of its former calamities, should still lie, as it were, in wait for the follies and dangerous excesses of the over-powerful Roman people; so that he thought it the wisest course to have all outward dangers removed, when they had so many inward ones among themselves.

Thus Cato, they say, stirred up the third and last war against the Carthaginians.

A. H. Clough and William W. Godwin, trans., *Plutarch's Lives*, 5 vols. (New York: The Colonial Company, Limited, 1905), II, 317-318, 321-322, 350-351.

Study Questions

1. How did Cato deal with his servants? What qualities did he look for in slaves? Why was that noteworthy?

2. What did Cato think "as requisite as a second body"? Given that Rome had no television networks or newspapers, why was that such an important skill?

3. In what major war had his "breast [been] covered with scars"? How old was he then?

4. Why do you think it remarkable that Cato only drank water in the army? Why did he do so?

5. Why did Cato think war with Carthage necessary? How did he convince the Senate? What was Nasica's argument?

6. In your own words, and using Cato as the model, describe the ideal Roman.

JULIUS CAESAR from THE CIVIL WAR

  Born of one of Rome's old patrician families, Julius Caesar (100-44 B.C.) received an excellent education and exhibited throuhout his life an outstanding intellect, wit and gift for oratory. His literary gifts were such that even Cicero, who otherwise hated Caesar, admired them. Caesar's father was a brother-in-law of Marius and Julius grew up in the era of civil strife between the Marians and the supporters of Sulla. He learned at an early age the lesson that the people could be used to break the Senate's control of government.

  Caesar's first office was as quaestor in 68 and he then served in several other offices, including governor of Further Spain. It was when Caesar returned from Spain in 60 expecting to receive the consulship that he, along with Crassus and Pompey, came together as the First Triumvirate. The arrangement was sealed with a marriage between Caesar's daughter, Julia, and Pompey and turned out to be a love match.

  In 59, Caesar embarked on what would be a nine-year campaign in Gaul which he described in his <u>Commentaries</u>. Under a courageous chieftain named Vercingetorix, the Gauls resisted fiercely, but Caesar's passion for efficiency and discipline and his sheer tenacity finally brought even that brave warrior to his knees by 51.

  The Triumvirate was renewed in 56 and Pompey and Crassus were guaranteed the consulship. Crassus was also assigned Syria, where he was killed in 53, a year after Julia's death. With their deaths, the alliance between Pompey and Caesar began to unravel. Caesar had left his interests in Rome in the hands of a patrician named Clodius who headed a gang of thugs. A rival gang, apparently acting on orders from Pompey who became sole consul in 52, killed Clodius and the breech became irreparable.

Roman Republic. 509 - 27 B.C.

In 49, Caesar, wanting to stand for the consulship and feeling that the conquest of Gaul gave him every right to that office, crossed the Rubicon, the river marking the boundary between Cisalpine Gaul and Italy. He was violating a specific directive from the Senate, now in Pompey's control, and by doing so he was declaring war on Pompey. He overran Italy, raided the treasury in Rome (most of it, the spoils of Gaul, he had won) and turned first to Spain and then to Pompey and the Senate who had fled to Greece. There, at Pharsalus in Thessaly, in August 48 B.C., he defeated them. It is that battle which he describes here, referring to himself in the third person.

[marginal note: *Fighting for Caesar not Rome*]

In Caesar's army there was a recalled veteran named Crastinus, who in the previous year had been chief centurion of the Tenth legion in his service, a man of outstanding valour. When the signal was given, he said: 'Follow me, you who were formerly in my company, and give your general the service you have promised. Only this one battle remains; after it, he will recover his position, and we our freedom.' Looking at Caesar, 'General,' he said, 'today I shall earn your gratitude, either dead or alive.' So saying, he ran out first from the right wing, followed by about 120 crack troops, volunteers from the same century.

Between the two armies there was just enough space left for them to advance and engage each other. Pompey, however, had told his men to wait for Caesar's onset, and not to move from their positions or allow the line to be split up. He was said to have done this on the advice of Gaius Triarius, with the intention of breaking the force of the first impact of the enemy and stretching out their line, so that his own men, who were still in formation, could attack them while they were scattered. He also thought that the falling javelins would do less damage if the men stood still than if they were running forward while the missiles were discharged. Moreover, Caesar's troops, having to run twice the distance, would be out of breath and exhausted. It appears to us that he did this without sound reason, for there is a certain eagerness of spirit and an innate keenness in everyone which is inflamed by desire for battle. Generals ought to encourage this, not repress it; nor was it for nothing that the practice began in antiquity of giving the signal on both sides and everyone's raising a war-cry; this was believed both to frighten the enemy and to stimulate one's own men.

Our men, on the signal, ran forward with javelins levelled; but when they observed that Pompey's men were not running to meet them, thanks to the practical experience and training they had had in earlier battles they checked their charge and halted about halfway, so as not to approach worn out. Then after a short interval they renewed the charge, threw their javelins and, as ordered by Caesar, quickly drew their swords. Nor indeed did the Pompeians fail to meet the occasion. They stood up to the hail of missiles and bore the onset of the legions; they kept their ranks, threw their javelins, and then resorted to their swords. At the same time the cavalry all charged forward, as instructed, from Pompey's left wing, and the whole horde of archers rushed out. Our cavalry failed to withstand their onslaught; they were dislodged from their position and gave ground a little. Pompey's cavalry thereupon pressed on the more hotly and began to deploy in squadrons and surround our line on its exposed flank. Observing this, Caesar gave the signal to the fourth line which he had formed of single cohorts. They ran forward swiftly to the attack with their standards and charged at Pompey's cavalry with such force that none of them could hold ground. They all turned, and not only gave ground but fled precipitately to the hilltops. Their withdrawal left all the archers and slingers exposed, and, unarmed and unprotected, they were killed. In the same charge the cohorts surrounded the Pompeians who were still fighting and putting up a resistance on the left wing, and attacked them in the rear.

At the same time Caesar gave the order to advance to the third line, which had done nothing and had stayed in its position up till then. As a result, when fresh and unscathed troops took the place of the weary, while others were attacking from the rear, the Pompeians could not hold out, and every one of them turned tail and fled. Caesar was not wrong in thinking that the victory would originate from those cohorts which had been stationed in a fourth line to counteract the cavalry, as he had declared in cheering on his men; for it was by these first that the cavalry were repulsed, it was by these that the Pompeian left wing was surrounded and the rout started. When Pompey, however, saw his cavalry routed, and observed that part of his forces on which he most relied in a state of panic, having no confidence in the rest he left the field; he rode straight to the camp and said to the centurions he had posted on guard at the praetorian gate, loudly, so that the soldiers could hear: 'Watch the camp and defend it strenuously, if there should be any reverse. I am going round to the other gates to make sure of the guard on the camp.' So saying, he went to his tent, doubting his chances of success and yet awaiting the outcome.

The Pompeians were driven back in their retreat inside the rampart. Caesar, thinking that they should be given no respite in their panic, urged his men to take advantage of the generosity of fortune and storm the camp. Even though it was extremely hot--for the engagement had gone on until midday--his men were ready to undertake any toil, and obeyed his order. The camp was being zealously defended by the cohorts left to guard it, and more fiercely still by the Thracian and native auxiliaries. For the troops who had fled from the field, terrified and exhausted, mostly dropped their weapons and military standards and had more thought for continuing their flight than for the defence of the camp. Nor indeed could those who had taken up their position on the rampart hold out any longer against the hail of missiles. Overcome by their wounds, they abandoned their posts and at once, led by their centurions and tribunes, fled to the hilltops near the camp.

* * * * * * *

At dawn Caesar ordered all those who had settled on the hill to come down from the higher ground on to the plain and throw down their weapons. They did this without demur; then they threw themselves to the ground with their hands outstretched, weeping, and begged him for their lives. He reassured them, told them to get up, and spoke briefly to them about his own leniency, to alleviate their fears. He spared them all and charged his own soldiers to see to it that none of them suffered any physical violence or lost any part of his property. These matters taken care of, he ordered the other legions to come from the camp to join him, and the ones which he brought with him to go back to camp and rest in their turn. He arrived at Larissa on the same day.

<u>Caesar: The Civil War</u>, translated by Jane F. Mitchell (Penguin Classics, 1967), copyright (c) Jane F. Mitchell, 1967 (New York: Penguin Books, 1976), 152-154, 155.

Study Questions

1. *From the Crastinus story, what kind of loyalty did Caesar elicit from his men? What cause is Crastinus willing to die for? (Crastinus was killed from a sword thrust full in his face.)*

2. *Describe the course of the battle.*

3. *How did Caesar treat Pompey's veterans? Why, do you think? (In other words, might some motive other than generosity, explain his conduct?)*

CATULLUS, POEMS

The greatest of Rome's lyric poets, Catullus, (84-54 B.C.) came to Rome from northern Italy as a young man and fell in with a circle of artists and intellectuals. He delighted in them and often wrote poems to and about them. He also fell in love with Clodia, the wife of a prominent politician and sister of Julius Caesar's henchman, Clodius. She is the "Lesbia" of his poems, a woman totally unworthy of his love. The third poem in this set came after he had discovered her infidelity.

Catullus writes in the tradition of the great Greek lyricist Sappho. There is intense emotion but also the controlled intelligence of the classic mind at its very best.

Bid Me To Live

To sit where I can see your face
And hear your laughter come and go
Is greater bliss than all the gods
Can ever know.

The bright dream carries me away:
Watching your lips, your hair, your cheek,
I have so many things to say,
Yet cannot speak.

I look, I listen, and my soul
Flames with a fire unfelt before
Till sense swims, and I feel and see
And hear no more ...

How rank this ease of lotus land:
I feel death in its dreamy spell.
The dreaming towers of Babylon
--How soon they fell.

My True Love Hath My Heart

There never was a woman who could say,
And say it true,
That she was loved of any, O my love,
As I love you.
There never was a loyal promise given
Faithful and free,
As loyalty to you, because I love you,
Is given from me.

Miser Catulle

Poor poet, let your folly sleep:
The past is dead: bury it deep.
Time was your love neath sunny sky
Beckoned to you as she went by,
And your fond merriment could stir
An equal happiness in her.
The passion that you lent her then
Mocked the mere loves of common men.
Sunny the skies, and every day
Was summer --- till she turned away.

Turn from her then yourself, nor strive
In futile misery to live.
Pursue no more the hope that flies:
No more remember love that dies.
Be resolute: make your heart hard ---
Goodbye, my dear: I've said the word.
My heart is steeled, my love shall sleep,
Nor seek the kiss you'd rather keep.

But you when heart and hand forsake ---
Yours is the hard heart that will break.
Who will make love when I am gone?
Call you his dear, his fair, his own?
Where's the heart now your heart adores?

Whose lips shall print themselves on yours
And leave their mark on them? ---
But stay!
Turn from her, poet, turn away.

E. A. Havelock, *The Lyric Genius of Catullus* (New York: Russell & Russell, 1967), 13, 27, 53.

Study Questions

1. *Compare these poems to those of Theocritus.*

2. *What resolution is he making in the third poem?*

MARCUS TULLIUS CICERO from
ON MORAL DUTIES

The man who gives his name to the Republic's last century is not a Pompey, a Caesar, nor a Sulla. It is a man who never commanded armies nor conquered worlds. Cicero (106-43 B.C.) was a brilliant orator whose wit and intelligence could galvanize a Senate, a jury or the Roman mob. He was warm, sensitive, vain, sometimes a bit pompous, stubborn and utterly courageous. He would defy tyrants, flatter other writers, mourn deeply the loss of his beloved daughter, counsel a friend, verbally rip Marc Antony to shreds, and lavishly praise a Pompey or even a Caesar. Utterly devoted to the ideals of the Republic, he would put duty before expediency, truth and justice before personal gain. It is Cicero who is humanitas, the Man Thinking whose nobility of character and range of intellect have been a hallmark of human excellence ever since.

Born into a wealthy family at Arpinum, Cicero was educated at Rome for a public career. By his mid-thirties, he had become Rome's leading lawyer. He was elected praetor in 66 and as consul in 63 he put down a conspiracy against the government with some severity. He was a supporter of Pompey although he was not happy with the First Triumvirate. He came back to Rome under Caesar and then, following Caesar's assassination, attacked Marc Antony in a series of fourteen vitriolic speeches called the "Philippic Orations." The "Philippics" sealed his doom. Antony had Cicero murdered on December 7, 43. His head and hands were then cut off and nailed to the Rostra in the Forum where Antony's wife, Fulvia, would pierce with a needle that tongue that had so eloquently vilified her husband.

As was the usual practice, Cicero published his speeches. He also left over 900 letters which cover everything from advice on governing a province to announcing the birth of a son. He was a Stoic and he popularized that philosophy. He embraced the Stoic *ideal of a brotherhood of Man based on Reason. The following excerpt from his* On Moral Duties *reveals that ideal applied to ethics.*

But to return to my rule.

Well, then, to take something away from someone else --- to profit by another's loss --- is more unnatural than death, or destitution, or pain, or any other physical or external blow. To begin with, this strikes at the roots of human society and fellowship. For if we each of us propose to rob or injure one another for our personal gain, then we are clearly going to demolish what is more emphatically nature's creation than anything else in the whole world: namely, the link that unites every human being with every other. Just imagine if each of our limbs had its own consciousness and saw advantage for itself in appropriating the nearest limb's strength! Of course the whole body would inevitably collapse and die. In precisely the same way, a general seizure and appropriation of other people's property would cause the collapse of the human community, the brotherhood of man. Granted that there is nothing unnatural in a man preferring to earn a living for himself rather than for someone else, what nature forbids is that we should increase our own means, property and resources by plundering others.

Indeed this idea --- that one must not injure anybody else for one's own profit --- is not only natural law, an international valid principle: the same idea is also incorporated in the statutes which individual communities have framed for their national purposes. The whole point and intention of these statutes is that one citizen shall live safely with another; anyone who attempts to undermine that association is punished with fines, imprisonment, exile, or death.

The same conclusion follows even more forcibly from nature's rational principle, the law that governs gods and men alike. Whoever obeys this principle --- and everyone who wants to live according to nature's laws must obey it --- will never be guilty of coveting another man's goods or taking things from someone else and appropriating them for himself. For great-heartedness and heroism, and courtesy, and justice, and generosity, are far more in conformity with nature than self-indulgence, or wealth, or even life itself. But to despise this latter category of things, to attach no importance to them in comparison with the common good, really does need a heroic and lofty heart.

In the same way, it is more truly natural to model oneself on Hercules and undergo the most terrible labours and troubles in order to help and save all the nations of the earth than (however superior you are in looks or strength) to live a secluded, untroubled life with plenty of money and pleasures. And mankind was grateful to Hercules for his services; popular belief gave him a place among the gods. That is to say, the finest and noblest characters prefer a life of dedication to a life of self-indulgence: and one may conclude that such men conform with nature and are therefore incapable of doing harm to their fellow-men.

A man who wrongs another for this own benefit can be explained in two different ways. Either he does not see that what he is doing is unnatural, or he refuses to agree that death, destitution, pain, the loss of children, relations, and friends are less deplorable than doing wrong to another person. But if he sees nothing unnatural in wronging a fellow-man, is he not beyond the reach of argument? --- he is taking away from human beings all that makes them human. If, however, he concedes that this ought to be avoided, yet still regards death, destitution, and pain as even more undesirable, he is mistaken. He ought not to concede that any damage, either to his person or to his property, is worse than a moral failure.

So everyone ought to have the same purpose: to identify the interest of each with the interest of all. Once men grab for themselves, human society will completely collapse. But if nature prescribes (as she does) that every human being must help every other human being, whoever he is, just precisely because they are all human beings, then --- by the same authority --- all men have identical interests. Having identical interests means that we are all subject to one and the same law of nature: and, that being so, the very least that such a law enjoins is that we must not wrong one another. This conclusion follows inevitably from the truth of the initial assumption.

If people claim (as they sometimes do) that they have no intention of robbing their parents or brothers for their own gain, but that robbing their other compatriots is a different matter, they are not talking sense. For that is the same as denying their common interest with their fellow-countrymen, and all the legal or social obligations that follow therefrom: a denial which shatters the whole fabric of national life. Another objection urges that one ought to take account of compatriots but not of foreigners. But people who put forward these arguments subvert the whole foundation of the human community - and its removal means the annihilation of all kindness, generosity, goodness, and justice: which is a sin against the immortal gods, since they were the creators of the society which such men are seeking to undermine. And the tightest of the bonds uniting that society is the belief that robbery from another man for the sake of one's personal gain is more unnatural than the endurance of any loss whatsoever to one's person or property - or even to one's very soul. That is, provided that no violation of justice is involved: seeing that of all the virtues justice is the sovereign and queen.

<u>Cicero: Selected Works</u>, translated by Michael Grant (Penguin Classics, 1960, 1965, 1971), copyright (c) Michael Grant, 1960, 1965, 1971 (New York: Penguin Books, 1971), 166-168.

Study Questions

1. *Why is it "unnatural" to profit by another's loss?*

2. *What is the relationship between natural law and the individual's conduct?*

3. *Which is preferable - the labors of a Hercules to save the earth or "doing one's own thing"? Why?*

4. *May the rational man withdraw from public service? Explain.*

5. Is there a difference between robbing one's parents and robbing a stranger?

6. Would Cicero find it permissible to sell a car with a slightly defective battery without telling the prospective buyer? Why or why not?

7. How would Cicero have reacted to Christianity?

8. What modern international body is based on the principles in the last paragraph?

ROMAN EMPIRE. 27 B.C. - 476 A.D.

In 27 B.C., Augustus ceremoniously closed the doors of the two-headed god, Janus, thus formally ushering in a period of profound peace called the Pax Romana that would last until 180 A.D. Then he set about making such reforms as would preserve that peace.

First, he kept the facade of republicanism. The Senate continued to meet and there were still elections for tribunes and consuls, but real power lay in the hands of Augustus who bore an old honorific title, "*princeps*", *first citizen.* He consulted an informal body of advisors called the "concilium princeps". The Senate then simply ratified what had already been decided upon by Augustus and his advisors.

The provincial administration was reorganized and a hierarchical civil service was established wherein the holding of public office depended simply on ability. Thus, a professional bureaucracy was created that would take on a life --- and pride --- of its own, independent of the princeps. By further extending citizenship, Augustus made access to public office universally possible. Before the end of the Pax Romana, the emperor's office itself would be occupied by a North African and a Spaniard. He also centralized the military under himself and stationed garrisons all along Rome's frontiers. He reformed and standardized the coinage, gave Rome a fire department, sanitation program and an efficient postal system. In order to give employment to the poor and to beautify Rome, he embarked on an ambitious building program which left Rome, as he said, "a city clothed in marble". Believing that the disorders of the last century were due at least partly to the breakdown of the family and hence, of that old Roman virtue, *pietas,* he took steps to restore the stability of the family by, among other things, legislating strongly against adultery. Unhappily he was forced by his own law to exile his own beloved daughter, Julia, for that crime.

The major flaw in Augustus' system was that he had no male heir of his own body to succeed him. His stepson, Tiberius, was a morose, suspicious, thoroughly unlovable sort, but in the absence finally of any other candidate, he had no choice but to name him. What also weakened the throne was that "princeps" wasn't legally an office and in a strict sense, Augustus could not hand it on to an heir. The Senate allowed him to do so but the ambiguity and thus the inherent weakness of the title would plague Augustus' successors. Augustus created a Praetorian Guard to protect the emperor's person. In the absence of a clear principle of succession, however, the Guard shortly turned from guarding the emperor's person to guarding the office, thus giving the army a key role in the making and unmaking of emperors.

The Julio-Claudian dynasty inaugurated by Augustus provided a few strange sorts like Nero and Caligula who would give even cruelty a bad name. Most of them, however, were capable administrators. Under Vespasian (69-79 A.D.) and his successors, the Flavians, the Augustan system became an open monarchy when Vespasian named his sons, Titus and Domitian, to succeed him. They were cruel too but they kept the legions in line and thus secured peace.

The Flavians were succeeded by the Antonines, the "Five Good Emperors" --- benevolent, wise, absolute in all but name. The last of them, Marcus Aurelius (d. 180), was, second to Cicero, Rome's finest Stoic thinker.

The Pax Romana ushered in a Golden Age adorned by such men as the poets Virgil and Horace, Juvenal the satirist, Ovid, and Livy, whose history of Rome, like Virgil's _Aeneid_ celebrated the new age ushered in by Augustus. There were the historians Suetonius and Tacitus and the satirist Petronius who were critical of what Rome had become. Typical of the general feeling of the age was the _Ars Pacis,_ a majestic altar built under Augustus dedicated not to Rome nor to Augustus but to peace itself. Upon it were sculpted reliefs of animals, crops and people engaged in agriculture --- the arts of peace.

The Roman peace rested on more than just legions. It was firmly grounded in Roman law, a flexible system rooted in experience and in the methods and principles of Greek philosophy. Two sets of men, praetors and jurisconsults, were responsible for changing the Twelve Tables from a set of customs governing an essentially agrarian society into a rational instrument that could secure justice for a multi-racial, cosmopolitan world. As in administration, the Romans improvised. From Greek philosophy they borrowed the dialectic which enabled them to develop a science of law. They learned to differentiate kinds of cases and to group them according to common traits. They devised new remedies for various wrongs so that the punishment began to be more appropriate to the crime. And they looked carefully at motive rather than simply at an act, realizing that wrong rested in the will of the doer, not merely in his overt action.

Roman law evolved from four sources. First, there were the Twelve Tables which had carefully balanced the claims of the individual against those of the community. Then, there was the legislation passed by the Senate during the Republic and third, there were the edicts of the individual emperors from Augustus on. Finally, and fundamentally, there was Stoicism with its insistence on the innate rationality and thus the brotherhood of all men. Regardless of race or customs or geographical location, Stoicism gave Roman lawyers a tool that was flexible and yet had universal application.

There were three categories in Roman law. The first was *jus naturale*, the natural law of the Stoics, what the reasonable man would discern as just and orderly. Secondly, there was *jus locale* or local law. Rome never had any intention of changing anyone's customs as long as they didn't interfere with anyone else or with the peace of the empire itself. Hence, local law was allowed to operate under the umbrella of the third category, *jus gentium*, the law of the nations, Rome's imperial law. The result was the creation of a sense of "Romanitas", the sense of a single civilization bound together by a law which was based on Reason. Romanitas then was synonymous with civilization itself. To be able to say "*Civis Romanus sum*" --- "I am a Roman citizen" --- was to say that a man was civilized, fully ordered, complete.

The Pax Romana also brought prosperity to the provinces. Peace opened new lands in Britain, Gaul, Spain, and Germany to immigration --- and thus to Romanization. From Augustus on, slavery diminished partly because peace brought a decline in

THE ROMAN EMPIRE UNDER AUGUSTUS

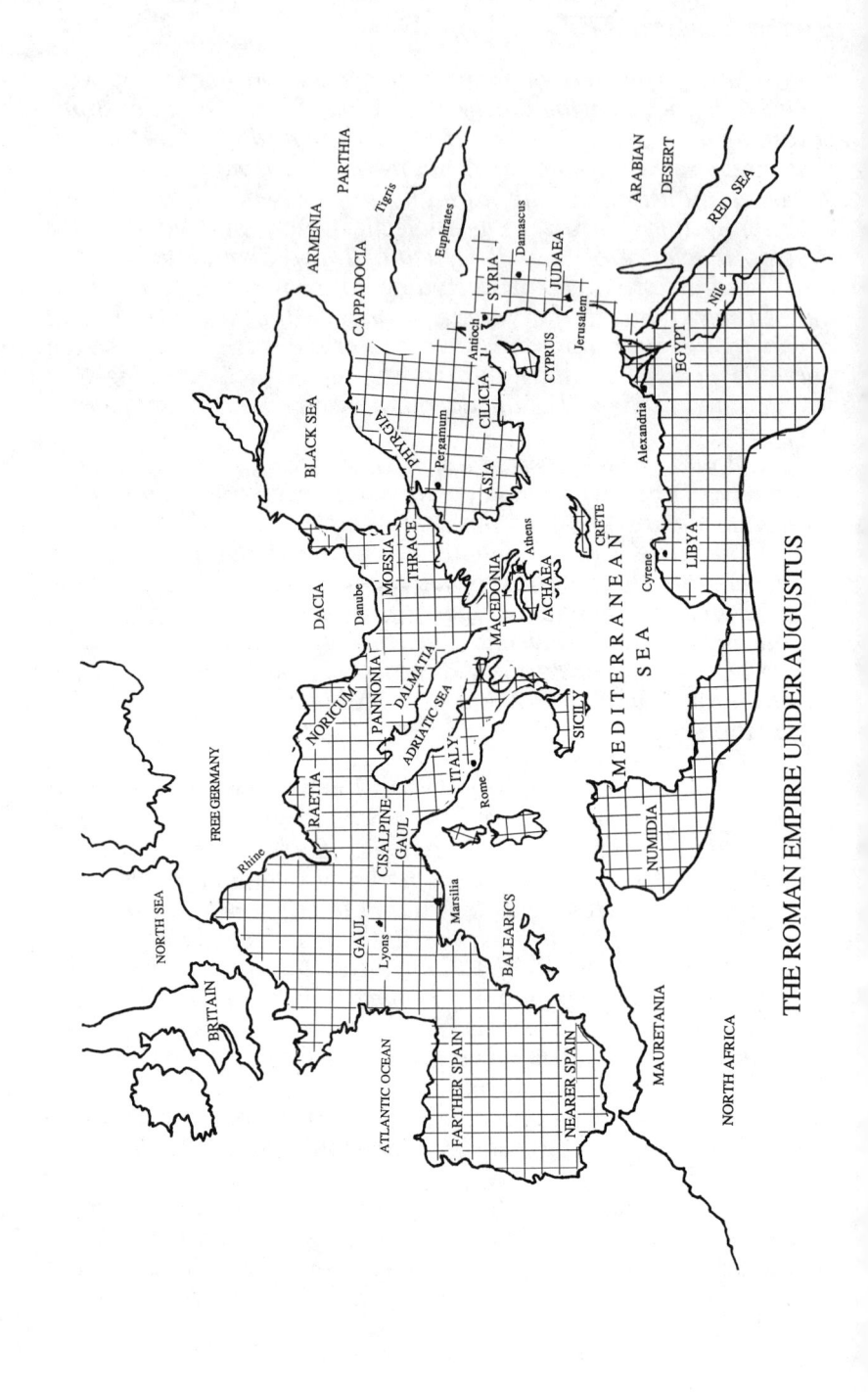

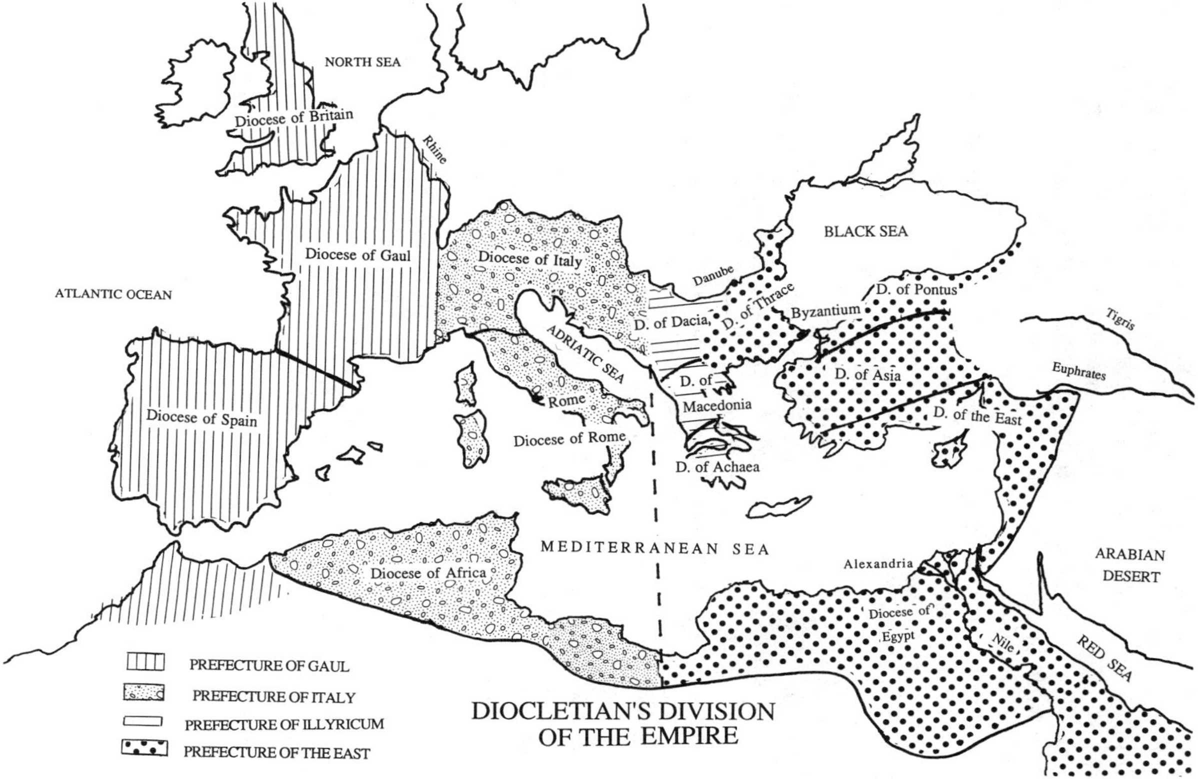

DIOCLETIAN'S DIVISION
OF THE EMPIRE

captives and also because Roman law had always made manumission fairly easy. Thus, the small independent farm, replacing the large slave-dependent latifundium, again became the norm in Western agriculture. Copper, iron, lead, tin and gold-mining flourished. So too did lively pottery and textile industries. The woolen industry in Britain started under the Romans and olives were introduced into Spain and northern Africa and they, along with Syria, produced tons of oil. Egypt's grain along with that of Britain and Belgium, wines from Italy, Gaul and the Danube crisscrossed Europe. As trade and industry flourished, new towns sprang up, often deliberately built on the spoked-wheel design of Rome with temples, fountains, public buildings, theatres, baths and new guilds.

The expansion and stabilization of the army, especially under the Antonines contributed to this. The garrisons on the frontier had to be clothed, fed, housed and entertained. Often too when legionnaires retired, they tended to remain and settle in the area in which they had served. They had learned skills in the army which they then used, along with their retirement pay, to set themselves up in business. Markets, then towns, grew up around the garrisons, and Rome's roads became a commercial lifeline linking little outposts with each other, the bigger cities and with the capital itself. Roman culture was thereby spread so thoroughly that in 212, the emperor, Caracalla, granted citizenship to all free men within the empire.

As the Pax Romana facilitated the growth of agriculture, industry and trade, however, Rome itself and even Italy gradually ceased to be the economic heart of the empire. New cities in Britain, Gaul and Germany eclipsed the older Mediterranean centers as the manufacture of pottery, glass and bronzeware moved away from places like Arrentium and Capua to Lyons and Cologne and tinware from Gaul drove Italian wares from the market.

The peaceful and prosperous age of the Antonines ended in 180 A.D. with the death of Marcus Aurelius. His son and successor, Commodus, was a cruel man who was murdered. That began a series of bitter civil wars which ended in 193 with the establishment of the Severan dynasty. Although Septimus Severus, the founder of the dynasty, was able to restore some stability, his

Roman Empire. 27 B.C. - 476 A.D.   151

successors were unable to control the legions and when the last of the Severi was murdered in 235, civil war again broke out. Between 235 and 284, so many military commanders tried to seize power that they were known as "the barracks emperors". Within less than fifty years, twenty different men ascended the throne, making the average reign incredibly short. Civil war opened the way for invasions from both Persia in the east and along the Rhine and Danube frontiers in the west. And the legions fought each other at least as often as they fought the invaders.

Meanwhile, as might be expected, public order simply broke down. Soldiers who should have protected the people turned to pillaging the countryside, demanding to be quartered in private homes and given livestock and supplies. Insolent, arrogant local and imperial officials added to the grief but often they were in a bind too. Tax collectors, responsible for collecting a certain quota from their areas, were often forced to make up the deficit from their own pockets. Judges and police officials whose pay was in arrears would take bribes. The result was that people often fled or became outlaws.

In the midst of this turmoil, in 284, the imperial chair was seized by a soldier named Diocletian. The empire's malaise was drastic --- and it was a drastic remedy that Diocletian applied to heal it. That remedy came in two forms. First, recognizing that the restoration of strength had to begin at the top, he completely did away with the fiction of "princeps". He arrogated to himself not merely the trappings of an Oriental despot but claimed to be the face of God on earth. Elaborate ceremonial and court ritual removed the emperor from even the gaze of the ordinary mortal. Persian eunuchs ran the palace and those entering the emperor's presence, prostrated themselves and kissed the hem of his robes. All of this had a purpose. By isolating and exalting the emperor's office, by making it a divine monarchy, his authority would be unquestioned and he could then embark on the second wing of his reforms.

Realizing that the empire was now too large and heterogeneous for one man to easily govern, Diocletian split it into two halves, then halved again each half. This quartering of the empire was called a Tetrarchy. Diocletian himself assumed control of the Eastern half and named a co-augustus (the title had become synonymous with emperor) to rule the Western half from Rome. Each quarter or prefecture was further subdivided into from three to five dioceses and the dioceses into provinces and then latifundia and metropolitanates. Provincial governors were deprived of the military powers which had allowed them to wreak such havoc and confined them to only civil and administrative duties.

The turmoil under the barracks emperors had had devastating economic consequences. They had responded by devaluing the coinage, thus sending prices and interest rates skyward. Commerce had been disrupted and mines exhausted in the attempt to supply gold and silver. Craftsmen, merchants and artisans left devastated regions. The drying up of trade and industry left whole cities and roads desolated and harbors decaying. In response to these conditions, Diocletian issued an edict on maximum prices and wages, setting a lid on both. That edict was almost immediately a failure because it was unrealistic and unenforceable. He also passed an edict that in effect locked into their occupations those people involved in the growing, preparation and transportation of food and other essential commodities. And the occupation was by law hereditary. Imperial offices also became hereditary. Roman society thus became stratified and inflexible.

In 305, Diocletian resigned and ordered his co-augustus in Rome to do the same. Under the tetrarchal system, a caesar in each half was to ascend to the office of augustus and name a caesar in his turn. That happened but then civil war erupted again. Out of this, in a battle at Milvian Bridge in 311, the Western caesar, Constantine, triumphed. Like Diocletian, his capital was not in Rome but in the East. According to legend, Constantine, in a single day, walked a circuit around the ancient Greek city of Byzantium, straddling the straits separating Asia from Europe. The circuit he walked then became the wall of his new capital, named, of course, Constantinople. It was that city now, not Rome, which became the political center of the Roman Empire. Thus, there was an implied recognition that Rome had now become a political backwater.

Constantine continued the pattern of reform set by Diocletian. He reunited the empire legally under himself but the

Roman Empire. 27 B.C. - 476 A.D.

East-West split would remain despite the efforts of later emperors to heal it. In later centuries, the Eastern half emerged as the wealthy, brilliant Byzantine Empire.

The decline in the Western empire continued. The increasing devastation of the provinces increased the difficulty of feeding the cities. Free tenant farmers, if they were not killed by invaders or plague or famine, simply fled their lands leaving large tracts deserted. Landlords who had the resources, reclaimed as much of this land as they could and turned them into large self-sufficient estates --- the precursors of the medieval manors. Small farmers, poor, propertyless and too weak to stand alone against the ravages of civil war, invasion, inflation, brigands and the tyranny of imperial officials often turned to these landowners for relief. In return for protection and security, they relinquished their freedom and became clients and finally serfs.

The Western provinces fell into the hands of Germanic tribes who seized the remains of Rome and then infused them with their own vigor to create the myriad splendors of Europe's Middle Ages. In 476 A.D., an Ostrogothic chieftain, Odavacar, sacked Rome and deposed its last "emperor," Romulus Augustulus, hence, the date traditionally used for the "fall" of Rome in the West. More accurately, the centers of power had simply shifted --- to Byzantium in the East and to hundreds of chieftains exercising local powers in the West.

You will note in this chapter that after the selection from Marcus Aurelius who died in 180 A.D., there is nothing. Does that mean that in the crises of the third and fourth centuries, there was no intellectual and artistic activity --- as there had been, for instance, in the earlier crisis-laden last century of the Republic? By no means.

In the third century, an Egyptian thinker, Plotinus (205-270), brought about a sort of revived Platonism. This Neo-Platonism conceived of a Trinity of One, Mind and Soul. The Soul purged by the Mind might find a union with the One. Dry and austere, what Neo-Platonism offered was an escape from the world --- as distant from the civic involvement of classical humanism as one could get.

Much of Rome's intellectual and artistic energy, however, now was given to a vibrant young religion, Christianity.

Suggested Readings

1. Barnes, T. D., *The New Empire of Diocletian and Constantine* (Cambridge, Mass.: Harvard University Press, 1982). Studies the attempts at recovery by these two rulers following the anarchy of the barracks emperors.

2. Carcopino, Jerome, *Daily Life in Ancient Rome* (London: G. Routledge & Sons, Ltd., 1941). This classic covers all phases of Roman society in the early Empire.

3. Clarke, M. L., *The Roman Mind* (Cambridge, Mass: Harvard University Press 1956). Covers the period from Cicero to Marcus Aurelius.

4. Gibbon, Edward, *Decline and Fall of the Roman Empire* (New York: Modern Library, 1932). The student should attempt this at some point in his career. Besides being one of the great masterpieces of English literature, it is also a brilliant analysis of one of the great problems in Western history.

5. Jones, A. H. M., *Augustus*, (New York: Norton, 1970). A superb treatment of the Augustan system of government.

6. _____, *The Decline of the Ancient World* (New York: Holt, Rinehart and Winston, 1966).

7. Katz, Solomon, *The Decline of Rome* (Ithaca, New York: Cornell University Press, 1955). A sound introduction to the turmoil of the later Empire.

8. West, D. A. and Woodman, A. J., *Poetry and Politics in the Age of Augustus* (New York: Cambridge University Press, 1984). Shows the relationship between politics and art in the Augustan age.

9. White, Lynn, ed., *The Transformation of the Roman World* (Berkeley: University of California Press, 1966). A collection of essays on the transformation of the classical world and the emergence of the early Middle Ages.

CICERO from THE LAWS

The genius of Roman law lay in its flexibility and rationalism. Augustus' administrative and legal reforms were in large part derived from Cicero's vision of a single universal state governed by something like Plato's philosopher-king. His humanistic faith in the human brotherhood was the foundation of a legal system that has shaped Western institutions and values for nearly twenty-one centuries.

True law is right reason in agreement with nature; it is of universal application, unchanging and everlasting; it summons to duty by its commands, and averts from wrongdoing by its prohibitions. And it does not lay its commands or prohibitions upon good men in vain, though neither have any effect on the wicked. It is a sin to try to alter this law, nor is it allowable to attempt to repeal any part of it, and it is impossible to abolish it entirely. We cannot be freed from its obligations by senate or people, and we need not look outside ourselves for an expounder or interpreter of it. And there will not be different laws at Rome and at Athens, or different laws now and in the future, but one eternal and unchangeable law will be valid for all nations and all times, and there will be one master and ruler, that is, God, over us all, for he is the author of this law, its promulgator, and its enforcing judge. Whoever is disobedient is fleeing from himself and denying his human nature, and by reason of this very fact he will suffer the worst penalties, even if he escapes what is commonly considered punishment...out of all the material of the philosophers' discussions, surely there comes nothing more valuable than the full realization that we are born for Justice, and that right is based, not upon men's opinions, but upon Nature. This fact will immediately be plain if you once get a clear conception of man's fellowship and union with his fellow-men. For no single thing is so like another, so exactly its counterpart, as all of us are to one another. Nay, if bad habits and false beliefs did not twist the weaker minds and turn them in whatever direction they are inclined, no one would be so like his own self as all men would be like all others.

And so, however, we may define man, a single definition will apply to all. This is a sufficient proof that there is no difference in kind between man and man; for if there were, one definition could not be applicable to all men; and indeed reason, which alone raises us above the level of the beasts and enables us to draw inferences, to prove and disprove, to discuss and solve problems, and to come to conclusions, is certainly common to us all, and, though varying in what it learns, at least in the capacity to learn it is invariable. For the same things are invariably perceived by the senses, and those things which stimulate the senses, stimulate them in the same way in all men; and those rudimentary beginnings of intelligence to which I have referred, which are imprinted on our minds, are imprinted on all minds alike; and speech, the mind's interpreter, though differing in the choice of words, agrees in the sentiments expressed. In fact, there is no human being of any race who, if he finds a guide, cannot attain to virtue.

The similarity of the human race is clearly marked in its evil tendencies as well as in its goodness. For pleasure also attracts all men; and even though it is an enticement to vice, yet it has some likeness to what is naturally good. For it delights us by its lightness and agreeableness; and for this reason, by an error of thought, it is embraced as something wholesome. It is through a similar misconception that we shun death as though it were a dissolution of nature, and cling to life because it keeps us in the sphere in which we were born; and that we look upon pain as one of the greatest of evils, not only because of its cruelty, but also because it seems to lead to the destruction of nature. In the same way, on account of the similarity between moral worth and renown, those who are publicly honoured are considered happy, while those who do not attain fame are thought miserable. Troubles, joys, desires and fears haunt the minds of all men without distinction, and even if different men have different beliefs, that does not prove, for example, that it is not the same quality of superstition that besets those races which worship dogs and cats as gods, as that which torments other races. But what nation does not love courtesy, kindliness, gratitude, and remembrance of favours bestowed? What people does not hate and despise the haughty, the wicked, the cruel, and the ungrateful? Inasmuch as these considerations prove to us that the whole human race is bound together in unity, it follows, finally, that knowledge of the principles of right living is what makes men better...

We are so constituted by Nature as to share the sense of Justice with one another and to pass it on to all men. And in this whole discussion I want it understood that what I shall call Nature is [that which is implanted in us by Nature]; that, however, the corruption caused by bad habits is so great that the sparks of fire, so to spek, which Nature has kindled in us are extinguished by this corruption, and the vices which are their opposites spring up and are established. But if the judgments of men were in agreement with Nature, so that, as the poet says, they considered "nothing alien to them which concerns mankind," then Justice would be equally observed by all. For those creatures who have received the gift of reason from Nature have also received right reason, and therefore they have also received the gift of Law, which is right reason applied to command and prohibition. And if they have received Law, they have received Justice also. Now all men have received reason; therefore all men have received Justice.

C. Warren Hollister, ed., <u>Landmarks of the Western Heritage</u>, 2 vols. (New York: John Wiley and Sons, Inc., 1973), I, 137-138.

Study Questions

1. *Why is it a sin to try to alter true law? Why is it impossible to abolish it entirely?*

2. *Why need we not look outside ourselves for an interpreter of the law?*

3. *Why is there no need for different laws for every part of the Empire?*

Roman Empire. 27 B.C. - 476 A.D.

4. *In what sense does the man who breaks the law not escape punishment? What is the source of the law?*

5. *What proof is there that Justice is based not on men's opinions but on Nature?*

6. *What things prove the similarity of the human race?*

7. *Upon what is law based?*

VIRGIL from THE AENEID

 Publius Vergilius Maro's life (70-19 B.C.) spanned the troubled later days of the Republic and the inauguration of the Pax Romana under Augustus. He was born in Mantua in northern Italy and received a good classical education. He moved to Rome where he may first have met Octavian and then moved on to Naples. A shy, scholarly man who hated the noise of big cities and the intrigues of the court, Virgil nevertheless was attracted to Augustus' court by the personality of Augustus himself. Virgil began the <u>Aeneid</u> the year after the battle at the Bay of Actium, when he was forty and Augustus was in the first year of his reign. He finished eleven years later when he was near death and on his deathbed ordered its destruction. Luckily, Augustus saw to it that that part of the poet's will was not carried out.

 The legend of Aeneas was known to the Romans. Aeneas leaves Troy as it is being sacked and burned by the Achaeans. Under the guidance of Juno (Hera in Greek mythology), he travels west, lands at Carthage on the North African coast where Dido, the queen of Carthage, falls in love with him. He tarries with her until Juno reminds him of his duty and he journeys to Latium where he defeats the Latin hero, Turnus, and then marries Lavinia, the daughter of the Latin king. Thereby, the Trojan race is merged with the Latin to create a new race, the Roman. Rome, the city of Aeneas, is a new Troy reborn from the ashes of the old.

 In the following excerpt, Aeneas journeys into the underworld where his father, Anchises, reveals his destiny and that of the city he will found to Aeneas.

"In the beginning know that heaven and earth,
The rivery plains, the glittering orb of the moon,

Roman Empire. 27 B.C. - 476 A.D.

And the Titanic stars were animated
By a Spirit within, and a Mind interfused
Through every fiber of the universe
Gave vital impulse to its mighty form.
From these there spring the races of men and beasts,
The birds that fly, and all the strange shapes of creatures
The sea brings forth beneath its marbled surface.
Their life-force is drawn from fire, their creative seeds
Are of heavenly source, except as they are clogged
By the corrupting flesh, and dulled by their earthly
Habiliments, and limbs imbued with death.
From these derive our fears and our desires,
Our grief and joy, nor can we compass the whole
Aura of heaven shut as we are in the prison
Of the unseeing flesh. And furthermore,
When on the last day we are lost to the light,
We do not shed away all evil or all the ills
The body has bequeathed to us poor wretches,
For many flaws cannot but be ingrained
And must have grown hard through all our length of days.
Therefore we souls are trained with punishment
And pay with suffering for old felonies-
Some are hung up helpless to the winds;
The stain of sin is cleansed for others of us
In the trough of a huge whirlpool; or with fire
Burned out of us--each one of us we suffer
The afterworld we deserve: and from thence are sent
Through wide Elysium, and some few maintain
Ourselves in the Fields of Bliss, until length of days
When time has come full circle, cleanses us
To corruption's very core and leaves a pure
Element of perception, a spark of the primal fire.
After the cycle of a thousand years
God summons all these in a great procession
To the waters of Lethe, so that when they visit
The sky-encircled earth, being bereft
Of memory, they may begin to want
The body on again."

      So spoke Anchises
And he led his son and the Sibyl both together
Into the midst of the chattering throng and took

His stand on a mound from which he could review
The whole of that long line and recognize
Each passing face.

"Come then, I shall show you the whole span
Of your destiny, I shall make manifest
What glory lies in store for the seed of Dardanus,
And what posterity, Italian-born,
Your blood shall fill, illustrious spirits all,
And heirs-to-be of our name. Do you see that youth
Leaning upon his yet unpointed spear?
Nearest he is to the light of day--so the lot
Has chosen--he will be the first to rise
To upper air with Italian blood in his veins-
His name is Silvius, an Alban name,
He is your son--to be born after your death-
Your wife Lavinia late in her life will rear him
Out in the woods, a king and father of kings:
Our ruling house in Alba Longa traces
Its origin from him. Then next is Procas
The pride of Trojan people; then Capys; Numitor;
Then Silvius Aeneas, bringing your name
Back into use, and equally distinguished
In piety and warfare, if ever he shall sit On Alba's throne--
O look what splendid youths!
What strength of build--see how their brows are shaded
With cinctures of the civic oak-leaf? They
Shall build Nomentum for you and Gabii, Fidenae's city and the mountain fortress Of Collatia; they shall build you Pometii
And Inuus, Bola and Cora, with their camps.
These sites are nameless --- they shall give them names.
And Romulus, too, the son of Mars shall come,
His grandfather at his side --- that Romulus
Sprung from the blood of Assaracus, and his mother
Is to be Ilea, named from Troy and she
Is to bring him up --- do you see the double plumes
That start from his helmet? --- see how even now
He is marked out by his divine father,
With his own emblem, for the Upper World? Behold, my son!
Under his tutelage
Our glorious Rome shall rule the whole wide world,
Her spirit shall match the spirit of the gods;
Round seven citadels shall she build her walls;

In her breed of heroes blest--as the goddess Cybele,
Charioted and wearing a towered crown,
Parades through the cities of Phrygia rejoicing
In all her brood of gods, her hundred grandsons
All heaven-dwellers, holders of the height!
Now turn the gaze of your eyes this way --- look!
Look at this people, your own Roman people.
Here is Caesar and all Iulus' line,
Destined to pass beneath the great arch of the sky;
Here is the very man whom you have heard
So often promised you, Augustus Caesar,
Your child of the Divine who shall refound
A golden age for Latium --- in those lands,
Those very lands where Saturn once was king,
Who shall extend the frontier of our rule
Beyond the Garamantians and the Indians
(A land that lies outside the track of stars,
Outside the course of the year and of the sun,
Where Atlas the sky-bearer humps on his shoulder
The spinning pole of the world with its inlay
Of blazing constellations).
And even now,
In expectation of his coming, the realm
Of Caspia quakes and the regions round Maeotis
Quiver in fear of the prophetess of the Gods,
And at the sevenfold mouth of the river Nile
A welter of confusion seethes.

From *The Aeneid*, translated by Patric Dickinson. Copyright (c) 1961 by Patric Dickinson (copyright (c) 1961 by Patric Dickinson. Reprinted by arrangement with NAL Penguin Inc., New York, New York), 140-143.

Study Questions

1. Noting the words "...and a Mind interfused/Through every fiber of the universe," how does Virgil's conception of the universe differ from Homer's?

2. Are all the dead treated alike? Explain.

3. *How are our "old felonies" dealt with in Hell?*

4. *What is the effect of the waters of Lethe?*

5. *Who are the "seed of Dardanus"? (Dardanus was the legendary founder of Troy.)*

6. *Who is to be Aeneas' son?*

7. *What will Romulus do?*

8. *What are to be Augustus' accomplishments?*

9. *Compare Virgil's underworld with Homer's. With the Christian afterlife.*

VIRGIL, ECLOGUE IV

Virgil was the son of a farmer and his deep love for the land emerges in the four books of the Georgics, *a kind of practical guide on farming. He talks about cattle breeding, beekeeping, when to plant and when to harvest. While he doesn't mince the hardships of a farmer's life, the poverty, the hard work and the frequent failures, his point is that the rural life is the surest path to contentment.*

The Eclogues *preceded the* Georgics. *Sometimes called the* Bucolics, *these ten short little pastoral poems celebrate the joys and sorrows of the country and the simple, unaffected folk who live there. The fourth eclogue is like the other nine in that respect but there is a good reason why the Christian Middle Ages had a special affection for it.*

Muses of Sicily, essay we now
A somewhat loftier task! Not all men love
Coppice or lowly tamarisk: sing we woods,
Woods worthy of a Consul let them be.
Now the last age by Cumae's Sibyl sung
Has come and gone, and the majestic roll
Of circling centuries begins anew:
Justice returns, returns old Saturn's reign,
With a new breed of men sent down from heaven.
Only do thou, at the boy's birth in whom
The iron shall cease, the golden race arise,
Befriend him, chaste Lucina; 'tis thine own Apollo reigns.
And in thy consulate,
This glorious age, O Pollio, shall begin,
And the months enter on their mighty march.
Under thy guidance, whatso tracks remain
Of our old wickedness, once done away,
Shall free the earth from never-ceasing fear.

He shall receive the life of gods, and see
Heroes with gods commingling, and himself
Be seen of them, and with his father's worth
Reign o'er a world at peace. For thee, O boy,
First shall the earth, untilled, pour freely forth
Her childish gifts, the gadding ivy-spray
With foxglove and Egyptian bean-flower mixed,
And laughing-eyed acanthus.
Of themselves,
Untended, will the she-goats then bring home
Their udders swollen with milk, while flocks afield
Shall of the monstrous lion have no fear.
Thy very cradle shall pour forth for thee
Caressing flowers.
The serpent too shall die,
Die shall the treacherous poison-plant, and far
And wide Assyrian spices spring.
But soon
As thou hast skill to read of heroes' fame,
And of thy father's deeds, and inly learn
What virtue is, the plain by slow degrees
With waving corn-crops shall to golden grow,
From the wild briar shall hang the blushing grape,
And stubborn oaks sweat honey-dew. Nathless
Yet shall there lurk within of ancient wrong
Some traces, bidding tempt the deep with ships,
Gird towns with walls, with furrows cleave the earth.
Therewith a second Tiphys shall there be,
Her hero-freight a second Argo bear;
New wars too shall arise, and once again
Some great Achilles to some Troy be sent.
Then, when the mellowing years have made thee man,
No more shall mariner sail, nor pine-tree bark
Ply traffic on the sea, but every land
Shall all things bear alike: the glebe no more
Shall feel the harrow's grip, nor vine the hook;
The sturdy ploughman shall loose yoke from steer,
Nor wool with varying colours learn to lie;
But in the meadows shall the ram himself,
Now with soft flush of purple, now with tint
Of yellow saffron, teach his fleece to shine.
While clothed in natural scarlet graze the lambs.
'Such still, such ages weave ye, as ye run,'

Sang to their spindles the consenting Fates
By Destiny's unalterable decree.

Assume thy greatness, for the time draws nigh,
Dear child of gods, great progeny of Jove!
See how it totters --- the world's orbed might,
Earth, and wide ocean, and the vault profound,
All, see, enraptured of the coming time!
Ah! might such length of days to me be given,
And breath suffice me to rehearse thy deeds,
Nor Thracian Orpheus should out-sing me then,
Nor Linus, though his mother this, and that
His sire should aid--Orpheus Calliope,
And Linus fair Apollo. Nay, though Pan,
With Arcady for judge, my claim contest,
With Arcady for judge great Pan himself
Should own him foiled, and from the field retire.

Begin to greet thy mother with a smile,
O baby-boy! ten months of weariness
For thee she bore: O baby-boy, begin!
For him, on whom his parents have not smiled,
Gods deem not worthy of their board or bed.

James Rhoades, trans., *The Poems of Virgil* (London: Oxford University Press, 1962). Reprinted by permission of Oxford University Press), 401-403.

Study Questions

1. *Explain the first four lines. What kind of "woods" is Virgil going to sing of? What does he mean by that?*

2. *Who is the boy Virgil is referring to? Who are the "new breed of men sent down from heaven"?*

3. *What are the characteristics of the world newly at peace?*

4. *Why did Christians later have a special regard for this poem?*

HORACE, ODE

Quintus Horatius Flaccus (65-8 B.C.) is best known for his odes, a Greek lyric form that he managed to adapt to Latin.

He came from Venusia in the Greek part of southern Italy. His father, a freed ex-slave, saw to it that his son had the best education available and even had him sent to Athens to study philosophy. While he was in Greece, Julius Caesar was assassinated and Horace joined with Brutus and Cassius in the cause of "freedom". He was at the battle of Philippi in 42 B.C. and escaped but he returned home to find his father dead and the family property confiscated.

In 39, however, Octavian declared a general amnesty and in the following year, Virgil, who had come to know and admire Horace's works, introduced him to Maecenas, Octavian's most trusted advisor in civil affairs. Maecenas granted Horace a small estate near Rome, thus relieving him of poverty. When the split occurred between Octavian and Antony, Horace remained loyal to Octavian, even after Octavian, as Augustus, turned Rome into an autocracy.

While he probably had no great affection for the vanished Republic, he no doubt questioned some of Augustus' reforms and especially the softness and self-indulgence he thought they were inducing in the sons of Romulus. Like Livy, there is a melancholy, a longing for a Golden Age when Romans were morally better.

Roman, you may be innocent of guilt,
Yet you shall pay for each ancestral crime,

Until our mouldering temples are rebuilt
And the gods' statues cleansed of smoke and grime.

Only as servant of the gods in heaven
Can you rule earth. The seed of action is
Theirs, and the fruit. Slighted, have they not given
Suffering Italy multiple miseries?

Monaeses and Pacorus have now twice
Bruised our ill-starred assaults. Loot from our tents
Has made them jubilant and enhanced the price
Of their poor necklaces and ornaments.

And, ridden by civil faction, Rome came near
To her annihilation and eclipse
When Dacia, linked with Egypt, made us fear
Her archers as we did the other's ships.

This age has proved fertile in evil. First
It stained the marriage vow, and then the home,
And thence pure blood; and from this fouled source burst
The river of ruin that has flooded Rome.

Watch the grown girl. She revels in being taught
Dances from Asia Minor; she perfects
The arts of provocation; her one thought
From top to tingling toe is lawless sex.

Soon she's pursuing the young philanderers
Among her husband's guests. Careless of whom
She chooses, hugger-mugger she confers
The illicit pleasure in a half-lit room.

Only the husband seeming not to note,
At any man's commmand she leaves her place,
Pedlar or captain of some Spanish boat
Whoever pays the price of her disgrace.

Pyrrhus, Antiochus, Hannibal - the young Romans who brought such generals to their knees
And dyed the sea with Punic blood, were sprung
From parents of a different mould from these.

They were a hardy generation, good
Farmers and warriors, brought up to turn

The Sabine furrows with their hoes, chop wood
And lug the faggots home to please a stern

Mother at evening when the sun relieves
The tired ox of the yoke and draws the shifting
Shadows down the mountainside and leaves
The pleasant darkness as his parting gift.

Time corrupts all. What has it not made worse?
Our grandfathers sired feebler children; theirs
Were weaker still - ourselves; and now our curse
Must be to breed even more degenerate heirs.

James Michier, trans., *The Odes of Horace* (New York: Orion Press, 1963), 189-193.

Study Questions

1. *Why has Italy suffered "multiple miseries"?*

2. *Who are Pyrrhus, Antiochus and Hannibal? What kind of Romans defeated them?*

3. *What does Horace see for Rome's future?*

OVID from THE ART OF LOVE

Publius Ovidius Naso (43 B.C. - 17 A.D.) was born in central Italy and trained for an official career but he found the life of Augustan Rome more to his liking. Where Virgil was nowhere happier than enjoying the quiet peace of his farm, Ovid would have been bored to death. He enjoyed the bustle and noise of the city and, for a time, he also enjoyed Augustus' favor. The Augustan revolution had harked back to the austere, sturdier morality of the Republic and although Ovid tried to be pious, his poetry was gay, sensuous, frivilous and amoral. His <u>Metamorphoses</u> went through Greek and Roman mythology, providing him with some rather racy stories. <u>The Art of Love</u> is a delightful description of the amoral life of Augustus' court as well as a helpful little how-to book on getting and keeping a girlfriend.

The end of Ovid's life was rather sad. Augustus exiled him from Rome. For what isn't clear. It is somewhat doubtful that <u>The Art of Love</u>, as alien as it was to Augustus' own ideas of morality, was the cause. It is possible that Ovid's exile may have had some thing to do with Julia, Augustus' daughter, who was exiled for adultery. In any case, Ovid was sent to Romania on the west coast of the Black Sea. From there, he petitioned several times to be returned to Rome, to the fun and excitement, the glamour and glitter of the city he loved. His appeals went unheeded and he died in exile in the year 17 A.D.

First, my raw recruit, my inexperienced soldier,
Take some trouble to find the girl whom you really can love.
Next, when you see what you like your problem
      will be how to win her.
Finally, strive to make sure mutual love will endure.
That's as far as I go, the territory I cover,
Those are the limits I set: take them or leave them alone.

While you are footloose and free to play the
        field at your pleasure,
Watch for the one you can tell, "I want no other but you!"
She is not going to come to you floating down
        from the heavens:
For the right kind of a girl you must keep using your eyes.
Hunters know where to spread their nets for
        the stag in his covert,
Hunters know where the boar gnashes his teeth in the glade.

* * * * * * *

The theater's curve is a very good place for
        your hunting,
More opportunity here, maybe, than
        anywhere else.
Here you may find one to love, or possibly
        only have fun with,
Someone to take for a night, someone to have and to hold.
Just as a column of ants keeps going and
        coming forever,
Bearing their burdens of grain, just as the flight of the bees
Over the meadows and over the fields of the
        thyme and the clover
So do the women come, thronging the festival games,
Elegant, smart, and so many my sense of judgment is troubled.
        Hither they come, to see; hither they come, to be seen.
This is a place for the chase, not the chaste, and Romulus knew
        it.

* * * * * * *

Furthermore, don't overlook the meetings when horses are
        running;
In the crowds at the track opportunity waits.
There is no need for a code of finger-signals
        or nodding,
Sit as close as you like; no one will stop you at all.
In fact, you will have to sit close - that's one of the rules, at a
        race track. Whether she likes it or not, contact is part of
        the game.
Try to find something in common, to open the conversation;
Don't care too much what you say, just so that every one hears.

Roman Empire. 27 B.C. - 476 A.D.

Ask her, "Whose colors are those?" - that's
good for an opening gambit.
Put your own bet down, fast, on whatever she plays.
Then, when the gods come along in procession, ivory, golden,
Outcheer every young man, shouting for Venus, the queen.
Often it happens that dust may fall on the
      blouse of the lady.
If such dust should fall, carefully brush it away.
Even if there's no dust, brush off whatever
      there isn't.
Any excuse will do: why do you think you have hands?
If her cloak hangs low, and the ground is
      getting it dirty,
Gather it up with care, lift it a little, so!
Maybe, by way of reward, and not without her indulgence,
You'll be able to see ankle or possibly knee.
Then look around and glare at the fellow who's sitting behind
      you,
Don't let him crowd his knees into her delicate spine.
Girls as everyone knows, adore these little attentions:

        * * * * * * *

Let your mistresses hear nothing but what they desire.
You have not come to one bed in the name of
      the law, but more freely.
Love is your warrant and bond, love holds the office of law.
Bring her courtesies, and flattering words,
      and endearments,
Words that are sweet to the ear; make her be glad you are
      there.
I do not lecture the rich in my role of
      professor of loving:
If you have presents to bring, you have no need of my art.
"Here is something for you!" A man who can
      say that has genius!
I give up, I retire; he can learn nothing from me.
I am a poor man's poet, because I was always a
      poor man;
Loving, I made no gifts, only a present of words.
Poor men should watch their step and poor men should watch
      their language,

Poor men should learn to bear more than the rich would
    endure.
I remember a time when I pulled my girl's hair
    in my anger:
How many days did that cost? More than I like to recall.
I did not know that I tore her dress, and I
    still do not think so:
Still, she said that I did; who do you think had to pay?
So, if you are wise, avoid the mistakes of
    your teacher,
Let my experience help, save you both time and expense.
Fight with the Parthian hordes, but keep the
    peace with your lady,
Have some fun, and enjoy all the
    inducements of love.
If she is somewhat rude, and none too polite
    to your loving,
Stick it out, endure; one of these days she'll be kind.
Gently, gently move, when you try to bend the
    bough over:
Don't make a show of your strength, or the bough will break in
    your hand.

Gently, gently float, and go along with the river:
Rivers are not to be won forcing your way upstream.
Kindness, the trainers say, will tame even
    lions and tigers,
Little by little the bull learns to submit to the plough.

       * * * * * * *

What about sending her poems? A very
    difficult question.
Poems, I am sorry to say, aren't worth so much in this town.
Oh, they are praised, to be sure; but the girls want something
    more costly. Even illiterates please, if they have money
    to burn.
Ours is a Golden Age, and gold can purchase
    you honors,
All the "Golden Mean" means is, gold is the end.
Homer himself, if he came attended by all of
    the Muses,
With no scrip in his purse, would be kicked out of the house.

There are a few, very few, bright girls with a
        real education,
Some (perhaps) here and there, willing to give it try.
So, go ahead, praise both: the worth of the
        song matters little
Just so you make it sound lovely while reading aloud.
Whether or not she can tell one kind of verse
        from another,
If there's a line in her praise she will assume, "It's a gift!"
What you were planning to do, provided it
        serves your advantage,
Get her to think of first, get her to take the lead.
There may be one of your slaves, to whom you
        have promised his freedom;
Have him appeal to her, give him the gift in her name.
If you release a slave from chains or the
        threat of a flogging,
What you intended to do, make her beholden to you.

Make the gain your own, but let her have all
the credit;
You lose nothing, and she gains in her sense of largesse.
But, whoever you are, if you're truly anxious
        to hold her,
See that she thinks you are held, stunned by her beauty and
        charm.
If she's in Tyrian dress, then praise her
        Tyrian dresses;
If in the Coan mode, say that the Coan is best.
Is she in gold? let her be more dear than her golden apparel;
Is she in wool? approve woolen, becoming to her.
If she appears in her slip, cry out, "You
        inflame me with passion!"
Ask, in a timid voice, "Aren't you afraid you'll be cold?"
Praise the new part in her hair, and praise
        the way she has curled it;
Praise her dance and her song; cry
        "Encore!" at the end.
Also, her ways in bed you should speak of with adulation,
Calling them out of this world, praising the joys of the night.
Though she is wild and fierce, untamed as any Medusa,
She will be gentle and kind when the right love is near.

Don't give yourself away, if you have to
    resort to deception,
Don't let a gesture or look spoil the effect of your words.
Art is effective, concealed; but once it is
    out in the open
Brings, as it should, disgrace, takes all your credit away.

Rolfe Humphries, trans., *Ovid. The Art of Love* (Bloomington: Indiana University Press, 1957), 106, 109, 135, 138-139.

Study Questions

1. What exhortation does Ovid give his pupil in the first paragraph?

2. Why is the theatre a good place to go "hunting"? What are women compared with? Explain the line "This is a place for the chase, not the chaste".

3. Why is the horse track a good place for impressing a girl? Why should one cheer Venus? What "little attentions" might one bestow on a girl here?

4. How should one talk to one's girlfriend? How should one treat her? What happened to Ovid when he treated his girl roughly?

5. Is sending poetry a good idea? Explain. Why should you get the slave you intended to free anyway to appeal to your mistress?

6. What is he advising in the last section?

7. Do you think this advice would work with any woman? Do you think Ovid is a "male chauvinist" or simply a good student of human nature? Explain.

PETRONIUS from SATYRICON

Almost nothing is known of the author of the Satyricon. Whoever Petronius was, he had a deft hand for satire, as the following excerpt shows. The "nouveau riche", the man who had profited by Augustus' reforms, had become rich and had not acquired any grace in the process, is the target of the Satyricon. Trimalchio is crude, immoral, naive, ill-bred and something of a huckster, the kind of person it grieved men like Livy and Horace and Virgil to see "gracing" the city of Romulus and Aeneas. Here he tells his guests how he came into his wealth.

But to come back to the living. Make yourselves at home, friends. For I was once just as you are now, but I raised myself to this on my own merits. The heart makes the man, and all the rest is rubbish. "I buy well, I sell well," although some people say differently. Happiness! I'm just bursting with it. What, still blubbing, you snuffler? I'll give you what for to whine about! As I was saying, self-help brought me to my fortune. I came out of Asia no bigger than this candlestick. In fact day by day I measured myself by it, and rubbed my lips with the lamp-oil to get a bit of hair on my muzzle all the quicker. All the same, I was my master's cherub for fourteen years. Nothing disgraceful in doing what the master bids. And I did my mistress's pleasure as well. You know what I mean. But hush, hush, I am not one to boast. Finally, as the gods would have it, I turned master in the house, and there I was, his master's brains. The gist of it was that he made me joint-heir with Caesar, and I came into an estate, nobleman's size. Nobody is satisfied with next to nothing. I was burning to do business. To cut a long story short, I built five ships, got a cargo of wine, worth its weight in gold in those days, and sent them to Rome. You would think it was a put-up job; every single ship was wrecked. That's the truth, I'm not making it up. In one day Neptune swooped thirty millions. Was I downhearted? No, I assure you, I felt the loss as if it was nothing. I built some more, bigger and better, more successful, and everybody said I was an intrepid fellow. You know, a big ship has a lot of staying power. Once again I shipped wine, bacon, beans, Capuan perfume, and slaves. This time Fortunata[1] did the right thing; she sold her jewels, her wardrobe, everything, and slipped a hundred gold pieces in my hand. This was the leaven of my pile. There's no delay when the gods are on to something. In one trip I rounded off a good ten million. I promptly bought up all my patron's estates. I built a house, I bought slaves and livestock; whatever I touched grew like a honeycomb. When I was getting more income than the whole country, I threw in my hand. I retired from business and began money-lending among freedmen. I was completely unwilling to carry on my affairs, but I was encouraged by an astrologer who happened to light on our town. He was a little Greek; name of Serapa, and well in with the gods. He told me things I had forgotten, he explained it all from the needle and thread onwards; he knew what I had in my guts. He might well have told me what I had for supper the day before. You would have thought he'd never left my side. You remember, don't you Habinnas - I think you were on the spot - "You took your wife from a certain place. You are unlucky in your friends. You never get the gratitude you deserve. You own vast estates. You nourish a viper in your bosom,' and - though I oughtn't to tell you this - he said I had thirty years, four months and two days left to live. Moreover I am soon to come into a legacy. My horoscope says so. And if I can extend my farms as far as Apulia, I shall have done well enough in this life. In the meantime, while Mercury watches over me, I have built this house. You know it was a mere hut; it's a palace now. Four dining-rooms, twenty bedrooms, two marble colonnades, an upper storeroom, a bedroom I sleep in myself, a nest for my viper[2], a first-rate porter's lodge, and accommodation for all my guests. Just let me mention that when Scaurus came here he would go nowhere else, and his people have a house, by the seaside. There are a great many other things I will show you quite soon. Believe me, you have a penny, you're worth a penny; have something, and you will be someone. That's how your friend who was a frog is now a king. Now, Stichus, bring

---

[1] Trimalchio's wife.
[2] Trimalchio's references to Fortunata are not flattering.

me the grave-clothes in which I wish to be buried, and bring the perfumes and a sample from the jar that shall be poured over my bones."

Stichus did not delay fetching a white winding-sheet and a robe into the dining-room. Trimalchio asked us to feel whether they were made of good wool. He added with a smile, "Take care, Stichus, that the mice and moths don't get at them, or I'll burn you alive. I want to be carried out in style, so that everybody blesses me."

Then he opened a pot of spikenard, anointed us all with it, and said, "I hope I like it as much when I'm dead as now I'm alive."

He had them pour the wine into a bowl.

"Just make-believe you are guests at my funeral," he said.

The thing was becoming utterly nauseating when Trimalchio, by now far gone in the most bestial drunkenness, ordered in a fresh lot of entertainers - horn-blowers. Propped up by a number of cushions, he stretched himself on the edge of his couch.

"Pretend I'm dead," he said. "Play something nice."

The horn-blowers sounded a funeral march. The undertaker's man in particular, the most respectable-looking of them all, blew with such force that he roused the entire neighbourhood. Watchmen patrolling the district, under the impression that Trimalchio's house was on fire, suddenly broke down the door and started about their duty with water, hatchets and considerable uproar.

We seized this most welcome opportunity, gave Agamemnon the slip, and fled as fast as we could, as if from a real blaze.

Paul Dinnage, trans., *The Satyricon of Petronius* (London: Spearman & Calder, 1953), 72-75.

Study Questions

1. In what condition did Trimalchio come from Asia? Why did he rub his lips with lamp oil? What clue does that give you to his intelligence?

2. What does he think happiness is?

3. What kind of "work" did he perform for his master? His mistress?

4. How did Trimalchio turn "master in the house"? Why do you think his master willed the estate to him?

5. What did he invest his wealth in? What happened to it?

6. Who helped him on his second venture? Why?

7. What had been Fortunata's relationship to Trimalchio?

8. What had Serapa the astrologer told him? How seriously did Trimalchio take it?

9. By what measure does Trimalchio assess the value of his life?

10. What seems to be his idea of fun? What is the result of his "funeral"?

MARCUS AURELIUS ANTONINUS
from MEDITATIONS

Born at Rome, Marcus Aurelius (121-180 A.D.) was trained by his uncle and guardian, the Emperor Antoninus Pius (reigned 138-161). He was converted to Stoicism and then studied philosophy and law. He married Pius' daughter, Faustina, and then succeeded him as emperor in 162.

His reign was a tumultuous one. There were earthquakes, floods, epidemics, threatened revolt in Britain, the usual hostilities from the Parthians in the east and from German barbarians in the north and west. In 175, Faustina died and he was faced with revolt in Asia. He was preoccupied again with war along the Danube in 180 when he caught some disease and died.

The Meditations *was never meant to be a philosophical treatise. It is a kind of spiritual diary, the expression of a profoundly good man communing with his own soul. Stoicism could be fairly arid and dogmatic but in the hands of this man, there is a warmth and humanity about it. He is sometimes inconsistent and uncertain but always direct and simple.*

Men seek out retreats for themselves in the country, by the seaside, on the mountains, and thou too art wont to long above all for such things. But all this is unphilosophical to the last degree, when thou canst at a moment's notice retire into thyself. For nowhere can a man find a retreat more full of peace or more free from care than his own soul --- above all if he have that within him, a steadfast look at which and he is at once in all good ease, and by good ease I mean nothing other than good order. Make use then of this retirement continually and regenerate thyself. Let thy axioms be short and elemental, such as when set before thee of all trouble, and send thee away with no discontent at those things to which thou art returning.

Why with what art thou discontented? The wickedness of men? Take this conclusion to heart, that rational creatures have been made for one another; that forbearance is part of justice; that wrong-doing is involuntary; and think how many ere now, after passing their lives in implacable enmity, suspicion, hatred, and at daggers drawn with one another, have been laid out and burnt to ashes --- think of this, I say, and at last stay thy fretting. But art thou discontented with thy share in the whole? Recall the alternative: Either Providence or Atoms! and the abundant proofs there are that the Universe is as it were a state. But is it the affections of the body that shall still lay hold on thee? Bethink thee that the Intelligence, when it has once abstracted itself and learnt its own power, has nothing to do with the motions smooth or rough of the vital breath. Bethink thee too of all that thou hast heard and subscribed to about pleasure and pain.

But will that paltry thing, Fame, pluck thee aside? Look at the swift approach of complete forgetfulness, and the void of infinite time on this side of us and on that, and the empty echo of acclamation, and the fickleness and uncritical judgment of those who claim to speak well of us, and the narrowness of the arena to which all this is confined. For the whole earth is but a point, and how tiny a corner of it is this the place of our sojourning! and how many therein and of what sort are the men who shall praise thee!

From now therefore bethink thee of the retreat into this little plot that is thyself. Above all distract not thyself, be not too eager, but be thine own master, and look upon life as a man, as a human being, as a citizen, as a mortal creature. But among the principles readiest to thine hand, upon which thou shalt pore, let there be these two. One, that objective things do not lay hold of the soul, but stand quiescent without; while disturbances are but the outcome of that opinion which is within us. A second, that all this visible world changes in a moment, and will be no more; and continually bethink thee to the changes of how many things thou hast already been a witness. 'The Universe mutation: Life--opinion.'

* * * * * *

Note that all that befalls befalleth justly. Keep close watch and thou wilt find this true, I do not say, as a matter of sequence merely but as a matter of justice also, and as would be expected from One whose dispensation is based on desert. Keep close watch, then, as thou has begun, and whatsoever thou doest, do it as only a good man should in the strictest sense of that word. In every sphere of activity safeguard this.

Harbour no such opinion as he holds who does thee violence, or as he would have thee hold. See things in all their naked reality.

Thou shouldest have these two readinesses always at hand; the one which prompts thee to do only what thy reason in its royal and lawmaking capacity shall suggest for the good of mankind; the other to change thy mind, if one be near to set thee right, and convert thee from some vain conceit. But this conversion should be the outcome of a persuasion in every case that the thing is just or to the common interest--and some such cause should be the only one--not because it is seemingly pleasant or popular.

All that befalls either so befalls as thou art fitted by nature to bear it or as thou art not fitted. If the former, take it not amiss, but bear it as thou art fitted to do. If the latter, take not that amiss either, for when it has destroyed thee, it will itself perish. Howbeit be assured that thou art fitted by nature to bear everything which it rests with thine own opinion about it to render bearable and tolerable, according as thou thinkest it thy interest or thy duty to do so.

If a man makes a slip, enlighten him with loving-kindness, and shew him wherein he hath seen amiss. Failing that, blame thyself or not even thyself.

Whatever befalls thee was set in train for thee from everlasting, and the interplication of causes was from eternity weaving into one fabric thy existence and the coincidence of this event.

Reprinted by permission of the publishers and The Loeb Classical Library from C. R. Haines, trans., *The Communings with Himself of Marcus Aurelius Antoninus* (Cambridge: Harvard University Press, 1979), 67-71, 75, 263.

Study Questions

1. What is the most peaceful retreat a man can have?

2. Why do men do wrong? How should we treat wicked men?

3. How does Marcus Aurelius treat popularity (fame)?

4. Summarize the two principles one should keep in mind. What two "readinesses" should we keep at hand?

EARLY CHRISTIANITY

The story of Jesus of Nazareth is simple. He was born of Jewish parents about 4 B.C. in Bethlehem in the Roman province of Judea, spent his childhood in Nazareth in Galilee and then, about the age of thirty, he began a public career of teaching. About three years later, he was delivered by Jewish leaders to the Roman procurator of Judea, Pontius Pilate, a mediocrity who was terrified of large, noisy crowds, and Pilate condemned him to death by crucifixion. According to Christian faith three days thereafter, Jesus rose from the dead; forty days after that, he ascended into heaven; and ten days later, his closest disciples, filled with what they claimed was the Holy Spirit, began to spread his teachings.

Two themes already familiar to the Roman world ran through Jesus' teachings --- the brotherhood of Man and the universality of God. Jesus added a unique touch, however, to both. To the Stoic idea of a universal brotherhood based on Reason, Jesus added the command that his followers care for each other and that they truly love one another. The idea of God also changed. What Jesus offered was a God who not only created the world but who loved it enough to invite men to address him as Father and moreover, who would intervene in human history and send his Son, Jesus, into the world and allow him to suffer death in order to bring men not merely to a rational understanding of God but a full, loving union with him as his sons.

Christianity didn't spread like a prairie fire but its growth was persistent. Conditions in the Roman world itself account for this. First, as has already been seen, there was nothing radically new in Jesus' teachings. Even the idea of a Trinity, which Christians themselves would have a difficult time with, could be found among the religious beliefs of Rome's Etruscan founders. Not only doctrine but also in ritual, there was little that was unique. A sacrificial victim and meal, a baptism, a slaughtered and then risen God, a personal resurrection --- all of these had parallels in the mystery religions Rome was already familiar with. And Christianity's idea of a universal God for all men squared nicely with Rome's own heterogeneous and universal empire. Also, there was an appeal not only to the poor and lonely but also to the intellectual who found classical philosophy rather arid. A God who was loving Father was simply more satisfying than a philosophy that could offer nothing more than serenity and peace of mind.

There were other factors as well. Christianity appeared during the Pax Romana. The upheavals of war were not there to inhibit or disrupt the travels of such peripatetic missionaries as St. Paul, for instance. Rome's roads, her postal system, the existence of not one but two universal languages, Latin and Koine, allowed easy initial contact and facilitated sustained communication between the apostles and their converts. Also, the Roman was tolerant, broad-minded. He would be the last to persecute someone merely for his religious beliefs, regardless of how outlandish he might have thought them --- and that attitude was reflected in his law. Finally, Christians were persecuted and "the blood of martyrs really was the seed of the Church." Romans were accustomed to a wide variety of religious sects and philosophies but they were not accustomed to people who were willing to die for such things. The martyrs would at first attract curiosity, then interest, then often conversion.

Persecutions there were but they were sporadic and local. Even the notorious persecution under Nero in which Peter and Paul were killed was confined to the city of Rome itself and generated more sympathy than hostility. If Rome had no doctrinal or ritual problems with Christianity, the question arises, why were Christians persecuted at all? One reason was that they were believed to engage in immoral and indecent acts. Since they ate the body and blood of Jesus, some people thought they were cannibals. Secondly, the middle classes who had profited by Augustus' reforms were also irritated by the early communism of the Christians, arising from their willingness to take literally Christ's command to give their goods to the poor and follow him. Thirdly, "love thy neighbor," if brought into the military, could have been disastrous on the frontiers. And finally and most importantly, Christianity struck at that most laudable and Roman virtue, *pietas*. To the Roman, devotion to the state was

Early Christianity

inextricably linked with religion. The Christian not only separated the two but looked forward to the second coming of Jesus and the establishment of his kingdom, an event which many of them expected to happen shortly. The Christians' loyalty to Rome thus was at least suspect. For the Roman, religion was never a matter of beliefs or ethics. It was simply a ritual and all he asked was for some kind of external observance to placate the gods who protected Rome. The Christians who refused even such small tokens of ritual were regarded by the Romans as atheists who could bring the wrath of the gods down on Roman heads. Roman culture was eclectic. It readily welcomed ideas, goods, values from the ends of the known world. The Christian, however, was exclusive. He insisted on worshiping only one god, and the Roman would think him at least dangerously narrow-minded.

Gradually, however, Romans overcame their fears of Christianity as they realized that Jesus and Caesar were not rivals. The emperor Trajan (98-117 A.D.) hated Christians but he forbade his governors to hunt them down. Most pagans by Diocletian's time were accustomed to living side by side with Christians and they were probably as relieved as Christians themselves by Constantine's Edict of Milan in 313 granting religious toleration to Christianity. In 381, Theodosius I made Christianity the official religion of the Roman Empire and the state then turned to persecuting pagans. Unhappily, the administrative reforms of Diocletian and Constantine gave the state far more efficient machinery for carrying out these persecutions than had ever been used against Christians.

Meanwhile the Church had been evolving an organizational structure which would survive Rome's fall. As the apostles spread the Gospel, their converts came together in what St. Paul described as a church (the Greek <u>ecclesia</u>). After an apostle such as Paul had established the faith in the community, he would often name a bishop to take his place as he moved on. The job of the bishop was twofold; he was to preach and spread the Gospel, encourage the new believers, preside over baptisms and the celebration of the Last Supper and resolve disputes among them (no small job as Paul's epistles reveal). Secondly, he was also to care for their physical needs --- arrange care for the sick, the elderly, widows and orphans. Thus, from the outset, the clergy's role was not merely a spiritual but also a secular one.

No one bishop had any more authority than any other. Ultimately, all of them owed their authority to one of the apostles; hence, we speak of Apostolic Succession. By the time of Theodosius' edict, five major bishoprics had emerged --- at Jerusalem, Alexandria, Antioch, Constantinople and at Rome. Of these, the bishop or "patriarch" of Constantinople had the most clout simply because his seat was in the capital. But the bishop of Rome had a special prestige and affection for two reasons. First, it had been into the Pax Romana that God had sent His Son and at a time when Rome, not Constantinople, had ruled the world. Clearly, Rome then had a preeminent role to play in God's plan. Secondly, St. Peter had been martyred at Rome and whatever real authority he may or may not have had, Peter clearly had been chosen by Jesus to play a special and leading role. Hence, it was Peter's successors alone who were addressed affectionately as "papa" or "father." Ultimately, as the political split between the Eastern and Western empires widened, so would the rift between the Roman and Byzantine churches. And as Roman political authority waned in the West, the bishops of Rome would feel compelled to step into the ensuing vacuum. Then too, as the bishops of Rome took leading roles in the doctrinal disputes of the fourth and fifth centuries, more and more Christians came to view them as indeed the heads of the Church. Eventually Pope Gregory I (590-610) took responsibility for the entire Western church by designating bishops and sending them out as far as Britain to preach. In taking the title "servant of the servants of God," Gregory was in fact laying claim to jurisdiction over the entire Church. The patriarch in Constantinople, however --- and bishops throughout the Byzantine world --- would ignore him, and even many Western bishops would take his claim lightly.

Christianity also borrowed from Rome the tools by which to frame its law and its doctrine. Roman legal terminology, procedures and principles were incorporated by the Church in its canon law and in the courts which enforced that law. Her doctrine too was shaped by Greco-Roman philosophy.

The earliest and easily the most serious dispute within the Church came in its first generation and was between Peter and Paul. To Peter, Jesus was the Jewish Messiah and, except for baptism and the Last Supper, early Christianity resembled simply

Early Christianity

a Jewish reform sect. And it would have remained that had it not been for the conversion of Paul. A native of the thriving, cosmopolitan city of Tarsus, Paul moved easily in the Hellenized Roman world. To Paul, Judaism had simply paved the way for the Messiah, who was Jesus, and Jesus had, by his death and resurrection, redeemed all men, Gentiles as well as Jews. According to Christian tradition, the issue was resolved by a dream or vision of Peter in which he saw a sheet lowered from heaven laden with foods which by Jewish law were "unclean". The message clearly was that the "food" of the Gospel was to be made available to those who ate unclean foods, non-Jews as well as Jews.

At issue between Peter and Paul was the wider problem of the proper relationship between Christianity and the Roman world. At first, the early Christians simply rejected that rational humanism which so characterized classical thought. A second-century Father, Tertullian, rhetorically asked, "What has Athens to do with Jerusalem? The Academy with the Church?" That hostility to all things Roman was understandable. The Romans had, after all, crucified Christ and then persecuted his followers, albeit fitfully. The sensuous verses of Ovid, the poetry of Virgil celebrating the earthly Rome, even the scintillating wit and wisdom of Cicero had little merit to the Christian who looked for the second coming of Christ.

There was another facet, however, which encouraged accommodation and assimilation. Jesus had, after all, ordered his followers to "Render unto Caesar the things that are Caesar's." Clearly, there were things that were properly Caesar's. St. Paul had thought there was much good in Greco-Roman thought and in the fourth century, St. Jerome (340-419) not only knew but dearly loved the writings of Cicero, Virgil and Terence. His translation of the Old and New Testaments into the vulgar or common Latin of his day reveals him not only as a theologian but also as a competent linguist. This <u>Vulgate</u> would remain the Church's official Bible until the Reformation in the sixteenth century.

Even before the <u>Vulgate</u>, Christians had the texts of the Bible and a clergy to teach them. But controversies over doctrine threatened the unity of the Church from its very foundation. Ultimately, most of these disputes derived from the dual nature of

Jesus. He had claimed to be both God --- infinite, immortal, immutable, omniscient --- and Man, finite, mortal, changeable --- a logical impossibility. And the Christian was still, after all, a Roman, heir to the rationalism of the Hellenistic world. In the third century, a priest in Alexandria, Arius (c. 250-336), began to attract followers with his teaching that Jesus was merely a man inspired by God but not divine nor co-eternal with the Father. Though condemned by the Council of Nicea in 325 as a heresy --- a teaching contrary to orthodox doctrine --- Arianism would have a long life ahead of it. It was condemned again by the Council of Chalcedon in 451 which insisted that Jesus is truly God and Man and that both the divine and human natures are joined together in his person. Yet variations of the heresy would appear in both the Eastern and Western churches well into the Middle Ages.

The full fusion of classical thought and Christian faith came from one of the warmest, most attractive of the Church Fathers, Augustine of Hippo (354-430). A good part of Augustine's enduring charm comes from his <u>Confessions</u>, the first autobiography in Western literature. In it, Augustine describes his own spiritual journey to God and reveals a soul immersed in the culture and philosophy of the classical world, a soul tormented, growing, searching and finally able to find solace only in God. Augustine's second great work, the <u>City of God</u>, like the <u>Confessions</u>, reveals his intimacy with classical learning much of which he thought could be used to support Christian faith. He rejects Plato's idea that knowledge and virtue are the same. Augustine, like Aristotle, believed that virtue lay in the will but, unlike Aristotle, Augustine believed in a will corrupted by sin. Thus, it is simply easier for us to commit an evil act than a good one. Augustine's view of the perpetual conflict between the corrupt lower world and the pure world of the spirit was to become one of the foundations of medieval thought.

Another cardinal shaper of medieval life and thought appeared about a century after St. Augustine. This was St. Benedict (480-543), the founder of Western monasticism. Theodosius' edict established the Church as a major political institution but not all Christians were happy with that. They would never have considered leaving the Church but they did yearn for a deeper, closer relationship with God than seemed available in the institutional Church. So they often would go off alone into the desert as hermits (from <u>eremos</u>, desert) and lead

Early Christianity

lives of often extreme asceticism. Asceticism is the subordination of physical pleasures, even necessities, to free the soul for a mystical union with God and is not uniquely Christian. It can be found in many cultures for many centuries before Christ. The hermits would fast, practice celibacy and self-flagellation and do various other penances. Egypt was the first home of Christian hermits and then St. Basil (c. 329-379) established a rule that became the standard for monastic life in the Eastern church.

The first monastery in the West was established by St. Benedict at Monte Casino, south of Rome. Benedict's Rule reveals the Roman concern for order, discipline, moderation and flexibility. The monks were required to pray and to work. The "work" in the Rule was to have immense significance. First, it marked a sharp break from the classical attitude toward manual labor which had been done only by slaves. Labor was to be embraced joyfully for the love of God. It therefore had great dignity. Secondly, the manual labor commanded by the Rule resulted ultimately in the development of new agricultural techniques and machinery, the use of crop rotation and the use of water and windmills. Monastic experiments in stock breeding would produce the medieval war-horse, an animal that would have made Julius Caesar envious had he seen it in Gaul.

The intellectual "work" of the monks involved the preservation and copying of manuscripts, not only sacred texts such as the Scriptures and the writings of the Fathers, but literally anything the monks could lay hands on. Often these texts would be adorned with gold leaf so that the page literally shone; it was "illuminated," and these illuminated manuscripts, the work of unknown monks, became one of the most beautiful artistic expressions of the Middle Ages.

Under the influence of Cassiodorus (490-575) who entered Monte Casino after a political career, the monasteries became centers for the preservation of classical learning. Cassiodorus also insisted that the quality of the clergy would be improved by higher education along classical lines. In other words, the classical trivium (logic, rhetoric and grammar) and the quadrivium (arithmetic, geometry, astronomy and music) were brought into the monasteries. Separated from the world, yet drawing the world to itself, the Benedictine monastery would preserve much of the learning of the classical world. But more --- it would also become the inn, dispensary, hospital, law court and above all, the school of the Middle Ages.

Suggested Readings

1. Benko, S., *Pagan Rome and Early Christians* (Bloomington: Indiana University Press, 1984). One of the better studies showing the evolution of Christianity against its Hellenistic and Jewish background.

2. Brown, P., *Augustine of Hippo* (Berkeley: University of California Press, 1967). Perhaps the best biography of the saint.

3. Chadwick, O., *The Making of the Benedictine Ideal* (Washington, D.C.: St. Anselm's Abbey, 1981). Stresses the personality of St. Benedict in the making of the Benedictine ideals.

4. Davies, J. G., *The Early Christian Church* (New York: Holt, Rinehart, and Winston, 1965). An excellent introduction to the first five centuries of Church history.

5. Jaeger, Werner, *Early Christianity and Greek Paideia* (Cambridge, Mass: Belknap Press of Harvard University Press, 1961). Shows the continuity between classical and Christian ideas.

6. Knowles, David., *Christian Monasticism* (New York: McGraw-Hill, 1969). Traces the development of monasticism through the mid-twentieth century.

7. MacMullen, R., *Christianizing the Roman Empire* (New Haven: Yale University Press, 1984). The growth of the Christian Church from a Roman perspective.

8. Richards, Jeffrey, *Consul of God: The Life and Times of Gregory the Great* (London, Boston: Routledge & Kegan Paul, 1980). The first biography of this important pope in over seventy years.

From the SERMON ON THE MOUNT

What the Gospel of St. Matthew gives as a single sermon may in fact be a compilation of Jesus' teachings uttered in various places at different times.

Blessed are the poor in spirit, for theirs is the kingdom of heaven.

Blessed are the meek, for they shall possess the earth.

Blessed are they who mourn, for they shall be comforted.

Blessed are they who hunger and thirst for justice, for they shall be satisfied.

Blessed are the merciful, for they shall obtain mercy.

Blessed are the clean of heart, for they shall see God.

Blessed are the peacemakers, for they shall be called children of God.

Blessed are they who suffer persecution for justice' sake, for theirs is the kingdom of heaven.

Blessed are you when men reproach you, and persecute you, and, speaking falsely, say all manner of evil against you, for my sake.

Rejoice and exalt, because your reward is great in heaven; for so did they persecute the prophets who were before you.

You are the salt of the earth; but if the salt loses its strength, what shall it be salted with? It is no longer of any use but to be thrown out and trodden underfoot by men.

You are the light of the world. A city set on a mountain cannot be hidden. Neither do men light a lamp and put it under the measure, but upon the lamp-stand, so as to give light to all in the house. Even so let your light shine before men, in order that they may see your good works and give glory to your Father in heaven.

Matthew, Ch. 5:1-16

In this manner therefore shall you pray:

Our Father who art in heaven, hallowed be thy name.

Thy kingdom come, thy will be done, on earth, as it is in heaven.

Give us this day our daily bread.

And forgive us our debts, as we also forgive our debtors.

And lead us not into temptation, but deliver us from evil

Matthew, Ch. 6:8-13.

* * * * * * *

SAINT PAUL from FIRST LETTER TO THE CORINTHIANS

Saul was born in the city of Tarsus in Cilicia. He was educated in Greek and learned the trade of his father, tent-making. In addition to the Pharasaic education he received at home he also journeyed as a young man to Jerusalem for further studies in the law. He returned to Tarsus before the beginning of Jesus' public life. He returned again to Palestine and was present at the stoning of the first Christian martyr, St. Stephen, and thereafter, he zealously persecuted Christians. The high priest commissioned him to go to Damascus to arrest Christians and bring them bound to Jerusalem. As he approached Damascus, however, he was blinded by a strong light and thrown from his horse. He heard Jesus addressing him, was converted to Christianity, changed his name to Paul and then became the apostle to the Gentiles, non-Jews.

On his second missionary journey, Paul had preached first to the Jews of Corinth where he encountered hostility and then to the Gentiles there among whom he made many converts. On his third missionary journey, a group of the new Corinthian Christians visited him at Antioch with news of disorders there. The First Letter was written to address those problems.

If I should speak with the tongues of men and of angels, but do not have charity, I have become as a sounding brass or a tinkling cymbal. And if I have prophecy and know all mysteries and all knowledge, and if I have all faith so as to remove mountains, yet do not have charity, I am nothing. And if I distribute all my goods to feed the poor, and if I deliver by body to be burned, yet do not have charity, it profits me nothing.

Charity is patient, is kind; charity does not envy, is not pretentious, is not puffed up, is not ambitious, is not self-seeking, is not provoked; thinks no evil, does not rejoice over wickedness, but rejoices with the truth; bears with all things, believes all things, hopes all things, endures all things.

Charity never fails, whereas prophecies will disappear, and tongues will cease, and knowledge will be destroyed. For we know in part and we prophecy in part; but when that which is perfect has come, that which is imperfect will be done away with. When I was a child, I spoke as a child, I felt as a child, I thought as a child. Now that I have become a man, I have put away the things of a child. We see now through a mirror in an obscure manner, but then face to face. Now I know in part, but then I shall know even as I have been known. So there abide faith, hope and charity, these three; but the greatest of these is charity.

1 Corinthians, 13, 1-10, 13

<u>Holy Bible,</u> Confraternity - Douay edition (New York: Catholic Book Publishing Company, 1957).

Study Questions

1. *From this, describe the Christian hero. How does this differ from the classical hero?*

2. *Compare the view of God (in the Lord's Prayer) with the view of God in Homer, Plato, Stoicism.*

THE EDICT OF MILAN

According to the historian Eusebius, the night before the battle at Milvian Bridge in 311, Constantine had a dream in which he saw a cross and heard the words, "By this sign you shall conquer." The next morning he ordered his soldiers to imprint the cross on their shields and armor. He won the battle, he believed, with the help of the Christian God, and two years later he issued the Edict of Milan in gratitude.

Vision or not, by 313, it would have been impossible to ignore Christians. They were no longer a minor nuisance. The highest ranks of both the military and civilian services were now filled with Christians, and Diocletian's persecution of them had met with stout resistance. Constantine was essentially a usurper whose claim to the imperial throne was no more valid than that of the man he had defeated. He needed the support of people who had power. The Edict of Milan held the olive branch out to just such people. Thus, the Edict, in granting legal toleration to Christianity and further spurring its growth, is even more an indication that it had already become so powerful a force that an emperor would oppose it only at his peril. The Edict then was motivated at least in part by political opportunism. In return for toleration, the Church was expected to back Constantine's accession, which it did, thus beginning that blurring of Church and state authority known as Caesaropapism. Further, in 326, Constantine ordered leading churchmen to convene a council in the city of Nicea to settle the dispute that had arisen out of Arianism. After ordering the council, Constantine remained scrupulously aloof from its deliberations. But would his successors in similar instances? Moreover, the Church's endorsement of Constantine for the Edict remained just that. But what a powerful Church gave an even more powerful Church might some day withdraw if political interests clashed with the Church's. The mutual backscratching could become a mutual gouging.

Constantine's interest in Christianity was not completely political, however. Although he was not baptized until just before his death, he was extremely generous to the Church. One of the many gifts he gave was the Lateran Palace in Rome which would remain the papal residence until the fourteenth century. Under his influence, Christianity became not merely a very strong religion but the leading one.

When we, Constantine and Licinius, Emperors, met at Milan in conference concerning the welfare and security of the realm, we decided that of the things that are of profit to all mankind, the worship of God ought rightly to be our first and chiefest care, and that it was right that Christians and all others should have freedom to follow the kind of religion they favoured; so that the God who dwells in heaven might be propitious to us and to all under our rule. We therefore announce that, notwithstanding any provisions concerning the Christians in our former instructions, all who choose that religion are to be permitted to continue therein, without any let or hindrance, and are not to be in any way troubled or molested. Note that at the same time all others are to be allowed the free and unrestricted practice of their religions; for it accords with the good order of the realm and the peacefulness of our times that each should have freedom to worship God after his own choice; and we do not intend to detract from the honour due to any religion or its followers. Moreover, concerning the Christians, we before gave orders with respect to the places set apart for their worship. It is now our pleasure that all who have bought such places should restore them to the Christians, without any demand for payment.

You are to use your utmost diligence in carrying out these orders on behalf of the Christians, that our command may be promptly obeyed, for the fulfillment of our gracious purpose in establishing public tranquility. So shall that divine favour which we have already enjoyed, in affairs of the greatest

Early Christianity 199

moment, continue to grant us success, and thus secure the happiness of the realm.

Henry Bettenson, *Documents of the Christian Church*, 2nd ed. (London: Oxford University Press, 1963. Reprinted by permission of Oxford University Press), 22.

Study Questions

1. *Why have Constantine and Licinius decided to issue this Edict?*

2. *What are the exact provisions of the Edict?*

3. *What is to be the position of other non-Christian religions?*

THEODOSIUS I (reigned 379-395) EDICT ON CATHOLIC AND HERETIC

It is our desire that all the various nations which are subject to our Clemency and Moderation, should continue in the profession of that religion which was delivered to the Romans by the divine Apostle Peter, as it hath been preserved by faithful tradition; and which is now professed by the Pontiff Damasus and by Peter, Bishop of Alexandria, a man of apostolic holiness. According to the apostolic teaching and the doctrine of the Gospel, let us believe the one deity of the Father, the Son and the Holy Spirit, in equal majesty and in a Holy Trinity. We authorize the followers of this law to assume the title of Catholic Christians; but as for the others, since, in our judgment, they are foolish madmen, we decree that they shall be branded with the ignominious name of heretics, and shall not presume to give to their conventicles the name of churches. They will suffer in the first place the chastisement of the divine condemnation, and in the second the punishment which our authority, in accordance with the will of Heaven, shall decide to inflict.

Bettenson, _Documents of the Christian Church_, 2nd ed., 31.

Study Questions

1. What, according to Theodosius, must all his subjects believe? How does this edict differ from the Edict of Milan?

2. How does he characterize those who don't believe this? What two punishments will they suffer?

3. What status does this edict give to Christianity? What will now be the relationship between Church and state?

SAINT JEROME'S DREAM

Jerome was educated in Rome in the classics which, as this story shows, he came to love deeply. But as he tells us here, whenever he turned to Cicero or Virgil for solace, he was overwhelmed with guilt. He was in Antioch about 375 when he had the vision he describes here, and for a time after this vision, he lived the life of an ascetic in the desert near Antioch studying the Scriptures and learning Hebrew. He returned to the city in 378, became a priest and then went to Constantinople to study with a Greek Father, Gregory of Nazianzus. He was then called to Rome by the pope who named him as papal secretary and it was at his request that Jerome turned the rather defective translation of the Scriptures into the famed <u>Vulgate Bible</u>. He had Greek manuscripts to help him with the New Testament and the help of scholarly Jews in making the translation of the Old but complete accuracy was not possible without the help of modern linguistic and textual scholarship. Jerome also wrote stories of the saints, thus beginning a kind of literary genre called "hagiography" that was extremely popular in the Middle Ages.

Jerome tells of his vision in a work entitled "The Virgin's Profession" which advocates the monastic life for women. This and other similar writings did much to popularize monasticism in the West.

Many years ago for the sake of the kingdom of heaven I cut myself from home, parents, sister, relations, and, what was harder, from the dainty food to which I had been used. But even when I was on my way to Jerusalem to fight the good fight there, I could not bring myself to forego the library which with great care and labour I had got together at Rome. And so, miserable man that I was, I would fast, only to read Cicero afterwards. I would spend long nights in vigil, I would shed bitter tears called from my inmost heart by the remembrance of my past sins; and then I would take up Plautus again. Whenever I returned to my right senses and began to read the prophets, their language seemed harsh and barbarous. With my blind eyes I could not see the light; but I attributed the fault not to my eyes but to the sun. While the old serpent was thus mocking me, about the middle of Lent a fever attacked my weakened body and spread through my inmost veins. It may sound incredible, but the ravages it wrought on my unhappy frame were so persistent that at last my bones scarcely held together.

Meantime, preparations were made for my funeral; my whole body grew gradually cold, and life's vital warmth only lingered faintly in my poor throbbing breast. Suddenly, I was caught up in the spirit and dragged before the Judge's judgment seat; and here the light was so dazzling and the brightness shining from those who stood around so radiant that I flung myself upon the ground and did not dare to look up. I was asked to state my condition and replied that I was a Christian. But He who presided said: "Thou liest: thou art a Ciceronian, not a Christian 'For where thy treasure is there will thy heart be also.'" Straightway I became dumb, and amid the strokes of the whip --- for he had ordered me to be scourged --- I was even more bitterly tortured by the fire of conscience, considering with myself the verse: "In the grave who shall give thee thanks?" Yet for all that I began to cry out and to bewail myself saying: "Have mercy upon me, O Lord, have mercy upon me"; and even amid the noise of the last my voice made itself heard. At last the bystanders fell at the knees of Him who presided and prayed him to pardon my youth and give me opportunity to repent of my error, on the understanding that the extreme of torture should be inflicted on me if ever I read again the works of Gentile authors. In the stress of that dread hour I should have been willing to make even larger promises and taking oath I called upon His name: "O Lord, if ever again I possess worldly books or read them, I have denied Thee."

After swearing this oath I was dismissed and returned to the upper world. There, to the surprise of all, I opened my eyes again and they were so drenched with tears that my distress convinced even the incredulous. That this experience was no sleep nor idle dream, such as often mocks us, I call to witness the judgment seat before which I fell and the terrible verdict which I feared. May it never be my lot again to come before such a court as that! I profess that my shoulders were black and blue, and that I felt the bruises long after I awoke from my sleep. And I acknowledge that henceforth I read the books of God with a greater zeal than I had ever given before to the books of men.

F. A. Wright, trans., "The Virgin's Profession" in *Fathers of the Church* (London: George Routledge & Sons, Ltd., 1928), 254-255.

Study Questions

1. Why had Jerome cut himself off from parents, sister and "dainty food"? What sort of life had he taken up? What one thing could he not give up?

2. From whom would he seek comfort? How much help was it?

3. Describe his dream. Why was he whipped? By whom? Who interceded for him? With what argument?

4. What view of God is given here? What is the attitude toward secular (classical) learning?

5. What evidence is there that this was no dream?

TERTULLIAN on "WOMEN'S DRESS"

*Tertullian (c. 155 - c. 220) was a North African convert to Christianity and became a priest. He had no use for Greek philosophy but he had been trained in law and turned his brilliant mind and pen to a defense of Christianity against both pagans and heretics. In an *Apology*, he shows point by point how every part of Roman legal procedure was violated in the persecution of Christians. His use of Latin rather than the Greek still being used by the Church earned him the title, "founder of ecclesiastical Latin".*

The extract below may not please a modern feminist but Tertullian's audience may not have been upset by it at all. Christianity was imperiled not only from persecution but, more insidiously, from heresy. It is always easy to compromise, to find excuses to slip back into pre-Christian behavior. It is this that Tertullian is really worried about.

If there lingered on earth a faith equal to the reward of that faith which is looked for in the skies, not one of you, my beloved sisters, I am sure, as soon as she knew the living God and realized her own, that is woman's, condition, would ever have desired to dress in joyful, not to say in boastful, guise. She would, rather, pass her days in squalor and put on the garb of mourning, proclaiming herself an Eve sad and repentant, and by the amendment of her dress seeking to expiate more fully that which she inherits from Eve, the ignominy, I mean, of the first sin and the odium of bringing ruin upon mankind. In pain and anguish, woman, thou dost bring forth: towards thy husband thou must turn, and he is thy master. And do you not know that you are Eve? The judgment of God upon your sex endures even to-day; and with it inevitably endures your position of criminal at the bar of justice. You are the gateway of the Devil; you are the unsealer of the forbidden tree; you are the first rebel against the divine law; you are she who persuaded him whom the Devil was not strong enough to attack. So easily did you shatter the image of God in man. Because of your reward, which was death, even the Son of God had to die.

Is not a skin tunic, then, sufficient for you? Why think of further adornments? Come now, if at the beginning of the world there had been men of Miletus shearing sheep, Chinese spinning silk from trees, Tyrians dyeing, Phrygians embroidering, Babylonians busy at the loom; if then there had been pearls shining white, rubies flashing red, and gold starting from the ground, together with the desire to possess it; if the mirror, too, already had won its boundless licence of deceit, would Eve, methinks, have coveted any of these things, a woman expelled from Paradise and now in the bonds of death? Well, then, if she wishes to live again, she must not desire nor know things which she had to and knew not when she was alive. Therefore, all such gauds are but the baggage of a woman condemned to death, invented, as it were, to grace her funeral procession.

Those, indeed, who first devised these things are held to be damned and sentenced to the penalty of death; for they were the angels who fell from heaven upon the daughters of men, and thereby added fresh shame to woman kind. Certain substances well hidden and many arts not well revealed they then first brought out into the light for the benefit of an age much less skillful than ours. They laid bare the working of metals, they divulged the qualities of herbs, they made known the power of incantations, they directed curious research even to the interpretation of the stars. But as a special and, as it were, peculiar gift for women, they offered them the instruments of female pride. They brought the flashing stones that give to necklaces their varied hues, the golden bracelets that are clasped about the arm, the artificial dyes that add colour to white wool, and even the dark powder which enhances the effect of eyelids and eyelashes. The quality of these devices we can tell at once by the quality and condition of their inventors. Sinners could not teach nor offer anything conducive to righteousness, wanton lovers anything conducive to chastity, renegades anything conducive to the fear of God.

F. A. Wright, trans., "Women's Dress" in *Fathers of the Church* (London: George Routledge & Sons, Ltd., 1928), 52-53.

Study Questions

1. *What kind of dress should women wear? Why?*

2. *How does Tertullian regard industries such as dyeing, weaving, embroidery? How have craftsmen especially beguiled women?*

From the RULE of SAINT BENEDICT

Benedict of Nursia (480-543) was born of a noble Roman family and fled the immorality of Rome to live a life of solitude, prayer and penance in a cave. After three years, an ascetic group asked him to be their governor. Benedict consented but found them a rather intractable lot and left with a tiny group of followers to establish the monastery at Monte Casino. The <u>Rule</u> he established has guided religious foundations down to our own time. It also enabled the Benedictine monastery to become a major institution of the Middle Ages.

The <u>Rule</u> calls for monks to live in poverty, chastity and obedience and to work hard, pray often and talk little. The abbot was also bound by the <u>Rule</u>. The word itself derived from "abba," meaning "father" but it was the authority of the Roman paterfamilias that Benedict had in mind. The abbot was elected by his fellow monks but, once elected, his authority was absolute.

Central to the <u>Rule</u> were labor and prayer. Although it may sound a bit harsh to our relaxed age, the <u>Rule</u> was meant to do away with the excessive asceticism and individualism of earlier monastic experiments. Benedict intended to impose a discipline that was rigorous but at the same time realistic and one that would best enable the monk to do what he had come to the monastery for in the first place --- to come to a close union with God.

The qualities necessary for an abbot.--The abbot who is worthy to rule over a monastery ought always to bear in mind by what name he is called and to justify by his life his title of superior. For he represents Christ in the monastery, receiving his name from the saying of the apostle:[1] "Ye have received

---
[1] St. Paul

the Spirit of adoption, whereby we cry, Abba, Father" [Rom. 8:15]. Therefore the abbot should not teach or command anything contrary to the precepts of the Lord, but his commands and his teaching should be in accord with divine justice. He should always bear in mind that both his teaching and the obedience of his disciples will be inquired into on the dread day of judgment. For the abbot should know that the shepherd will have to bear the blame if the Master finds anything wrong with the flock. Only in case the shepherd has displayed all diligence and care in correcting the fault of a restive and disobedient flock will he be freed from blame at the judgment of God, and be able to say to the Lord in the words of the prophet: "I have not hid thy righteousness within my heart; I have declared thy faithfulness and thy salvation" [Ps. 40:10]; but "they despising have scorned me" [Ezek. 20:27]. Then shall the punishment fall upon the flock who scorned his care and it shall be the punishment of death. The abbot ought to follow two methods in governing his disciples: teaching the commandments of the Lord to the apt disciples by his words, and to the obdurate and the simple by his deeds. And when he teaches his disciples that certain things are wrong, he should demonstrate in his own life by not doing those things, lest when he has preached to others he himself should be a castaway [1 Cor. 9:27], and lest God should sometime say to him, a sinner: "What hast thou to do to declare my statutes, or that thou shouldest take my covenant in thy mouth? Seeing that thou hatest instruction, and castest my words behind thee" [Ps. 50:16, 17], or "Why beholdest thou the mote that is in thy brother's eye, but considerest not the beam that is in thine own eye?" [Matt. 7:3]. Let there be no respect of persons in the monastery. Let the abbot not love one more than another, unless it be one who excels in good works and in obedience. The freeman is not to be preferred to the one who comes into the monastery out of servitude, unless there be some other good reason. But if it seems right and fitting to the abbot, let him show preference to anyone of any rank whatsoever; otherwise let them keep their own places. For whether slave or free, we are all one in Christ [Gal. 3:28] and bear the same yoke of servitude to the one Lord, for there is no respect of persons with God [Rom. 2:11]. For we have special favor in His sight only in so far as we excel others in all good works and in humility. Therefore, the abbot should have the same love toward all and should subject all to the same discipline according to their respective merits. In his discipline the abbot should follow the rule of the apostle who says: "Reprove, rebuke, exhort" [2 Tim. 4:2]. That is, he should suit his methods to the occasion, using either threats or compliments, showing himself either a hard master or a loving father, according to the needs of the case. Thus he should reprove harshly the obdurate and disobedient, but the obedient, the meek, and the gentle he should exhort to grow in grace. We advise also that he rebuke and punish those who neglect and scorn his teaching. He should not disregard the transgressions of sinners, but should strive to root them out as soon as they appear, remembering the peril of Eli, the priest of Siloam [1 Sam. chaps. 1-4]. Let him correct the more worthy and intelligent with words for the first or second time, but the wicked and hardened and scornful and disobedient he should punish with blows in the very beginning of their fault, as it is written: "A fool is not bettered by words" [cf. Prov. 17:10]; and again "Thou shalt beat him with the rod, and shalt deliver his soul from hell" [Prov. 23:14].

The abbot should always remember his office and his title, and should realize that as much is entrusted to him, so also much will be required from him. Let him realize how difficult and arduous a task he has under taken, to rule the hearts and care for the morals of many persons, who require, one encouragements, another threats, and another persuasion. Let him so adapt his methods to the disposition and intelligence of each one that he may not only preserve the flock committed to him entire and free from harm, but may even rejoice in its increase...

Silence is to be kept after completorium.--The monks should observe the rule of silence at all times, but especially during the hours of the night. This rule shall be observed both on fast-days and on other days, as follows: on other than fast days as soon as the brothers rise from the table they shall sit down together, while one of them reads from the Collations or the lives of the fathers or other holy works. But the reading at this time shall not be from the Heptateuch or from the books of the Kings, which are not suitable for weak intellects to hear at this hour and may be read at other times. On fastdays the brethren shall assemble a little while after vespers, and listen to readings from the Collations. All shall be present at this reading except those who have been given other duties to be done at this time, and after the reading of four or five pages, or as much as shall occupy an hour's time, the whole congregation shall meet for completorium. After completorium no one shall be allowed to speak to another, unless the abbot has to give a command to some one; and in these cases such speaking as is necessary shall be done quietly and gravely. If anyone breaks this rule of silence he shall be severely disciplined.

* * * * * * *

The order of divine worship during the day.--The prophet says: "Seven times a day do I praise thee" [Ps. 119:164]; and we observe this sacred number in the seven services of the day; that is, matins, prime, terce, sext, nones, vespers, and completorium; for the hours of the daytime are plainly intended here, since the same prophet provides for the nocturnal vigils, when he says in another place: "At midnight I will rise to give thanks unto thee" [Ps. 119:62]. We should therefore praise the Creator for his righteous judgments at the aforesaid times: matins, prime, terce, sext, nones, vespers, and completorium; and at night we should rise to give thanks unto Him.[2]

The daily labor of the monks.--Idleness is the great enemy of the soul, therefore the monks should always be occupied, either in manual labor or in holy reading. The hours for these occupations should be arranged according to the seasons, as follows: From Easter to the first of October, the monks shall go to work at the first hour and labor until the fourth hour, and the time from the fourth to the sixth hour shall be spent in reading. After dinner, which comes at the sixth hour, they shall lie down and rest in silence; but anyone who wishes may read, if he does it so as not to disturb anyone else. Nones shall be observed a little earlier, about the middle of the eighth hour, and the monks shall go back to work,

---

[2]Matins, about daybreak; prime, the first part of the day; terce, the third part of the day; sext, the sixth part of the day; nones, the ninth part of the day; vespers in the evening; completorium, or compline, was the last service. Vigils were held during the night.

laboring until vespers. But if the conditions of the locality or the needs of the monastery, such as may occur at harvest time, should make it necessary to labor longer hours, they shall not feel themselves ill-used, for true monks should live by the labor of their own hands, as did the apostles and the holy fathers. But the weakness of human nature must be taken into account in making these arrangements. From the first of October to the beginning of Lent, the monks shall have until the full second hour for reading, at which hour the service of terce shall be held. After terce, they shall work at their respective tasks until the ninth hour. When the ninth hour sounds they shall cease from labor and be ready for the service at the second bell. After dinner they shall spend the time in reading the lessons and the psalms. During Lent the time from daybreak to the third hour shall be devoted to reading, and then they shall work at their appointed tasks until the tenth hour. At the beginning of Lent each of the monks shall be given a book from the library of the monastery which he shall read entirely through. One or two of the older monks shall be appointed to go about through the monastery during the hours set apart for reading, to see that none of the monks are idling away the time, instead of reading, and so not only wasting their own time but perhaps disturbing others as well. Anyone found doing this shall be rebuked for the first or second offense, and after that he shall be severely punished, that he may serve as a warning and an example to others. Moreover, the brothers are not to meet together at unseasonable hours. Sunday is to be spent by all the brothers in holy reading, except by such as have regular duties assigned to them for that day. And if any brother is negligent or lazy, refusing or being unable profitably to read or meditate at the time assigned for that, let him be made to work, so that he shall at any rate not be idle. The abbot shall have consideration for the weak and the sick, giving them tasks suited to their strength, so that they may neither be idle not yet be distressed by too heavy labor.

Oliver J. Thatcher and Edgar Holmes McNeal, eds., *A Source Book for Medieval History* (New York: Charles Scribner's Sons, 1905), 435-437, 450, 464, 467-468.

Study Questions

1. What responsibility does an abbot have for his monks?

2. What methods ought he use in governing his monks? How should different social ranks be treated?

3. How should discipline be decided upon?

4. How many times a day do monks pray? From this, what can you guess about the way in which people told time?

5. Describe the labor of the monks.

SAINT AUGUSTINE from THE CONFESSIONS

Augustine (354-430 A.D.) was born in what is now Algeria. His father, a minor civil servant, was pagan, but his mother, Monica, was a devout Christian. Since his family was poor and obscure, his only avenue to success was a classical education. After a basic education in the local schools, focussed mostly on memorization of texts from Cicero, Virgil, Horace and other classical writers, Augustine traveled to nearby Carthage at the age of seventeen to continue his education. There he mastered rhetoric and took a mistress with whom he lived for thirteen years and sired a son, Adeodatus. He also began to flirt with Manicheanism which taught that the universe was a battleground between Good and Evil. It was a convenient philosophy for it relieved him of moral responsibility. Whatever evil he did was not his own fault but the fault of a principle of Evil.

He became a teacher of rhetoric first at Tagaste, then Carthage and then Rome. At the same time he became increasingly dissatisfied with Manicheanism and conditions in Rome weren't terribly good --- his students wouldn't pay their fees. So in 384, with his mistress, son and mother, he went to Milan to gain a reputation, wealth and a rich wife. His mother found a suitable wife for him in a girl who would not reach marriageable age for two years. (Monica apparently never suggested that he marry his mistress whose name, incidentally, Augustine does not mention in his <u>Confessions</u>.) Augustine dismissed the mistress with whom he had lived for so long and promptly took another.

Meanwhile he had been falling more and more under the influence of Ambrose, the bishop of Milan. It was Ambrose's command of Augustine's discipline --- rhetoric --- that first attracted him to Ambrose. Soon, however, it was not merely how Ambrose spoke but what he said that began to move Augustine. What triggered his conversion to Christianity, however, was the song of a child, the event described below. Augustine was baptized by Ambrose in 387, ordained a priest in 391 and named auxiliary bishop of Hippo four years later.

The *Confessions* describes his struggle between his spiritual ideals and his sensual and material self. Some of the Manichean tension between a principle of Good and Evil never entirely left him. He never forgot his childhood theft of the pears. It showed him the innate weakness of the human will.

HE COMMITS THEFT WITH HIS COMPANIONS, NOT URGED ON BY POVERTY, BUT FROM A CERTAIN DISTASTE OF WELLDOING.

Theft is punished by Thy law, O Lord, and by the law written in men's hearts, which iniquity itself cannot blot out. For what thief will suffer a thief? Even a rich thief will not suffer him who is driven to it by want. Yet had I a desire to commit robbery, and did so, compelled neither by hunger, nor poverty, but through a distaste for welldoing, and a lustiness of iniquity. For I pilfered that of which I had already sufficient, and much better. Nor did I desire to enjoy what I pilfered, but the theft and sin itself. There was a pear-tree close to our vineyard, heavily laden with fruit, which was tempting neither for its color nor its flavor. To shake and rob this some of us wanton young fellows went, late one night (having, according to our disgraceful habit, prolonged our games in the streets until then), and carried away great loads, not to eat ourselves, but to fling to the very swine, having only eaten some of them; and to do this pleased us all the more because it was not permitted. Behold my heart, O my God; behold my heart, which Thou hadst pity upon when in the bottomless pit. Behold, now, let my heart tell Thee what it was seeking there, that I should be gratuitously wanton, having no inducement to evil but the evil itself. It was foul, and I loved it. I loved to perish. I loved my own error --- not that for which I erred, but the error itself. Base soul, falling from Thy firmament to utter destruction --- not seeking aught through the shame but the shame itself?

* * * * * * *

But now, the more ardently I loved those whose healthful affections I heard of, that they had given up themselves wholly to Thee to be cured, the more did I abhor myself when compared with them. For many of my years (perhaps twelve) had passed away since my nineteenth, when, on the reading of Cicero's <u>Hortensius</u>, I was roused to a desire for wisdom; and still I was delaying to reject mere worldly happiness, and to devote myself to search out that of which not the finding alone, but the bare search, ought to have been preferred before the pleasures of the body, though encompassing me at my will. But I, miserable young man, supremely miserable even in the very outset of my youth, had entreated chastity of Thee, and said, "Grant me chastity and continency, but not yet." For I was afraid lest Thou shouldest hear me soon, and soon deliver me from the disease of concupiscence, which I desired to have satisfied rather than extinguished. And I had wandered through perverse ways in a sacrilegious superstition; not indeed assured thereof, but preferring that to the others, which I did not seek religiously, but opposed maliciously.

And I had thought that I delayed from day to day to reject worldly hopes and follow Thee only, because there did not appear anything certain whither to direct my course. And now had the day arrived in which I was to be laid bare to myself, and my conscience was to chide me. "Where art thou, O my tongue? Thou saidst that for an uncertain truth thou wert not willing to cast off the baggage of vanity. Behold, now it is certain, and yet doth that burden still oppress thee; whereas they who neither have so worn themselves out with searching after it, nor yet have spent ten years and more in thinking thereon, have had their shoulders unburdened, and gotten wings to fly away." Thus was I inwardly consumed and mightily confounded with a horrible shame, while Pontitianus was relating these things. And he, having finished his story, and the business he came for, went his way. And to myself, what said I not within myself? With what scourges of rebuke lashed I not my soul to make it follow me, struggling to go after Thee! Yet it drew back; it refused, and exercised not itself. All its arguments were exhausted and confuted. There remained a silent trembling; and it feared, as it would death, from the flow of that custom whereby it was wasting away even to death.

* * * * * * *

I was saying these things and weeping in the most bitter contrition of my heart, when, lo, I heard the voice as of a boy or girl, I know not which, coming from a neighboring house, chanting and oft repeating, "Take up and read; take up and read." Immediately my countenance was changed, and I began most earnestly to consider whether it was usual for children in any kind of game to sing such words; nor could I remember ever to have heard the like. So, restraining the torrent of my tears, I rose up, interpreting it no other way than as a command to me from Heaven to open the book, and to read the first chapter I should light upon. For I had heard of Antony, that, accidentally coming in while the gospel was being read, he received the admonition as if what was read were addressed to him, "Go and sell that thou hast, and give to the poor, and thou shalt have treasure in heaven; and come and follow me." And by such oracle was he forthwith converted unto Thee. So quickly I returned to the place where Alypius was sitting; for there had I put down the volume of the apostles, when I rose thence. I grasped, opened, and in silence read that paragraph on which my eyes first fell - "Not in rioting and drunkenness, not in chambering and wantonness, not in strife and envying; but put ye on the Lord Jesus Christ, and make not provision for the flesh, to fulfill the lusts thereof." No further would I read, nor did I need; for instantly, as the sentence ended - by a light, as it were, of security infused into my heart - all the gloom of doubt vanished away.

J. Oates Whitney, ed., "Confessions" in *Basic Writings of Saint Augustine*, 2 vols. (New York: Random House, 1948), I, 23-24, 120, 126-127.

Early Christianity

Study Questions

1. Who is Augustine's audience?

2. Why did he steal the pears?

3. Describe his relationship with God in his thirty-first year.

4. How is that relationship changed by the child's song? What is the song?

SAINT AUGUSTINE from CITY OF GOD

In 410, the Visigothic chieftain, Alaric, attacked and sacked Rome. Some Romans were convinced that the disaster was a result of pagan gods punishing Rome for deserting them for Christianity. Augustine wrote <u>City of God</u> to refute that. According to him, Rome, even though she had survived for over a millennium, was nonetheless an earthly city, a city of men and thus transient and, like all things of earth, doomed to decay. Alaric's sack was no punishment but simply a part of the natural course of things. The wise man would put his faith not in a city of men, for the ideal state can never be realized on this earth, but only in heaven, in the city of God. The decline of Rome then was unimportant and should not distress the Christian at all. Not that a Christian should reject the earthly city. It is after all a reality that he must face. But he must bend it to fit the Christian pattern. The Church then must not neglect the state but must guide it to protect men from their own sinful natures.

There are two important ideas in this article. One is Augustine's idea that history has a goal --- a point. The Christian is in the city of men in order to transform it, to bring the world to the city of God, not to detach himself from it.

The second is his view of human nature. He will use the word "predestination" but he doesn't mean by that what John Calvin will mean in the sixteenth century. He simply means that God knows what choices we will make but he leaves our wills free to make those choices nonetheless. Also, when he speaks of Adam and Eve's "evil will" and "corrupted nature" he means simply that we do not always act on the basis of Reason or "conscience," that it is as easy for a highly educated person to commit evil as for an illiterate.

Our first parents fell into open disobedience because already they were secretly corrupted; for the evil act had never been done had not an evil will preceded it. And what is the origin of our evil will but pride? For "pride is the beginning of sin." And what is pride but the craving for undue exaltation? And this is undue exaltation, when the soul abandons Him to whom it ought to cleave as its end, and becomes a kind of end to itself. This happens when it becomes its own satisfaction. And it does so when it falls away from that unchangeable good which ought to satisfy it more than itself. This falling away is spontaneous; for if the will had remained steadfast in the love of that higher and changeless good by which it was illumined to intelligence and kindled into love, it would not have turned away to find satisfaction in itself, and so become frigid and benighted. The woman would not have believed the serpent spoke the truth, nor would the man have preferred the request of his wife to the command of God, nor have supposed that it was a venial transgression to cleave to the partner of his life, even in a partnership of sin. The wicked deed, then, --- that is to say the transgression of eating the forbidden fruit, --- was committed by persons who were already wicked.

* * * * * * *

Of these two first parents of the human race, then, Cain was the first-born, and he belonged to the city of men; after him was born Abel, who belonged to the city of God. For as in the individual the truth of the apostle's statement is discerned, "that is not first which is spiritual, but what which is natural, and afterward that which is spiritual," whence it comes to pass that each man, being derived from a condemned stock, is first of all born of Adam evil and carnal, and becomes good and spiritual only afterwards, when he is grafted into Christ by regeneration: so was it in the human race as a whole. When these two cities began to run their course by a series of deaths and births, the citizen of the city of God, predestinated by grace, elected by grace, by a grace a stranger below, and by grace a citizen above. By grace --- for so far as regards himself he is sprung from the same mass, all of which is condemned in its origin: but God, like a potter (for this comparison is introduced by the apostle judiciously, and not without thought) of the same lump made one vessel to honor, another to dishonor. But first the vessel to dishonor was made, and after it another to honor. For in each individual, as I have already said, there is first of all that which is reprobate, that from which we must begin, but in which we need not necessarily remain; afterwards is that which is well-approved, to which we may by advancing attain, and in which, when we have reached it, we may abide. Not, indeed, that every wicked man shall be good, but that no one will be good who was not first of all wicked; but the sooner any one becomes a good man, the more speedily does he receive this title, and abolish the old name in the new. Accordingly, it is recorded of Cain that he built a city, but Abel, being a sojourner, built none. For the city of the saints is above, although here below it begets citizens, in whom it sojourns till the time of its reign arrives, when it shall gather together all in the day of the resurrection; and then shall the promised kingdom be given to them, in which they shall reign with their Prince, the King of the ages, time without end.

Whitney J. Oates, ed., "City of God" in *Basic Writing of St. Augustine*, 2 Vols. (New York: Random House, 1948), II, 257, 275-276.

Study Questions

1. *How do we learn that there is a city of God?*

2. *Why was the eating of food in the Garden not a small nor light thing? What really was at stake?*

3. *How does Augustine explain the sin of Adam and Eve?*

4. *Describe Augustine's view of human nature. How is human nature perfected?*

5. *Describe his view of history.*

GREGORY I'S INSTRUCTION TO AUGUSTINE, 601 A.D.

Gregory (reigned 590-604) was the first pope to call himself "servant of the servants of God," thereby claiming authority over the entire Church. That claim of course was ignored by the Eastern Church, as he no doubt knew it would be, but in the West, he underlined his responsibility for and authority over other bishops by sending missionaries to preach the Gospel. One of these was Augustine, sent to convert the pagans of Britain. The following letter, sent to Augustine via the Abbot Mellitus, beautifully illustrates Gregory's belief that the Church should not abolish Germanic practices and rituals but adapt them to Christian usages. Gregory knew that while men, even Christian men, might be impatient for new converts, God and God's Church had all of eternity. And real Christian values would require generations, even centuries, to take root.

Gregory's instructions would encourage the Germanization of the Western Church, another factor in the growing rift with the Eastern Byzantine Church which was becoming increasingly Orientalized.

When these messengers had left, the holy father Gregory sent after them letters worthy of our notice, which show most clearly his unwearying interest in the salvation of our nation. The letters run as follows:

'To our well loved son Abbot Mellitus: Gregory, servant of the servants of God.

'Since the departure of yourself and your companions, we have been somewhat anxious, because we have received no news of the success of your journey. Therefore, when by God's help you reach our most reverend brother, Bishop Augustine, we wish you to inform him that we have been giving careful thought to the affairs of the English, and have come to the conclusion that the temples of the idols in that country should on no account be destroyed. He is to destroy the idols, but the temples themselves are to be aspersed with holy water, altars set up, and relics enclosed in them. For if these temples are well built, they are to be purified from devil-worship, and dedicated to the service of the true God. In this way, we hope that the people, seeing that its temples are not destroyed, may abandon idolatry and resort to these places as before, and may come to know and adore the true God. And since they have a custom of sacrificing many oxen to devils, let some other solemnity be substituted in its place, such as a day of Dedication or the Festivals of the holy martyrs whose relics are enshrined there. On such occasions they might well construct shelters of boughs for themselves around the churches that were once temples, and celebrate the solemnity with devout feasting. They are no longer to sacrifice beasts to the Devil, but they may kill them for food to the praise of God, and give thanks to the Giver of all gifts for His bounty. If the people are allowed some worldly pleasures in this way, they will more readily come to desire the joys of the spirit. For it is certainly impossible to eradicate all errors from obstinate minds at one stroke, and whoever wishes to climb to a mountain top climbs gradually step by step, and not in one leap. It was in this way that God revealed Himself to the Israelite people in Egypt, permitting the sacrifices formerly offered to the Devil to be offered thenceforward to Himself instead. So He bade them sacrifice beasts to Him, so that, once they became enlightened, they might abandon a wrong conception of sacrifice, and adopt the right. For, while they were to continue to offer beasts as before, they were to offer them to God instead of to idols, thus transforming the idea of sacrifice. Of your kindness, you are to inform our brother Augustine of this policy, so that he may consider how he may best implement it on the spot. God keep you safe, my very dear son.

'Dated the seventeenth of June, in the nineteenth year of the reign of our most devout Lord and Emperor Maurice

Early Christianity

Tiberius Augustus, and the eighteenth after his Consulship. The fourth indiction.'

Leo Sherley-Price, trans., <u>Venerable Bede, A History of the English Church and People</u> (Baltimore: Penguin Books, 1965), 86-87.

Study Questions

1. *What is Abbot Mellitus' function? From the reading, can you determine who this Augustine is and why Gregory might be writing to him?*

2. *How should Augustine treat pagan temples, sacrifices and idols? How does Gregory justify his policy?*

3. *Name three or four pagan (Germanic) practices that have been "baptized" by the Church. (You might think of our Christmas and Easter celebrations especially.) How would Gregory feel about our commercialization of Christmas?*

4. *Notice how Gregory dates this letter (in the last paragraph). What does this reveal about the calendar?*

EARLY MIDDLE AGES

The people whose migrations contributed so much to the decline of the Roman Empire originally inhabited northern Germany, southern Sweden and Denmark and the Baltic area. The term "German" describes a linguistic group, but apart from language there was little ethnic solidarity among them. The Visigoths and Ostrogoths on the Rhine-Danube frontier lived a settled, agrarian life and early on accepted Arian Christianity. The Franks in Gaul and the Lombards in Italy became fairly Romanized, others like the Angles and Saxons remained rather primitive.

Since they left no written records of their own, for centuries our chief source of information on the early Germans came from Roman sources such as Caesar's <u>Commentaries</u> and particularly from the historian Tacitus, who while he admired many of their qualities, nonetheless regarded them as barbarians. Recent research, however, is revealing highly intelligent, energetic people.

The Germans had no notion of state. It was the tribe or folk that united them. Law was unwritten custom and each tribe had its own set of customs. Since a breech of custom was regarded as a personal injury, it was up to the individual who had been wronged to get satisfaction himself. There was no notion that crime was committed against something as vague as the "state". Common to all of them was the <u>wergild</u> or man-money paid by the murderer to the victim's family in homicide cases. They also made use of trial by ordeal or by combat. The tribe was led by a king or tribal chieftain. This was normally an hereditary office but the king was also elected from among the strongest and bravest clan in the tribe. Theoretically at least, if the chief left a weak son to succeed him, the tribe could bypass the heir and elect someone else. The king in some southern tribes was the head of the <u>comitatus</u> or war band, the bravest warrior in the tribe.

Early Middle Ages 225

In 496, the king of the Franks, Clovis (reigned 481-511), got baptized. His conversion apparently came about when he decided that the Christian God was better at helping him win battles than his pagan gods were. Baptism didn't change his behavior nor that of his men much but it was important because Clovis and his successors would give the Church entree into their lands. The dynasty Clovis founded was called the Merovingian, after Merovich, a legendary ancestor.

The Merovingian kings immediately after Clovis expanded into eastern Gaul. Clovis had established the old Roman garrison town of Paris as his capital but the center of government was literally wherever the king happened to be at the moment. Merovingian authority extended as far as the king could physically reach. There was no uniform administration. Local custom, not the king's writ, held sway throughout his kingdom. There was also a custom that was to prove fatal to the Merovingians. When a father died, he left his inheritance to all his sons rather than simply to the eldest. And the Merovingians had lots of healthy sons. These fell to fighting each other over who got what and as they did so they weakened each other so badly that, by the end of the seventh century their own subjects had contemptuously dubbed them "les rois fainéants", the do-nothing kings. As the kings weakened, power tended to slip into the hands of an official called a "major domus", the head, or mayor of the palace. In the early eighth century, the mayor of one of these Merovingian kingdoms, Austrasia, Pepin II of Heristal (687-714), forcibly brought the other two, Burgundy and Neustria, under his control. That unity was forged just in the nick of time, for the Christian civilization of Western Europe was about to be threatened by a new and dangerous enemy from the southeast, Islam.

Islam

The founder of Islam, Mohammed, was born in 570 in the bustling city of Mecca in Arabia. When he was forty years old, according to religious accounts, Mohammed began receiving revelations from God. These revelations were the Quran.

Except for a tiny handful of followers, Mecca rejected Mohammed. But in 622, the city of Medinah some 250 miles to the north, invited Mohammed to come and mediate a dispute between Arab and Jewish merchants there. He accepted the *invitation and went to Medinah. This is the "hejira" (which somewhat inaccurately translates as "flight"), the beginning of the Islamic era. In Medinah, Mohammed established Islam not only as a religion but also as a political system based on the Quran. Then, with Medinah as his base, all of Arabia, including Mecca, was brought into a single Islamic community.*

Mohammed died in 632 and his followers began to spread Islam northward. This was not really a sudden "sweeping out" of ignorant tribesmen wielding a scimitar in one hand and the Quran in the other. There had long been a vigorous caravan trade between the Arabs and the Near East. The Arabs were fully aware of the wealth that lay there --- and that, perhaps, as much as religious fervor --- fired them. Moreover, religious heresy in the Byzantine Empire automatically was politicized and vice versa, since the church was a department of the Byzantine state. And there was plenty of both political and religious discontent in the Near East. This the Arabs were able to take advantage of and city after city in Syria, Palestine and Egypt fell to them. They then swept eastward and conquered Persia. Meanwhile another Arabic army moved across North Africa, crossed Gibraltar in 712, conquered Visigothic Spain and in 719 overran the Pyrenes to conquer Europe.

You will recall, however, that Pepin of Heristal had united the Merovingian kingdoms under his own king. It was that Pepin's son (and also mayor), Charles (717-741), who was faced with repelling the Islamic invasion. In a battle in 732 near Tours, Charles "hammered" at the Muslims, defeated them and got the nickname Charles "Martel", the Hammer. No one knew it then, of course, but the Battle of Tours was to be the most significant battle in the Middle Ages. First, it saved Christian civilization in Europe. That in itself was important enough. But almost as important, all that Charles did was defeat the Muslims, not destroy them. Neither he nor his immediate successors would be able to dislodge them from Spain. As a result Islamic science and philosophy, mathematics and medicine would be able to enrich Europe as soon as it was rich and self-confident enough to reach into those treasures. Under the Ummayid dynasty with its capital at Cordova, Jewish and Christian merchants mingled freely with Islamic scholars from as far as Baghdad. Toledo became the center through which Hindu, Greek, Persian and even Chinese learning, filtered through Islam, would reach the West.

Early Middle Ages

All that still lay in the future, however. Charles Martel's son and successor as mayor was Pepin the Short. Pepin's father had been king in fact but not in name. Pepin wanted the title as well as the reality of kingship but there was still a reigning Merovingian whom Pepin had no desire to murder. In 751, Pepin was acclaimed by the great lords and magnates as king and he promptly abolished the office of mayor. He thus had one of the props of regal authority according to Germanic custom but, lacking royal blood, Pepin still felt that authority to be on shaky ground.

At this point, by a happy coincidence, Pope Stephen II had a serious problem. Lombards from northern Italy who were Arians had been pressing southward toward Rome. In 753, the Pope approached Pepin to seek help against the Lombards. To guarantee that help, he gave Pepin an added assurance of legitimacy --- he annointed him king of the Franks. In 754, Pepin defeated the Lombards and in 756, on a second successful campaign, he awarded the Papacy a large tract of land extending from the Byzantine exarchate of Ravenna at the head of the Adriatic Sea diagonally through northern and central Italy down to Rome.

But there was more. In the Donation, the Papacy acquired a good bit of real estate, and thus wealth and power. The claim Gregory I had made to authority over the Church --- or at least the Western half of it --- could now become a reality.

What Pepin got from the alliance was the support of the Church for his crown. Henceforth, heredity and the approval of the people would be less important than the Church's anointing of the ruler. The ruler would be a priest-king. Equally important, however, the Church now became part of secular administration. After Pepin abolished the office of mayor, he established parishes. Through the Church, loyalty to the king could easily be linked with religious devotion.

Art and Thought

The period from the fall of Rome to Charlemagne is often referred to by the unhappy term "Dark Ages," but as the excerpts in this chapter show, the term hardly fits.

One of the finest minds in all of Western history came out of Rome in the sixth century. This was Boethius. His translations of Aristotle's works on logic, arithmetic and geometry were important in the development of medieval education and his treatise on music was being used at Oxford as late as the eighteenth century. It was his <u>Consolation of Philosophy</u>, however, written while Boethius awaited execution, that endeared him to later generations.

Byzantine culture left its imprint on Italy, especially in Ravenna. Later Roman art tended to lose the realism and the interest in perspective and precision of earlier ages. It became more spiritualized, more representational. The human body was the home of the soul, hence the body became stiff and one-dimensional, the eyes tended to become rather large, and drapery tended to lose its flowing, natural quality. This style is found in the breathtakingly beautiful mosaics of the churches in Ravenna, but it would somewhat affect the illuminated manuscripts of Western Europe as well. Benedictine monasticism found an especially congenial home in Ireland. It was these monks who would produce the incomparable <u>Book of Kells</u> whose highly stylized, decorative motifs strongly resemble Byzantine styles.

Irish-Celtic culture, with its close connections with the Roman Church, centered at monasteries, such as Lindisfarne and York, permeated the British Church. From such monasteries as Jarrow and Wearmouth came missals, used in the Mass, and psalters, containing the psalms and other prayers, commentaries on the Scriptures and Church Fathers, sermons, illuminated texts, the poetry of Caedmon, law codes and, from Lindisfarne, a beautiful Gospel book.

From Jarrow came Bede (673-735), whose scholarship and piety make him one of the best-loved authors of the Middle Ages. His <u>Ecclesiastical History of the English Nation</u> is our best source for the history of Britain from the fall of Rome to Bede's own day. And it was Bede who began the practice of dating events from the birth of Christ as "anno domini" (the year of Our Lord), viz., A.D. Bede shared St. Augustine's view of history as the story of God's redemptive plan being worked out through human events.

So did his fellow historian Gregory of Tours, the author of *History of the Franks*, chronicling the story of the Franks to the early eighth century. Like Bede, Gregory was careful to check and balance his sources and like Bede, too, for Gregory the veracity of a story depended upon the virtue of the source. God would not permit a good person to tell a falsehood, even inadvertently.

In addition to the histories, there was a lively tradition of sagas --- sets of oral stories, woven together into a unified whole around the figure of a king or hero. Out of these sagas came the first story written in English, *Beowulf*, written by one or possibly several monks in Northumbria, possibly at Bede's Jarrow. Though childishly simple --- there's little development of character, the plot is unremarkable and the setting is downright gloomy --- it has been hailed as a masterpiece. It beautifully weaves together Christian and pagan elements providing a vivid picture of the society out of which it came. Although it is about the conflict between good and evil, there is little of Christianity in it. The highest virtue is loyalty to the "gesith" or war band, and humility is notable by its absence as the heroes boast of their great deeds. Nor is charity remarkable. It is fighting, feasting and bragging which preoccupy the warriors --- not thoughts of justice or peace.

Suggested Readings

1. Dawson, Christopher, *The Making of Europe* (New York: Macmillan Company, 1957). Stresses the role of Christianity in shaping early medieval civilization.

2. Duby, Georges, *The Early Growth of the European Economy* (London: Weidenfeld and Nicolson, 1974). By a leading French medievalist.

3. Lot, Ferdinand, *The End of the Ancient World* (New York: Harper & Row, 1961). An examination of the economic and social reasons for Rome's decline.

4. Runciman, S., *Byzantine Civilization* (New York: Meridian Books, 1956). A scholarly and readable survey of medieval Europe's neighbor.

5. Southern, R. W., *The Making of the Middle Ages* (New Haven: Yale University Press, 1953). A brief and highly readable survey.

6. Thrupp, Sylvia, ed., *Early Medieval Society* (New York: Appleton-Century-Crofts, 1967). Discusses the Christianization of the Germans.

TACITUS from GERMANIA

Tacitus (55-120 A.D.) was born in the little town of Narbonensis, served as a senator, a consul (in 97) and governor of Asia (112-113). He resembles a Roman of the old Republic, committed to duty, to serving the New Order that Rome had now become, and he would serve it under both good and bad emperors, Nero and Domitian, for instance, or Nerva and Trajan.

The autocracy probably bore hardest on senators and Tacitus no doubt had to bite back cries of outrage when the Senate was forced to endorse the works of tyrants. In his <u>Histories</u> and again in the <u>Germania</u> he tends to be a bit harsh on Rome. He contrasts the Romans often unfavorably with the Germans. The Germans, he says, love freedom and think lightly of precious metals nor do they think debauchery fashionable. Women are chaste and the children may be naked and dirty but home life itself is pure. Yet he does not idealize the Germans either. They are indolent, quarrelsome, they drink a lot ("they extract a juice from barley or grain") and have a ridiculous propensity for war.

In this excerpt, he describes the "comitatus" or war band, the "wergild" and Germanic notions of hospitality.

13

No business, public or private, is transacted except in arms. But it is the rule that no one shall take up his arms until the State has attested that he is likely to make good. When that time comes, one of the chiefs or the father or a kinsman equips the young warrior with shield and spear in the public council. This with the Germans is the equivalent of our toga-- the first public distinction of youth. They cease to rank merely as members of the household and are now members of the state. Conspicuous ancestry or great services rendered by their fathers can win the rank of chief for boys still in their teens. They are attached to the other chiefs, who are more mature and approved, and no one blushes to be seen thus in the ranks of the companions. This order of companions has even its different grades, as determined by the leader, and there is intense rivalry among the companions for the first place by the chief, among the chiefs for the most numerous and enthusiastic companions. Dignity and power alike consist in being continually attended by a corps of chosen youths. This gives you consideration in peace-time and security in war. Nor is it only in a man's own nation that he can win name and fame by the superior number and quality of his companions, but in neighbouring states as well. Chiefs are courted by embassies and complimented by gifts, and they often virtually decide wars by the mere weight of their reputation.

14

On the field of battle it is a disgrace to the chief to be surpassed in valour by his companions, to the companions not to come up to the valour of their chief. As for leaving a battle alive after your chief has fallen, that means lifelong infamy and shame. To defend and protect him, to put down one's own acts of heroism to his credit--that is what they really mean by 'allegiance'. The chiefs fight for victory, the companions for their chief. Many noble youths, if the land of their birth is stagnating in a protracted peace, deliberately seek out other tribes, where some war is afoot. The Germans have no taste for peace; renown is easier won among perils, and you cannot maintain a large body of companions except by violence and war. The companions are prodigal in their demands on the generosity of their chiefs. It is always 'give me that war-horse' or 'give me that bloody and victorious spear'. As for meals with their plentiful, if homely, fare, they count simply as pay. Such open-handedness must have war and plunder to feed it. You will find it harder to persuade a German to plough the land and to await its annual produce with patience than to challenge a foe and earn the prize of wounds. He thinks it spiritless and slack to gain by sweat what he can buy with blood.

21

A man is bound to take up the feuds as well as the friendships of father or kinsman. But feuds do not continue unreconciled. Even homicide can be atoned for by a fixed number of cattle or sheep, and the satisfaction is received by the whole family. This is much to the advantage of the community, for private feuds are peculiarly dangerous side by side with liberty.

No nation abandons itself more completely to banqueting and entertainment than the German. It is accounted a sin to turn any man away from your door. The host welcomes his guest with the best meal that his means allow. When supplies run out, the host takes on a fresh role; he directs and escorts his guest to a new hostelry. The two go on, uninvited, to the nearest house. It makes no difference; they are welcomed just as warmly. No distinction is ever made between acquaintance and stranger as far as the right to hospitality is concerned. As the guest takes his leave, it is usual to let him have anything he asks for; the host, too, is no more shy in asking. They take delight in presents, but ask no credit for giving them and admit no obligation in receiving them. There is a pleasant courtesy in the relations between host and guest.

<u>Tacitus: On Britain and Germany</u> translated by H. Mattingly (Penguin Classics, 1958), copyright (c) H. Mattingly, 1958 (Baltimore, Maryland: Penguin Books, 1960), 111-113, 118-119.

Study Questions

1. Why do you think the Germans conduct business only in arms? Why do you think a visiting head of state is still given a military salute when he comes to Washington, D.C.?

2. How is a boy received into manhood? What is the chief characteristic of manhood?

3. *How do chiefs choose their followers? How do followers choose their chiefs? Describe the bond between them. How is rank determined?*

4. *How do the Germans regard agriculture?*

5. *How are feuds reconciled?*

6. *Describe German hospitality.*

THE TRIAL BY ORDEAL

As Christianity had adapted to classical Rome and had assimilated much of Rome's law and philosophy, so too did it act pretty much the same way when it came into contact with Germanic customs. The Church's involvement in this trial by the hot iron may strike us as a bit un-Christian but it was perfectly in line with the directive of Gregory I: "...whoever wishes to climb to a mountain top climbs gradually step by step, and not in one leap." What strikes us as a cruel and irrational way of determining guilt did not seem so to the people involved. Indeed, they would have scorned a religion that asked them to use other methods and the Church would have lost any chance at all of gentling and softening their manners.

Ordeal By Hot Iron

(1) First the priest says the prescribed mass; then he has the fire lighted, and blesses the water and sprinkles it over the fire, over the spectators, and over the place where the ordeal is to be held; then he says this prayer:

(2) O Lord, our God, the omnipotent Father, the unfailing Light, hear us, for thou art the maker of all lights. Bless O God, the fire which we have sanctified and blessed in thy name, thou who hast illumined the whole world, that we may receive from it the light of thy glory. As thou didst illumine Moses with the fire, so illumine our hearts and minds that we may win eternal life.

(3) Then he shall say the litany....

(4) The prayers....

(5) Then the priest approaches the fire and blesses the pieces of iron, saying: O God, the just judge, who are the author of peace and judgest with equity, we humbly beseech thee so to bless this iron, which is to be used for the trial of this case, that if this man is innocent of the charge he may take the iron in his hand, or walk upon it, without receiving harm or injury; and if he is guilty this may be made manifest upon him by thy righteous power; that iniquity may not prevail over justice, nor falsehood over truth.

(6) O Lord, the holy Father, we beseech thee by the invocation of thy most holy name, by the advent of thy Son our Lord Jesus Christ, and by the gift of the Holy Spirit, the comforter, to bless these pieces of iron to the manifestation of thy righteous judgment, that they may be so sanctified and dedicated that thy truth may be made known to thy faithful subjects in this trial. In the name of our Lord Jesus Christ, etc.

(7) Omnipotent God, we humbly beseech thee that in the trial which we are about to make, iniquity may not prevail over justice, nor falsehood over truth. And if anyone shall attempt to circumvent this trial by witchcraft or dealing with herbs, may it be prevented by thy power.

(8) May the blessing of God the Father, Son, and Holy Spirit descend upon these pieces of iron, that the judgment of God may be manifest in them.

(9) Then this psalm shall be said on behalf of the accused: Here my prayer, O Lord, and give ear unto my cry....

(10) Prayer: Hear, we beseech thee, O Lord, the prayer of thy suppliants, and pardon those that confess their sins, and give us pardon and peace.

(11) Then those who are to be tried shall be adjured as follows: I adjure you (name), by omnipotent God who made heaven and earth, the sea, and all that in them is, by Jesus Christ his Son, who was born and suffered for us, by the Holy Spirit, by the holy Mary, the Mother of

God, and by all the holy angels, apostles, martyrs, confessors, and virgins, that you do not yield to the persuasions of the devil and presume to take the iron in your hand, if you are guilty of the crime of which you are accused, or if you know the guilty person. If you are guilty and are rash enough to take the test, may you be put to confusion and condemned, by the virtue of our Lord Jesus Christ, and by the sign of his holy cross. But if you are innocent of the crime, in the name of our Lord Jesus Christ and by the sign of his holy cross, may you have faith to take this iron in your hand; and may God, the just judge, keep you from harm, even as he saved the three children from the fiery furnace and freed Susanna from the false accusation; may you go through the ordeal safe ... and may the power of our Lord be made manifest in this day.

(12) Then he who is about to be tried shall say: In this ordeal which I am about to undergo, I put my trust rather in the power of God the omnipotent Father to show his justice and truth in this trial, than in the power of the devil or witchcraft to circumvent the justice and truth of God.

(13) Then the man who is accused takes the sacrament and carries the iron to the designated place. After that the deacon shall bind up his hand and place the seal upon it. And until the hand is unwrapped [i.e., at the end of three days] the man should put salt and holy water in all his food and drink.

Oliver J. Thatcher and Edgar Holmes Mc Neal, eds., *A Source Book for Medieval History* (New York: Charles Scribner's Sons, 1905), 404-406.

Study Questions

1. *What is the person being tried required to do? How is guilt or innocence determined?*
2. *Why does the priest ask God's blessing on the fire, the iron and the accused? What attitude does this indicate about God's involvement in human affairs?*
3. *What is the attitude toward physical pain?*

GREGORY OF TOURS from HISTORY OF THE FRANKS

Gregory (538-594) grew up in Clermont in the Loire valley on the southern limit of Frankish colonization where his father had a large estate. He was educated but probably not in the seven liberal arts, for he betrays a total ignorance of them and it is possible that they simply were not available in Gaul during his lifetime.

Powerful family connections in the Church made a clerical career an obvious choice and after 573, Gregory lived at Tours where he became bishop. Tours had five roads centering in it so that most of the trade of the rich Loire valley passed through it. Tours was also the center of devotion to St. Martin, a Roman soldier who had given his cloak to a beggar who turned out to be Christ. As bishop, Gregory was in charge of St. Martin's cult. The crippled, the sick, the devout came to his tomb for healing and sometimes for political refuge. As with Bede's Jarrow, it is possible that everyone who mattered or who was going anywhere passed through Tours at one time or other. Gregory also traveled a good bit, met kings, bishops and other influential personages. Thus, he had access to a considerable amount of information.

Gregory's view of history is like Bede's. It is God's plan being worked out through human agency. Thus, Gregory accepts miracles and, like Bede, he will assume that a virtuous person is telling him the truth. Both men also assume the Augustinian sense that history is going someplace, i.e., to the coming of Christ's kingdom.

The following is Gregory's account of the baptism of Clovis.

The queen did not cease to urge him to recognize the true God and cease worshiping idols. But he could not be influenced in any way to this belief, until at last a war arose with the Alamanni, in which he was driven by necessity to confess what before he had of his free will denied. It came about that as the two armies were fighting fiercely, there was much slaughter, and Clovis's army began to be in danger of destruction. He saw it and raised his eyes to heaven, and with remorse in his heart he burst into tears and cried: "Jesus Christ, whom Clotilda asserts to be the son of the living God, who art said to give aid to those in distress, and to bestow victory on those who hope in thee, I beseech the glory of thy aid, with the vow that if thou wilt grant me victory over these enemies, and I shall know that power which she says that people dedicated in thy name have had from thee, I will believe in thee and be baptized in thy name. For I have invoked my own gods, but, as I find, they have withdrawn from aiding me; and therefore I believe that they possess no power, since they do not help those who obey them. I now call upon thee, I desire to believe thee, only let me be rescued from my adversaries." And when he said this, the Alamanni turned their backs, and began to disperse in flight. And when they saw that their king was killed, they submitted to the dominion of Clovis, saying: "Let not the people perish further, we pray; we are yours now." And he stopped the fighting, and after encouraging his men, retired in peace and told the queen how he had had merit to win the victory by calling on the name of Christ. This happened in the fifteenth year of his reign.

Then the queen asked saint Remi, bishop of Rheims, to summon Clovis secretly, urging him to introduce the king to the word of salvation. And the bishop sent for him secretly and began to urge him to cease worshiping idols, which could help neither themselves nor any one else. But the king said: "I gladly hear you, most holy father; but there remains one thing: the people who follow me cannot endure to abandon their gods; but I shall go and speak to them according to your words." He met with his followers, but before he could speak the power of God anticipated him, and all the people cried out together: "O pious king, we reject our mortal gods, and we are ready to follow the immortal God whom Remi preaches." This was reported to the bishop, who was greatly rejoiced, and bade them get ready the baptismal font. The squares were shaded with tapestried canopies, the churches adorned with white curtains, the baptistery set in order, the aroma of incense spread, candles of fragrant odor burned brightly, and the whole shrine of the baptistery was fulled with a divine fragrance: and the Lord gave such grace to those who stood by that they thought they were placed amid the odors of paradise. And the king was the first to ask to be baptized by the bishop. Another Constantine advanced to the baptismal font, to terminate the disease of ancient leprosy and wash away with fresh water the foul spots that had long been borne. And when he entered to be baptized, the saint of God began with ready speech: "Gently bend your neck, Sigamber; worship what you burned; burn what you worshipped." The holy bishop Remi was a man of excellent wisdom and especially trained in rhetorical studies, and of such surpassing holiness that he equaled the miracles of Silvester. For there is extant a book of his life which tells that he raised a dead man. And so the king confessed all-powerful God in the Trinity, and was baptized in the name of the Father, Son and holy Spirit, and was anointed with the holy ointment with the sign of the cross of Christ. And of his army more than 3000 were baptized. His sister also, Albofled, was baptized, who not long after passed to the Lord. And when the king was in mourning for her, the holy Remi sent a letter of consolation which began in this way: "The reason of your mourning pains me, and pains me greatly, that Albofled your sister, of good memory, has passed away. But I can give you this comfort, that her departure from the world was such that she ought to be envied rather than mourned." Another sister also was converted, Lanthechild by name, who had fallen into the heresy of the Arians, and she confessed that the Son and the holy Spirit were equal to the Father, and was anointed.

Ernest Brehaut, trans., *History of the Franks* (New York: W. W. Norton & Company, Inc., 1969), 39-41.

Study Questions

1. Clotilda is the queen and Clovis' wife. What was her religion? What did she have to do with Clovis' conversion?

2. *Why did Clovis become a Christian? How did Clovis think his people would react to his conversion? What, in fact, did happen?*

3. *Why does Gregory call Clovis "another Constantine"?*

4. *What major miracle had Remi accomplished before this?*

5. *Who else was baptized with Clovis?*

From the QURAN

    Mohammed was the son of Abdullah of the powerful Quraysh clan in Mecca. His father died when he was quite young and Mohammed then came under the protection first of his grandfather and then of an uncle. This uncle took Mohammed with him in a number of merchant caravans carrying goods from the Yemen and other districts of Arabia into Syria and Lebanon. There, Mohammed came into contact with both Christianity and Judaism. Later he made that same journey for a wealthy widow named Khadijeh, fifteen years his senior, whom he married.

    Every year during the month of Ramadan, Mohammed had the habit of going off with his family into the desert to meditate. It was there when he was in his fortieth year, that, according to Muslim tradition, he began to receive revelations from God through the angel Gabriel. These revelations centered on two major points. First, instead of the many gods believed in by the Arabs, there was only one god, Allah (i.e., al lah, the One). Secondly, although Allah had revealed his nature and his will through prophets such as Noah, Abraham, Moses and Jesus, men have always forgotten or ignored their words. Allah nonetheless is compassionate and reveals himself one last time through one last prophet, Mohammed. Those who submit to this revelation, the Quran (Muslim=one who submits, from Islam=the act of submitting) are saved; all others are damned. The Quran was not like the Christian Bible, a book written by men albeit inspired by God. Rather, it is the everlasting, unchanging word of God and thus analogous to the person of Jesus.

    The Quran is arranged in "surahs" --- from the longest to the shortest. There is, however, a short opening surah --- a kind of Islamic "Lord's Prayer." No worship, public or private, is complete without it nor will any contract or business agreement omit it.

243

In the name of God, the Beneficent, the Merciful.

1. In the name of God, Most Gracious, Most Merciful.

2. Praise be to God, The Cherisher and Sustainer of the Worlds;

3. Most Gracious, Most Merciful;

4. Master of the Day of Judgment.

5. Thee do we worship,
   And Thine aid we seek.

6. Show us the straight way,

7. The way of those on whom Thou hast bestowed Thy Grace,
   Those whose (portion)
   Is not wrath,
   and who go not astray.

* * * * * * *

The following is from the twenty-fourth surah.

35. God is the Light
    Of the heavens and the earth.
    The parable of His Light
    Is as if there were a Niche
    And within it a Lamp:
    The Lamp enclosed in Glass:
    The glass as it were
    A brilliant star:
    Lit from a blessed Tree,
    An Olive, neither of the East nor of the West,
    Whose Oil is well-nigh Luminous,
    Though fire scarce touched it: Light upon Light!
    God doth guide
    Whom He will
    To His Light:

God doth set forth Parables
For men: and God
Doth know all things.

A. Yusuf Ali, trans., *The Holy Quran* (Baltimore: Amana Corp., 1983), 14-15, 907-908.

Study Questions

1. *Compare the first surah, the cardinal prayer in Islam with the "Lord's Prayer." How is God addressed in the two prayers? What does the petitioner ask for in each?*

2. *How are light and darkness used in the second passage?*

3. *Can you find parallels in Christian and Jewish texts with the "light" surah?*

DONATION OF PEPIN, 756

This Donation was not Pepin's to give to the pope nor to anyone. Technically, it belonged to the Byzantine Empire. Thus, Pepin by granting it and Stephen in accepting it, were snubbing their noses at Byzantium, knowingly. The pope had the most to gain. By seeking and accepting help from Pepin he was in fact denying the authority of the Byzantine Empire to protect and thus to rule Rome or anything in the West. By extension he was also asserting, again, his independence from the Byzantine Church. Stephen had shrewdly sought the help of a power who could protect the Church but one who, at least for the time being, could not overwhelm her. But there was more. In the Donation, the Papacy acquired a good bit of real estate, and thus wealth and power. The Donation was to become the foundation for the powerful Papal States of the Middle Ages and Renaissance. The claim Gregory I had made to authority over the Church, or at least the Western half of it, could now become a reality.

What Pepin got from the Donation was the support of the Church for his crown. Henceforth, heredity and the approval of the people would be less important than the Church's anointing of the ruler. Equally important, the Church now became part of the secular administration. Through the Church, loyalty and service to the king could be linked with religious devotion.

The most Christian king of Franks (Pepin) dispatched his counselor Fulrad, venerable abbot and prelate to receive these cities, and then he himself straightway returned to France with his army. The aforesaid Fulrad met the representative of King Aistulf at Ravenna, and went with them through the various cities of the Pentapolis and of Emilia receiving their submission and taking hostages from each and bearing away with him their chief men and the keys of their gates. Then he went to Rome, and placed the keys of Ravenna

Early Middle Ages

and of the other cities of the exarchate along with the grant of them which the king had made, in the confession of St. Peter, thus handing them over to the apostle of God [Peter] and to his vicar the holy pope and to all his successors to be held and controlled forever.

Oliver J. Thatcher and Edgar Holmes McNeal, eds., *A Source Book for Medieval History* (New York: Charles Scribner's Sons, 1905), 104-105.

Study Questions

1. *Locate the Donation on a map.*

2. *Who do you think King Aistulf is?*

3. *Who is Fulrad? What does his appearance here tell us about the activities of Benedictine monks?*

4. *At this point, Byzantium was far more powerful than either Pepin or the pope. Why didn't the Byzantine government react very strongly --- with force, even --- to this Donation? In short, why did Pepin and the pope get away with it?*

5. *What future dangers are there in this Donation for both Pepin's and Stephen's descendants?*

BOETHIUS from CONSOLATION OF PHILOSOPHY

Anicius Manlius Severinus Boethius (c. 480 - c. 525) was born into an old and aristocratic family which had converted to Christianity in the fourth century. His father died when Boethius was still a child but he had the finest of classical educations primarily from a man named Symmachus. It was Symmachus who introduced Boethius to the liberal arts and also to his daughter, Rusticiana, whom Boethius married and of whom he speaks so reverently in the <u>Consolation</u>.

At a very early age, Boethius came to the attention of the Ostrogothic king, Theodoric, who in 493 had overthrown and murdered Odavacar. Theodoric soon made Boethius the head of his whole civil service. True to the ancient Roman tradition of <u>pietas</u> --- and consistent with the ideals of Greek and Roman philosophy --- Boethius viewed public office not as an opportunity to acquire fame but as a duty. Thus, it was inevitable that he would make enemies at a court riddled with intrigue and self-aggrandizement.

Theodoric was a Christian but an Arian. At first, he was able to live amicably in the city of St. Peter, the center of orthodoxy. In 484, the pope's condemnation of the Byzantine patriarch had inaugurated a schism which divided not only the Eastern and Western churches but also the two halves of the empire. That had allowed Theodoric a pretty free and independent hand in Italy. In 519, the schism ended and while he no doubt tried to remain aloof from the political and ecclesiastical bickerings, Boethius' sympathies lay with a united and orthodox empire. The end of the schism also turned Theodoric from an independent king to a mere invader and heretic. A renewed persecution of Arians in the East further incensed the king. The time was ripe for Boethius' enemies to move. Evidence, no doubt false, was produced implicating him in the recent election of the pro-Eastern pope, John I. He was arrested and then tortured and bludgeoned to death in 524 or 525. His beloved teacher Symmachus and Pope John I were also killed.

Under Symmachus, Boethius had developed a passion for philosophy. He wanted to translate all of Aristotle into Latin, and, while he was not able to accomplish that whole task, he did put Aristotle's works on logic into Latin accompanied by his own commentaries on these works. The historical importance of this cannot be over-emphasized. It was only through Boethius that knowledge of Aristotle was able to survive in the West. The vocabulary of the medieval scholar would be drawn directly from Boethius' translations and commentaries.

It was while he was in prison awaiting execution that he wrote the beloved <u>Consolation</u>. In the form of Platonic dialogue, Boethius imagines that Philosophy, as a woman, appears to him and they discuss good and evil, fortune, free will as against God's foreknowledge, and the nature of happiness. To the age-old question of why good men suffer at least as much, or more, than evil men do, Boethius answers that to God, all is an Eternal Now. We do act with total freedom and the ultimate meaning of our lives is in the hands of an ever-present, caring God, not an indifferent force.

The <u>Consolation</u> draws on Stoicism, Neo-Platonism and, of course, Aristotle. But as he faced death, Boethius was less concerned with the details of philosophical speculation than with the comfort to be gained from meditation. It is then aimed not at the specialist but at the ordinary man trying to lead a good life in a world that often is not good.

"In all the care with which they toil at countless enterprises, mortal men travel by different paths, though all are striving to reach one and the same goal, namely, happiness, which is a good which once obtained leaves nothing more to be desired. It is the perfection of all good things and contains in itself all that is good; and if anything were missing from it, it couldn't be perfect, because something would remain outside it, which could still be wished for. It is clear, therefore, that happiness is a state made perfect by the presence of everything that is good, a state, which, as we said, all mortal men are striving to reach though by different paths. For the desire for true good is planted by nature in the minds of men, only error leads them astray towards false good."

"Some men believe that perfect good consists in having no wants, and so they toil in order to end up rolling in wealth. Some think that the true good is that which is most worthy of respect, and so struggle for position in order to be held in respect by their fellow citizens. Some decide that it lies in the highest power, and either want to be rulers themselves, or try to attach themselves to those in power. Others think that the best thing is fame and busy themselves to make a name in the arts of war or peace. But most people measure the possession of the good by the amount of enjoyment and delight it brings, convinced that being abandoned to pleasure is the highest form of happiness. Others again confuse ends and means with regard to these things, such as people who desire riches for the sake of power and pleasure, or those who want power for the sake of money or fame. So it is in these and other such objectives that the aim of human activity and desire is to be found, in fame and popularity which appear to confer a kind of renown, or in a wife and children which men desire for the sake of the pleasure they give. And as for friendship, the purest kind is counted as a mark not of good fortune, but of moral worth, but all other friendship is cultivated for the sake of power or pleasure."

"Now, it is clear that physical endowments are aspects of higher blessings: for clearly bodily strength and size give a man might; beauty and speed give him renown; and health gives him pleasure. And through all of this it is clear that the only thing men desire is happiness. Each man considers whatever he desires above all else to be the supreme good. We have already the supreme good as happiness; so that the state which each man desires above all others is judged by him to be one of happiness."

* * * * * * *

"As to where it is to be found, then, you should think as follows. It is the universal understanding of the human mind that God, the author of all things, is good. Since nothing can be conceived better than God, everyone agrees that that which has no superior is good. Reason shows that God is so good that we are convinced that His goodness is perfect. Otherwise He couldn't be the author of creation. There would have to be something else possessing perfect goodness over and above God, which would seem to be superior to Him and of greater antiquity. For all perfect things are obviously superior to those that are imperfect. Therefore, to avoid an unending argument, it must be admitted that the supreme God is to the highest degree filled with supreme and perfect goodness. But we have agreed that perfect good is true happiness; so that it follows that true happiness is to be found in the supreme God."

* * * * * * *

"But the greatest cause of my sadness is really this - the fact that in spite of a good helmsman to guide the world, evil can still exist and even pass unpunished. This fact alone you must surely think of considerable wonder. But there is something even more bewildering. When wickedness rules and flourishes, not only does virtue go unrewarded, it is even trodden underfoot by the wicked and punished in the place of crime. That this can happen in the realm of an omniscient and omnipotent God who wills only good, is beyond perplexity and complaint."

"It would indeed be a matter of infinite wonder," she said, "it would be something more horrible than any outrage, if, as you reckon, in the well-ordered house of so great a father the worthless vessels were looked after at the expense of the precious ones, which grew filthy. But it is not so."

* * * * * * *

"First then," she said, "that the good are always strong and that the wicked always bereft of all power, these are facts you will be able to see, the one being proved by the other. For since good and evil are opposites, the weakness of evil is shown by establishing the strength of good, and vice versa. So to strengthen your confidence in my teaching, I will proceed along both ways and prove my assertions doubly."

"Now, there are two things on which all the performance of human activity depends, will and power. If either of them is lacking, there is no activity that can be performed. In the absence of the will, a man is unwilling to do something and therefore does not undertake it; and in the absence of the power to do it, the will is useless. So that if you see someone who wants to get something which he cannot get, you can be sure that what he has been lacking is the power to get what he wanted."

"It is obvious," I said, "and cannot be denied."

"And if you see a man who has done what he wanted, you will hardly doubt that he had the power to do it, will you?"

"No."

"Therefore, men's power or ability is to be judged by what they can do, and their weakness by what they can't do."

"I agree."

"Do you, then, remember how earlier in the argument we reached the conclusion that the instinctive direction of the human will, manifested through a variety of pursuits, was entirely towards happiness?"

"I remember that this was proved as well."

"And you recall that happiness is the good itself and similarly that since they seek happiness, all men desire the good?"

"Not so much recall it, as hold it fixed in my mind."

"So that without any difference of instinct all men, good and bad alike, strive to reach the good."

"Yes, that follows."

"But surely men become good by acquiring goodness?"

"Yes."

"So that good men obtain what they are looking for?"

"It seems so."

"But if the wicked obtained what they want - that is goodness - they could not be wicked?"

"No."

"Since, then, both groups want goodness, and one obtains it and the other doesn't, surely there can be no doubt of the power of the good and the weakness of the bad?"

"Yes, for what follows is also obvious; from what I have already admitted it follows that the good are powerful and the bad weak."

* * * * * * *

"Think of the extent of the weakness impeding the wicked. It is not as if the prizes they failed to win were mere sports trophies. The quest in which they fail is the quest for the highest and most important of all things, and success is denied these wretched men in the very pursuit they toil at night and day to the exclusion of all else, the same pursuit in which the strength of the good stands out."

"If a man by walking could reach a point beyond which there was nowhere for him to go, you would consider him the champion at walking. In the same way you must judge the man who achieves the goal of all endeavour, beyond which there is nothing, to be supreme in power. The opposite of this is also true; those who do not gain it are obviously lacking all power."

"For I ask you, what is the cause of this flight from virtue to vice? If you say it is because they do not know what is good, I shall ask what greater weakness is there than the blindness of ignorance. And if you say that they know what they ought to seek for, but pleasure sends them chasing off the wrong way, this way too, they are weak through lack of self control because they cannot resist vice. And if you say they abandon goodness and turn to vice knowingly and willingly, this way they not only cease to be powerful, but cease to be at all. Men who give up the common goal of all things that exist, thereby cease to exist themselves. Some may perhaps think it strange that we say that wicked men, who form the majority of men, do not exist; but that is how it is. I am not trying to deny the wickedness of the wicked; what I do deny is that their existence is absolute and complete existence. Just as you might call a corpse a dead man, but couldn't simply call it a man, so I would agree that the wicked are wicked, but could not agree that they have unqualified existence. A thing exists when it keeps its proper place and preserves its own nature. Anything which departs from this ceases to exist, because its existence depends on the preservation of its nature."

"To the objection that evil men do have power, I would say that this power of theirs comes from weakness rather than strength. For they would not have the power to do the evil they can if they could have retained the power of doing good. This power only makes it more clear that they can do nothing, for if, as we concluded a short time ago, evil is nothing, it is clear that since they can only do evil, the wicked can do nothing."

<u>Boethius: The Consolation of Philosophy</u>, translated by V. E. Watts (Penguin Classics, 1969), copyright (c) V. E. Watts, 1969 (New York: Penguin Books, 1969), 79-80, 99-100, 116-122 passim.

Study Questions

1. What are all men striving for? What mistakes do they make in getting it? How, alone, is the goal to be attained?

2. Name at least two other people who have said the same or nearly the same thing.

3. Why is God the true happiness?

4. *How does Boethius handle the question of why "in spite of a good helmsman to guide the world, evil can still exist and even pass unpunished"?*

5. *Why do wicked men not truly exist?*

SAINT BEDE from A HISTORY OF THE ENGLISH CHURCH AND PEOPLE

When he was seven, Bede's (673-734) parents placed him in the care of the monastery at Jarrow. Bede's natural love of scholarship and his piety were encouraged by the abbots there who themselves were men of learning and holiness. In his <u>Lives of the Abbots</u> Bede tells us of the active share that everyone took in the life of work and prayer that regulated the monastery.

His <u>History</u> covers the centuries when, in the wake of Rome's withdrawal from Britain, Angles, Saxons and Jutes sent the native Celts into the remote, inaccessible regions along the Atlantic coast where they were harried by Irish pirates. Saint Patrick was one of their victims and then returned to convert the Irish to Christianity. In Devon, Cornwall, Wales and Cumberland, Romanized Britons clung tenaciously to their native customs and to the Christian faith they had already received and they tended to look down on the customs and beliefs of their heathen neighbors. Harassed by enemies, they were isolated too from the rest of Christendom. Later, when these enemies were converted to Christianity by missionaries such as the Augustine sent by Pope Gregory I, the Celtic Christians tended to look upon their Roman Christianity too as barbaric. The Celtic Church was primarily monastic wherein supreme authority was vested in an abbot. The Roman Church was diocesan, placing highest authority in a bishop. Celtic missionaries had been men of great piety and had gained many converts but the Celtic Church was not capable of administering a vast nationwide church. The issue was joined when the two churches disagreed on the date for celebrating Easter. That matter was settled at the Council of Whitby in 664 when the Celtic clergy decided to follow Rome. The spiritual unity would generate a national unity. Sixty years after Bede's death, when the Danes invaded, King Alfred was able to unite many races into a single nation on the basis of that religious unity.

Bede as a Benedictine monk belonged to the Roman Church but he was entirely sympathetic to the passionate piety of the Celtic missionaries. He began his History in 731, and the very conception of the project was formidable. Bede faced great limitations. The Jarrow library had Greek and Latin theology books but few models for writing history. Bede tried to get at all available records, written and verbal, local traditions and stories, whatever might illumine the past. He visited Lindisfarne and other monastic houses and his friend Egbert, Archbishop of York, but most of his time was spent at Jarrow. Despite his limitations, however, Bede is remarkably accurate. He painstakingly tried to verify facts, to get them in order, to interpret them correctly, and recent research shows that he made very few errors.

What strikes the modern reader perhaps the most is Bede's acceptance of miracle, and we wonder if he could have been that naive. What people perceive as miraculous reveals much about themselves, their way of seeing the world. To Bede's world, all of history was in God's hands. That God should intervene in his creation, that he should instruct, protect, chastise his creatures did not strike the Christians of Bede's time as at all strange. And perhaps if we find that odd, it is only because our faith is less than theirs.

Cuthbert, the man of God who had lived a solitary life on Farne Island before he became a bishop, was succeeded by a venerable man named Ethelwald. The latter, who had received the priesthood many years previously in the monastery of Ripon, adorned the office worthily by his doings. To illustrate his virtue and the kind of life that he led more clearly, I will relate a miracle of his that was told me by one of the brethren for whose benefit it as performed; this was the venerable priest and servant of Christ Guthfrid, who subsequently became abbot, and ruled the church of Lindisfarne where he had been brought up.

"I came with two other brothers to Farne Island," he said, "wishing to speak with the most reverend Father Ethelwald. We were greatly inspired by his discourse, and when we had asked his blessing and were returning homewards, while we were in the middle of the sea, the calm weather that was favouring our crossing suddenly changed.

There followed a storm of such ferocity and violence that sail and oars were useless, and we expected nothing but death. Having struggled unavailingly against the wind and waves for a long time, we looked back to see whether it were practicable to fight our way back to the island we had left, but round the storm was equally violent on all sides, so that there was no hope of escape. But as we looked into the distance, we saw Father Ethelwald, the beloved of God, come out of his cell on Farne to watch our progress, for he had heard the roar of the gale and raging of the sea, and had come out to discover what would happen to us. When he saw us in distress and despair, he fell on his knees to the Father of our Lord Jesus Christ, and prayed for our safety. Directly his prayer was ended, the raging sea grew calm, the severity of the storm lessened on all sides, and a following wind bore us over the sea towards the land. As soon as we had reached the shore and dragged our small boat out of the water, the wind that had dropped awhile for our sakes at once began to blow again, and continued strongly all that day. So we realized that the short interval of calm had been granted by the mercy of heaven at the prayer of the man of God so that we might escape."

The man of God remained on Farne Island for twelve years and died there, but he was buried on the island of Lindisfarne in the church of the blessed Apostle Peter next to the bodies of the above-mentioned bishops. These events took place in the time of King Alfrid, who succeeded his brother Egfrid as King of the Northumbrians, and reigned for eighteen years.

<u>Bede: A History of the English Church and People</u>, translated by Leo Sherley-Price (Penguin Classics, 1955, 1968), copyright (c) Leo Sherley-Price, 1955, 1968 (Baltimore: Penguin Books, 1965), 265-266.

Study Questions

1. *How has Bede learned of this story? Why does he relate it?*

2. *What story in the Gospel does this remind you of? Do you think perhaps there is a direct connection between the two?*

From BEOWULF

The story of Beowulf is this: For twelve years, the monster Grendel has ravaged the great hall of the Danish king, Hrothgar, carrying off and devouring his thanes. From over the sea, Beowulf, nephew of Higelac, king of the Geats, hears of Hrothgar's distress and sails to Denmark with fourteen trusted followers. In a desperate struggle, Beowulf wounds the monster, and Grendel, howling with pain and rage, retreats to his den and dies.

A great banquet is held to celebrate Beowulf's victory but the next night, Grendel's mother comes to avenge her son's death. She seizes one of Hrothgar's nobles and devours him. Beowulf pursues her to her den near the bottom of the sea where he sees the dead Grendel. He slays the mother and then takes Grendel's head back with him in triumph. Beowulf then leaves Denmark laden with gifts and honors.

Beowulf in time becomes king of the Geats and rules for fifty years. Then his own land is ravaged by a dragon. Beowulf challenges him and in that battle, both the dragon and Beowulf are slain. The poem ends with a tribute to Beowulf's bravery, goodness and generosity.

The following excerpt tells of the epic struggle between Beowulf and Grendel.

No thought had the monster of deferring the matter,
But on earliest occasion he quickly laid hold of
A soldier asleep, suddenly tore him,

Bit his bone-prison, the blood drank in currents,
Swallowed in mouthfuls: he soon had the dead man's
Feet and hands, too, eaten entirely.

Nearer he strode then, the stout-hearted warrior
Snatched as he slumbered, seizing with handgrip,
Forward the foeman foined with his hand;
Caught he quickly the cunning deviser,
On his elbow he rested. This early discovered
The master of malice, that in middle-earth's regions,
'Neath the whole of the heavens, no handgrapple greater
In any man else had he ever encountered:
Fearful in spirit, faint-mooded waxed he,
Not off could betake him; death he was pondering,
Would fly to his covert, seek the devils' assembly:
His calling no more was the same he had followed
Long in his lifetime. The liege-kinsman worthy
Of Higelac minded his speech of the evening,
Stood he up straight and stoutly did seize him.
His fingers crackled; the giant was outward,
The earl stepped farther.
The famous one minded
To flee away farther, if he found an occasion,
And off and away, avoiding delay,
To fly to the fen-moors; he fully was ware of
The strength of his grapple in the grip of the foeman.
'Twas an ill-taken journey that the injury-bringing,
Harrying harmer to Heorot wandered:
The palace re-echoed; to all of the Danemen,
Dwellers in castles, to each of the bold ones,
Earlmen, was terror. Angry they both were,
Archwarders raging. Rattled the building;
'Twas a marvellous wonder that the wine-hall withstood then
The bold-in battle, bent not to earthward,
Excellent earth-hall; but within and without it
Was fastened so firmly in fetters of iron,
By the art of the armorer. Off from the sill there
Bent mead-benches many, as men have informed me,
Adorned with gold-work, where the grim ones did struggle.
The Scylding wise men weened ne'er before
That by might and main-strength a man under heaven
Might break it in pieces, bone-decked, resplendent,
Crush it by cunning, unless clutch of the fire
In smoke should consume it. The sound mounted upward
Novel enough; on the North Danes fastened

A terror of anguish, on all of the men there
Who heard from the wall the weeping and plaining,
The song of defeat from the foeman of heaven.
Heard him hymns of horror howl, and his sorrow
Hell-bound bewailing.
He held him too firmly
Who was strongest of main-strength of men of that era.

XIII.

Grendal Is Vanquished.

For no cause whatever would the earlmen's defender
Leave in life-joys the loathsome newcomer,
He deemed his existence utterly useless
To men under heaven. Many a noble
Of Beowulf brandished his battle-sword old,
Would guard the life of his lord and protector,
The far-famed chieftain, if able to do so;
While waging the warfare, this wist they but little,
Brave battle-thanes, while his body intending
To slit into slivers, and seeking his spirit:
That the relentless foeman nor finest of weapons
Of all on the earth, nor any of war-bills
Was willing to injure; but weapons of victory
Swords and suchlike he had sworn to dispense with.
His death at that time must prove to be wretched,
And the far-away spirit widely should journey
Into enemies' power.
This plainly he saw then
Who with mirth of mood malice no little
Had wrought in the past on the race of the earthmen
(To God he was hostile), that his body would fail him,
But Higelac's hardy henchman and kinsman
Held him by the hand; hateful to other
Was each one if living.
A body-wound suffered
The direful demon, damage incurable
Was seen on his shoulder, his sinews were shivered,
His body did burst. To Beowulf was given
Glory in battle; Grendel from thenceward
Must flee and hide him in the fen-cliffs and marshes,
Sick unto death, his dwelling must look for

Unwinsome and woful; he wist the more fully
The end of his earthly existence was nearing,
His life-days' limits. At last for the Danemen,
When the slaughter was over, their wish was accomplished.
The comer-from-far-land had cleansed then of evil,
Wise and valiant, the war-hall of Hrothgar,
Saved it from violence. He joyed in the night-work,
In repute for prowess; the prince of the Geatmen
For the East-Danish people his boast had accomplished,
Bettered their burdensome bale-sorrows fully,
The craft-begot evil they erstwhile had suffered
And were forced to endure from crushing oppression,
Their manifold misery. 'Twas a manifest token,
When the hero-in-battle the hand suspended,
The arm and the shoulder (there was all of the claw of
Grendel together) 'neath great-stretching hall-roof.

Jno. Lesslie Hall, trans., *Beowulf* (Boston: D.C. Heath & Co., 1893), 27-29.

Study Questions

1. How does Grendel react to Beowulf's strength?

2. What weapons do Grendel and Beowulf fight with? Why? What peculiar quality does Grendel possess that makes it necessary for Beowulf to fight him in this way?

3. How does Beowulf mortally wound Grendel?

4. What trophy is left behind? Compare the account of this battle with Homer's story of the battle between Hector.

CHARLEMAGNE

Pepin the Short's son and heir was Charles who succeeded his father in 768. So outstanding are his achievements that he gives his name (in Latin, Carolus) to the entire dynasty and to an age. This is Charles the Great, Charlemagne.

He was easily the greatest warrior of the Middle Ages. He fought in over fifty campaigns. Many of these were over a period of thirty years in what is now northern Germany against the Saxons.

His second area of concern lay toward the Pyrenees and Muslim Spain. He fought several campaigns there; sometimes he won and some times he lost. Thus, the judgment of the Battle of Tours was confirmed. One of these campaigns became the background for the famous Song of Roland *written much after Chalemagne's death which provided the model for medieval chivalry.*

The third area was Italy. In 773 and 774, the Arian Lombards again threatened the Papacy. Charlemagne rode south, defeated them, added Lombardy to his empire and was crowned king of the Lombards. By 805, his empire included all of continental Europe except Spain, Scandinavia, southern Italy and Slavic fringes in the east.

Meanwhile in the year 800, he had received a title commensurate with this vast empire. According to his biographer, Einhard, Pope Leo III had received terrible abuse from the people of Rome. Charlemagne intervened on his behalf and restored Leo to the papal chair. In return, after Mass on Christmas Day, Leo placed a crown on Charlemagne's head and hailed him as Augustus and Emperor, thus recognizing him as head of not merely a Germanic realm but a revived Roman Empire, centered now not in Constantinople or even Rome but in

Charlemagne's capital. What did Charlemagne get from this? Unlike his father, there was no question of his right to rule in 768 and certainly not thirty-two years later. The Church had been central to his administration before 800 and would be so afterward. In bestowing the title of Emperor on him, the pope was giving Charlemagne something he had no legal right to grant anyone. Actually, what Charlemagne was getting was very little and he himself protested that had he known what the pope had planned, he would have heard Christmas Mass elsewhere. He had seen himself as ordained of God to protect Christ's Church, and he would do so without gouging the Church. But would his descendants? Worse, a crown granted by one pope could be withdrawn by another. Would his descendants have to some day sacrifice the interests of state to those of a powerful Papacy? His coronation gave Charlemagne more to worry about than to glory in.

The manner in which Charlemagne administered his empire drew on Germanic custom and his own genius and lay the pattern for medieval, and modern, governments. Under the Merovingians, a Frankish aristocracy had emerged. It was these warrior-aristocrats who became a cornerstone of Chalemagne's government. About 250 of these counts possessing full military and judicial powers for life, governed at the local level. They could be removed for misconduct; otherwise they were the link between the local authorities and the central government. They also provided the backbone of Chalemagne's army. Margraves having authority over sensitive border areas called "marks" had wider powers simply because they were more vulnerable.

There were also missi dominici *(agents of the lord, viz., Charlemagne). These were usually pairs of men, one lay, the other clergy, who administered Charlemagne's capitularies. The capitularies overrode local custom and somewhat resembled the relationship between American federal and state law. The* missi *had authority to investigate judicial, financial and clerical activities. They held courts to regulate crime and settle local disputes. They assisted the poor, encouraged education and checked the power of the counts and margraves. The* missi *were wholly dependent on Charlemagne and were rotated regularly to prevent their acquiring a base of power from which to threaten him.*

Industry and trade also flourished under Charlemagne. He stabilized the currency, the silver denier, and merchants carried it from Russia to England and to Constantinople. Trade fairs at Pavia and Paris attracted merchandise from England and ports such as Marseilles carried on a lively trade with Muslims in Spain and North Africa. Charlemagne welcomed Jews who provided a merchant class and acted as middlemen to markets throughout the Near East. One of the most prized commodities in the Near East, in fact, was a broadsword manufactured at Cologne.

Ease in trading with the two major world powers was possible because Charlemagne's relations with them were cordial, even warm. His relations with the Islamic caliph, Harun al-Rashid, were particularly close. Harun, one of the wisest, most capable caliphs in medieval Islamic history, saw in Charlemagne not the barbaric ruler of a backward state but a colleague, and the correspondence between the two rulers shows a mutual high regard. With Byzantium, despite the coronation in 800, relations were warm and trade flourished.

A key factor in Charlemagne's administration was that he had a capital, Aachen. Even when he was absent, business could still be done. The palace was a low, unpretentious building, rather plain by Byzantine and Islamic standards. At one end of the palace was a school headed by a Northumbrian monk, Alcuin of York. From about 781 until his death in 804, Alcuin was the chief architect of a Carolingian renaissance. Alcuin's school trained the <u>missi</u>, copied books and manuscripts and there developed the clear, precise style of writing called <u>minuscule</u>, which used lower-case letters in contrast to the Roman script which used only capitals. Alcuin and Charlemagne were convinced that a Christian ruler's job was to provide peace, justice and security so that the salvation of his subjects might the more easily be accomplished. In order to further that end, his subjects needed to know the will of God. Hence, they were not content merely with educating an elite corps of officials. Rather, schools, usually attached to cathedrals and monasteries, were established throughout the realm. The main object was to establish basic literacy among the clergy, to train priests and even some nobles who would then enlighten the laity. The core of the curriculum, however, was always the trivium and quadrivium; thus, it was not merely the preservation of religious learning that *was encouraged but also the classics. In order to know logic, for instance, the student needed Boethius' translations of Aristotle; for geometry, Euclid was required and for rhetoric, Cicero and Virgil. Always it was the pursuit of clarity, analysis and careful definition, of correct argumentation that was sought. It was these scholars who were laying the foundation for medieval Scholasticism.*

One of the remarkable things about this cultural revival was its international quality. Alcuin, of course, represented Britain but there were also Lombards, Germans, Spaniards and of course Frenchmen. The visual arts especially illustrate this. The influence of the Irish is evident in the illustrations of the <u>Gospel Book of Charlemagne</u>. But perhaps the masterpiece is the <u>Utrecht Psalter</u> done at Reims between 820 and 840. (Its present home is at the University of Utrecht in Holland; hence, the name.) There is a lively, almost playful quality about the human figures. Byzantine as well as Celtic influences are present in the text. Another exquisite text, the <u>Daqulf Psalter</u>, shows the beginning of what became a traditional technique of enlarging and adorning the initial letter of certain psalms. Collections of canon law and of Frankish law, commentaries on the Bible and on the Church Fathers poured from the scriptoria of schools established by Alcuin and his colleagues. These texts were often bound in leather or wooden covers overlaid with worked ivory and set with precious gems. By Charlemagne's death in 814, not only the institutions but more importantly the attitudes and patterns of thought of a literate Christian society had been so thoroughly established as to withstand even the invasions of the ninth and early tenth centuries.

Charlemagne left the empire to his son, Louis the Pious, an inept sort. The empire was really too big to be governed by a single man without a bureaucracy such as the Romans had had. Without the force of Charlemagne's personality to bind them together, local counts, margraves and bishops simply assumed judicial, military and financial functions. Before Louis died in 840, he divided the empire among his three sons. But after his death, the three fell to fighting each other. In 843, they agreed to the Treaty of Verdun by which the eastern and most Germanic part went to Louis the German. Lothair got the "middle kingdom" which, lacking any defensible borders and political or linguistic unity, almost immediately broke up into many petty little principalities which would be fought over down into the twentieth century. The western third, the core of modern France, went to Charles the Bald. In 987, the leading magnates elected one of Charles' descendants, Hugh Capet, a king. Hugh made Paris his capital and founded a dynasty that would last until 1871.

Real power in all three kingdoms was in the hands of local chieftains who were not quite strong enough to withstand the onslaught of invaders who began striking Europe even before the Treaty of Verdun. They came from three directions. Along the southern coastal areas, Muslim pirates from North Africa called Saracens raided and pillaged. But that really is all they did. They did not launch any major invasion. From the east came Slavs. In 962, the last major Slavic force, the Magyars, were defeated and then absorbed into Christian Europe.

Easily the most terrifying were the Norsemen, or Normans, or Vikings in the last great migration out of Scandinavia. Driven by overpopulation, crop failures and possibly too by the search for commercial contacts, Vikings sailed down the rivers of Russia to Constantinople where their beautifully crafted goods were in demand on Byzantine markets. They reached Ireland, Greenland and probably got as far as Long Island Sound, New York. They reached Sicily and established a Norman kingdom there which would be one of the most formidable powers in the Mediterranean. In 911, a Viking chieftain named Rollo subdued a large area at the mouth of the Seine which came to be called Normandy (the Normans' land). Charles the Simple, unable to oust the Normans, recognized Rollo as duke of Normandy and Rollo and his followers were soon baptized as Christians. It was one of Rollo's descendants, William I, who would conquer England in 1066. By then, Normandy had become one of the most powerful and settled feudal states in Western Europe.

The ninth-century invasions did a lot of physical damage, but unlike the invasions which contributed to Rome's fall, these invaders were absorbed by the civilization they encountered. Like the Vikings, the Magyars too accepted Christianity. And the invasions moreover contributed to the development of that most characteristic medieval institution, feudalism.

Suggested Readings

1. Barraclough, G., *The Crucible of Europe: The Ninth and Tenth Centuries in European History* (London: Thames and Hudson, 1976). Sees those centuries as most critical in the development of Western civilization.

2. Duckett, E. S., *Alcuin: Friend of Charlemagne* (New York: Macmillan, 1951). A light and readable biography of the supervisor of the palace school.

3. Jones, Gwyn, *A History of the Vikings* (New York, London: Oxford University Press, 1968). A comprehensive view of the Vikings using the latest archaeological findings.

4. Riche, P., *Life in the World of Charlemagne* (trans., J. McNamara, (Philadelphia: University of Pennsylvania Press, 1978). A wonderful study of all facets of life in the Carolingian world.

5. White, Lynn, *Medieval Technology and Social Change* (Oxford: Clarendon Press, 1962). Now a classic on technological advances in the Carolingian period.

EINHARD from LIFE OF CHARLEMAGNE

Very little is known of Charlemagne's biographer. He was born in the valley of the river Main and educated at the monastery of Fulda, <u>the</u> center of learning in Carolingian times and a major intellectual center throughout the Middle Ages. About 791 or 792, the abbot of Fulda persuaded Charlemagne to bring Einhard to his court.

Although Einhard served as Charlemagne's advisor and did a number of errands, he never achieved high office under him. It was not until the reign of Charlemagne's son, Louis the Pious, that Einhard became the king's secretary and was loaded with honors and benefices. He retired from the court in 828 probably because of the violent quarrels between Louis and his three sons and died in 840.

His biography of Charlemagne was composed between 817 and 836. Besides his own personal memories and those of his colleagues at the palace school, Einhard, as Louis' secretary, had access to the <u>annales royales</u> which furnished material on Charlemagne's military campaigns and political activities. His most serious problem was how to write a biography. Plutarch was no doubt unknown to him but he did have Suetonius' <u>Lives of the Caesars</u> on which he relied rather heavily.

Einhard's purpose clearly was to praise Charlemagne. Nonetheless, his account does have the ring of historical truth. Interestingly, Einhard's idea that biography was essentially a vehicle to praise the subject rather than a vehicle to reveal unvarnished truth remained the norm until well into the nineteenth century.

Accordingly war was begun against [the Saxons,] and was waged for thirty-three years with great fury; more, however, to the disadvantage of the Saxons than of the Franks. It could doubtless have been brought to an end sooner, had it not been for the faithlessness of the Saxons. It is hard to say how often they were conquered, and, humbly submitting to the King, promised to do what was enjoined upon them, gave without hesitation the required hostages, and received the officers sent them from the King. They were sometimes so much weakened and reduced that they promised to renounce the worship of devils, and to adopt Christianity, but they were no less ready to violate these terms than prompt to accept them, so that it is impossible to tell which came easier to them to do; scarcely a year passed from the beginning of the war without such changes on their part. But the King did not suffer his high purpose and steadfastness --- firm alike in good and evil fortune - to be wearied by any fickleness on their part, or to be turned from the task that he had undertaken; on the contrary, he never allowed their faithless behavior to go unpunished, but either took the field against them in person, or sent his counts with an army to wreak vengeance and exact righteous satisfaction. At last, after conquering and subduing all who had offered resistance, he took ten thousand of those that lived on the banks of the Elbe, and settled them, with their wives and children, in many different bodies here and there in Gaul and Germany. The war that had lasted so many years was at length ended by their acceding to the terms offered by the King; which were renunciation of their national religious customs and the worship of devils, acceptance of the sacraments of the Christian faith and religion, and union with the Franks to form one people.

* * * * * * *

Charles was large and strong, and of lofty stature, though not disproportionately tall (his height is well known to have been seven times the length of his foot); the upper part of his head was round, his eyes very large and animated, nose a little long, hair fair, and face laughing and merry. Thus his appearance was always stately and dignified, whether he was standing or sitting; although his neck was thick and somewhat short, and his belly rather prominent; but the symmetry of the rest of his body concealed these defects. His gait was firm, his

Charlemagne

whole carriage manly, and his voice clear, but not so strong as his size led one to expect. His health was excellent, except during the four years preceding his death, when he was subject to frequent fevers; at the last he even limped a little with one foot. Even in those years he consulted rather his own inclinations than the advice of physicians, who were almost hateful to him; because they wanted him to give up roasts, to which he was accustomed, and to eat boiled meat instead. In accordance with the national custom, he took frequent exercise on horseback and in the chase, accomplishments in which scarcely any people in the world can equal the Franks. He enjoyed the exhalations from natural warm springs, and often practiced swimming, in which he was such an adept swimmer that none could surpass him; and hence it was that he built his palace at Aix-la-Chapelle, and lived there constantly during his latter years until his death. He used not only to invite his sons to his bath, but his nobles and friends, and now and then a troop of his retinue or bodyguard, so that a hundred or more persons sometimes bathed with him.

* * * * * * *

Charles was temperate in eating, and particularly so in drinking, for he abominated drunkenness in anybody, much more in himself and those of his household; but he could not easily abstain from food, and often complained that fasts injured his health. He very rarely gave entertainments, only on great feastdays, and then to large numbers of people. His meals ordinarily consisted of four courses, not counting the roast, which his huntsmen used to bring in on the spit; he was more fond of this than any other dish. While at table, he listened to reading or music. The subjects of the readings were the stories and deeds of olden time: he was fond, too, of St. Augustine's books, and especially of the one entitled "The City of God." He was so moderate in the use of wine and all sorts of drink that he rarely allowed himself more than three cups in the course of a meal. In summer, after the midday meal, he would eat some fruit, drain a single cup, put off his clothes and shoes, just as he did for the night, and rest for two or three hours. He was in the habit of awaking and rising from bed four or five times during the night. While he was dressing and putting on his shoes, he not only gave audience to his friends, but if the Count of the Palace told him of any suit in which his judgment was necessary, he had the parties brought before him forthwith, took cognizance of the case, and gave his decision, just as if he were sitting on the judgment seat. This was not the only business that he transacted at this time, but he performed any duty of the day whatever, whether he had to attend to the matter himself, or to give commands concerning it to his officers.

Charles had the gift of ready and fluent speech, and could express whatever he had to say with the utmost clearness. He was not satisfied with command of his native language merely, but gave attention to the study of foreign ones, and in particular was such a master of Latin that he could speak it as well as his native tongue; but he could understand Greek better than he could speak it. He was so eloquent, indeed, that he might have passed for a teacher of eloquence. He most zealously cultivated the liberal arts, held those who taught them in great esteem, and conferred great honors upon them. He took lessons in grammar of the deacon Peter of Pisa, at the time an aged man. Another deacon, Albin of Britain, surnamed Alcuin, a man of Saxon extraction, who was the greatest scholar of the day, was his teacher in other branches of learning. The King spent much time and labor with him studying rhetoric, dialectics, and especially astronomy; he learned to reckon, and used to investigate the motions of the heavenly bodies most curiously, with an intelligent scrutiny. He also tried to write, and used to keep tablets and blanks in bed under his pillow, that at leisure hours he might accustom his hand to form the letters; however, as he did not begin his efforts in due season, but late in life, they met with ill success.

Samuel Epes Turner, tr., *Life of Charlemagne* by *Einhard*, (Ann Arbor: University of Michigan Press, 1964), 30-32, 50-51, 52-54.

Study Questions

1. *How had the Saxons provoked war with the Franks? What terms did Charlemagne impose on them whenever he defeated them? How was the Saxon problem finally settled?*

2. *In your own words, describe Charlemagne physically and mentally. How well-educated was he?*

From a CAPITULARY OF CHARLEMAGNE

The following shows the thoroughness Charlemagne gave to every detail of government.

The most serene and most Christian lord emperor Charles has chosen from his nobles the wisest and most prudent men, archbishops and some of the other bishops also, together with venerable abbots and pious laymen, and has sent them throughout his whole kingdom; through them he would have all the various classes of persons mentioned in the following sections live strictly in accordance with the law. Moreover, where anything which is not right and just has been enacted in the law, he has ordered them to inquire into this most diligently and to inform him of it; he desires, God granting, to reform it.

And let no one, through cunning craft, dare to oppose or thwart the written law, as many are wont to do, or the judicial sentence passed upon him; or to do injury to the churches of God, or the poor, or the widows, or the wards, or any Christian. But all shall live entirely in accordance with God's precept, justly and under a just rule, and each one shall be admonished to live in harmony with his fellows in his business or profession. The canonical clergy ought to observe in every respect a canonical life without heeding base gain; nuns ought to keep diligent watch over their lives; laymen and the secular clergy ought rightly to observe their laws without malicious fraud; and all ought to live in mutual charity and perfect peace.

And let the *missi* themselves make a diligent investigation whenever any man claims that an injustice has been done to him by any one, just as they desire to deserve the grace of omnipotent God and to keep their fidelity pledged to him, so that in all cases, every where, they shall, in accordance with the will and fear of God, administer the law fully and justly in the case of the holy churches of God and of the poor, of wards and widows, and of the whole people. And if there shall be anything of such a nature that they, together with the provincial counts, are not able of themselves to correct it and to do justice concerning it, they shall, without any reservations, refer this, together with their reports, to the judgment of the emperor. The straight path of justice shall not be impeded by any one on account of flattery or gifts, or on account of any relationship, or from fear of the powerful.

Concerning the fidelity to be promised to the lord emperor he has commanded that every man in his whole kingdom, whether ecclesiastic or layman, each according to his vow and occupation, shall now pledge to him as emperor the fidelity which he has previously promised to him as king and all of those who have not yet taken any oath shall do likewise, down to those who are twelve years old.

And that it shall be announced to all in public, so that each one may know, how great and how many things are comprehended in that oath; not merely, as many have thought hither to, fidelity to the lord emperor as regards his life, and not introducing any enemy into his kingdom out of enmity, and not consenting to, or concealing another's faithlessness to him; but that all may know that this oath contains in itself the following meaning:

First, that each one voluntarily shall strive, in accordance with his knowledge and ability, to live entirely in the holy service of God in accordance with the precept of God and in accordance with his own promise, be cause the lord emperor is unable to give to all individually the necessary care and discipline.

Secondly, that no man, either through perjury or any other wile or fraud, or on account of the flattery or gift of any one, shall refuse to give back or dare to abstract or conceal a serf of the lord emperor, or a district, or land, or anything that belongs to him; and that no one shall presume, through perjury or other wile, to conceal or abstract his fugitive serfs belonging to the fisc, who wrongly and fraudulently claim that they are free.

That no one shall presume to rob or in any way do injury fraudulently to the churches of God, or to widows or orphans or pilgrims; for the lord emperor himself, after God and his saints, has constituted himself their protector and defender.

That no one shall dare to lay waste a benefice of the lord emperor, or to make it his own property.

That no one shall presume to neglect a summons to war from the lord emperor; and that no one of the counts shall be so presumptuous as to dare to excuse any one of those who owe military service, either on account of relationship, or flattery, or gifts from any one.

That no one shall presume to impede in any way a ban or command of the lord emperor, or to dally with his work, or to impede or to lessen or in any way to act contrary to his will or commands. And that no one shall dare to neglect to pay his dues or tax.

That no one, for any reason, shall make a practice in court of defending another unjustly, either from any desire of gain when the cause is weak, or by impeding a just judgment by his skill in reasoning, or by a desire of oppressing when the cause is weak....

The oath to the emperor should include the observance of all those things mentioned above.

* * * * * * * *

And we command that no one in our whole kingdom shall dare to deny hospitality either to rich or poor, or to pilgrims; that is, no one shall deny shelter and fire and water to pilgrims traversing our country in God's name, or to any one traveling for the love of God or for the safety of his own soul. If, moreover, any one shall wish to serve them further, let him expect the best reward from God, who himself said, "And whoso shall receive one such little child in my name receiveth me"; and elsewhere, "I was a stranger, and ye took me in."

Concerning messengers coming from the lord emperor: the counts and centenarii shall provide most carefully, as they desire the grace of the lord emperor, for the missi who are sent out, so that they may go through their provinces without any delay. The emperor commands all, everywhere, to see to it that the missi are not hindered anywhere, but are sent forward with the utmost dispatch and provided with such things as they may require

In our forest no one shall dare to steal our game. This has already been many times forbidden; we now again strictly forbid it for the future. If one would keep his fidelity pledged to us, let him take heed to his conduct....

Finally, we desire that all our commands should be made known throughout our whole realm by means of the missi now sent forth, whether these commands be directed to those connected with the Church - bishops, abbots, priests, deacons, canons, monks or nuns - with a view of securing the observance of our ban or decrees, or whether we would duly thank the citizens for their good will, or request them to furnish aid, or to correct some matter....

James Harvey Robinson, ed., *Readings in European History*, 2 vols. (Needham Heights, Massachusetts: Silver, Burdett and Ginn, Inc., 1904), I, 139-143.

Study Questions

1. What kind of men have been chosen to serve as *missi dominici*? Why is a written law something that "many are wont" to oppose or thwart in this age?

2. What are the duties of the *missi*?

3. Describe the oath of fidelity to Charlemagne. (What are its terms?) Who is to take it? What kind of people are meant by the term "man"? Who is not included in that word?

4. *Who is to aid the missi?*

5. *What appears to be Charlemagne's relationship with the Church?*

THE STRASSBOURG OATHS, 842

After Louis the Pious' death in 840, his three sons fought over their inheritance. In 842, two of them, Louis, who had established a power base in the eastern part, and Charles, who had established himself in the west, came together and made an alliance against their brother, Lothair. The interesting thing about this oath is the language. Each brother took the oath in the language of his brother's followers, the <u>lingua teudisca</u>, an early form of German, and in the <u>lingua romana</u>, the ancestor of modern French. Notice how the Latin is being merged with the native speech.

So Lewis and Charles came together at Argentaria, which is called Strassburg in the common tongue, and there took the oaths which are given below, Lewis speaking in the lingua romana and Charles in the lingua teudisca.

... Lewis, being the elder, took the oath first, as follows:

Pro deo amur et pro christian poblo et nostro commun salvament, d'ist di in avant, in quant deus savir et podir me dunat, si salvaraeio cist meon fradre Karlo et in aiudha et in cadhuna cosa, si cum om per dreit son fradra salvar dist, in o quid il mi altresi fazet, et ab Ludher nul plaid numquam prindrai, qui meon vol cist meon fradre Karle in damno sit.[1]

When Lewis had finished, Charles took the oath in the lingua teudisca:

In godes minna ind in thes christanes folches ind unser bedhero gehaltnissi, fon thesemo daga frammordes, so fram so mir got geuuicai indi mahd furgibt, so haldih thesan minan bruodher, soso man mit iirehtu sinan bruodher scal, in thiu thaz er mig so sama duo, indi mit Ludheren in nohheiniu thing ne gegango, the minan uuilon imo ce scadhen uuerdhen.

And this is the oath which the followers of each took in their own tongues:

Lingua teudisca:

Si Lodhuuigs sagrament, que son fradre Karlo iurat, conervat, et Karlus meos sendra de suo part non los tanit, si io returnar non l'int pois: ne io ne neuls, cui eo returnar int pois, in nulla aiudha contra Lodhuuuig nun li iv er.[2]

Lingua teudisca:

---

[1] Literal translation of the *lingua romana*, the *lingua teudisca* being the same with the names changed:
"By God's love and by this Christian people and our common salvation, from this day forth, as far as God gives me to know and to have power, I will so aid this my brother Charles in each and every thing as a man ought to aid his brother, in so far as he shall do the same for me; and I will never have any dealings with Lothar that may by my wish injure this my brother Charles."

[2] Literal translation of the *lingua romana*, the same as the other with the names changed:
"If Lewis keeps the oath which he swore to his brother Charles, and Charles, my lord, on his part does not keep it, if I cannot prevent it, then neither I nor anyone whom I can prevent shall ever defend him against Lewis."

Oba Karl then eid, then er sinermo bruodher Luhuuuige gesuor, geleistit, indi Ludhuuuig min herro then er imo gesuor forbrihchit, ob ih inan es iruuenden ne mag: noh ih noh thero nohhein, then ih es iruuenden mag, uuidhar Karl imo ce follusti ne uuirdhit.

Oliver J. Thatcher and Edgar Holmes McNeal, eds., *A Source Book for Medieval History* (New York: Charles Scribner's Sons, 1905), 61-62.

Study Question

1. *Exactly what are the two brothers obligating themselves to?*

TREATY OF VERDUN

A year after the Strassbourg Oaths, all three brothers agreed to this treaty.

Charles met his brothers at Verdun and there the portions of the empire were assigned. Ludwig received all beyond the Rhine, including also Speier, Worms, and Mainz on this side of the Rhine; Lothar received the land bounded [by that of Ludwig on the west, and] by a line followed along the lower Rhine, the Scheldt, and the Meuse, then through Cambrai, Hainault, Lomme, including the counties east of the Meuse, to where the Saone flows into the Rhone, then along the Rhone to the sea, including the counties on both sides of the Rhone; the rest as far as Spain, went to Charles.

Thatcher and McNeal, 63.

Study Question

1.   *Locate the boundaries of the three kingdoms on a map.*

THE NORSEMEN INVADE EUROPE

In their fleet little ships called <u>knorrs</u>, the Vikings were able to travel down inland waterways as easily as on the open seas. This article shows why they were so feared.

---

(885) In December of this same year Carloman was accidentally killed while on a boar hunt. As soon as Emperor Charles (the Fat) received tidings of this, he made a hasty journey and came to Pontion; and all the men of Carloman's kingdom went to him there and submitted to his sway....

On the twenty-fifth of July the whole host of the Northmen forced their way to Rheims. Their ships had not yet come, so they crossed the Seine in boats they found there, and quickly fortified themselves. The Franks followed them. All those who dwelt in Neustria and Burgundy gathered to make war upon the Northmen. But when they gave battle it befell that Ragnold, duke of Maine, was killed, with a few others. Therefore, all the Franks retreated in great sorrow and accomplished nothing.

Thereupon the rage of the Northmen was let loose upon the land. They thirsted for fire and slaughter; they killed Christian people and took them captive and destroyed churches; and no man could resist them.

Again the Franks made ready to oppose them, not in battle, but by building fortifications to prevent the passage of their ships. They built a castle on the river Oise at the place which is now called Pontoise, and appointed Aletramnus to guard it. Bishop Gauzelin fortified the city of Paris.

In the month of November the Northmen entered the Oise, and besieged the castle the Franks had built. They cut off the water supply from the castle's garrison, for it depended on the river for water and had no other. Soon they who were shut up in the castle began to suffer for lack of water. What more need be said? They surrendered on condition that they be allowed to go forth unharmed. After hostages had been exchanged, Aletramnus and his men went to Beauvais. The Northmen burned the castle and carried off all that had been left by the garrison, who had been permitted to depart only on condition that they would leave everything behind except their horses and arms.

Elated with victory, the Northmen appeared before Paris and at once attacked a tower, confident that they could take it quickly because it was not yet fully fortified. But the Christians defended it manfully and the battle raged from morning till evening. The night gave a truce to fighting and the Northmen returned to their ships. Bishop Gauzelin and Count Odo worked with their men all night long to strengthen the tower against assaults. The next day the Northmen returned and tried to storm the tower, and they fought fiercely till sunset. The Northmen had lost many of their men and they returned to their ships. They pitched a camp before the city And laid siege to it and bent all the energies to capture it. But the Christians fought bravely and stood their ground.

James Harvey Robinson, ed., *Readings in European History*, 2 vols. (Needham Heights, Massachusetts: Silver, Burdett and Ginn, Inc., 1904), I, 165-166.

Study Questions

1. How did the Franks fare in battle with the Norsemen at Rheims? How did they treat the defeated?

2. How then did the Franks prepare to resist them? How did that tactic work?

3. What was the outcome of the battle at Paris? Describe the role of Bishop Gauzelin.

MEDIEVAL SOCIETY

In medieval theory, human society was divided into three categories --- the men who prayed, men who fought and men who worked. The men who prayed were obviously the clergy. We now turn to the other two categories, the nobility, those who fought and then to those who worked, everybody else.

Men Who Fight

The nobility were embraced by the feudal system. Although the roots of feudalism lay deep in the latter days of the Roman Empire, the great impetus for its development came in response to the invasions of the ninth century. One man clearly could not stand alone against the invaders so he would seek the protection of a stronger man --- perhaps a descendant of one of Charlemagne's counts or dukes, for instance. The stronger man, aware that he, too, could not face the invaders alone, was quite willing to offer his protection to the first man in return for the latter's military service. He would become a lord to the first man who would then become his vassal. In addition to pledging protection, however, the lord also granted his vassal a "fief" (from *beneficium*) in return for the vassal's pledge of homage and fealty. The fief was normally land but it could also be an office or a set of rights. In the case of land, it was expected that the vassal would "subenfeoff" or subdivide the fief and create vassals of his own. The terms "lord" and "vassal" then described a relationship. Thus, while a man was a vassal to Lord A, he would be the lord to his own vassals C and D who in turn could also "subenfeoff" and be lords over other vassals and so on. To complicate matters, however, a man might hold several fiefs, might thus be a vassal and owe military service to two or possibly even three lords. What did a vassal do if two of his lords started fighting each other? To get around this, vassals could swear liege homage to one of their lords. One would, of course, chose one's liege lord carefully --- a *close relative, perhaps, or the lord who was the most powerful or possibly a lord who was in the Church, a bishop or a monastery, for then the obligation to protect would extend beyond the grave in the form of prayers for the vassal's soul.*

Technically, a vassal did not own his fief. Only God owned land. Rather, he held it on condition of service. If the vassal could not or would not perform the required service, the fief would escheat or revert back to the lord who might then grant it to someone else. Obviously, when the vassal died, the bond was broken. Neither the lord nor the vassal usually wanted escheat to happen, though. Thus, the vassal usually willed his fief with its attached obligations to his eldest son and, in return for an act of homage and fealty, the lord simply regranted the fief. Similarly, when the lord died, all his vassals were expected to swear homage to his heir, on pain of escheat. If the vassal had no male heir or his sons were minors, the lord had the right to appoint guardians for his children and protect his widow, which he often did by arranging her remarriage to another of his vassals.

The root of the feudal bond was military service but they didn't fight quite all the time. Sometimes peace broke out and military obligations were then commuted into payments in goods or other kinds of services. There were aids, gifts of various sorts, hospitality was required if the lord showed up at the vassal's castle and ransom payments were owed if the lord was captured. And there was the obligation to attend court. Court had three functions --- ceremonial, judicial and consultative --- and often all three were combined. The ceremonial function was simply to let everyone know that the lord had powerful vassals whom he could call up at will. It was to impress --- and intimidate --- but it was also an occasion for jousting tournaments, parades, feasting, races and just plain fun and display. The feudal court's judicial function came into play when there were disputes between a lord and his vassals or between vassals themselves. In the absence of strong central government, justice was in the hands of barons whose law was custom, not a king's writ. Nonetheless, a lord could not exercise arbitrary authority over his vassals.

The third function of the court was consultative. A lord was expected to parley (from the French word parler) with his vassals on any matter that concerned them. He could not, for instance, arbitrarily decide to go on a campaign and order his vassals into battle. He had to consult with them on strategy and the minutiae of waging a campaign. Their rights, too, the lord was expected to protect. He could not, for instance, demand services or aids of them that were unreasonable. Out of these parleys would, of course, come modern parliaments.

Although warfare was as chronic in the Middle Ages as it is in our own time, its scale was far more limited. First, the feudal contract itself was partly the reason. Most contracts obligated vassals to fight for only about 40 days of the year. Many knights of course were willing to carry on a campaign for far longer than that. And that brings up the second reason. Wars were not fought necessarily for any strategic or political objective but in order to gain glory and plunder. When they had enough of one or the other, or both, technically they could go home. Third, only the nobility by law could fight. While civilians often suffered horribly, the actual waging of combat engaged only a small percentage of the population. Fourth, both the methods of transport and the range of weapons were limited. A horse can cover a limited amount of terrain in a day and supplies moved by even slower, mule-driven carts or were carried by people. Roads were muddy quagmires or dusty and rutted --- where they existed. Then, too, while medieval swords, maces, spears and battle-axes were beautifully crafted, they could still only harm one person at a time and had to be used at close range. Fifth, medieval armor made the knight almost invulnerable but it weighed up to 75 and 80 pounds and made movement slow and cumbersome. Sixth, the bulwark of medieval defense was the castle which was nearly invincible. In the wake of the ninth-century invasions, they began to be built of stone and near or over a source of water. The only realistic way they could be taken was by siege and the burden of that fell more on the attackers than the defenders. Seventh, command was not hierarchical. Even a king was essentially no more than a feudal lord and bound thereby to parley with his nobles on whether or not to wage the war and then how to wage it. Finally, the Church tried to enforce peace with the Peace of God and the Truce of God, restricting warfare to certain days of the week and times of the year.

Feudalism may strike the modern observer as disorganized only because authority was in the hands of hundreds of individual barons rather than a single centralized government. Law was custom and could vary from one barony to another. Nonetheless, it did provide stability and two very important assumptions gave it a fundamental unity. One was that law, thus government, rested on an agreement between vassal and lord, ruler and ruled. The second was that any human law should mirror Divine Law as articulated through God's Church and through the custom of a Christian people. Both assumptions would remain fundamental to the development of modern Western law.

Men Who Work

The economic base of feudalism was the manor. Any one fief might contain many manors. The manor resembled the old Roman latifundium out of which it had evolved. Self-sufficient and self-sustaining, the manor was worked by peasants. The lord's castle dominated the manor but the center of the peasants' life was the village. Like the nobility, peasants had varying rights and responsibilities. Most of them were agricultural laborers but there were coopers, wheelwrights, carpenters, tanners, candle makers, a miller to grind wheat into flour, weavers and masons. There were different types of peasant. The lowest was the serf who was bound to the land and could not leave it without his lord's permission and the payment of a fee. On the other hand, the lord could not dispossess the serf nor separate him from his wife and children. Above the serf was the villein and above that was the freeman who was not bound to the land, but as long as he stayed on it he was subject to the lord's jurisdiction. Each peasant's holding consisted of strips scattered throughout the three fields. In this way, land could be more equitably distributed among the peasants so that each peasant had both fertile and nonfertile strips. They worked cooperatively with everyone plowing, sowing and reaping at the same time.

From the Benedictine monks, the peasants learned the use of water and windmills. The invention of a heavy metal wheeled plow also allowed them to cut a deeper furrow than the Mediterranean scratch plows of Roman times. The heavier plow was better suited to the rich loams of northern and western Europe. Finally, the invention of a horse collar or yoke allowed the utilization of the horse to pull that plow. From the monasteries also came the three-field system. The arable land on

Medieval Society

the manor would be divided into three large fields so that crops could be sown twice a year, in spring and again in the fall, while the third field was left fallow or turned to pasture in order to give it a rest. In this way, it was possible to increase the yield, perhaps by as much as a third and to produce a greater variety of crops.

There were a number of taxes and dues which varied from manor to manor. First, was the corvée or labor service such as planting, shearing sheep, harvesting, cutting wood and the like. Second, there were banalities, fees the lord charged for the use of his facilities, his wine press, his bakery, water mill, and so on. Third, the peasant also owed a capitation or head tax to his lord. And then there was a taille paid in produce. This was usually about a tenth of his produce. These dues were fixed, however, and they did not go up as productivity increased. Thus, it was very possible for some peasants to become rather wealthy.

The life of the medieval peasant was harsh and tedious. He was at the beck and call of his lord and worked long hours. Yet it wasn't oppressive by medieval standards. The peasant had a greater job security than most of us will ever know. He was illiterate but so were most of the nobility. His cottage was ill-furnished, without glass windows, ill-ventilated and ill-lighted. But the same might be said of his lord's cold, damp, gloomy castle. His entertainments were few and boisterous. There was a kind of field hockey, an early form of bowling, boxing and in the winter, ice skating. And for the peasant, as well as his lord, there was the Church --- sermons, mystery and miracle plays at the local fairs, the elaborate processions and rituals on feast days and the baptisms, weddings and funerals that broke the tedium of daily life.

As productivity increased, more diverse crops could be developed, diets were diversified and enriched and with that population increased. It was to the mutual advantage of both the lord and his peasants to drain marshes and clear wooded areas and bring them under cultivation. In return for more land from which he could extract rents, the lord was quite willing to allow the peasants greater freedom as they moved further away from the castle. He was even willing to allow them to sell their excess produce at local markets, called "fairs," from which he, of course, could derive a percentage of the profits. Very simply, the greater the technological improvements, the freer the peasants became.

The Towns

The fair was a busy place to which goods were brought to be exhibited, bought and sold. It might meet once or twice a month or three or four times a week, depending on the area's wealth. Its location was carefully chosen --- at the junction of roads or riverways, or near a monastery or a castle which could offer protection to the merchants and their goods. In fact, some early fairs were originally *fau bourgs*, meaning "outside the wall or castle." As the fairs became permanent they evolved structures for protecting their new, specifically mercantile interests. At that point, the fair had become a new kind of thing, quite distinct from the manor. It had become a town.

Not all medieval towns came about in this way. Some of them, like Narbonne, Marseilles, Lyons, Cologne, York and the cities of Italy, were founded in Roman times and although trade may have trickled off in the troubles of the later empire, it had never really stopped. The stability and order wrought by feudalism and the wealth --- and enlarged population --- provided by the new agricultural technology revived trade again in these ancient cities.

People in the towns were organized in guilds. A craft guild was an association of craftsmen or artisans who produced the same kind of good or service as, for example, bakers, dyers, brewers, coppersmiths, etc. No one could practice a trade unless he was licensed with a guild. The purposes of the guild were to regulate competition among their own members and also to protect the consumer from shoddy or overpriced merchandise. There were many guild regulations to prevent poor workmanship. The slightest appearance of fraud was to be avoided; in Venice, for instance, it was forbidden to sell plated metalware. The London bakers guild had to periodically warn its members against baking stones into their loaves to make them heavier, thus increasing their prices.

The guild also set prices and wages, outlawed competition through advertising and price-cutting and regulated the behavior of its members. It also jealously guarded their manufacturing secrets. In Florence, the secret of making silk brocade was so zealously guarded that for a long time it could be gotten only in that city. In Venice, if a worker in possession of trade secrets fled for any reason to a foreign territory, he had to be tracked down and killed, lest he divulge the information.

The guild also took care of widows and orphans, supplied funeral expenses for its poorer members, and granted dowries to poorer girls. The guild cared for its sick and some even had their own hospitals. It also built chapels, donated windows to the town cathedral and actually helped in the construction of the building and provided schools for the members' children. And each guild had its own patron saint and "livery" or distinctive costume.

There were three kinds of people in a guild. There was the apprentice, the boy who was learning the trade. Apprenticeships could begin as young as six or seven years. Their length varied but the norm was about seven years. Having served his apprenticeship, the boy could then become a journeyman (from the French *journée*=day), literally a day laborer. The journeyman could make and market the good, and many people found this a satisfying enough life, but he could not take on apprentices until he had produced a masterpiece acceptable to the guild. The day he was accepted as a master must have been one of the most thrilling in a man's life, for it really was not merely his masterpiece, but the man himself who was accepted into the company of the best. It was the masters who governed the guild, but more. It was representatives of the major guilds that governed the town itself.

The town's governing council regulated the life of the town itself and negotiated with the local lord or with the king. Their main goal was to get and then maintain their independence, viz., the right to make their own laws and have their own courts to deal with contracts, debts, bankruptcy and various other business transactions that feudal law had nothing to do with. They also wanted the right to select their own mayor and other public officials and the right to levy and collect taxes and other tolls. Initially, kings and lords were reluctant to grant such extensive rights but they soon realized that greater rights almost invariably increased a town's wealth and attracted more people, who could be taxed. In other words, the charters which they granted guaranteeing a town's liberties often worked to their benefit as well as the town's.

In the eleventh century, merchant guilds had developed in some of the greater towns. A merchant guild was a group of men engaged in long-distance trade. Because it often involved a large expenditure of capital and because of the risks of piracy, brigandage, shipwreck and, in some cases, the spoilage of goods, this trade was in the hands of groups of men who would pool their investments and then share both the risks and the profits. This foreign trade was dominated by the great city-states of Italy --- Florence, Milan, Genoa, Pisa and Naples. But the leader was Venice whose caravans were bringing silk from China and Mongolia to the West by the thirteenth century. Relatively easy access to the sea lanes of the Adriatic and Mediterranean and thus to the markets of the Byzantine and Islamic worlds gave the Italians the edge in international trade until the fourteenth century when the Turks closed many of those markets.

Before then, however, a fleet would leave an Italian port laden with goods from all over Europe. Before any ship in that fleet returned it would stop at perhaps dozens of different "factories", deposit several kinds of goods and take on others. A factory was a walled district in a foreign port containing warehouses, offices, a church and the houses of the factors. Each city-state needed to negotiate with the local government for the right to establish a factory and to trade in specific commodities. Usually this required the payment of a handsome fee for the license to trade and in any one port there were likely to be two or three European, usually Italian, factories. The competition between the Italians for these licenses could get fairly rough and involve a good bit of deceit and skullduggery, for the Byzantine and Near Eastern --- and the Chinese and Persian --- trade was lucrative indeed. And far-flung. Venice and her near rival, Florence, established factories not only in such old trading centers as Alexandria, Antioch, Tyre, Sidon, Cyprus, Rhodes and, of course, Constantinople, but also at Trebizond and Sinope on the southern shores of the Black Sea, Tabriz in northwestern Persia and even at Peking. Paper, indigo and cotton from Egypt, precious dyes, woods and linens from the Levant, spices from Persia and China, carpets from Asia Minor, hides, pepper and other spices from North Africa, found their way to the markets of Europe.

Medieval Society

The largest of these international markets were the fairs in the county of Champagne. Goods from literally all over the world appeared in the Champagne fairs which the counts of Champagne astutely encouraged. Eventually the Champagne fairs died out because European merchants brought back more than mere goods. They also brought back new marketing methods they had learned from the Arabs. These included the use of double-entry bookkeeping, the use of checks and banking. Instead of sending several wagons filled with goods to Champagne and then return home with wagons filled with money or other valuable goods, a merchant would find it cheaper --- and safer --- to keep a single representative there to handle his interests. The Arabs also gave the Europeans that ancestor of the modern calculator, the abacus. And in the crowded, busy bazaars of the East, Europeans learned the uses of algebra, of nautical instruments like the astrolabe and more accurate maps. They also acquired more refined tastes and habits. Though never more than a tiny percentage of the total population, these wealthy merchants eventually taught Europeans to use forks and knives rather than their fingers to eat and to wipe their greasy hands on napkins rather than on the dog lying under the table. Books, poetry and music from the Near East would also enter Europe and contribute to a renaissance in the twelfth century. Too, kings soon realized that an alliance with wealthy towns could relieve them of the need to rely on the feudal nobility. Wealth could be taxed and taxes could buy soldiers who, as long as the pay held out, were more dependable than the nobles with their various entrenched privileges and rights. In the alliance between kings and towns lay the foundations of the modern centralized state.

Suggested Readings

1. Barber, Richard W., *The Knight and Chivalry* (London: Longmans, 1970). A good introduction to the world and the values of the nobility.

2. Bautier, Robert-Henri, *The Economic Development of Medieval Europe* (New York: Harcourt, Brace, Jovanovich, 1971). The development of trade, industry and banking in the medieval world.

3. Brooke, C., *The Structure of Medieval Society* (London: Thames and Hudson, 1971). A beautiful little introduction to all phases of medieval society.

4. Duby, Georges, *Rural Economy and Country Life in the Medieval West*. Trans. C. Postan (Columbia: University of South Carolina Press, 1968). The best treatment of medieval peasant life.

5. _____, *William Marshall: The Flowering of Chivalry* (New York: Pantheon Books, 1985). Story of a commoner who became one of the most powerful lords of England and the intimate of kings.

6. Ganshoff, F. L., *Feudalism* (New York: Harper, 1964). The best concise treatment of feudalism.

7. Gies, Joseph and Frances, *Life in a Medieval Castle* New York: Harper Colophon Books, 1974).

8. _____, *Life in a Medieval City* (New York: Harper Colophon Books, 1969). Nicely illustrated studies of the nobility and the towns.

9. Keen, Maurice, *The Pelican History of Medieval Europe* (Harmondsworth: Penguin, 1969). A good and brief survey.

10. Kelly, Amy, *Eleanor of Aquitaine and the Four Kings* (Cambridge: Harvard University Press, 1950). The twelfth century from the perspective of one of its most prominent personalities.

11. Lopez, R. S., *The Commercial Revolution of the Middle Ages* (Englewood Cliffs, N.J.: Prentice Hall, 1971). Medieval commercial and industrial development in a highly readable text.

12. Rowling, Marjorie, *Everyday Life in Medieval Times* (New York: Putnam, 1968). Deals with all levels of medieval life.

13. Strayer, Joseph R., *Western Europe in the Middle Ages* (Englewood Cliffs, N.J.: Prentice Hall, 1974). An excellent, readable text by an outstanding scholar.

14. White, Lynn, *Medieval Technology and Social Change* (Oxford: Clarendon Press, 1962). Studies the impact of technological advances on social patterns.

FEUDAL CHARTER, 1110

By the early twelfth century, when this contract was made, feudalism had evolved as the normal political system of most of Western Europe. Its language, habits of mind, values, and specific institutions were well established by 1110. Thus, there is no phrase here that is accidental or incidental.

In the name of the Lord, I, Bernard Atton, viscount of Carcassonne, in the presence of my sons, Roger and Trencavel, and of Peter Roger of Barbazan, and William Hugo, and Raymond Mantellini and Peter de Vitry, nobles, and of many other honorable men, who had come to the monastery of St. Mary of Grasse in honor of the festival of the August St. Mary. Since Lord Leo, abbot of the said monastery, asked me, in the presence of all those above mentioned, to acknowledge to him the fealty and homage for the castles, manors, and places which the patrons, my ancestors, held from him and his predecessors and from the said monastery as a fief, and which I ought to hold as they held, I have made to the lord abbot Leo acknowledgment and done homage as I ought to do.

Therefore, let all present and to come know that I, the said Bernard Atton, lord and viscount of Carcassonne, acknowledge verily to thee, my Lord Leo, by the grace of God abbot of St. Mary of Grasse, and to thy successors, that I hold and ought to hold as a fief, in Carcassonne, the following: that is to say, the castles of Confoles, of Leocque, of Capendes (which is otherwise known as St. Martin of Sussagues); and the manors of Mairac, of Albars, and of Musso; also, in the valley of Aquitaine, Rieux, Traverina, Herault, Archas, Servians, Villatritoes, Tansiraus, Presler, and Cornelles.

Moreover, I acknowledge that I hold from thee and from the said monastery, as a fief, the castle of Termes in

Narbonne; and in Minerve, the castle of Ventaion, and the manors of Cassanolles, and of Ferral and Aiohars; and in Le Roges, the little village of Longville; for each and all of which I render homage and fealty with hands and mouth to thee, my said Lord Abbot Leo and to thy successors; and I swear upon these four gospels of God that I will always be a faithful vassal to thee and to thy successors and to St. Mary of Grasse in all things in which a vassal is required to be faithful to his lord; and I will defend thee, my lord, and all thy successors, and the said monastery, and the monks present and to come, and the castles and manors and all your men and their possessions against all malefactors and invaders, of my own free will and at my own cost, and so shall my successors do after me; and I will give to thee power over all the castles and manors above described, in peace and in war, whenever they shall be claimed by thee or by thy successors.

Moreover, I acknowledge that, as a recognition of the above fiefs, I and my successors ought to come to the said monastery at our own expense, as often as a new abbot shall have been appointed, and there do homage and return to him the power over all the fiefs described above. And when the abbot shall mount his horse, I and my heirs, viscounts of Carcassonne, and our successors ought to hold the stirrup for the honor of the dominion of St. Mary of Grasse; and to him and all who come with him, to as many as two hundred beasts, we should make the abbot's purveyance in the borough of St. Michael of Carcassonne, the first time he enters Carcassonne, with the best fish and meat, and with eggs and cheese, honorably, according to his will, and pay the expense of shoeing the horses, and for straw and fodder as the season shall require.

And if I or my sons or their successors do not observe towards thee or thy successors each and all the conditions declared above, and should come against these things, we desire that all the aforesaid fiefs should by that very fact be handed over to thee and to the said monastery of St. Mary of Grasse and to thy successors.... I, therefore, the aforesaid Lord Leo, by the grace of God abbot of St. Mary of Grasse, receive the homage and fealty for all fiefs of castles and manors and places which are described above, in the way and with the agreements and understandings written above; and likewise I concede to thee and thy heirs and their successors, the viscounts of Carcassonne, all the castles and manors and places aforesaid, as a fief.... And I promise by the religion of my order to thee and thy heirs and successors, viscounts of Carcassonne, that I will be a good and faithful lord concerning all those things described above....

Made in the year of the Incarnation of the Lord 1110, in the reign of Louis [VI]. Seal of Bernard Atton, viscount of Carcassonne, seal of Raymond Mantellini, seal of Peter Roger of Barbazan, seal of Roger, son of the said viscount of Carcassonne, seal of Peter de Vitry, seal of Trencavel, son of the said viscount of Carcassonne, seal of William Hugo, seal of Lord Abbot Leo, who has accepted this acknowledgment of the homage of the said viscount.

And I, the monk John, have written this charter at the command of the said Lord Bernard Atton, viscount of Carcassonne, and of his sons, on the day and year given above, in the presence and witness of all those named above.

J. H. Robinson, ed., *Readings in European History* (Needham Heights, Massachusetts: Silver, Burdett, and Ginn, Inc., 1904), I, 180-182.

Study Questions

1. Who is the lord? Who is the vassal?

2. Who are Peter Roger of Barbazan, William Hugo, Raymond Mantellini and Peter de Vitry, *i.e.*, why are they mentioned by name? What is their function? Why is it necessary to indicate that they are nobles?

3. Why has Bernard Atton come to the monastery? Who has just died?

4. Describe Bernard Atton's fief. How many castles, manors and villages does he hold?

Medieval Society

5. *Can you describe "homage and fealty with hands and mouth"?*

6. *What clauses recognize the right of escheat?*

7. *Describe precisely the hospitality Bernard owes his lord.*

8. *Who is the monk John?*

SURVEY OF DUES from HURSTBOURNE PRIORY

The following list of rents is typical of what would have been owed by peasants on a large English manor. A "hide" is 120 acres.

Here are recorded the dues which the peasants must render at Hurstbourne. First from every hide they must render 40 pence at the autumnal equinox, and 6 church 'mittan' of ale and 3 sesters of wheat for bread, and they must plough 3 acres in their own time, and sow them with their own seed, and bring it to the born in their own time, and give 3 pounds of barley as rent, and mow half an acre of meadow as rent in their own time, and make it into a rick, and supply 4 fothers of split wood as rent, made into a stack in their own time, and supply 16 poles of fencing as rent likewise in their own time, and at Easter they shall give 2 ewes with 2 lambs --- and we reckon 2 young sheep to full-grown sheep --- and they must wash the sheep and shear them in their own time, and work as they are bidden every week except three --- one at midwinter, the second at Easter, the third at the Rogation Days.

David C. Douglas and George W. Greenway, eds., <u>English Historical Documents</u> (London: Eyre and Spottiswoode, 1953), II, 816.

Study Questions

1. What dues would fall under the heading of "corvée"?

2. Recalling that the rent comes from the hide, not from the individual peasant, in what cases might it have been excessive? When might it have been fairly easy to come up with? This survey is about 1050. Do you think the rent would have been affected by the Norman Conquest sixteen years later? (See next chapter.) Explain.

ARTICLES OF THE SPURRIERS GUILD OF LONDON

The following illustrates the habits and concerns of a group of medieval artisans. Spurriers, as the name implies, made spurs.

Be it remembered, that on Tuesday, the morrow of St. Peter's bonds, in the nineteenth year of the reign of King Edward III, the articles underwritten were read before John Hammond, mayor, Roger de Depham, recorder, and the other aldermen; and seeing that the same were deemed befitting, they were accepted and enrolled in these words.

In the first place, that no one of the trade of spurriers shall work longer than from the beginning of the day until curfew rings out at the church of St. Sepulcher, without Newgate; by reason that no man can work so neatly by night as by day. And many persons of the said trade, who compass how to practice deception in their work, desire to work by night rather than by day; and then they introduce false iron, and iron that has been cracked, for tin, and also they put gilt on false copper, and cracked.

And further, many of the said trade are wandering about all day, without working at all at their trade; and then, when they have become drunk and frantic, they take to their work, to the annoyance of the sick, and all their neighborhood as well, by reason of the broils that arise between them and the strange folk who are dwelling among them. And then they blow up their fires so vigorously, that their forges begin all at once to blaze, to the great peril of themselves and of all the neighborhood around. And then, too, all the neighbors are much in dread of the sparks, which so vigorously issue forth in all directions from the mouths of the chimneys in their forges.

By reason thereof it seems unto them that working by night should be put an end to, in order to avoid such false work and such perils; and therefore the mayor and the aldermen do will, by the assent of the good folk of the said trade and for the common profit, that from henceforth such time for working, and such false work made in the trade, shall be forbidden. And if any person shall be found in the said trade to do the contrary hereof, let him be amerced, the first time in forty pence, one half to go to the use of the Chamber of the Guildhall of London, and the other half to the use of the said trade; the second time, in half a mark; and the third time, in ten shillings, to the use of the same Chamber and trade; and the fourth time, let him forswear the trade forever.

Also, that no one of the said trade shall hang his spurs out on Sundays, or on any other days that are double feasts; but only a sign indicating his business; and such spurs as they shall so sell, they are to show and sell within their shops, without exposing them without or opening the doors or windows of their shops, on the pain aforesaid.

Also, that no one of the said trade shall keep a house or shop to carry on his business, unless he is free of the city; and that no one shall cause to be sold, or exposed for sale, any manner of old spurs for new ones, or shall garnish them or change them for new ones.

Also, that no one of the said trade shall take an apprentice for a less term than seven years, and such apprentice shall be enrolled according to the usages of the said city.

Also, that if any one of the said trade, who is not a freeman, shall take an apprentice for a term of years, he shall be amerced as aforesaid.

Also, that no one of the said trade shall receive the apprentice, serving man, or journeyman of another in the same trade, during the term agreed upon between his master and him, on the pain aforesaid.

Also, that no alien of another country, or foreigner of this country, shall follow or use the said trade, unless he is enfranchised before the mayor, aldermen, and chamberlain; and that, by witness and surety of the good folk of the said trade, who will go surety for him, as to his loyalty and his good behavior.

Also, that no one of the said trade shall work on Saturdays, after nones has been run out in the city; and not from that hour until the Monday morning following.

J. H. Robinson, ed., *Readings in European History*, (Boston: Ginn and Company, 1904) I, 409-411.

Study Questions

1. Why are these articles being read before the mayor and aldermen?

2. How long a work day shall the spurriers have? Why don't they want anyone working after dark?

3. Why doesn't the guild want inferior metals ("false iron", cracked iron, gilt copper)?

4. What kind of workers have become troublesome? What have they been doing that is particularly dangerous? What measures are being resolved upon to put an end to this nuisance?

5. Why do you think the guild doesn't want anyone to hang his spurs out on Sundays or other days that are double feasts? What is the guild trying to prevent?

6. Can you explain the phrase, "unless he is free of the city"?

7. What is the purpose of not selling old spurs for new ones or garnishing them?

8. What is the term of apprenticeships in the spurriers guild?

Medieval Society

9. What provision does the guild make regarding spurriers from other countries? What is a "foreigner of this country"?

10. How long is the weekend?

DECREES OF THE HANSEATIC LEAGUE, 1260-1264

In the twelfth century, two great trading networks had developed in northern Europe. One linked England with the cities of Flanders. English raw wool would be shipped to places like Bruges, Ghent, Antwerp and Brussels where the great textile guilds would turn it into finished cloth and then ship it back to England or markets in the rest of Europe.

The second network was actually much wider. The cities of the Hanse extended from London in the west to Novgorod in the east and included places like Danzig, Cologne, Hamburg and Bruges. The dominant member of the Hanseatic League, however, was Lubeck. The League negotiated trading rights and offered the members mutual security. Eventually in the fourteenth century, the League branched out into other parts of Germany, Italy, France and even Spain and Portugal. Furs, textiles, copper, iron, dried fish, grain, flax, hemp, wines, timber, pitch and salt were carried in League ships for sale at fairs where they had special exemptions from local fees.

This excerpt illuminates some of their problems.

We wish to inform you of the action taken in support of all merchants who are governed by the law of Lubeck.

(1) Each city shall, to the best of her ability, keep the sea clear of pirates, so that merchants may freely carry on their business by sea. (2) Whoever is expelled from one city because of a crime shall not be received in another. (3) If a citizen is seized [by pirates, robbers, or bandits] he shall not be ransomed, but his sword-belt and knife shall be sent to him [as a threat to his captors]. (4) Any merchant ransoming him shall lose all his possessions in all the cities which have the law

of Lubeck. (5) Whoever is proscribed in one city for robbery or theft shall be proscribed in all. (6) If a lord besieges a city, no one shall aid him in any way to the detriment of the besieged city, unless the besieger is his lord. (7) If there is a war in the country, no city shall on that account injure a citizen from the other cities, either in his person or goods, but shall give him protection. (8) If any man marries a woman in one city, and another woman from some other city comes and proves that he is her lawful husband, he shall be beheaded. (9) If a citizen gives his daughter or niece in marriage to a man [from another city], and another man comes and says that she is his lawful wife, but cannot prove it, he shall be beheaded.

This law shall be binding for a year, and after that the cities shall inform each other by letter of what decisions they make.

Oliver J. Thatcher and Edgar Holmes McNeal, eds., *A Source Book for Medieval History* (New York: Charles Scribner's Sons, 1905), 611-612.

Study Questions

1. Why does each city --- and not the League itself --- have the responsibility for dealing with pirates?

2. What's the purpose of #2?

3. Why is the ransoming of captives so strictly forbidden?

4. What practice are #8 and #9 trying to stop?

WILLIAM FITZ-STEPHEN, A DESCRIPTION OF MEDIEVAL LONDON, 1173

William Fitz-Stephen's view of London is as valuable for its picture of a thriving medieval metropolis as it is for his own civic pride.

Of the Site Thereof

Among the noble cities of the world that Fame celebrates the City of London of the Kingdom of the English, is the one seat that pours out its fame more widely, sends to farther lands its wealth and trade, lifts its head higher than the rest. It is happy in the healthiness of its air, in the Christian religion, in the strength of its defence, the nature of its site, the honour of its citizens, the modesty of its matrons; pleasant in sports; fruitful of noble men....

Of the Strength of the City

It has on the east the Palatine Castle, very great and strong, of which the ground plan and the walls rise from a very deep foundation, fixed with a mortar tempered by the blood of animals. On the west are two towers very strongly fortified, with the high and great wall of the city having seven double gates, and towered to the north at intervals. London was walled and towered in like mannner on the south, but the great fishbearing Thames river which there glides, with ebb and flow from the sea, by course of time has washed against, loosened, and thrown down those walls. Also upwards to the west the royal palace is conspicuous above the same river, an incomparable building with ramparts and bulwarks, two miles from the city, joined to it by a populous suburb.

Medieval Society

Of Gardens

Everywhere outside the houses of those living in the suburbs are joined to them, planted with trees, the spacious and beautiful gardens of the citizens.

Of Pasture and Tilth

Also there are, on the north side, pastures and a pleasant meadow land, through which flow river streams, where the turning wheels of mills are put in motion with a cheerful sound. Very near lies a great forest, with woodland pastures, coverts of wild animals, stags, fallow deer, boars and wild bulls. The tilled lands of the city are not of barren gravel but fat plains of Asia, that make crops luxuriant, and fill their tillers' barns with Ceres' sheaves.

Of Schools

In London three principal churches have by privilege and ancient dignity, famous schools; yet very often by support of some personage, or of some teachers who are considered notable and famous in philosophy, there are also other schools by favour and permission. On feast days the masters have festival meetings in the churches. Their scholars dispute, some by demonstration, others by dialectics; some recite enthymemes, others do better in using perfect syllogisms. Some are exercised in disputation for display, as wrestling with opponents; others for truth, which is the grace of perfectness. Sophists who feign are judged happy in their heap and flood of words. Others paralogize. Some orators, now and then, say in their rhetorical speeches something apt for persuasion, careful to observe rules of their art, and to omit none of the contingents. Boys of different schools strive against one another in verses, and contend about the principles of grammar....

Of the Ordering of the City

Those engaged in the several kinds of business, sellers of several things, contractors for several kinds of work, are distributed every morning into their several localities and shops. Besides, there is in London on the river bank, among the wines in ships and cellars sold by the vintners, a public cook shop; there eatables are to be found every day, according to the season, dishes of meat, roast, fried and boiled, great and small fish, coarser meats for the poor, more delicate for the rich, of game, fowls, and small birds....Outside one of the gates there, immediately in the suburb, is a certain field, smooth (Smith) field in fact and name. Every Friday, unless it be a higher day of appointed solemnity, there is in it a famous show of noble horses for sale. Earls, barons, knights, and many citizens who are in town, come to see or buy....In another part of the field stand by themselves the goods proper to rustics, implements of husbandry, swine with long flanks, cows with full udders, oxen of bulk immense, and woolly flocks....To this city from every nation under heaven merchants delight to bring their trade....This city...is divided into wards, has annual sheriffs for its consuls, has senatorial and lower magistrates, sewers and aqueducts in its streets, its proper places and separate courts for cases of each kind, deliberative, demonstrative, judicial; has assemblies on appointed days. I do not think there is a city with more commendable customs of church attendance, honour to God's ordinances, keeping sacred festivals, almsgiving, hospitality, confirming betrothals, contracting marriages, celebration of nuptials, preparing feasts, cheering the guests, and also in care for funerals and the interment of the dead. The only pests of London are the immoderate drinking of fools and the frequency of fires. To this may be added that nearly all the bishops, abbots, and magnates of England are, as it were, citizens and freemen of London; having there their own splendid houses, to which they resort, where they spend largely when summoned to great councils by the king or by their metropolitan, or drawn thither by their own private affairs.

C. Warren Hollister, ed., *Landmarks of the Western Heritage*, 2 Vols., 2nd ed. (New York: John Wiley and Sons, Inc., 1973), I, 258-261.

Medieval Society

Study Questions

1. *Where does William place London in relation to such cities as Venice, Constantinople, Jerusalem and Florence?*

2. *There are gardens, pastures, meadows, forests and "tilled lands" within the city. What does that tell us about the way in which some of the citizens earn their living?*

3. *How many "principal" schools are there? Where are they? What does this tell us about popular entertainment as well? Is there a parallel for such entertainments as these in modern American life?*

4. *Describe the Friday fair at Smith field.*

5. *What are the only pests in London?*

THE DEVELOPMENT OF MEDIEVAL STATES

One of the most remarkable achievements of the Middle Ages was the laying of the foundations of the modern state. As we have already seen, the breakdown of the Roman Empire had seen too the disappearance in Western Europe of a centralized state and its gradual replacement by feudal baronies. The most powerful of lords was able to exercise power only over a relatively few people. Yet it was out of the feudal system and a revived interest in Roman law, particularly in the towns, that the medieval state would emerge.

Medieval kings were essentially feudal lords. Their armies were their vassals, who had rights that the king, as lord, could not infringe upon. Yet if a king wanted to be a real king, he needed revenue, courts of law, police and military powers, a bureaucracy, the means to extend royal authority and to provide security to the very lowest peasant in his realm. He needed to be able to make war and peace, supply a currency and to raise and lead armies, rights that his vassals incidentally also had.

England

In the invasions of the ninth century, Britain had been attacked frequently by Danes. The seven Anglo-Saxon kingdoms were united under the king of Wessex, the remarkable Alfred the Great (871-899). Under continued pressure from the Danes, Alfred and his successors lay the foundations for a system of local government directly responsible to the king. England was divided into shires and each shire had a "reeve" directly responsible to the king.

From 1014 until 1042, England was part of a vast Scandinavian empire. Under Canute (1016-1035), who was king of England and after 1030 was also king of Norway, England became the center of that empire. Canute ruled with a <u>witan gamout</u> or council of the great men --- thegns, ealdormen, etc. ---

The Development of Medieval States 313

of the realm which met several times a year. Canute and his successor, Edward the Confessor (1035-1066), held more power than any of their contemporaries on the continent.

When Edward died without an heir, England's throne was disputed by two men, Edward's brother-in-law, Harold Godwin, and William I, duke of Normandy, to whom Edward had actually promised it. With the pope's blessing and the <u>witan gamout's</u> support, William invaded England and defeated and killed Harold at the battle of Hastings in 1066. The rest of the island was subdued and the lands divided among William himself, his Norman barons and the Church, and William required all feudal lords to swear allegiance to him as their liege lord. Norman feudalism thus was introduced into England. However, he kept the Anglo-Saxon institution of the shire reeve and actually expanded his duties. The shire reeve, or sheriff, caught and punished criminals, presided over the shire court where local customs were enforced, collected revenues for the king, preserved order and raised an army when the king ordered it. He was appointed by the king but received no pay. Thus began the pattern, continued into the nineteenth century, of making local people responsible for governing their own communities, but also of restricting public service to the wealthy who could afford the time.

William also retained the <u>witan gamout</u> and another Anglo-Saxon device, the "writ," a brief order written by a royal clerk by which the king could be kept in communication with every part of his realm. He also introduced the Norman inquest, or formal inquiry. The most famous of these was the <u>Domesday</u> survey, ordered in 1085. The resulting <u>Domesday Book</u> allowed William to tax and allot feudal services fairly. It also gives us an invaluable source of information on the life of the ordinary Englishman of the eleventh century.

Under William's sons, William Rufus (1089-1099) and Henry I (1100-1135), the conflict between Anglo-Saxon custom and Norman feudal law became apparent. Complicating matters were the overlapping jurisdictions of Church and commercial law. It was under Henry I that the process of shaping all of these into a single common law began to emerge. The <u>witan gamout</u> became the Great Council which met three times a year, as opposed to the king's small, private or Privy Council which advised him on a day-to-day basis. The chief officials on the Privy Council were the Chancellor who sent out the royal writs, a treasurer or head of the Exchequer, (so-called because he recorded accounts collected by the sheriffs on a checkered cloth), and a chief Justiciar who sent out circuit court judges to try cases in royal courts, thereby increasing royal power. Under Henry I, juries were used to give evidence but they did not yet render verdicts.

Henry I's death was followed by civil war. The claim of Henry's daughter Matilda, married to Geoffrey of Anjou, was disputed by her cousin Stephen. The civil war, a particularly nasty thing, was settled in 1151 when Matilda relinquished the throne to Stephen but only for his lifetime. It would be her heir, not his, who would succeed Stephen.

Matilda's son was Henry II. His patrimony was Normandy and Anjou, plus Maine and Touraine through his father. But he also married Eleanor, heiress to the rich counties of Aquitaine, Poitiers and Gascony. And besides England, Henry II also had claims to Scotland and Wales. Thus, when Henry II ascended to the English throne in 1154, he was the most powerful ruler in Western Europe.

Henry's most important achievements came in the area of law. The customs of the community --- common law --- were underwritten by the king's writ. The justiciars traveled from place to place to hear civil and criminal cases, and since they would often find it convenient to apply customs from one area to other places, common law shortly became unified. At the same time, the idea of the "king's peace" became current. Any breach of peace offended the king and it was the king who would preserve it. To that end, Henry ordered his sheriffs to have juries conduct inquests and draw up lists of known or suspected criminals who would then be tried by royal circuit judges who would come to the community at regular times throughout the year. Wherever they sat, there sat, in effect, the king, and any of his subjects could seek remedy in his courts. What Henry was doing was placing royal courts above feudal or even Church courts. Most Englishmen welcomed this simply because royal justice was notably cheaper, fairer and more efficient. But Henry did run head-on into a conflict with the Church on just that issue when he locked horns with his Archbishop of Canterbury, Thomas à Becket. While Thomas was a wholly sympathetic character, especially after his

The Development of Medieval States

murder, few Englishmen regretted Henry's reforms. Occasionally too, when a problem arose that involved a specific area or group of people, Henry would order an "assize," literally, a sitting of the people involved. Whatever decision they reached then had the force of royal law. Law then actually was the creation of the English people acting with their king.

Henry's sons, however, were far less interested in the details of managing. Richard I (1189-1199), the Lionheart, saw in England merely a source of revenue for his military capers. Shortly after he was crowned, he joined the Holy Roman Emperor, Frederick Barbarossa, and Philip Augustus of France in the Third Crusade and fought with his royal colleagues almost as much as he did the Turks. He was held captive by Frederick and was released a short six months before he died.

Interestingly, ministers and judges trained under Henry II capably managed England in Richard's absence. Thus, by the time Richard's brother, John I (1199-1216), succeeded him, Englishmen had a good bit of experience in managing their own affairs without a lot of interference from the king. This was John's undoing. An unreasonably suspicious man who saw plots where none could possibly have existed, John also inherited a financial problem. His father's wars in France and Richard's enormous ransom had depleted the Exchequer. In 1204, John also lost Normandy to Philip Augustus and then tried fitfully and unsuccessfully to regain it. His incompetence as a soldier would have diminished him in the eyes of his nobles anyway but to worsen matters, he took scutage, a tax paid by nobles in lieu of military service. Scutage itself would have been acceptable had John been willing to renew the campaign but he gave one excuse after another for not doing so. When he finally did go to war, he lost again to Philip at the battle of Bouvines in Flanders in 1214.

Meanwhile the Church had also become his enemy, primarily because he had refused to accept Pope Innocent III's candidate, Stephen Langton, to the see of Canterbury. Innocent had responded by excommunicating John, thus throwing into doubt the legitimacy of royal courts. John had also angered the towns by extorting tolls and duties and threatening to revoke their charters of self-government.

Bouvines was the last straw. Led by Langton (John had been forced to accept him finally) and William Marshall, the doughty old Earl of Pembroke, the chief lay and Church lords forced John to meet them in a meadow called Runnymede in June 1215 where he signed Magna Carta --- the Great Charter, the cornerstone of English and American liberties. In signing it, John bound himself and every English king thereafter under the rule of law.

Magna Carta was an outgrowth, a result of a process that had been maturing for over a century. Englishmen were not about to abolish royal authority. Quite the contrary! Royal judges enforcing royal law which was rational, even-handed and moreover, derived from the customs of the common folk of England, suited Englishmen quite well. Even under a fairly weak king such as Henry III (1216-1272), respect for royal law and royal courts promoted respect for the crown itself. Under Edward I (1272-1307) a single law, common law, "self-government by the king's command," ran throughout every shire in England.

France

When Hugh Capet, Count of Paris, was crowned in 987, his kingdom was the tiny Ile-de-France stretching from Laon to Orleans and centered at Paris. Even over that, his authority was divided among vassals, several of whom possessed greater holdings than he. Hugh and his successors achieved very little at first but they survived. Each king crowned his successor, thus weakening the principle of election, and by shrewd marriages, and also perhaps because they were too weak to be taken seriously, they hung on to what they had and gradually even enlarged it a bit. Even so, Louis VI (1108-1137) was called "le roi de Saint Denis" because his realm was really no more than Paris and St. Denis. The connection of the Capetians with St. Denis was important, however. According to tradition, St. Denis who had proselytized the area around Paris and had been martyred, had crowned Clovis, and the holy oil with which he had been anointed was carefully preserved in the abbey there. It was under St. Denis' banner, the "oriflamme," that Hugh and his successors marched into battle. As insignificant as they may have been then, the Capetians alone would be able to claim a truly national loyalty.

It was Louis VI who began to expand royal power by curbing the power of the great barons in his own duchy. He also began to flesh out a royal administration by relying on trusted and capable men, often drawn from the ranks of the petty nobility. One of these was Abbot Suger, who would lay the pattern for Gothic architecture. Also, his court began to look like a regular instrument of government. By the time he died, it was even hearing cases from outside the Ile-de-France. His most brilliant coup, however, was the marriage of his son, the future Louis VII, to Eleanor, heiress to the vast duchy of Aquitaine. Unhappily, Louis' divorce from Eleanor would send that lady and her stupendous dowry into the arms of the future king of England, Henry II.

Under Philip Augustus (1180-1223), however, the Ile-de-France became the most formidable power in France. After squelching a baronial plot to seize the crown, Philip secured Artois and Vermandois in the north. His greatest rival, however, was his powerful vassal the king of England, who controlled about half of what would someday be France. Philip wrested Normandy from King John in 1204, as we have already seen, and within two years he had also gained Maine, Anjou and Touraine, thus trebling the size of his kingdom.

Philip Augustus also devised an efficient administration using members of the clergy and the urban middle class. He would sometimes go to the defense of a town or a bishop or monastery threatened by a secular lord. In this way he was tying two powerful and wealthy institutions, the Church and the towns, to the monarchy. Each province had its own customs and institutions but royal officials (called <u>baillis</u> in the north and <u>seneschals</u> in the south) linked the provinces with the government in Paris. Appointed and paid by the king, they had full judicial, financial and military authority in their districts. The massive enlargement of the royal domain obviously carried with it a substantial increase in royal revenues.

Philip's successor, the saintly Louis IX (1226-1270), prohibited private warfare among his nobles and issued other ordinances without seeking their consent. A currency produced by a royal mint circulated throughout the realm. The thirteenth-century French kings were creating a professional royal bureaucracy marked by diversity at the local level and centralization at the top. They also began to control the organs of justice as more and more cases were taken from feudal courts into the king's. Moreover, it became possible to appeal a decision in a feudal court to the king's court. The highest court was the king's parliament in Paris but often the kings would meet in local parliaments to settle problems involving a specific area or group of people. Like the English assize, the local parliament's decision had the backing of royal law behind it. Nothing like the English common law evolved but the essentials of the system remained intact until 1789.

By war, diplomacy, prudent marriages and inheritances, Philip's descendants added Poitou, Provence and Languedoc to the royal domain. By the end of the thirteenth century, the French king was stronger than any one or any group of nobles who might oppose him.

Holy Roman Empire

In 910, the most powerful magnates in what was left of Charlemagne's eastern empire came together and elected one of themselves as king. The man chosen was Conrad, duke of Franconia. No one meant for Conrad to act like a real king, but the little muscle flexing he did induced the nobles to bypass his heir at Conrad's death. They elected Henry I, the Fowler (919-936), Duke of Saxony.

Once king, Henry, like Conrad, worked to expand his authority over the nobles who had elected him. He began to use officials called "ministeriales," officials appointed by and paid by him and exercising judicial and military functions. Henry's son, Otto I (936-973), expanded the use of the ministeriales. Taking Aachen as the site of his coronation in order to associate himself with Charlemagne, Otto deliberately tied the Church to the crown. He asserted the right to "invest" bishops and abbots with the ring and staff of pastoral authority. This is called "lay investiture" --- a layman invests someone in clerical office. They could not take office without these and they gave Otto feudal homage for the lands connected with the office. Thus, every major churchman was also Otto's vassal. At this point, few people even in the Church itself thought it was terribly wrong. Powerful lords and princes everywhere used lay investiture. If anything, the use of the Church to enforce royal, as against feudal authority, was a better

The Development of Medieval States

guarantor of peace and order and a better defense against the Magyar invaders from the East. Many of the ministeriales were churchmen, and the bulk of Otto's army came from church lands.

In 955, Otto inflicted a crushing defeat on a major Magyar force at the battle of Lechfeld. Not only did Otto then appear as the savior of Christendom, a worthy successor to Charlemagne, but also to Charlemagne's title. In 962, therefore, Otto was crowned by the pope as Holy Roman Emperor. His marriage to Adelaide, Countess of Tuscany, bordering the Papal States, along with the title established him as the protector of the Papacy --- a role that would bedevil both sides for centuries.

In 1035, Henry III rode into Rome to settle a disputed election. He named as his candidate Bruno, Bishop of Toul and, backed by Henry's troops, Bruno won. He took the name Leo IX and began that series of reforms which culminated in the Investiture Contest. (See next chapter.) The conflict with the Papacy left the Empire in disarray. The real winners were the secular princes --- the hundreds of principalities, duchies and bishoprics which held sway over rather small areas.

Developing a centralized government in Germany was much more complicated than in England or France. One asset the kings of the Ile-de-France had had was that they were too insignificant to be taken seriously until it was too late for the nobility to oppose them. But the German princes had had a taste of imperial power wielded at their own expense and they had no great desire to let it be repeated. Since there was no accepted principle of succession either, the death of the emperor invariably brought on disputes. To worsen matters, the title itself and its associations with Charlemagne and his empire, involved the emperors time and again in Italian affairs and thus with the Papacy. When Conrad III died in 1152, the chaos was so terrible that the seven electors --- the princes who chose the emperor --- elected a very strong ruler, Frederick Barbarossa, Duke of Swabia.

Frederick (1152-1190) tried to unite his squabbling nobles as the French kings had by using his family domain, Swabia, as a power base. He ordered all the nobles in Swabia to swear liege homage to him and then used ministeriales to exercise royal authority much as William the Conqueror had done in England. Then, outside Swabia, he made alliances with lay princes by which they recognized that they held their fiefs of the emperor but in return for wide military and judicial powers in those fiefs. But at an assembly at Roncaglia, Italy, in 1158, Frederick made it quite clear that private warfare was forbidden not only in Italy but throughout the empire. Great churchmen were also his vassals and when they died, because of the vow of celibacy, their estates automatically reverted to him. Unable to resist the lure of Italy, however, and believing that their interminable squabbles had made them nicely vulnerable, Frederick attacked. What he missed was that those squabbling city-states did value their independence and that even the Papacy, fearing renewed German interference in northern Italy, was willing to throw its weight behind the towns. After a terrible defeat at the battle of Legnano in 1176 in which feudal cavalry were defeated for the first time by town infantry, Frederick was forced to concede independence to the Italian towns. Legnano was the signal for Frederick's clergy and nobility to reassert their independence too.

Italy was costly, yet its allure invited continued German intervention. Frederick Barbarossa's grandson and heir, Frederick III (1212-1250), was a conscientious administrator. The "wonder of the world" to his contemporaries, he forbade personal warfare, brought all castles under royal control and replaced town officials with royal governors. His Constitutions of Malfi in 1231 put both feudal and church courts under royal jurisdiction and even churchmen accused of crimes were to be tried in royal rather than church courts. The towns were also subordinated to the crown. The University of Naples founded by Frederick in 1224 trained officials for the royal bureaucracy in Roman legal principles. His financial experts regulated the collection of customs, public works, trade, agriculture and greatly increased royal revenues. Frederick was able even to tax his people without too much fuss.

Again, though, there was Italy. Frederick had a habit of concentrating on Sicily rather than Swabia and he was willing to grant large concessions to his German towns and princes in return for their support of his Italian policy. As a result, imperial authority was badly weakened and when Frederick died, lay and church lords again held sway over a fragmented empire. The only realistic claimant to the universal government of Latin Christendom was ironically, the Emperor's old enemy, the Papacy.

Suggested Readings

1. Barraclough, G., *The Origins of Modern Germany* (Oxford: B. Blackwell, 1946). Still a standard text on the medieval Holy Roman Empire.

2. Fawtier, R., *The Capetian Kings of France* (New York: St. Martin's Press, 1960). A highly readable introduction to the subject.

3. Hallam, E., *Capetian France, 987-1328* (London, New York: Longmans, 1980). An excellent survey of the medieval French monarchy.

4. Holt, J. C., *Magna Carta* (Cambridge: University Press, 1965). The best recent analysis of that document.

5. Howarth, D., *1066: The Year of the Conquest* (New York: Viking Press, 1978). A lively account of the Norman conquest from the perspective of Normans, Scandinavians and English. Utterly delightful reading.

6. Petit-Dutaillis, Charles, *The Feudal Monarchy in France and England* (New York: Harper & Row, 1964). Compares the development of the monarchies in those two states.

7. Sayles, G. O., *The Medieval Foundations of England* (New York: Barnes & Noble, 1961). Traces the foundations of political and social institutions to the end of the twelfth century.

8. Strayer, J. R., *On the Medieval Origins of the Modern State* (Princeton, N. J.: Princeton University Press, 1970). Shows how elements of medieval state building survive in modern institutions.

From the DOMESDAY BOOK

The Domesday survey is one of the most remarkable records of the Middle Ages. Not since Roman times had any ruler ordered such a thorough and far-reaching census, nor would its parallel be seen again until the nineteenth century.

Domesday is a tribute to the energy and curiosity of the man who ordered it, William the Conqueror, but it also attests the fairly advanced state of Anglo-Saxon institutions which William found in England. Not only had Anglo-Saxon kings divided England into shires but they had minted a coinage and were able to collect substantial amounts of silver from a tax called the Danegeld, so-called because it had originally been levied to buy off marauding Danish invaders. Even at this early point, the Danegeld was beginning to come from an economy turned toward wool.

The survey was launched at Christmas 1085 and completed the following year. All of England (except for the north which still eluded Norman control) was divided into seven districts to each of which were assigned three or four commissioners whose task was to verify information given by tenants-in-chief about their holdings. All land was held by William directly or indirectly. Below the king were his tenants-in-chief. Bishops and abbots were often in this category. They also included Norman barons who had swept aside the Anglo-Saxon nobility. Below the tenants-in-chief were the under-tenants.

The name of the survey is itself interesting. It refers to the Day of Judgment from which there is no appeal. Nor was there to be any appeal from this. At first, there was a good bit of resentment about Domesday. In the civil war between Matilda and Stephen (1135-1151), however, property changed hands rather frequently. In order to end the disputes peaceably, Henry II, when he ascended to the throne in 1154, went back to

The Development of Medieval States

Domesday to certify who rightly held what. Many times thereafter, it was Domesday that was the final arbiter in property disputes.

The document below may well be unintelligible without an explanation of terms. The term "hide" was used for tax purposes and was 120 acres. A "plough" is a team of eight oxen and the plough itself. A "mill" is a water mill used for grinding wheat. A "villager" is a peasant with the most land; a "smallholder" held a bit less and a "cottager" held very little or no land, only his own cottage. A "slave" owed personal service and could not buy or sell of his own choice nor could he change his work or home without permission. The term "in lordship" indicates that Roger de Raismes held Dedham directly from the king as a tenant-in-chief. "Then" is before 1066; "now" is in 1086.

Dedham is a beautiful town located in Essex which came to prominence on the wool trade.

Roger (de Raismes) holds DEDHAM DELHAM in lordship, which Aelfric Kemp held as a manor, for 2 1/2 hides. Then 7 villagers, now 5; always 24 smallholders. Then 4 slaves, now 3. Then 2 ploughs in lordship, now 3. Then among the men 10 ploughs, now 5. Woodland, 250 pigs; meadow, 40 acres; then 1 mill, now 2. Then 2 cobs, now 10; then 5 cows, now 3; then 40 sheep, now 100; then 25 pigs, now 30. Value always 12. Of this manor, Gerald holds 30 acres. Value 10 s. in the same assessment.

Thomas Hinde, ed., *The Domesday Book* (London: Century Hutchinsons, Ltd., 1985), 98.

Study Questions

1. Who held Dedham before the Conquest? What has happened to the number of smallholders since 1066? Of villagers? Of slaves?

2. *Looking at the number of ploughs, and also at the establishment of another mill since 1066, what particular crop seems to have been expanded?*

3. *What has happened to the number of livestock? In terms of land use, what direction does this manor seem to be heading in? (Look at the sheep.)*

4. *Who do you think Gerald is? What status did he have before 1066? What do you think he's doing now?*

From MAGNA CARTA, 1215

Following King John's defeat at the Battle of Bouvines in 1214, his nobles stood on the brink of revolt. Moody, cruel and sometimes even sadistic, John had not been forgiven for his loss of Normandy to Philip Augustus in 1204, nor had England sympathized with him at all in his quarrel with Pope Innocent III over the appointment of Stephen Langton as Archbishop of Canterbury. Although in 1213 John had been forced to accept Langton, his stand regarding the Church had not enhanced his position with the latter nor with his barons.

The truth is John was not a bad king. He was intelligent, fair, he relied on superior officials such as William Marshall, Earl of Pembroke, and Geoffrey Fitz Peter, his chief Justiciar, and he was generous to the poor. But he was also unlucky. He followed his brother, Richard, who had spent most of his ten-year reign crusading. In his absence, Englishmen had governed themselves --- as Henry II had in fact taught them to do. John understandably thought kings did that job and he ran up against nobles who were getting used to managing shire affairs on their own. They perhaps could have endured John's taxes and fines had there been victories in France. But there had been only defeats and Bouvines was the last straw.

In March 1215, a group of lords met at Stamford and set out to capture a strategic royal castle at Northampton. They failed to take it but then they marched on London where they were welcomed by a group of citizens. Archbishop Langton acted as an intermediary between the two sides and a truce was arranged on May 27. On June 15, John and his advisors met the nobles in a meadow running along the river Thames, Runnymede. There he signed a draft agreement. Four days later, after Langton and others had touched it up, that document was converted into the Magna Carta.

It has been hailed as the charter of American and English liberties but it really only became that in future generations. In 1215, it was simply a bargain struck between a king and his subjects to redress grievances that were not only private but sometimes selfish.

John, by the grace of God, king of England, lord of Ireland, duke of Normandy and Aquitaine, count of Anjou, to the archbishops, bishops, abbots, earls, barons, justiciars, foresters, sheriffs, reeves, servants and all bailiffs and his faithful people greeting. Know that by the suggestion of God and for the good of our soul and those of all our predecessors and of our heirs, to the honor of God and the exaltation of holy church, and the improvement of our kingdom, by the advice of our venerable fathers Stephen, archbishop of Canterbury, primate of all England and cardinal of the holy Roman church, [and other churchmen]...and of the noblemen William Marshall, earl of Pembroke, [and others]....

In the first place we have granted to God, and by this our present charter confirmed, for us and our heirs forever, that the English church shall be free, and shall hold its rights entire and its liberties uninjured; and we will that it thus be observed; which is shown by this, that the freedom of elections, which is considered to be most important and especially necessary to the English church, we, of our pure and spontaneous will, granted, and by our charter confirmed, before the contest between us and our barons had arisen; and obtained a confirmation of it by the lord Pope Innocent III; which we will observe and which we will shall be observed in good faith by our heirs forever.

We have granted moreover to all free men of our kingdom for us and our heirs forever all the liberties written below, to be had and holden by themselves and their heirs from us and our heirs.

If any of our earls or barons, or others holding from us in chief by military service shall have died, and when he has died his heir shall be of full age and owe relief, he shall have his inheritance by the ancient relief; that is to say, the heir or heirs of an earl for the whole barony of an earl a hundred pounds; the heir or heirs of a baron for a whole barony a hundred pounds; the heir or heirs of a knight, for a whole knight's fee, a hundred shillings at most; and who owes less let him give less according to the ancient custom of fiefs.

If moreover the heir of any one of such shall be under age, and shall be wardship, when he comes of age he shall have his inheritance without relief and without a fine.

The custodian of the land of such a minor heir shall not take from the land of the heir any except reasonable products, reasonable customary payments, and reasonable services, and this without destruction or waste of men or of property....

No widow shall be compelled to marry so long as she prefers to live without a husband, provided she gives security that she will not marry without our consent, if she holds from us, or without the consent of her lord from whom she holds, if she holds from another....

No scutage or aid shall be imposed in our kingdom except by the common council of our kingdom, except for the ransoming of our body, for the making of our oldest son a knight, and for once marrying our oldest daughter, and for these purposes it shall be only a reasonable aid; in the same way it shall be done concerning the aids of the city of London.

And the city of London shall have all its ancient liberties and free customs, as well by land as by water. Moreover, we will and grant that all other cities and boroughs and villages and ports shall have all their liberties and free customs.

And for holding a common council of the kingdom concerning the assessment of an aid otherwise than in the three cases mentioned above, or concerning the assessment of a scutage we shall cause to be summoned the archbishops, bishops, abbots, earls, and greater barons by our letters under seal; and besides we shall cause to be summoned generally, by our sheriffs and bailiffs all those who hold from us in chief, for a certain day, that is at the end of forty days at least, and for a certain place; and in all the letters of that summons, we will express the cause of the summons, and when the summons has thus been given the business shall proceed on the appointed day, on the advice of those who shall be present, even if not all of those who were summoned have come.

We will not grant to any one, moreover, that he shall take an aid from his free men, except for ransoming his body, for making his oldest son a knight, and for once marrying his oldest daughter; and for these purposes only a reasonable aid shall be taken.

No one shall be compelled to perform any greater service for a knight's fee, or for any other free tenement than is owed from it....

A free man shall not be fined for a small offence, except in proportion to the measure of the offence; and for a great offence he shall be fined in proportion to the magnitude of the offence, saving his freehold; and a merchant in the same way, saving his merchandise; and the villein shall be fined in the same way, saving his wainage, if he shall be at our mercy; and none of the above fines shall be imposed except by the oaths of honest men of the neighborhood.

Earls and barons shall only be fined by their peers, and only in proportion to their offence.

A clergyman shall be fined, like those before mentioned, only in proportion to his lay holding, and not according to the extent of his ecclesiastical benefice....

No constable or other bailiff of ours shall take anyone's grain or other chattels, without immediately paying for them in money, unless he is able to obtain a postponement at the good-will of the seller.

No constable shall require any knight to give money in place of his ward of a castle if he is willing to furnish that ward in his own person or through another honest man, if he himself is not able to do it for a reasonable cause; and if we shall lead or send him into the army he shall be free from ward in proportion to the amount of time by which he has been in the army through us.

No sheriff or bailiff of ours or any one else shall take horses or wagons of any free man for carrying purposes except on the permission of that free man.

Neither we nor our bailiffs will take the wood of another man for castles, or for anything else which we are doing, except by the permission of him to whom the wood belongs....

No free man shall be taken or imprisoned or dispossessed, or outlawed, or banished, or in any way destroyed, nor will we go upon him, nor send upon him, except by the legal judgment of his peers or by the law of the land.

To no one will we sell, to no one will we deny, or delay right or justice.

All merchants shall be safe and secure in going out from England and coming into England and in remaining and going through England, as well by land as by water, for buying and selling, free from all evil tolls, by the ancient and rightful customs, except in time of war, and if they are of a land at war with us; and if such are found in our land at the beginning of war, they shall be attached without injury to their bodies or goods, until it shall be known from us or from our principal Justiciar in what way the merchants or our land are treated who shall be then found in the country which is at war with us; and if ours are safe there, the others shall be safe in our land....

We will not make justiciars, constables, sheriffs or bailiffs except of such as know the law of the realm and are well inclined to observe it.

All barons who have founded abbeys for which they have charters of kings of England, or ancient tenure, shall have their custody when they have become vacant, as they ought to have....

All the bad customs concerning forests and warrens and concerning foresters and warreners, sheriffs and their servants, river banks and their guardians shall be inquired into immediately in each county by twelve sworn knights of the same county, who shall be elected by the honest men of the same county, and within forty days after the inquisition has been made, they shall be entirely destroyed by them, never to be restored, provided that we be first informed of it, or our Justiciar, if we are not in England.

We will give back immediately all hostages and charters which have been liberated to us by Englishmen as security for peace or for faithful service....

And immediately after the re-establishment of peace we will remove from the kingdom all foreign-born soldiers, cross-bow men, servants, and mercenaries who have come with horses and arms for the injury of the realm.

If anyone shall have been dispossessed or removed by us without legal judgment of his peers, from his land, castles, franchises, or his right we will restore them to him immediately....

All fines which have been imposed unjustly and against the law of the land, and all penalties imposed unjustly and against the law of the land are altogether excused, or will be on the judgment of the twenty-five barons of whom mention is made below in connection with the security of the peace, or on the judgment of the majority of them, along with the aforesaid Stephen, archbishop of Canterbury....

Since, moreover, for the sake of God, and for the improvement of kingdom, and for the better quieting of the hostility sprung up lately between us and our barons, we have made all these concessions; wishing them to enjoy these in a complete and firm stability for ever, we make and concede to them the security described below; that is to say, that they shall elect twenty-five barons of the kingdom, whom they will, who ought with all their power to observe, hold, and cause to be observed, the peace and liberties which we have conceded to them, and by this our present charter confirmed to them; in this manner, that if we or our Justiciar, or our bailiffs, or any one of our servants shall have done wrong in any way toward any one, or shall have transgressed any of the articles of peace or security; and the wrong shall have been shown to four barons of the aforesaid twenty-five barons, let those four barons come to us or to our Justicier, if we are out of the kingdom, laying before us the transgression, and let them ask that we cause that transgression to be corrected without delay. And if we shall not have corrected the transgression or, if we shall be out of the kingdom, if our Justicier shall not have corrected it within a period of forty days, counting from the time in which it has been shown to us or to our Justicier, if we are out of the kingdom; the aforesaid four barons shall refer the matter to the remainder of the twenty-five barons, and let these twenty-five barons with the whole community of the country distress and injure us in every way they can; that is to say by the seizure of our castles, lands, possessions, and in such other ways as they can until it shall have been corrected according to their judgment, saving our person and that of our queen, and those of our children; and when the correction has been made, let them devote themselves to us as they did before. And let whoever in the country wishes take an oath that in all the above-mentioned measures he will obey the orders of the aforesaid twenty-five barons, and that he will injure us as far as he is able with them, and we give permission to swear publicly and freely to each one who wishes to swear, and no one will we ever forbid to swear. All those, moreover, in the country who of themselves and their own will are unwilling to take an oath to the twenty-five barons as to distressing and injuring us along with the, we will compel to take the oath by our mandate, as before said....

Wherefore we will and firmly command that the Church of England shall be free and that the men in our kingdom shall have and hold all the aforesaid liberties rights and concessions, well and peacefully, freely and quietly, fully and completely, for themselves and their heirs, from us and our heirs, in all things and places, forever, so before said. It has been sworn, moreover, as well on our part as on the part of the barons, that all these things spoken of above shall be observed in good faith and without any evil intent. Witness the above named and many others. Given by our hand in the meadow which is called Runnymede, between Windsor and Staines, on the fifteenth day of June, in the seventeenth year of our reign.

C. Warren Hollister, ed., *Landmarks of the Western Heritage*, 2nd ed., 2 vols. (New York: John Wiley and Sons, Inc., 1969), I, 242-247.

Study Questions

1. What lands is John claiming that he no longer holds? Why is he claiming them?

2. In the first paragraph, what is apparently the motive for the Charter? Remember that John did not write this; he only signed it. Why do you think this kind of language is used?

3. What rights is John confirming for the Church?

4. What rights of inheritance are being confirmed to the nobility? What do you suppose John had been doing?

5. What rights are being confirmed to widows? What had John been doing?

6. When can scutage or aid be imposed? What slogan in the American Revolution arose from this clause?

7. What rights are being confirmed to towns?

8. What kind of people constitute a "common council of the kingdom"?

9. How shall fines be determined for freemen? Who fines nobles? Clergy?

10. Who alone may judge freemen?

11. If "hostages and charters" are to be given back immediately, what do you suppose John had been doing and why?

12. What are the twenty-five elected barons supposed to do? What is happening to the power of the monarchy at this point?

ELECTION OF HUGH CAPET, 987

In 987, the last direct descendant of Charlemagne, Louis V, died and many of the great lords attended his funeral. Before they left to go home, however, they met to consider what to do. The Archbishop of Rheims, Adalbero, didn't think they should choose a king until all the barons could meet. Most of the barons agreed but Charles of Lorraine, the late king's uncle, was unwilling to wait for a decision of all the barons and tried to get Adalbero to support his own claim to the throne. The archbishop put him off and this then is what happened.

Meanwhile the nobles of Gaul who had taken the oath came together at the appointed time at Senlis; when they had all taken their places in the assembly, the duke, *[Hugh Capet who was presiding at the meeting]* having made a sign to the archbishop of Rheims, the latter expressed himself as follows: "King Louis, of divine memory, left no children; we must therefore take counsel as to the choice of a successor, in order that the country shall not come to ruin through neglect and the lack of a pilot. Our deliberations on this subject were recently postponed, by common consent, in order that each one might here voice the sentiments with which God might inspire him, and that from all these individual opinions a general and collective decision might be reached.

"Now that we are once more assembled together, let us endeavor, in all prudence and rectitude, not to sacrifice reason and truth to our personal likes or dislikes. We know that Charles has his partisans, who claim that the throne belongs to him by right of birth. Regarding the question from this point of view, we reply that the throne cannot be acquired by hereditary right. Nor should one be placed upon it who is not distinguished alike by nobility of body and wisdom of mind, and by his good faith and magnanimity. We see in the annals of history rulers of illustrious origin deposed on account of their unworthiness, and replaced by incumbents of equal, or even of inferior, birth.

"And what is there to recommend Charles of Lorraine? He is feeble and without honor, faith, or character; he has not blushed to become the servitor of a foreign king *[the German emperor]*, nor to take to wife a girl of only knightly rank. How could the great duke bear that a woman belonging to the lowest rank of his vassals should be queen and rule over him? How could he give precedence to a woman, when his equals and even his superiors in birth bend the knee before him and place their hands beneath his feet? If you consider this matter carefully, you will see that Charles' fall has been brought about through his own fault rather than that of others.

"Make a choice, therefore, that shall insure the welfare of the state instead of being its ruin. If you wish ill to your country, choose Charles; if you wish to see it prosperous make Hugh, the glorious duke, king. Do not let yourselves be misled by your sympathy for Charles, nor blinded to the common good by hatred of the duke. For if you blame the good, how can you praise the bad? If you praise the bad, how despise the good? Remember the words of the Scripture: 'Woe unto them that call evil good, and good evil that put darkness for light, and light for darkness.' Choose the duke, therefore; he is the most illustrious among us by reason of his exploits, his nobility, and his military following. Not only the state, but every individual interest will find in him a protector. His great-heartedness will render him a father to you all. Who has ever fled to him for aid and been disappointed? Who that has been left in the lurch by his friends has he ever failed to restore to his rights?"

This discourse was received with universal applause, and by unanimous consent the duke was raised to the throne. He was crowned at Noyon on the first of June, by the archbishop and the other bishops, as king of the Gauls, the Bretons, the Danes (Normans?), the Aquitanians, the Goths, the Spaniards, and the Gascons. Surrounded by the nobles of the kingdom, he issued decrees and made laws according to royal custom, judging and disposing of all matters with success.

James Harvey Robinson, *Readings in European History*, 2 vols. (Needham Heights, Massachusetts: Silver, Burdett, and Ginn, Inc., 1904), I, 194-196.

Study Questions

1. *What right to the throne does Adalbero concede to Charles? How does he treat that right? Why doesn't he think Charles would be a good choice?*

2. *What does Hugh have to recommend him?*

3. *Of what peoples is Hugh crowned king? Do you think he is recognized by them all?*

4. *Can you guess what some of Hugh's problems are going to be?*

PHILIP AUGUSTUS ACQUIRES VERMANDOIS

A major thread that runs through French history down to the Revolution in 1789 is the perennial conflict between the nobility and the monarchy. A very young king or a weak one gave the nobles a chance to increase their own power at the monarchy's expense and rarely did they all resist the temptation. Here the young king opposes the claim of his very powerful count of Flanders to the district of Vermandois.

In the year of our Lord's Incarnation 1184, the fifth year of Philip Augustus' reign and the twentieth of his age, a dispute arose, as is not uncommon in times of change, between Philip, most Christian king of the French, and Philip, count of Flanders, about a certain district commonly called Vermandois.

The king claimed that all Vermandois, with its castles, villages, and vills, belonged by right of inheritance and succession to the kings of the French; and he offered to prove it all by the testimony of clergy and laity, --- archbishops, bishops, counts, viscounts, and other nobles.

The count of Flanders replied that he had held the land in question during the lifetime of the most Christian king Louis, of blessed memory, and had possessed it in peace, without any dispute, during many years, and was firmly resolved never to give it up so long as he lived. For the count believed that, since the king was but a lad, he could easily divert his mind from this project by promises and flattering words. Besides, it is said that many nobles were ready to support him; but, as the proverb says, "They are sons of the winds, they weave cobwebs."

At length Philip Augustus followed the advice of the princes and barons and called together all the nobles of his lands in the beautiful castle of Karnopolis, commonly called Compiegne. He took counsel with them, and collected a very large army at the city which is called Amiens.

When the count of Flanders heard of the king's coming his heart rejoiced. He collected an army to oppose Philip, directed his forces against his lord, the king, and swore by the strength of his arm that he could defend himself against all men. Thus in the fifth year of his reign and the twentieth of his age the king entered into that land with his army, which covered the face of the earth like locusts. When the count of Flanders saw the king's army, that it was very great and strong, his spirit was troubled, and the hearts of his people became as water, so that they sought safety in flight. Then the count took counsel with his own, and sent messengers to call to his presence Theobald, count of Blois, chief of the king's knights and sene schal of France, and William, archbishop of Rheims-- both uncles of the king, to whom the direction of affairs had been intrusted at this time because they were faithful to the king.

The count of Flanders used them as intermediaries and through them addressed the king in this wise: "Let thine anger toward us cease, Lord. Come to us in peaceful guise, and use our service as shall be pleasing in thy sight. The land which thou desirest, my lord king, Vermandois, with all the castles and vills belonging to it, I will restore to thee, my lord king, in its entirety, freely, and without delay. But if it shall please your royal majesty, I beg that the castle of St. Quentin and the castle of Peronne may be granted to me as a kingly gift to be held so long as I live. After my death they shall, without controversy, devolve upon thee or thy successors, the kings of the French."

When Philip, most Christian king of the French, had heard this message, he called together all the archbishops, bishops, abbots, counts, viscounts, and all the barons who had come with one accord to subdue the insolence of the count of Flanders and to humble his pride. He took counsel with them, and they answered as with one voice that this which the count of Flanders proposed to the king should be done. When this decision had been reached, the count of Flanders was introduced, and before all the nobles and the throng gathered there, he restored to Philip, the lawful king, the land he had so long wrongfully held; and then and there, after he had restored the land before them all, he put the king in possession of it.

Further, he promised the king upon his oath to make good, without delay, and according to the king's will, all the losses he had inflicted upon Baldwin, count of Hainault, and other friends of the king. And thus was peace restored between the king and the count as by a miracle, for it was concluded without shedding human blood. And when all the people heard of these things they were filled with great joy, and praised and blessed God who saves those who put their hope in him.

J. H. Robinson, ed., *Readings in European History* (Boston: Ginn and Company, 1904) I, 207-209.

Study Questions

1. How old is Philip Augustus now? How old was he when he became king?

2. Who initiates the quarrel? On what grounds? What does his age have to do with the Count of Flanders' action? What claim does the count make for Vermandois?

3. How much support does the king have?

4. Who act as intermediaries? What agreement is reached?

5. Why is the agreement hailed as a miracle? What does that tell us about the way in which such quarrels usually ended?

JEAN de JOINVILLE on LOUIS IX

Joinville, (1226-1270) a noble, served as seneschal of Champagne. He faithfully served Louis IX and was a witness to the disastrous crusade of Louis which he described in the <u>Histoire de Saint Louis</u>. To many people in the Middle Ages and afterwards, Louis was the archetype of the perfect Christian ruler.

This holy man loved God with all his heart, and followed Him in His acts; and this appeared in that, as God died for the love He bore His people, so did the king put his body in peril, and that several times, for the love he bore to his people; and such peril he might well have avoided, as you shall be told hereafter.

The great love that he bore to his people appeared in what he said during a very sore sickness that he had at Fontainebleau, unto my lord Lewis, his eldest son. "Fair son," he said, "I pray thee to make thyself beloved of the people of thy kingdom; for truly I would rather that a Scot should come out of Scotland and govern the people of the kingdom well and equitably than that thou shouldest govern it ill in the sight of all men." The holy king so loved truth, that, as you shall hear here after, he would never consent to lie to the Saracens as to any covenant that he had made with them.

Of his mouth he was so sober, that on no day of my life did I ever hear him order special meats, as many rich men are wont to do; but he ate patiently whatever his cooks had made ready and was set before him. In his words he was temperate; for on no day of my life did I ever hear him speak evil of any one; nor did I ever hear him name the Devil --- which name is very commonly spoken throughout the kingdom, whereby God, as I believe, is not well pleased.

* * * * * * *

The rule of his land was so arranged that every day he heard the hours sung, and a requiem mass without song; and then, if it was convenient, the mass of the day, or of the saint, with song. Every day he rested in his bed after having eaten, and when he had slept and rested, he said, privily in his chamber --- he and one of his chaplains together --- the office for the dead; and after he heard vespers. At night he heard complines.

* * * * * * *

And when he came back from church, he would send for us and sit at the foot of his bed, and make us all sit round him, and ask if there were any whose cases could not be settled save by himself in person. And we named the litigants; and he would then send for such and ask, "Why do you not accept what our people offer?" and they would make reply, "Sire, because they offer us very little." Then would he say, "You would do well to accept what is proposed, as our people desire." And the saintly man endeavoured thus, with all his power, to bring them into a straight path and a reasonable.

Ofttimes it happened that he would go, after his mass, and seat himself in the wood of Vincennes, and lean against an oak, and make us sit round him. And all those who had any cause in hand came and spoke to him, without hindrance of usher, or of any other person. Then would he ask, out of his own mouth, "Is there any one who has a cause in hand?" And those who had a cause in hand stood up. Then would he say, "Keep silence all, and you shall be heard in turn, one after the other." Then he would call my lord Peter of Fontaines and my lord Geoffry of Villette, and say to one of then, "Settle me this cause."

And when he saw that there was anything to amend in the words of those who spoke on his behalf, or in the words of those who spoke on behalf of any other person, he would himself, out of his own mouth, amend what they had said. Sometimes have I seen him, in summer, go to do justice among his people in the garden of Paris, clothed in a tunic of camlet, a surcoat of tartan without sleeves, and a mantle of black taffeta about his neck, his hair well combed, no cap, and a hat of white peacock's feathers upon his head. And he would cause a carpet to be laid down, so that we might sit round him, and all the people who had any cause to bring before him stood around. And then would he have their causes settled, as I have told you afore he was wont to do in the wood of Vincennes....

James Bruce Ross and Mary Martin McLaughlin, *Medieval Reader* (New York: Viking Press, 1949), 369-374.

Study Questions

1. *What seems to be the common opinion of the Scots?*

2. *Why does Joinville think it worth noting that Louis would not even lie to the Saracens (Muslims)?*

3. *How did Louis deal with litigants who appealed directly to him?*

4. *What does his behavior in the woods of Vincennes and in the gardens of Paris reveal about the relationship between Louis and his staff and with his subjects?*

SALIMBENE on "THE FOLLIES OF FREDERICK II"

Frederick's administrative successes and his involvement in Italy earned him harsh criticism. This account of him is by an Italian, Salimbene.

But know you that Frederick always delighted in having strife with the Church, and that he many times fought her, who had nourished, protected, and exalted him. Of faith in God he had none. He was a crafty man, wily, avaricious, lustful, malicious, and wrathful.

And yet at times he was a worthy man, when he wanted to prove his goodness and his generosity; then he was friendly, merry, full of sweetness and diligence. He could read, write, and sing, and make songs and music. He was a handsome, well-formed man, but only of middle height. I have seen him, and once I loved him, for he wrote on my behalf to Brother Elias, the minister general of the Franciscan order, to send me back to my father. He knew how to speak many and various languages. And, to put it briefly, had he been a good Catholic, and loved God, the Church, and his own soul, he would have had as his equals few emperors in the world. But since, as it is written, a little leaven leaveneth the lump, so he destroyed all his good qualities through this, that he persecuted the Church of God, which he would not have done, if he had loved God and his own soul.... So he was deposed from the imperial office, and died an evil death....

But now I have something to say about the follies of Frederick. His first folly was that he had the thumb of a notary cut off, because he spelled his name in a different way from what he wished. Frederick desired that the first syllable of his name be written "i," like this, Fridericus, and that notary had written it with an "e," Fredericus.

His second folly was that he wanted to find out what kind of speech and what manner of speech children would have when they grew up, if they spoke to no one beforehand. So he bade foster mothers and nurses to suckle the children, to bathe and wash them, but in no way to prattle with them or to speak to them, for he wanted to learn whether they would speak the Hebrew language, which was the oldest, or Greek, or Latin, or Arabic, or perhaps the language of their parents, of whom they had been born. But he laboured in vain, because the children all died. For they could not live without the petting and the joyful faces and loving words of their foster mothers. And so the songs are called "swaddling songs," which a woman sings while she is rocking the cradle, to put a child to sleep, and without them a child sleeps badly and has no rest.

His third folly was that, when he saw the land across the sea, the Holy Land, which God had so often praised, in that He called it "the land flowing with milk and honey," and the most excellent of all lands, it displeased him, and he said that the God of the Jews had not seen his own lands, namely, the Terra di Lavoro, Calabria, Sicily and Apulia. Other wise, He would not so often have praised the land that He promised and gave to the Jews....

His fourth folly was that he often sent a certain Nicholas, against his will, to the bottom of the Faro, and many times he returned. But Frederick wanted to discover whether or not he had really gone to the bottom and returned, so he threw his golden cup in the sea, where he thought it was deep est. And Nicholas plunged in, found the cup, and brought it to him, which astonished the emperor. But when Frederick wanted to send him back once again, Nicholas said, "Do not send me there again at any price, for the sea is so troubled in its depths, that if you send me I shall never return." The emperor sent him nevertheless, and he never returned. For at the times of tempests there are great fishes in the depths of the sea and also, as Nicholas himself reported, rocks and many wrecked ships....

Moreover, Frederick had other superstitions and curiosities and curses and incredulities and perversities and abuses, concerning which I have written in another chronicle.... For he was an Epicurean, and so whatever could be found in divine Scripture by him and by his wise men, which seemed to show that there is not other life after death, he found it all, for example, the words of the Psalms: "You will destroy them and you will not rebuild them" and the saying, "Their sepulchres will be their homes forever."....

The sixth curiosity and folly of Frederick, as I have said in my other chronicle, was that at a certain luncheon he had two men very well beaten, and then sent one of them to sleep and the other to hunt, and on the following evening, he had them defecate in his presence, because he wanted to know which of them had digested the better. And it was decided by the doctors that he who had slept had enjoyed the better digestion.

The seventh and last of his curiosities and follies was that, as I have also written in my other chronicle, when he was in a certain palace on a certain day, he asked Michael Scot, his astrologer, how far he was from the sky, and the astrologer told him how far it seemed to him. Then the emperor took him to other parts of the kingdom, as if for the sake of travel, and he remained for many months. Meanwhile, Frederick had ordered the architects or carpenters to lower the hall of the palace in such a way that no one could detect it. And thus it was done. When after many days, the emperor was staying in the same palace with his astrologer, as if beginning in another way, he asked him whether he was still as far from the sky as he had said the other time. After he had made his computation, the astrologer said that either the sky had been raised or certainly the earth had been lowered. And then the emperor knew that the astrologer spoke truly. I know and I have heard many other follies of Frederick, which for the sake of brevity I do not mention, and because it bores me to relate so many of his follies, and also because I hasten to speak of other things.

James Bruce Ross and Mary Martin McLaughlin, <u>The Portable Medieval Reader</u>, (New York: Viking Press, 1949), 365-368.

Study Questions

1. Describe Frederick's relationship with the Church. Do you think Salimbene is completely correct in attributing this to a lack of faith in God?

2. How had Salimbene come to know Frederick?

3. What experiment was he performing in his "second folly"? Why does Salimbene think the children died? Do you think he's right?

4. Why did Frederick think God had made a mistake about the "Holy Land"?

5. What was Frederick trying to find out in his "sixth folly"? In the "seventh folly"? What do you think of his methods? What does Salimbene think of them?

6. Compare this biographical sketch with that of Einhard on Charlemagne.

REFORM AND REVIVAL WITHIN THE CHURCH

In 910, William, the Duke of Aquitaine, perhaps fearing for the safety of his soul, founded a monastery at Cluny in Burgundy. He gave Cluny an unusual charter, freeing it from any secular or feudal obligations. It was to be entirely subordinate to the pope. All William asked in return was prayers for his soul.

Under the first two extraordinary abbots, Berno (910-927) and Odo (927-942), Cluny gained a reputation not only for its very strict observance of the Benedictine Rule but also for the scholarship and deep piety of its monks. As daughter monasteries sprouted throughout Europe, Cluny came to spearhead a movement for reform within the Church. The monks attacked what they saw as the three major evils in the Church: simony, the buying and selling of Church office; nepotism, the granting of office in return for favors either received or expected; and concubinage. Clunaic criticism of the Church did not mean that the Church was in any worse shape than hitherto. Concubinage, for instance, was not frowned upon as much as one might suppose. Church law had enjoined celibacy as a condition for ordination to the priesthood since the fourth century but by the tenth, most priests were married. Nepotism too was regarded as a "necessary evil" if indeed people regarded it as any kind of evil at all. Bishops and abbots were part of the feudal system. They held fiefs, they were themselves lords and vassals and most folks viewed the Church's involvement as downright salutary.

The Clunaic reform movement is evidence then not of greater corruption but that people's expectations for their own behavior and thus that of their clergy had risen. Moreover, the Papacy of the ninth and tenth centuries was in no position to lead a reform of anything. The plaything of the various factions in Roman politics, the Papacy had been frequently bought and sold, despite the Church's ban on simony, and the men who held the chair of St. Peter were often as debauched as the characters who placed them there.

Reform and Revival Within The Church

Inevitably, Cluny had to strike at its "protector," the Papacy. The reform of the Papacy began with a German emperor inspired by Clunaic ideals and convinced of his ability to control the Church, Henry III (1039-1056). In 1046, three equally unscrupulous characters were actually fighting in the streets of Rome for the throne of St. Peter. Henry summoned all three to a synod which then rejected all three of them. And on Christmas Day that year, Henry put one of his relatives on the papal throne as Clement II. Clement and his successor, also chosen by Henry III, died only a few months after taking office but the third, also named by Henry, was Bruno, Bishop of Toul, who took the name Leo IX (1048-1059), and it was Leo who would establish the Clunaic reform movement in the Papacy itself.

A year after his election, Leo summoned a council to be held in the French city of Rheims. There he deposed all bishops who were not present and insisted that churchmen swear homage to him as their liege lord, thus establishing the Papacy as the head of the entire clergy. Then he condemned simony and concubinage. By the time he died, he had established that reform of the Church would now come from the top --- the seat of St. Peter.

The next step was taken by Nicholas II (1059-1061). At a synod held in Rome the year of his election, Nicholas promoted some drastic reform legislation. There were the standard decrees against concubinage and simony. But there was more. One was a decree forbidding lay investiture, viz., the practice by which kings and lay nobles give the symbols of church office to those they had elevated to church office. Henceforth, bishops were to be chosen for their offices and invested with the insignia of that office only by other bishops. Nicholas' second decree stipulated that popes were to be chosen only by cardinals sitting as an electoral college. Henceforth, there was to be no lay interference in the election of the Vicar of Christ, not even from the Papacy's erstwhile protector, the emperor.

Through all this, in Rome, there had been a Clunaic monk named Hildebrand who had been gaining influence. Hildebrand was somewhat aloof, difficult to approach, a fiery orator and not terribly likable. He was also single-minded to the point of fanaticism, stubborn, abrasive, loyal, kind and egotistical. He was also convinced that, since the material world is subordinate to the spiritual, secular government ought then to be subject to the Papacy. Since the Church had been ordained for the spiritual guidance of all mankind, she should not only be separated from any lay influence or control but in fact should be supreme in Christian society. In 1073, Hildebrand became pope as Gregory VII (1073-1085).

The man he would tangle with, Henry IV (1056-1106), was cut from the same piece of cloth as he. Unless Henry could appoint bishops as ministeriales, he had no weapon at all against his powerful and not always loyal lay nobles. For two years, following his election as pope, Gregory VII followed a conciliatory policy toward Henry IV who had his hands full with a massive rebellion in Saxony. In 1075, however, he succeeded in establishing order and appointed two of his trusted favorites as bishops there. Gregory responded with a bull, <u>Dictatus Papae</u>, condemning lay investiture and he threatened to excommunicate Henry if he continued to use it.

Henry reacted by summoning a synod at Worms in 1076. There, his loyal bishops condemned the bull and renounced their obedience to "Brother Hildebrand" whom they called a "false monk" and "Antichrist". Gregory responded by excommunicating them and Henry IV, thus depriving them of office.

This was the signal for a general rebellion among the lay nobles in Germany who had resented the accretion of royal authority anyway. They demanded that Henry seek forgiveness of Gregory or they would depose him and elect a new emperor in his place. Faced with this, Henry developed a sudden case of contrition. When Gregory was informed of Henry's "malady," he too was put in rather a bind. He knew as well as anyone that Henry feared deposition and that, with that fear removed, he would again resort to lay investiture but as a priest, he had to forgive repentant sinners. Still, Gregory, the shrewd politician, while he no doubt trusted the mysterious workings of the Holy Spirit, took no chances and ordered Henry to meet him at a castle called Canossa in order to lift the ban of excommunication. Canossa belonged to the crusty old Countess Matilda of Tuscany, a dear friend of Gregory's, so that Henry was literally going to have to risk his life to save his soul. Nonetheless, he had little choice and he went. On the day appointed for the meeting in January 1077, however, there was no Gregory. Nor did he show up on the next day. Nor the next. Gregory was three days late. And not accidentally. Gregory had shown Henry, and all the Christian world, that the state, the world, would await the pleasure of the pope.

Canossa was a victory for the Church although Gregory died believing that he had failed God and his Church. Civil war continued to rage in Germany despite Henry's absolution. In 1085, having restored peace, Henry marched on Rome to depose Gregory but Gregory died before Henry could kill him. Thirty-seven years later, an agreement was reached between Henry's heir and the Papacy at Worms. By the Concordat, a prince was allowed to nominate a candidate to church office but it would be the pope or a papal representative who would invest him with the symbols of office.

The agreement at Worms was not really a clear-cut victory for either side. The Investiture Contest had, in fact, raised a fundamental issue --- how was Christian society to be rightly governed, by the Church with the pope as its head or the state with the emperor at the apex? That the two could share supreme power in two separate but equal spheres was unthinkable since society --- all being --- was viewed in a hierarchical Chain of Being where there could only be one, not two heads. The debate would force an interest in Roman law, already being studied at the University of Bologna, and a greater intellectual awakening in all spheres of knowledge, called by historians the Renaissance of the Twelfth Century.

Nonetheless, the real power of the Papacy grew dramatically in the eleventh and twelfth centuries. In 1095, Pope Urban II (1088-1099) went to Clermont, France, and called for a crusade to liberate the city of Jerusalem from the hands of Turkish Muslims, and the cry "God wills it" resounded throughout Europe.

The First Crusade, actually launched in 1096, did succeed in capturing Jerusalem in 1099. A fairly decent sort, Godfrey of Bouillon, then governed the city but his death a short time later led to wrangling among the other knights and the return of Turkish rule to the city in 1187. Other crusades to retake

Jerusalem in the twelfth century met with little success but that did little to diminish the prestige of the Papacy. As a religious enterprise, the Fourth Crusade called by Pope Innocent III in 1204, was a disaster. The crusaders, ferried across the Adriatic in Venetian ships, repaid their Venetian benefactors by sacking Constantinople. The Venetians then established their own Latin Empire of Constantinople which lasted until 1260. There had long been suspicion and distrust between the Eastern and Western churches but the Fourth Crusade made the breach irreparable. The assault of one Christian people upon another tended to give crusading a bad reputation in Europe. Often badly led by leaders who forever wrangled with each other, who had little knowledge of the geography, climate, language or cultures of the Near East, the crusaders often starved, died of strange diseases and were too often easily slaughtered by the Turks. Moreover, the cry "God wills it!" often justified nasty cruelty not only against non-Christians (Jews and Muslims) but against fellow Christians in Europe as well.

Still, as bad a name as crusading got, when Innocent III asked for a crusade against a heretical sect called the Albigensians he was readily joined not only by the French nobility but by Philip Augustus as well. Since they tended to concentrate in towns, as almost every medieval heresy did, there were economic and political gains to be made from the suppression of the Albigensians. Later in the century, however, when popes called for crusades against the emperor, Frederick II, there was little enthusiasm for an enterprise that clearly had far heavier political than religious motives behind it.

Not only in the Crusades, however, did the reformed Papacy exercise leadership. Pope Urban II also lay the foundations for the bureaucracy of the papal monarchy. He reorganized the writing office, the Chancery, and the financial office. The college of cardinals changed from being merely a body to elect the pope to a consultative body. These agencies along with the papal chapel became the Curia, the center of its bureaucracy, the highest legal court in the Church. From the Curia went legates (representatives) to the major courts of Europe to press the goals of reform. Curial legates were also empowered to hear legal appeals and the Papacy soon became the court of highest appeal in Europe. These papal legates and their methods of pursuing their ends were soon imitated by other princes. Very quickly, the language, tools and manners of modern diplomacy began to take shape --- the formal presentation of credentials, the immunity given to legates and to his correspondence by diplomatic pouch.

Many of these popes were also men of the highest probity and moral character. Their high principles as much as the vast power they wielded contributed to a higher moral tone throughout the clergy. By the end of the twelfth century simony and nepotism were becoming rare and clerical marriage had almost ceased.

The increased power of the Papacy ultimately worked against it. As the size of the papal bureaucracy grew and Church lawyers became increasingly concerned about technicalities, fees and climbing in their careers, the prestige of the Vicar of Christ also slipped. The high ideals of the reform movement, coupled with the Curia's greed and insensitivity to human pain led to religious movements springing from the people themselves. Sometimes these movements were heretical as in the case of the Albigensians of southern France who attacked the Church's hierarchy and the need for the sacraments. They also taught a dualism wherein everything material including the human body was evil, everything spiritual was good. Their attack on the material wealth of the clergy attracted townspeople and also nobles who welcomed an excuse to seize clerical properties.

Far more attractive, though, were two popular preachers, St. Dominic (1170-1221) and St. Francis of Assisi (1181-1226). St. Dominic, a Spaniard, founded a small group of followers specifically to combat Albigensianism. The Dominicans were a preaching order but to preach effectively, they first had to learn. So Dominic sent them to the universities for theological studies. Interestingly, the finest mind to come out of the Middle Ages belonged to a Dominican, St. Thomas Aquinas. The followers of St. Francis were not engaged in intellectual contests with heresy-- at least not at first. St. Francis was the son of a wealthy cloth merchant in Assisi and after an extravagant youth, underwent a sudden conversion. He gave away all he had to the poor, and dressed in a rough brown robe began to preach complete devotion to poverty and submission to the Gospel. His Franciscan order gained papal approval in 1221, five years after the Dominicans were recognized.

The Dominicans and Franciscans were friars (from frater=brother). They took the three monastic vows of poverty, chastity and obedience but they were not monks. Instead of withdrawing from the world they sought to be involved in it, to preach and to reform it. The vow of poverty was understood differently too. While the Benedictine monk owned nothing individually, his abbey frequently owned huge tracts of land. Neither the friar nor his order, on the other hand, owned anything. They were mendicants, beggars who would beg for even their daily bread. Also, too, they grew out of towns and retained a close connection with them. Many of their members came from the merchant class, whereas the monks drew largely from the nobility. Moreover, an abbey was often part of the feudal system; the friars were independent of any political ties.

By not only preaching but living Christianity, the friars gave the Church renewed vitality. Although it was the Papacy which had spearheaded reform, following Cluny's lead, the most vital impulse had passed now to new centers of power --- the towns, the universities in those towns and to the secular monarchs who were quick to recognize the possibilities in those towns for increasing their own power.

Suggested Readings

1. Barraclough, G., *The Medieval Papacy* (New York: Harcourt Brace & World, 1968). Nicely illustrated and balanced study of the growth of the papal administration.

2. Cowdrey, H. E. J., *The Clunaics and the Gregorian Reform* (Oxford: Clarendon Press, 1970). A bit difficult but worth the effort.

3. Finucane, R. C., *Soldiers of the Faith: Crusaders and Muslims at War* (New York: St. Martin's Press, 1983). For the Crusades from both points of view.

4. Hill, B. D., *Church and State in the Middle Ages* (New York: John Wiley, 1970). A readable examination of a very complex relationship.

Reform and Revival Within The Church

5. Lewis, Bernard, *The Muslim Discovery of Europe* (New York: W. W. Norton, 1982). For the crusades from the Muslim point of view.

6. Setton, K. M., *A History of the Crusades* (Philadelphia: University of Pennsylvania Press, 1955-1977). Perhaps the best starting point for a thorough study of the Crusades; also S. Runciman's, *A History of the Crusades*, 3 Vols. (Cambridge, England: University Press, 1951-1954).

7. Tellenbach, G., *Church, State and Christian Society at the Time of the Investiture Contest* (Oxford: B. Blackwell, 1948). A very good starting point for a study of the conflict. Sees it as the pivotal issue in medieval history.

8. Ullman, W., *A Short History of the Papacy in the Middle Ages* (London: Methuen, 1972). For the more advanced student.

From the 1059 REFORM DECREES

At the Lateran Council in 1059, Pope Nicholas II struck at an evil that was the cause of much that was wrong with the Church --- lay investiture, the control of Church offices by laymen.

---

1. On the death of a pontiff of the universal Roman church, first, the cardinal bishops,[1] with the most diligent consideration, shall elect a successor; then they shall call in the other cardinal clergy [to ratify their choice], and finally the rest of the clergy and the people shall express their consent to the new election.

2. In order that the disease of venality may not have any opportunity to spread, the devout clergy shall be the leaders in electing the pontiff, and the others shall acquiesce. And surely this order of election is right and lawful, if we consider either the rules or the practice of various fathers, or if we recall that decree of our predecessor, St. Leo, for he says: 'By no means can it be allowed that those should be ranked as bishops who have not been elected by the clergy, and demanded by the people, and consecrated by their fellow bishops of the province with the consent of the metropolitan.' But since the apostolic seat is above all the churches in the earth, and therefore can have no metropolitan over it, without doubt the cardinal bishops perform in it the office of the metropolitan, in that they advance the elected prelate to the apostolic dignity [that is, choose, consecrate, and enthrone him].

---

[1] The seven cardinal bishops were those of Palaestrina, Porto, Ostia, Turulum, Silva Candida, Albano, and Sabina.

3. The pope shall be elected from the church in Rome, if a suitable person can be found in it, but if not, he is to be taken from another church.

4. In the papal election --- in accordance with the right which we have already conceded to Henry and to those of his successors who may obtain the same right from the apostolic see --- due honor and reverence shall be shown our beloved son, Henry, king and emperor elect [that is, the rights of Henry shall be respected].

5. But if the wickedness of depraved and iniquitous men shall so prevail that a pure, genuine, and free election cannot be held in this city, the cardinal bishops with the clergy and a few laymen shall have the right to elect the pontiff wherever they shall deem most fitting.

6. But if after an election any disturbance of war or any malicious attempt of men shall prevail so that he who is elected cannot be enthroned according to custom in the papal chair, the pope elect shall nevertheless exercise the right of ruling the holy Roman church, and of disposing of all its revenues, as we know St. Gregory did before his consecration.

But if anyone, actuated by rebellion or presumption of any other motive, shall be elected or ordained or enthroned in a manner contrary to this our decree, promulgated by the authority of the synod, he with his counselors, supporters, and followers shall be expelled from the holy church of God by the authority of God and the holy apostles Peter and Paul, and shall be subjected to perpetual anathemas as Antichrist and the enemy and destroyer of all Christianity, nor shall he ever be granted a further hearing in the case, but he shall be deposed without appeal from every ecclesiastical rank which he may have held formerly. Whoever shall adhere to him or shall show him any reverence as if he were pope, or shall aid him in any way, shall be subject to like sentence. Moreover, if any rash person shall oppose this our decree and shall try to confound and disturb the Roman church by his presumption contrary to this decree, let him be cursed with perpetual anathema and excommunication, and let him be numbered with the wicked who shall not arise on the day of judgment. Let him feel upon him the weight of the wrath of God the Father, the Son, and the Holy Spirit, and let him experience in this life and the next the anger of the holy apostles, Peter and Paul, whose church he has presumed to confound. Let his habitation be desolate and let none dwell in his tents [Ps. 69:25]. Let his children be orphans and his wife a widow. Let him be driven forth and let his sons beg and be cast out from their habitations. Let the usurer take all his substance and let others reap the fruit of his labors. Let the whole earth fight against him and let all the elements be hostile to him, and let the powers of all the saints in heaven confound him and show upon him in this life their evident vengeance. But may the grace of omnipotent God protect those who observe this decree and free them from the bonds of all their sins by the authority of the holy apostles Peter and Paul.

I, Nicholas, bishop of the holy Catholic and apostolic church, have subscribed this decree which has been promulgated by us, as said above. I, Boniface, by the grace of God bishop of Albano, have subscribed. I, Peter, bishop of the church of Ostia, have subscribed. And other bishops to the number of seventy-six, with priests and deacons.

Oliver J. Thatcher and Edgar Holmes McNeal, *A Source Book for Medieval History* (New York: Charles Scribner's Sons, 1905), 129-131.

Study Questions

1. Who shall henceforth elect the popes?

2. Who can be a candidate for pope? Where shall the papal elections be held?

3. What concession is made to the emperor? Why, do you think?

4. What happens if an election cannot be held in Rome?

5. *What happens to anyone not elected in accordance with this decree?*

6. *Who is signing this decree? What kind of people are they? What kind of person who has hitherto had a great deal of interest in papal elections is not a party to this decree?*

7. *Describe the penalties connected with excommunication.*

DICTATUS PAPAE, 1075

This is the most extreme statement of papal authority made to date. Gregory was stubborn but this statement does not come from personal ambition or vanity. It must be read from his point of view --- to him, the Vicar of Christ had jurisdiction from God over men's immortal souls and that gave the pope then -- any pope --- authority not equal to an emperor's but far superior to it. As far as Gregory was concerned, he was fighting not his own battle but God's.

---

1. That the Roman church was founded by the Lord alone.

2. That only the Roman pontiff is rightly called universal.

3. That he alone can depose or reestablish bishops.

4. That his legate, even if of inferior rank, is above all bishops in council; and he can give sentence of deposition against them.

5. That the pope can depose the absent [i.e., those absent from his synods].

6. That, among other things, we ought not to remain in the same house with one whom he has excommunicated.

7. That it is permitted to him alone to establish new laws for the necessity of the time, to make new peoples into congregations, to make an abbacy of a canonic establishment and vice versa, to divide a rich bishopric and combine poor ones.

8. That he alone can use imperial insignia.

9. That all princes kiss the feet of the pope alone.

10. That his name alone is recited in the churches.

11. That his name is unique in the world.

12. That it is permitted to him to depose emperors.

13. That it is permitted to him to transfer bishops, under pressure of necessity, from one see to another.

14. That throughout the church, wherever he wishes, he can ordain a cleric.

15. That one ordained by him can be over the church of another, but not to perform service; and that he ought not to accept a superior rank from any bishop.

16. That no synod summoned by him ought to be called general.

17. That no chapter and no free canonry exists without his authority.

18. That his decision ought to be reviewed by no one, and that he alone can review the decisions of everyone.

19. That he ought to be judged by no one.

20. That no one may dare to condemn a man who is appealing to the apostolic see.

21. That the greater cases of every church ought to be referred to him.

22. That the Roman church *[i.e., the spokesman of the diocese of Rome: the pope]* has never erred nor will ever err, as the Scriptures bear witness.

23. That the Roman pontiff, if he has been canonically ordained, is indubitably made holy by the merits of the blessed Peter, as St. Ennodius, Bishop of Pavia, bears witness, with the support of many holy fathers, as we find in the decretals of the blessed pope Symmachus.

24. That by his precept and license subjects are permitted to accuse their lords.

25. That he can depose and reestablish bishops without a meeting of the synod.

26. That he who is not in concord with the Roman church [i.e., the Papacy] is not held to be a catholic.

27. That he can absolve the subjects of the unjust from their fealty.

Ewart Lewis, ed., *Medieval Political Ideas* (New York: Alfred A. Knopf, 1954), II, 380-381.

Study Questions

1. *Recalling the cool and often hostile relationship between the Eastern and Western churches, what is the purpose of #1 and #2?*

2. *Regarding #3, Gregory is saying that who cannot depose or reestablish bishops?*

3. *Would a college freshman representing the pope be able to depose an American bishop from his diocese?*

4. *What clauses are specifically directed against lay investiture?*

Reform and Revival Within The Church

5. *What is the relationship between secular and papal courts?*

6. *In what clauses does Gregory claim authority over secular princes?*

7. *What is meant by "papal infallibility"? Where does Gregory claim this?*

THE DEPOSITION OF GREGORY VII BY HENRY IV, 1076

Henry IV's response to <u>Dictatus Papae</u> was this.

Henry, king not by usurpation, but by the holy ordination of God, to Hildebrand, not pope, but false monk.

This is the salutation which you deserve, for you have never held any office in the church without making it a source of confusion and a curse to Christian men instead of an honor and a blessing. To mention only the most obvious cases out of many, you have not only dared to touch the Lord's anointed, the archbishops, bishops, and priests; but you have scorned them and abused them, as if they were ignorant servants not fit to know what their master was doing. This you have done to gain favor with the vulgar crowd. You have declared that the bishops know nothing and that you know everything; but if you have such great wisdom you have used it not to build but to destroy. Therefore we believe that St. Gregory, whose name you have presumed to take, had you in mind when he said: "The heart of the prelate is puffed up by the abundance of subjects, and he thinks himself more powerful than all others." All this we have endured because of our respect for the papal office, but you have mistaken our humility for fear, and have dared to make an attack upon the royal and imperial authority which we received from God. You have even threatened to take it away, as if we had received it from you, and as if the empire and kingdom were in your disposal and not in the disposal of God. Our Lord Jesus Christ has called us to the government of the empire, but he never called you to the rule of the church. This is the way you have gained advancement in the church: through craft you have obtained wealth; through wealth you have obtained favor; through favor, the power of the sword; and through the power of the sword, the papal seat, which is the seat of peace, and then from the seat of peace you have expelled peace. For you have incited subjects to rebel against their prelates by teaching them to despise the bishops, their rightful rulers. You have given to laymen the authority over priests, whereby they condemn and depose those whom the bishops have put over them to teach them. You have attacked me, who, unworthy as I am, have yet been anointed to rule among the anointed of God, and who, according to the teaching of the fathers, can be judged by no one save God alone, and can be deposed for no crime except infidelity. For the holy fathers in the time of the apostate Julian did not presume to pronounce sentence of deposition against him, but left him to be judged and condemned by God. St. Peter himself said: "Fear God, honor the king" [1 Pet. 2:17]. But you, who fear not God, have dishonored me, whom He hath established. St. Paul, who said that even an angel from heaven should be accursed who taught any other than the true doctrine, did not make an exception in your favor to permit you to teach false doctrines. For he says: "But though we, or an angel from heaven, preach any other gospel unto you than that which we have preached unto you, let him be accursed" [Gal. 1:8]. Come down, then, from that apostolic seat which you have obtained by violence; for you have been declared accursed by St. Paul for your false doctrines and have been condemned by us and our bishops for your evil rule. Let another ascend the throne of St. Peter, one who will not use religion as a cloak of violence, but will teach the life-giving doctrine of that prince of the apostles. I, Henry, king by the grace of God, with all my bishops, say unto you: "Come down, come down, and be accursed through all the ages."

Oliver J. Thatcher and Edgar Holmes McNeal, *A Source Book for Medieval History* (New York: Charles Scribner's Sons, 1905), 151-152.

Study Questions

1. Why does Henry address the pope as Hildebrand, not Gregory?

2. What does Henry accuse Gregory of doing?

3. What kinds of arguments does he use?

4. Given the two documents, who probably has the better argument? Explain.

CONCORDAT OF WORMS, 1122

Henry IV's son finally reached a compromise with Pope Calixtus II. The principle agreed upon here, however, did not entirely end the matter since there was still some doubt as to how it was to be applied.

Calixtus, bishop, servant of the servants of God, to his beloved son, Henry, by the grace of God emperor of the Romans, Augustus.

We hereby grant that in Germany the elections of the bishops and abbots who hold directly from the crown shall be held in your presence, such elections to be conducted canonically and without simony or other illegality. In the case of disputed elections you shall have the right to decide between the parties, after consulting with the archbishop of the province and his fellow-bishops. You shall confer the regalia of the office upon the bishop or abbot elect by giving him the sceptre, and this shall be done freely without exacting any payment from him; the bishop or abbot elect on his part shall perform all the duties that go with the holding of the regalia.

In other parts of the empire the bishops shall receive the regalia from you in the same manner within six months of their consecration, and shall in like manner perform all the duties that go with them. The undoubted rights of the Roman church, however, are not to be regarded as prejudiced by this concession. If at any time you shall have occasion to complain of the carrying out of these provisions, I will undertake to satisfy your grievances as far as shall be consistent with my office. Finally, I hereby make a true and lasting peace with you and with all of your followers, including those who supported you in the recent controversy.

The Promise of Henry V

In the name of the holy and undivided Trinity.

For the love of God and his holy church and of pope Calixtus, and for the salvation of my soul, I, Henry, by the grace of God, of the Romans, Augustus, hereby surrender to God and his apostles, Sts. Peter and Paul, and to the holy Catholic church, all investiture by ring and staff. I agree that elections and consecrations shall be conducted canonically and shall be free from all interference. I surrender also the possessions and regalia of St. Peter which have been seized by me during this quarrel, or by my father in his lifetime, and which are now in my possession, and I promise to aid the church to recover such as are held by any other persons. I restore also the possessions of all other churches and princes, clerical or secular, which I have, and promise to aid them to recover such as are held by any other persons.

Finally, I make true and lasting peace with Pope Calixtus and with the holy Roman church and with all who are or have ever been of his party. I will aid the Roman church whenever my help is asked, and will do justice in all matters in regard to which the church may have occasion to make complaint.

All these things have been done with the consent and advice of the princes whose names are written below; Adlebert, archbishop of Mainz; Frederick, archbishop of Cologne, etc.

Oliver J. Thatcher and Edgar Holmes McNeal, *A Source Book for Medieval History* (New York: Charles Scribner's Sons, 1905), 165-166.

Study Questions

1. How shall German bishops and abbots be elected? What role will the prince (emperor) play?

2. What will the prince give the bishop?

3. What things will the pope give to the new bishop?

4. Who won?

POPE URBAN II CALLS THE FIRST CRUSADE, 1095

When Pope Urban issued his call for a crusade to free the city of Jerusalem from the hands of the Turks, he tapped an enormous reservoir of religious enthusiasm which coincided with more mundane motives as well. In addition to the indulgence Urban promised, many knights, usually the younger sons of the nobility, hoped to carve out fiefs in the Holy Land. And since the expeditions would cost a small fortune in equipment and outfitting, burghers and bankers also hoped to profit. The pull of adventure, excitement, sometimes the desire to dodge responsibilities pulled pilgrims into the Crusade. And it was the pope alone who stood at the head of the Crusade, and thus made good his claim to lead Christian Europe. It was clearly the pope, not the emperor, who seemed to be the rightful head of Christendom.

"From the confines of Jerusalem and from the city of Constantinople a grievous report has gone forth and has repeatedly been brought to our ears; namely, that a race from the kingdom of the Persians, an accursed race, a race wholly alienated from God, 'a generation that set not their heart aright, and whose spirit was not steadfast with God,' has violently invaded the lands of those Christians and has depopulated them by pillage and fire. They have led away a part of the captives into their own country, and a part they have killed by cruel tortures. They have either destroyed the churches of God or appropriated them for the rites of their own religion. They destroy the altars, after having defiled them with their uncleanness.... The kingdom of the Greeks is now dismembered by them and has been deprived of territory so vast in extent that it could not be traversed in two months' time.

"On whom, therefore, is the labor of avenging these wrongs and of recovering this territory incumbent, if not upon you, -you, upon whom, above all other nations, God has conferred remarkable glory in arms, great courage, bodily activity, and strength to humble the heads of those who resist you? Let the deeds of your ancestors encourage and incite your minds to manly achievements:--the glory and greatness of King Charlemagne, and of his son Louis, and of your other monarches, who have destroyed the kingdoms of the Turks and have extended the sway of the holy Church over lands previously pagan. Let the holy sepulcher of our Lord and Saviour, which is possessed by the unclean nations, especially arouse you, and the holy places which are now treated with ignominy and irrevently polluted with the filth of the unclean. Oh, most valiant soldiers and descendants of invincible ancestors, do not degenerate, but recall the valor of your progenitors.

"But if you are hindered by love of children, parents, or wife, remember what the Lord says in the Gospel, 'He that loveth father or mother more than me is not worthy of me.' 'Every one that hath forsaken houses, or brethren, or sisters, or father, or mother, or wife, or children, or lands, for my name's sake, shall receive an a hundredfold, and shall inherit everlasting life.' Let none of your possessions retain you, nor solicitude for your family affairs. For this land which you inhabit, shut in on all sides by the seas and surrounded by the mountain peaks, is too narrow for your large population; nor does it abound in wealth; and it furnishes scarcely food enough for its cultivators. Hence it is that you murder and devour one another, that you wage war, and that very many among you perish in intestine strife.

"Let hatred therefore depart from among you, let your quarrels end, let wars cease, and let all dissensions and controversies slumber. Enter upon the road to the Holy Sepulcher; wrest that land from the wicked race, and subject it to yourselves. That land which, as the Scripture says, 'floweth with milk and honey' was given by God into the power of the children of Israel. Jerusalem is the center of the earth; the land is fruitful above all others, like another paradise of delights. This spot the Redeemer of mankind has made illustrious by his advent, has beautified by his sojourn, has consecrated by his passion, has redeemed by his death, has glorified by his burial.

"This royal city, however, situated at the center of the earth, is now held captive by the enemies of Christ and is subjected, by those who do not know God, to the worship of the heathen. She seeks, therefore, and desires to be liberated and ceases not to implore you to come to her aid. From you especially she asks succor, because, as we have already said, God has conferred upon you above all other nations great glory in arms. Accordingly, undertake this journey eagerly for the remission of your sins, with the assurance of the reward of imperishable glory in the kingdom of heaven."

When Pope Urban had urbanely said these and very many similar things, he so centered in one purpose the desires of all who were present that all cried out, "It is the will of God!" When the venerable Roman pontiff heard that, with eyes uplifted to heaven, he gave thanks to God and, commanding silence with his hand, said:

"Most beloved brethren, today is manifest in you what the Lord says in the Gospel, 'Where two or three are gathered together in my name, there am I in the midst of them'; for unless God had been present in your spirits, all of you would not have uttered the same cry; since, although the cry issued from numerous mouths, yet the origin of the cry was one. Therefore I say to you that God, who implanted this in your breasts, has drawn it forth from you. Let that then be your war cry in combats, because it is given to you by God. When an armed attack is made upon the enemy, let this one cry be raised by all the soldiers of God: 'It is the will of God! It is the will of God!' [Deus vult! Deus vult!]

"And we neither command nor advise that the old or feeble, or those incapable of bearing arms, undertake this journey. Nor ought women to set out at all without their husbands, or brothers, or legal guardians. For such are more of a hindrance than aid, more of a burden than an advantage. Let the rich aid the needy; and according to their wealth let them take with them experienced soldiers. The priests and other clerks, whether secular or regular, are not to go without the consent of their bishop; for this journey would profit them

Reform and Revival Within The Church

nothing if they went without permission. Also, it is not fitting that laymen should enter upon the pilgrimage without the blessing of their priests.

"Whoever, therefore, shall determine upon this holy pilgrimage, and shall make his vow to God to that effect, and shall offer himself to him for sacrifice, as a living victim, holy and acceptable to God, shall wear the sign of the cross of the Lord on his forehead or on his breast. When, indeed, he shall return from his journey, having fulfilled his vow, let him place the cross on his back between his shoulders. Thus shall ye, indeed, by this twofold action, fulfill the precept of the Lord, as he commands in the Gospel, 'He that taketh not his cross, and followeth after me, is not worthy of me.'"

Oliver J. Thatcher and Edgar Holmes McNeal, *A Source Book for Medieval History* (New York: Charles Scribner's Sons, 1905), 151-152.

Study Questions

1. *Urban's speech indicates an interesting perception of world geography. From what country does he think the invaders of the Holy Land have come? Where (what city) is the center of the earth?*

2. *Beside the obvious one of freeing the Holy Land from "the filth of the unclean," what other motive(s) does Urban give for going to Jerusalem?*

3. *Why does he think Europeans are waging war on each other? Given what he has just said about the behavior of the "unclean filth," is it likely that Crusaders who are murdering and devouring each other will give the Holy Land any greater peace?*

4. *How does he describe Jerusalem? How is that description going to affect preparations for the Crusade? How will it affect expectations of Palestine?*

5. *What reward does Urban offer those who go on the Crusade? Who ought not to go?*

INNOCENT III on PAPAL AUTHORITY, 1198

The apogee of the medieval Papacy came under Innocent III (1198-1216). An expert in canon law and a thoroughly good man, Innocent was as convinced as Gregory VII had been of the supremacy of the pope over other princes. And he wielded that power often and effectively. Philip Augustus of France was forced to take back the wife he had abandoned for another woman. John I of England was excommunicated when he refused to install Innocent's candidate, Stephen Langton, as Archbishop of Canterbury. Innocent arbitrated a dispute between two claimants for the imperial crown in Germany and his influence was felt as far as Scandanavia and Armenia.

The following is from a letter he wrote to the prior of a Tuscan abbey. Even in that pre-Galilean age, no one could miss the symbolism.

Innocent III to Acerbius, prior, and to the other clergy in Tuscany. As God, the creator of the Universe, set two great lights in the firmament of heaven, the greater light to rule the day, and the lesser to rule the night (Gen. 1:15, 16), so He set two great dignities in the firmament of the universal church, ... the greater to rule the day, that is, souls, and the lesser to rule the night, that is, bodies. These dignities are the papal authority and the royal power. And just as the moon gets her light from the sun, and is inferior to the sun in quality, quantity, position, and effect, so the royal power gets the splendor of its dignity from the papal authority.

J. H. Robinson, ed., <u>Readings in European History</u> (Boston: Ginn and Company, 1904) I, 208.

Study Questions

1. *On what grounds does Innocent claim papal supremacy?*
2. *Upon what is the legitimacy of kings based?*

ST. FRANCIS OF ASSISI, PRAYER

The continuing popularity of this little prayer may have as much to do with its psychological sanity as its devoutness.

Lord, make me an instrument of Thy peace.
Where there is hatred, let me sow love;
Where there is injury, pardon;
Where there is doubt, faith;
Where there is despair, hope;
Where there is darkness, light.

Lord, grant that I may not so much seek to be consoled as to console,
To be understood as to understand;
To be loved as to love.

For it is in giving that we receive,
In pardoning that we are pardoned,
And in dying that we are born to eternal life.

Study Questions

1. *Compare the view of God and of keep Man's relationship with him in this prayer with that in the "Dies Irae."*

2. *Compare the relationship between Man and God expressed here with that of any Greek hero and his gods.*

THE SCHOOLS AND SCHOLASTICISM

  There were four major factors leading to the development of the "new learning" of the twelfth century and to the universities where it was centered. First, towns by then, especially in Italy, had created a wealthy class who could not only afford books but dearly wanted and needed them. As urban life became increasingly complex, there was an ever greater demand for trained lawyers, administrators and bureaucrats. Moreover, they were interested in keeping land and sea routes open so that books and ideas flowed easily not only within Europe but between Europe and the Near East. Second, the Crusades, beginning in 1096, had opened up intellectual as well as commercial contacts with the Greek and Islamic worlds and third, the fall of the Spanish city of Toledo to Christian forces in 1085 opened a flood of Arabic treatises on science, mathematics, philosophy and medicine to Europe. Since its infancy, the central problem in Christianity had been to reconcile Faith and Reason. Happily, both Islamic and Jewish thinkers had been faced with the same dilemma. Two Islamic scholars, Avicenna (980-1036) and Averroes (1126-1198) of Cordova, had done commentaries on Aristotle's works in relationship to Islam. Moses Maimonides (1135-1204), a Jew, had made a similar reconciliation in his <u>Guide for the Perplexed</u>. In distinguishing the place of reason and the place of faith in reaching truth, Maimonides anticipated Thomas Aquinas by only a few decades. Finally, the Investiture Controversy itself sparked a good bit of speculation. In deciding whether it was the authority of the Church or the emperor which was supreme, scholars were faced with something of a dilemma. The Scriptures could be used to support either side and the Fathers were not united on the matter. Thus, thoughtful men were forced to go back beyond the Scriptures and the Fathers to Roman political theory. Europe's earliest schools were in monasteries where the heart of the curriculum was the classical trivium and quadrivium, the seven liberal arts. Although all learning ultimately culminated in the study of God, some monasteries such as Fulda and Jarrow (Bede's home) became major centers of learning of any kind.

With the increasing importance of towns, however, schools attached to cathedrals also became important. It was out of these cathedral schools that the university emerged. The word "universitas" means corporation or guild and the university --- then and now --- preserved many of the features of a craft guild. Students were organized initially according to their nation but they soon found they had more in common with others who shared their interests. So they soon organized as "colleges" of medicine, law and the like.

Student life in the Middle Ages was not terribly different from today. Letters survive of students writing home for money, worrying about exams and complaining of their food and lodging. Most of them were "upwardly mobile" and from what might be called a "middle class" --- sons of lesser knights, burghers, merchants and artisans who hoped to secure well-paying jobs in government or church service, in law, medicine or in trade.

There were some differences, however. First, there were no women. Women, especially noble and very wealthy women, were often educated but at home, not in a university. Secondly, medieval students especially in Italy, had far more power than today's student. Student guilds in some places hired the professors, paid their fees and demanded that they cover the syllabus in the agreed-upon time, that they demonstrate competence in both Latin and in their discipline and that they start and end lectures on time. Student guilds also existed to protect their members from the exorbitant rates charged at inns and boarding houses. Sometimes they were organized for sheer physical protection. The "town-gown" conflict was often bloody and many a student's voluminous gown concealed a dagger when he went down to the local tavern for ale. Merchants often saw students as arrogant scoundrels and the students often viewed the merchants as extortioners.

The lecture (from *lectio*=reading) was the standard method of imparting knowledge since books were so rare and expensive. The lecture and the exams were given in Latin hence, before a student could even enter the university he had to demonstrate competence in that language. The lecture would be *based on an authority such as Galen (in medicine), Justinian (in law), Aristotle or the Bible along with the professor's own interpretation and commentaries or glosses. An example of glosses are Peter Lombard's (d. 1160) Sentences, a compilation of basic theological principles. The students would copy out the lecture on waxed tablets and the information then would be committed to memory. There was little emphasis on independent research since it was felt that everything had been revealed and the scholar's job was simply to understand it.*

That was not, however, as stultifying as it may sound. With the increased wealth and political stability of Europe, there were new kinds of problems besetting people and there was greater access to classical, Jewish and Arabic works. The development of the University of Bologna illustrates this. As the commercial transactions of the Bolognese merchants became ever more sophisticated, they realized that neither feudal law nor the Church's canon law met their needs. So they fell back on that legal system which was nearest to them, the civil code of the Roman Empire. The emperor Justinian had, in the sixth century, codified Roman law and in the twelfth century, Irnerius, a teacher at Bologna, picked up that code and adjusted it to the needs of the city-state. While towns found Roman law useful so, too, did the monarchies which began to emerge in the eleventh and twelfth centuries. Roman law assumed centralized, monarchical government and now kings whose authority hitherto had been that of a mere liege lord over unruly vassals welcomed Roman law to provide a theoretical basis from which to build governments independent of, or at least less dependent, on the feudal levies.

Like Bologna, the University of Salerno also grew out of and reflected the needs of its town. It became the leading center for the study of medicine but Greeks and Jews had long been experimenting there with herbs and different possibilities in surgery. In the twelfth century, King Roger II of Sicily brought the study of medicine under royal control. The major medical texts were Hippocrates and the Roman physician, Galen. Under these influences, disease was, of course, viewed as an imbalance in the humors. Too, the understanding of human anatomy was based on Galen who had been squeamish about doing dissections on human cadavers. His anatomy was based on analogies he had drawn from dissecting animals, and the Church's own proscription of dissections reinforced that. As limiting as this was, however, Salerno had easy access to the medical lore of the non-Christian world including Jewish and Arabic medical treatises on anatomy and pharmacology.

The third major school was the University of Paris. The curriculum in any university revolved around the trivium and the quadrivium but the queen of all studies was theology and it was Paris that was the center of theological work. One's approach to the study of God affected one's approach to all that God had created. The use of logic to illumine the Christian faith was first attempted by Anselm of Bec who was Archbishop of Canterbury under Henry I. Asserting "I believe in order that I might know", Anselm began with faith and would use reason to explain that faith. For Anselm, reason was a partner, although a junior one, in reaching truth about God and, by extension, about anything else. What Anselm had done was to lay the foundations for Scholasticism.

Scholasticism took root at the University of Paris in the next century. It was an approach to learning, a method of inquiry and it possessed five major characteristics. First, it fused reason and faith. Second, it was authoritarian. If one quoted a Church Father, Aristotle or the Bible, for instance, that clinched the argument, but the more authorities one could marshal in support of one's argument, the more airtight it was. Third, it rested on logic, not sense experience, since the senses can deceive us and are in any case limited. Fourth, Scholasticism was ethical. There was the Platonic idea that knowledge should generate virtue. And fifth, it saw the universe as static, unchanging. The way Nature, including human nature, appears to us now is the way it has always been and will be. Thus, knowledge about Nature is also already there, not evolving. It increased, not through research and experimentation as it does in our day but through public debates.

All of this would seem to make Scholasticism rather rigid but it wasn't. For one thing, the "authorities" one relied on hadn't always agreed with each other. And secondly, there was a kind of explosion of texts of all kinds in the twelfth century. While knowledge itself might be finite, what the individual himself knew in a certain field dramatically expanded as these new texts became available and as the use of those new texts changed the method in which one approached and applied old materials. Third, there was a universality about knowledge. The knowledge required for a degree was specific but medieval scholarship was wide-ranging. Robert Grosseteste, for instance, an early figure in English science, wrote treaties on meteorology, the tides, colors, phonetics, the <u>Psalms</u>, <u>Gospels</u> and Paul's <u>Epistles</u>, commentaries on Aristotle's <u>Physics</u> and a number of philosophical and theological treatises. He also translated a number of Greek treatises into Latin, including Aristotle's <u>Nicomachean</u> Ethics. That kind of broad output was not uncommon.

By the time Paris became the center of theology, many of Aristotle's works had been translated and Arabic and Jewish, as well as Christian, commentaries on them rendered the atmosphere at Paris exciting as well as tense. There was intense disagreement over the problem of universals --- something most American students would find a little tedious now perhaps, but absolutely critical in the development of scientific thought. Essentially, it boiled down to whether the proper approach to a problem ought to be induction or deduction. Into this dispute came a rather cocky student named Peter Abelard. Abelard was something of a pain to his teachers because he questioned not only what they said but their very method of arriving at their conclusions. He was convinced that all knowledge, even knowledge of God, must begin not in faith, but in doubt. In a famous work called <u>Sic et Non</u> he posited about 150 articles of Christian faith and then very clearly and logically argued both for and against each one. What he aimed to do was not contradict Christian faith at all, but to make doctrine more precise. His insistence that even theology be studied according to the rules of formal logic was a fundamental point of Scholasticism. That meant that problems had to be carefully defined and divided into topics and subtopics and authorities had to be cited accurately.

Abelard's work and that of a famous Aristotelian scholar, Albertus Magnus, helped to shape the mind of St. Thomas Aquinas. In a massive work, the <u>Summa Theologica</u>, Thomas brings reason and faith together. He drew a sharp distinction between those truths which can be demonstrated through Reason such as the existence of God. Here, Thomas, following Aristotle,, began with Nature --- earth, trees, animals and reasoned back to an original source or cause of all things --- the Prime Mover or Unmoved Mover of Aristotle now identified by Thomas as God. There are also truths, though, which can only be apprehended through faith, such as the Trinity and the Incarnation. But even *those truths which are in the province of faith cannot be contrary to reason, nor can reason, rightly used, ever contradict faith.*

Thomas was also interested in how we know and established a new discipline called "epistemology." Nothing can be in the mind, he said, that is not first of all in the senses, an idea that would be developed in the seventeenth century by John Locke.

What Thomas Aquinas had done was to bring about a complete synthesis of reason and faith, of the learning of this world together with the faith of the other world. That synthesis was not only happening in theology, however. The arts of the Middle Ages --- especially Gothic cathedrals and the Divine Comedy of Dante --- also reflect it.

Suggested Readings

1. Brooke, Christopher, *The Twelfth Century Renaissance* (London: Thames and Hudson, 1969). The schools, artists, writers and theologians of an important and exciting century.

2. Copleston, F. C., *Aquinas* (Baltimore: Penguin Books, 1975). This leading Thomist's study is the best introduction to Aquinas.

3. Gilson, Etienne, *Heloise and Abelard* (Ann Arbor: University of Michigan Press, 1960). Treats the development of humanism from the background of one of the most vital figures of the Middle Ages.

4. *Reason and Revelation in the Middle Ages* (New York: Scribner's, 1939). A thorough and readable analysis of medieval thought.

5. Haskins, C., *The Rise of the Universities* (Ithaca, New York: Great Seal Books, 1957). A good beginning for the development of the schools.

6. _____, *The Renaissance of the Twelfth Century* (New York: Meridian Books, 1957). A classic that should not be ignored.

7. Knowles, David, *The Evolution of Medieval Thought* (Baltimore: Helicon Press, 1962). Perhaps the best introduction to the entire range of medieval ideas.

8. Lindberg, David, ed., *Science in the Middle Ages* (Chicago: University of Chicago Press, 1978). Collection of essays on various branches of medieval science.

9. Pieper, Josef, *Scholasticism* (New York: Pantheon Books, 1960). An intelligent, readable analysis.

10. Wieruszowski, Helen, *The Medieval University* (Princeton, New Jersey: Van Nostrand, 1966). A good survey on the origins and structure of the universities and the people who came to them.

FREDERICK BARBAROSSA PROTECTS STUDENTS, 1158

By the mid-twelfth century, rulers had become aware of how valuable universities could be in cementing their own power.

After a careful consideration of this subject by the bishops, abbots, dukes, counts, judges, and other nobles of our sacred palace, we, out of our piety, have granted this privilege to all scholars who travel for the sake of study, and especially to the professors of divine and sacred laws, namely: that they may go in safety to the places in which the studies are carried on, both they themselves and their messengers, and may dwell there in security. For we think it fitting that, so long as they conduct themselves with propriety, those should enjoy our approval and protection who, by their learning, enlighten the world and mold the life of our subjects to obey God and us, his minister. By reason of our special regard we desire to defend them from all injuries.

For who does not pity those who exile themselves through love for learning, who wear themselves out in poverty in place of riches, who expose their lives to all perils and often suffer bodily injury from the vilest men, --- yet all these vexatious things must be endured by the scholar. Therefore, we declare, by this general and ever-to-be-valid law, that in the future no one shall be so rash as to venture to inflict any injury on scholars, or to occasion any loss to them on account of a debt owed by an inhabitant of their province, --- a thing which we have learned is sometimes done, by an evil custom. And let it be known to the violators of this decree, and also to those who shall at the time be the rulers of the places where the offense is committed, that a fourfold restitution of property shall be exacted from all those who are guilty and that, the mark of infamy being affixed to them by the law itself, they shall lose their office forever.

Moreover, if any one shall presume to bring a suit against them on account of any business, the choice in this matter shall be given to the scholars, who may summon the accusers to appear before their professors, or before the bishop of the city, to whom we have given jurisdiction in this matter. But if, in sooth, the accuser shall attempt to drag the scholar before another judge, even though his cause is a very just one, he shall lose his suit for such an attempt.

We also order this law to be inserted among the imperial constitutions under the title, ne filius pro patre, etc.

Given at Roncaglia, in the year of our Lord 1158, in the month of November.

James Harvey Robinson, *Readings in European History*, 2 vols. (Needham Heights, Massachusetts: Silver, Burdett, and Ginn, Inc., 1904), I, 452-453.

Study Questions

1. *What problems apparently had university students been facing?*

2. *What may a student do if he is sued?*

STUDENT SONGS

The medieval student's life somewhat resembled that of a modern student's. He worried about rents, money to buy books, getting established in a career and above all, of course, his grades. Now and then, however, he went to the tavern and had a good time.

Let's Away With Study

Let's away with study,
    Folly's sweet.
Treasure all the pleasure
    Of our youth:
Time enough for age
    To think on Truth.
So short a day,
And life so quickly hasting,
And in study wasting
Youth that would be gay!

'Tis our spring that's slipping,
    Winter draweth near,
Life itself we're losing,
    And this sorry cheer
Dries the blood and chills the heart,
    Shrivels all delight.
Age and all its crowd of ills
    Terrifies our sight.
So short a day,
And life so quickly hasting,
And in study wasting
Youth that would be gay!

Let us as the gods do,
    'Tis the wiser part:
Leisure and love's pleasure
Seek the young in heart
Follow the old fashion,
    Down into the street!

Down among the maidens,
And the dancing feet!
So short a day,
And life so quickly hasting,
And in study wasting
    Youth that would be gay!

There for the seeing
Is all loveliness,
White limbs moving
Light in wantonness.
Gay go the dancers,
I stand and see,
Gaze, till their glances
Steal myself from me.
So short a day,
And life so quickly hasting,
And in study wasting
    Youth that would be gay!

* * * * * * *

This Song Wants Drink

Who has good wine should flagon it out
And thrust the bad where the fungus sprout;
Then must merry companions shout:
This song wants drink!

When I see wine into the clear glass slip
How I long to be matched with it;
My heart sings gay at the thought of it:
This song wants drink!

I thirst for a sup; come circle the cup:
This song wants drink!

James Bruce Ross and Mary Martin McLaughlin, eds., *Medieval Reader* (New York: Viking Press, 1961), 502-503, 509.

ST. ANSELM PROVES THE EXISTENCE OF GOD

The "Father of Scholasticism" (1033-1109) was born in northern Italy and became the Abbot of Bec in Normandy in 1078. Under his guidance, the monastic school there became a major center of learning. Later, Anselm became Archbishop of Canterbury and labored to promote Gregory VII's program of church reform in England.

Anselm was convinced that the Christian faith could be explained rationally but he also believed that faith was required first and then reason could explain faith. "I believe," he said, "in order that I might understand."

In the excerpt below, Anselm tries to prove the existence of God by reason alone. He makes the famous argument that God is that than which nothing greater can be conceived. To put it another way, if this "greatest thing" can exist in the mind, it must also then exist in reality.

And so, Lord, do thou, who dost give understanding to faith, give me, so far as thou knowest it to be profitable, to under stand that thou art as we believe; and that thou art that which we believe. And, indeed, we believe that thou art a being than which nothing greater can be conceived. Or is there no such nature, since the fool hath said in his heart, there is no God? (Psalms xiv.I). But, at any rate, this very fool, when he hears of this being of which I speak - a being than which nothing greater can be conceived - understands what he hears, and what he understands is in his understanding; although he does not understand it to exist.

For, it is one thing for an object to be in the understanding, and another to understand that the object exists. When a painter first conceives of what he will afterwards perform, he has it in his understanding, but he does not yet understand it to be, because he has not yet performed it. But after he has made the painting, he both has it in his understanding, and he understands that it exists, because he has made it.

Hence, even the fool is convinced that something exists in the understanding, at least, than which nothing greater can be conceived. For, when he hears of this, he understands it. And whatever is understood, exists in the understanding. And assuredly that, than which nothing greater can be conceived, cannot exist in the understanding alone. For, suppose it exists in the under standing alone: then it can be conceived to exist in reality; which is greater.

Therefore, if that, than which nothing greater can be conceived, exists in the understanding alone, the very being, than which nothing greater can be conceived, is one, than which a greater can be conceived. But obviously this is impossible. Hence, there is no doubt that there exists a being, than which nothing greater can be conceived, and it exists both in the understanding and in reality.

Reprinted from *Saint Anselm, Basic Writings*, by S. N. Deane, trans., 2nd ed. (by permission of The Open Court Publishing Company, La Salle, Illinois, 1968), 7-8.

Study Questions

1. *What is the relationship between Faith and Reason?*

2. *What is Anselm's proof for the existence of God?*

3. *Using the "painter" analogy, can you figure out the flaw in Anselm's argument?*

ABELARD from SIC ET NON

The son of a minor knight in Brittany, Abelard (1079-1142) became inflamed with a love of the new learning which was beginning to grip Europe in the early twelfth century. Not only were new texts making their way into Europe but old materials were being looked at with new eyes and new meanings and applications were being discovered in them. He went to study at the University of Paris which was full of famous teachers but had no established curriculum.

Abelard's first love was logic. He saw in it more than simply an intellectual tool. Rather, he thought it had universal application, in solving old problems, in acquiring new knowledge and most importantly in handling theology. Thus, he set out to master both logic and theology. Brilliant, brash, vain and a bit arrogant, he completed his studies in record time and then began stealing students from his former teachers.

Meanwhile he had made the acquaintance of Heloise, niece of a canon of Paris Cathedral. He got her pregnant and the affair could hardly be hushed up because his love poems to her were being sung all over Paris. Heloise had the child and Abelard was forced by the uncle to marry her, thus ending any chance for advancement in the Church. Heloise offered to go to a convent, thus irritating the uncle even more because he feared that Abelard might then repudiate her --- so he hired a gang of thugs to castrate Abelard. Abelard was forced to flee and he went as a monk to St. Denis where he stirred up trouble by criticizing some of the legends about the saint. He was forced to flee St. Denis (this was before Suger's time) and he finally ended at Cluny.

Abelard came to the University of Paris at a time when scholars were in a rather heated debate on the problem of universals. They fell into two camps, the Realists, deriving from Plato, and the Nominalists, coming from Aristotle. As dull and pedantic as the whole argument may seem to us, the fundamental

The Schools and Scholasticism

problem of how we ever come to know the truth of anything at all was at stake. If one considers the approach one takes to a chemistry problem and the very different way in which one tackles a term paper on Shakespeare, the importance of the debate will become clear. Now, we would tend to accept scientific observation as a "proof", but in the Middle Ages, even if scientific data had been widely available, it may not have been trusted. It was logic that was proof, not the evidence of our senses, which after all, can be deceptive.

The Realists argued that ideas have an independent existence of their own, being reflections of "forms" in the mind of God. The Nominalists argued that ideas exist only in the mind and have no independent existence of their own. All knowledge comes through sense experience, thus logic alone does not prove truth.

Abelard took a modified Nominalist position. Contentious and terribly arrogant, he delighted in ridiculing his teachers. But there was more to Abelard. In the Sic et Non, *he is demanding a careful and critical definition of argument. Like Socrates, he was convinced that true knowledge must begin in doubt.*

The following selection is not directly from the Sic et Non. *These are some of the 150 questions he raised for debate:*

Should human faith be based upon reason, or no?
Is God one, or no?
Is God a substance, or no?
Does the first Psalm refer to Christ, or no?
Is sin pleasing to God, or no? Is God the author of evil, or no?
Is God all-powerful, or no?
Can God be resisted, or no?
Has God free will, or no?
Was the first man persuaded to sin by the devil, or no?
Was Adam saved, or no?
Did all the apostles have wives except John, or no?
Are the flesh and blood of Christ in very truth and essence present in the sacrament of the altar, or no?
Do we sometimes sin unwillingly, or no?

Does God punish the same sin both here and in the future, or no?
Is it worse to sin openly than secretly, or no?

J. H. Robinson, ed., <u>Readings in European History</u>, (Boston: Ginn and Company, 1904) I, 451-452.

Study Question

1. *Take any one of the questions and argue it, both for and against, without using the Bible or faith as part of your argument.*

THOMAS AQUINAS from the
SUMMA THEOLOGICA

Thomas (1225-1274) was born of a noble family near Naples and educated at Monte Cassino, then at the University of Naples and then, after entering the Dominican order, he went to the University of Paris to study and eventually to teach theology. As a student, his slow, methodical analysis of questions gave people the impression that he was stupid and dull. Ironically, this genius whose intellect so towers over the ages got the nickname, "big dumb ox."

You will recall that about a century earlier, Abelard had insisted on subjecting even the truths of the Christian faith to a careful, logical analysis. And Abelard had raised howls of outrage. St. Bernard of Clairvaux had stormed that "Abelard is trying to prove everything so that no one will have to believe anything." Obviously, Bernard and many others had missed the point of Abelard's work. Since then, however, a treasury of works from Islamic and Jewish scholars in Spain had entered Europe. Many of these works were translations of and commentaries on Aristotle, works that neither Anselm nor Abelard had had. These had created a crisis. Aristotle seemed to be in conflict with Christian teaching, especially on the matter of God. To Aristotle, the cause of all things was the "prime mover", an abstract principle, not the Christian God who personally intervened in human history. Also, Aristotle had thought matter was eternal and that was in conflict with the Christian belief that God had created the world out of nothing. Moreover, while Aristotle had believed in the immortality of Soul, he had not thought the individual soul was immortal.

Aquinas' teacher was Albertus Magnus who was not satisfied with simple translations of Aristotle. The Fourth Crusade of 1204 had made available the original texts and it was from these that he worked. And Albertus totally absorbed

Aristotle's conviction that knowledge must be grounded in experience. That conviction he passed on to his pupil.

Thomas' great work is the <u>Summa Theologica</u>, a summary of theology and, by extension, a summary then of all knowledge. All his life, he was concerned with the basic problem of how to harmonize those things that are part of human learning (Reason) with those things which have been revealed to men by God through the Bible and the Church. How, in other words, does one bring Faith and Reason together without diminishing either one? What he did was to steer a middle path between the two and in doing that he did what the builders of the Gothic cathedral were doing. He was using the materials of human experience, in this case, Reason, and God's revelation as known through Faith to pull together an integrated, organic system of thought.

Thomas makes a sharp distinction between those truths that can be known through philosophy and those which are in the realm of faith. Philosophy is the logical explanation of nature; theology deals with revelation. But because both are aimed at Truth itself, they cannot logically contradict each other. Reason, however, is limited by Man's finite intellect. Thus, one can prove logically the existence of God. And Thomas offers his famous Five Proofs from experience --- and shaped by Aristotle --- to support that position. But Reason can go no further. It cannot prove the Trinity, for instance, nor the Incarnation. These truths come from revelation. The excerpt below summarizes the Five Proofs.

"Whether God Exists"

Objection 1. It seems that God does not exist; because if one of two contraries be infinite, the other would be altogether destroyed. But the name God means that He is infinite goodness. If, therefore, God existed, there would be no evil discoverable; but there is evil in the world. Therefore God does not exist.

Objection 2. Further, it is superfluous to suppose that what can be accounted for by a few principles has been produced by many. But it seems that everything we see in the world can be accounted for by other principles, supposing God did not exist. For all natural things can be reduced to one principle, which is nature; and all voluntary things can be reduced to one principle, which is human reason, or will. Therefore there is no need to suppose God's existence.

On the contrary, It is said in the person of God: I am Who am (Exod. iii. 14).

I answer that, The existence of God can be proved in five ways.

The first and more manifest way is the argument from motion. It is certain, and evident to our senses, that in the world some things are in motion. Now whatever is moved is moved by another, for nothing can be moved except it is in potentiality to that towards which it is moved; whereas a thing moves inasmuch as it is in act. For motion is nothing else than the reduction of something from potentiality to actuality. But nothing can be reduced from potentiality to actuality, except by something in a state of actuality. Thus that which is actually hot, as fire, makes wood, which is potentially hot, to be actually hot, and thereby moves and changes it. Now it is not possible that the same thing should be at once in actuality and potentiality in the same respect but only in different respects. For what is actually hot cannot simultaneously be potentially hot; but it is simultaneously potentially cold. It is therefore impossible that in the same respect and in the same way a thing should be both mover and moved, i.e., that it should move itself. Therefore, whatever is moved must be moved by another. If that by which it is moved be itself moved, then this also must needs be moved by another, and that by another again. But this cannot go on to infinity, because then there would be no first mover, and, consequently, no other mover, seeing that subsequent movers move only inasmuch as they are moved by the first mover; as the staff moves only because it is moved by the hand. Therefore it is necessary to arrive at a first mover, moved by no other; and this everyone understands to be God.

The second way is from the nature of efficient cause. In the world of sensible things we find there is an order of efficient causes. There is no case known (neither is it indeed, possible) in which a thing is found to be the efficient cause of itself; for so it would be prior to itself, which is impossible. Now in efficient causes it is not possible to go on to infinity, because in all efficient causes following in order, the first is the cause of the intermediate cause, and the intermediate is the cause of the ultimate cause, whether the intermediate cause be several, or one only. Now to take away the cause is to take away the effect. Therefore, if there be no first cause among efficient causes, there will be no ultimate, nor any intermediate, cause. But if in efficient causes it is possible to go on to infinity, there will be no first efficient cause, neither will there be an ultimate effect, nor any intermediate efficient causes; all of which is plainly false. Therefore it is necessary to admit a first efficient cause, to which everyone gives the name of God.

The third way is taken from possibility and necessity, and runs thus. We find in nature things that are possible to be and not to be, since they are found to be generated, and to be corrupted, and consequently, it is possible for them to be and not to be. But it is impossible for these always to exist, for that which can not-be at some time is not. Therefore, if everything can not-be, then at one time there was nothing in existence. Now if this were true, even now there would be nothing in existence, because that which does not exist begins to exist only through some thing already existing. Therefore, if at one time nothing was in existence, it would have been impossible for anything to have begun to exist; and thus even now nothing would be in existence--which is absurd. Therefore, not all beings are merely possible, but there must exist something the existence of which is necessary. But every necessary thing either has its necessity caused by another, or not. Now it is impossible to go on to infinity in necessary things which have their necessity caused by another, as has already proved in regard to efficient causes. Therefore we cannot but admit the existence of some being having of itself its own necessity, and not receiving it from another, but rather causing in others their necessity. This all men speak of as God.

The fourth way is taken from the gradation to be found in things. Among beings there are some more and some less good, true, noble, and the like. But more and less are predicated of different things according as they resemble in their different ways something which is the maximum, as a thing is said to be hotter according as it more nearly resembles that which is hottest; so that there is something which is truest, something best, something noblest, and, consequently, something which is most being, for those things that are greatest in truth are greatest in being, as it is written in Metaph. ii. Now the maximum in any genus is the cause of all hot things, as is said in the same book. Therefore there must also be something which is to all beings the cause of their being, goodness, and every other perfection; and this we call God.

The fifth way is taken from the governance of the world. We see that things which lack knowledge, such as natural bodies, act for an end, and this is evident from their acting always, or nearly always, in the same way, so as to obtain the best result. Hence it is plain that they achieve their end, not fortuitously, but designedly. Now whatever lacks knowledge cannot move towards an end, unless it be directed by the archer. Therefore some intelligent being exists by whom all natural things are directed to their end; and this being we call God.

Reply Obj. 1. As Augustine says: Since God is the highest good, He would not allow any evil to exist in His works, unless His omnipotence and goodness were such as to bring good even out of evil. This is part of the infinite goodness of God, that He should allow evil to exist, and out of it produce good.

Reply Obj. 2. Since nature works for a determinate end under the direction of a higher agent, whatever is done by nature must be traced back to God as to its first cause. So likewise whatever is done voluntarily must be traced back to some higher cause other than human reason and will, since these can change and fail; for all things that are changeable and capable of defect must be traced back to an immovable and self-necessary first principle, as has been shown.

"St. Thomas Aquinas: 'Whether God Exists'" in C. Warren Hollister, ed., *Landmarks of the Western Heritage*, 2 vols., 2nd ed. (New York: John Wiley and Sons, Inc., 1973) I, 271-273.

Study Questions

1. Which of the Five Proofs stems from Aristotle's idea of a Prime Mover? (*A Being which is itself uncreated but which brings everything else into existence.*)

2. Summarize the argument from motion.

MEDIEVAL CULTURE

Central to the way in which medieval people thought about themselves and their world was the idea of a Great Chain of Being. God, as Creator of all Being, of course, was at the top of the Chain. Then there were angels, then Man, then animals, then plants, and inanimate being. There were also gradations within each category. There were nine ranks of angels, for instance, and medieval men could clearly see that there was ranking in the animal world. An elephant, for instance, was clearly nobler than a mouse and in the plant world, an oak tree was finer than a thistle. A diamond in the inanimate world ranked above a piece of granite. Just so then, in the category of Man, there were rankings. To have told a medieval person that all men are "equal" would have invited his scorn and pity. Equally loved and saved by God, yes, but the peasant was no more the equal of a duke than a bramble was the equal of a giant redwood. Each person had a niche, a place, given him by God, with specific rights and duties attached to that niche. And when each man fulfilled his roles properly, society was regular, ordered. Often the human body was used as an analogy for the social and political order. The man is healthy when each part of the body performs the office proper to it. But if the hands should try to do the work of the head or the stomach do the work of the feet, then everything is in disarray.

That sense of everything having its proper place is illustrated in the Church's liturgy. The liturgy or the formal prayers, particularly those surrounding the Mass, of the Church had been developed in the fourth century by St. John Chrysostom and was then modified and added to over the centuries. It consisted of two parts --- the Ordinary which remained constant day after day, season after season. This included such things as the Kyrie, the Creed, Offertory, Consecration and Agnus Dei. The second part, the Propers, changed daily and included the introductory prayer or Collect, the Epistle and Gospel, the prayer which preceded the Offertory and the Communion anthem.

Gregorian chant was a fundamental part of the liturgy. Even though it was credited to Pope Gregory I, it was not developed until the eleventh and twelfth centuries. Chanted without instrumental accompaniment, it was monophonic, arhythmic and, while its primary object was to glorify God, it was sublimely pleasing to human ears as well. Gregorian chant accompanied the Mass but it was also part of the celebration of the sacraments. A sacrament is a visible outward sign --- in gestures and words--- that God's special graces have entered the soul. Without these special graces, it was felt, one could not be saved. In 1215, the number of sacraments was put at seven, the most important of which were baptism, confession, communion (the Eucharist), and extreme unction (the sacrament of the dying). One could be cut off from these sacraments by excommunication (literally, to be cut off from communication with the rest of the Christian community). Excommunication happened not for sin, because this could be forgiven in confession, but for things like heresy or deliberate defiance of the Church's law --- things that would cause other people to sin.

The Church touched every aspect of every individual's life from birth to death. But it didn't dominate so much as it infused people's lives. The Church was not just the clergy but the entire community and it was the faith, the aspirations, the habits and attitudes of all kinds of people --- scholars, peasants, nobles, saints and sinners that were reflected through and in the Church. The universality and diversity of the Church is particularly evident in medieval architecture. Until the twelfth century, most building had been done in the Romanesque style. As the name suggests, the Romanesque incorporated several features of Roman architecture --- vaulted ceilings, a rounded arch over the nave, or central part of the church and thick, short walls supporting a domed roof. There were few windows and these were small. Because they were often monastic buildings, the Romanesque style reflected the character of the Benedictine order. As the monastery was removed from the world but drew the world to itself, so the Romanesque building was often church, fortress, dispensary and, above all, school. A profusion of exterior sculpture depicted dragons, gargoyles, animals (both real and mythical), plants, geometric devices, peasants, kings and saints all in a riot of display. The interior of the building with its subdued light conveyed a sense of safety and sublime peace --- a refuge from the world, albeit still in it, as the monastery itself was.

The Gothic style is associated with Suger, Abbot of St. Denis (1122-1157). He was commissioned to reconstruct the old Carolingian abbey church of St. Denis. There was no mere coincidence in the choice of that church. First, it housed the veil of the Virgin which was venerated by pilgrims who brought money to St. Denis. Second, there was also an annual fair called the Lendit which also generated a good bit of wealth. And third, besides its close associations with Charlemagne, St. Denis was also closely linked with the present French monarchy. King Louis VII himself was present at the church's consecration in 1144.

Money and powerful patronage --- whether secular or religious --- was important because the Gothic building required a good deal of both. But it needed more. It needed masons, stone-cutters, roofers, sculptors, stained-glass makers, blacksmiths, carpenters. These, along with the wealth, could only be had in the towns. Thus, the Gothic cathedral, like the university, was an outgrowth of town life and indeed towns often competed with each other to build the tallest, most splendid cathedral.

The cathedral was also central to a town's economy. It was also a court, a marketplace, school and theatre. It took many years to build and would provide employment to generations of craftsmen. It would also attract pilgrims --- and money and trade --- for a long time. A town's decision then to build a cathedral was a prudent long-term financial investment.

Most importantly, the cathedral was a monument to faith --- but not a faith which gave security so much as a self-confident, energetic faith that soared. Abbot Suger was fascinated by light. The light of the sun made all natural life possible. The sun's light to Suger represented Divine Wisdom which makes all spiritual life possible and he wanted to fill his buildings with as much of that as he could. Windows, however, were a structural weakness. He solved this problem by creating very high thin walls supported by buttresses on the outside. With the flying buttresses taking the stress, Suger actually could build his walls as high as he wished and put just as many windows in them as he wished. The stained-glass windows allowed the church to be literally flooded with light and they and the sculpted figures on the facades and altars give one a sense of an extremely vital, lively world in which each carving, each image, each hinge and arch all have their own unique roles to play in glorifying God. The pitched roofs, the pointed arches, the ribbed vault, all draw the eye and the soul heavenward in a perfect harmonious whole.

Light also played a key role in the <u>Divine Comedy</u> of Dante Alighieri, an allegorical journey through Hell, Purgatory and then Heaven. Dante begins his descent into Hell on Good Friday and as he goes farther and farther from God Who is Wisdom and Love, the light grows dimmer and dimmer. The ascent toward God, culminating with the Beatific Vision in Paradise on Easter Sunday is accompanied by increasing brightness. As with Thomas' <u>Summa</u>, and the Gothic cathedral, so too does the <u>Comedy</u> provide a perfect synthesis, a gathering together of the knowledge and experience of this world to point the way and lead to the Divine. As Thomas took Aristotle for his guide, so does Dante use a classical teacher, the Roman poet Virgil, symbolizing human reason, to guide him through Hell and Purgatory. And it is human love, in the person of Beatrice, who leads Dante finally to Divine Love itself.

The other great poet of medieval literature, Geoffrey Chaucer, left us perhaps the best description in any language of his contemporaries. His <u>Canterbury Tales</u>, while it gives us characters who are nobles, millers, clerks, monks, nuns, physicians, parish priests, farmers and housewives are not mere types. They are also fully developed individuals in their own right. These pilgrims wending their way to the shrine of Thomas à Becket at Canterbury are Christian but they are also materialistic, sensual, sometimes hypocritical and even crude.

The <u>Canterbury Tales</u> is part of the lighter side of medieval life. <u>Chansons d'histoire</u> (songs of history) and <u>chansons des geste</u> (songs of deeds), and the songs of troubadours about courtly love delighted the upper classes. One of these was the <u>Roman de la Rose</u>, an elegant poem describing the course of courtly love. Bawdier songs and dances entertained the lower classes. University students sang songs in honor of spring, wine and their girlfriends, many of them in honor of the patron saint of students, the very mythical St. Golias.

All classes rubbed shoulders at the presentation of miracle, morality and mystery plays. Medieval drama developed out of the Church's liturgy. With the colorful vestments, the studied words

Medieval Culture

and gestures, the candles, incense and especially the drama of the Redemption itself at its core, the liturgy was a dramatic ongoing spectacle at all times. Perhaps about the time of Charlemagne, however, the clergy themselves began adding little personal touches of their own to some of the prayers. These little added things were called "tropes" and were usually in the form of a chanted dialogue, not terribly different from early Greek tragedy. And like Greek tragedy, eventually, these dialogues expanded and went out of the main church proper into the vestibule, then into the courtyard and then into the streets. Some of the players would even bring their little dramatic presentations from town to town and there were "hits" such as <u>Everyman</u> which personified Virtue and Vice in a war in which Virtue always triumphs. A mystery play such as <u>The Second Shepherds'</u> Play, dramatizing the announcement of Christ's birth to the shepherds was also popular. The joshing and horseplay rather push the religious elements to the background and illustrate the gradual secularization of themes.

One of the gentler influences on medieval thought and behavior was a greater interest in Mary, the mother of Jesus. The story of the development of devotion to Mary is interesting. Very little is said of her until about the end of the eleventh century. As a result, the status of women suffered. Tertullian's view that women are daughters of Eve and, as the weaker vessel, the cause of sin in the world, prevailed. Women were valued chiefly as part of the marriage bargain by which fiefs were consolidated and legitimate heirs produced. There long had been an element deriving from early Germanic culture, however, that allowed noblewomen especially a fairly wide scope for their talents. Thus, we hear of queens leading armies into battle, of women administering estates in their husband's absence, of women doctors (as well as midwives), and, in the towns, an occasional wife running a business following the death of her husband.

Contact with Islamic culture, both in Spain and in the Near East through the Crusades --- and through trade --- tended to soften the view of women. There was a lively poetic tradition in Islam of idealizing woman, of seeing her as the personification of virtue. The Church picked this up and associated it with the Virgin Mary, and there was a veritable explosion of popular devotion to her all over Europe. Mary "cults" appeared; stories were told of how she appeared to help people, miracles attributed to her became a part of the spiritual milieu of the period. St. Dominic apparently was given the Rosary by Mary herself to help in the fight against Albigensian heretics. It is no coincidence that the Gothic cathedrals themselves were very often named in her honor, Notre Dame. Devotion to Mary radically changed the view of all women. Noblewomen were associated with Mary, or at least with Virtue, and devotion to a pure and beautiful woman then could make the knight himself more virtuous. From being daughters of Eve, then, women were placed on a pedestal, revered for their moral beauty. It was out of this that courtly love came -- a love that was pure, chaste and ennobling.

Mary, as mother, tended to also humanize her son and the view of Jesus also tended to soften. He was still God, still Judge but now also a friend, a fellow-sufferer. The crucifixes of the period tell an interesting story. No longer is the body of Jesus stylized, often wearing the robes of a king with the cross merely as a background. Now it is the naked, suffering, bleeding Jesus truly nailed to a very real cross that appears. This realism, this increasing interest in the humanity of Christ and thus of Man was to be the hallmark of the Renaissance.

Suggested Readings

1. Brooke, C., *The Twelfth Century Renaissance* (London: Thames and Hudson, 1969). A nicely illustrated book.

2. Brooke, R. and C., *Popular Religion in the Middle Ages* (London: Thames and Hudson, 1984). A new and very readable book.

3. Duby, George, *The Age of the Cathedrals. Art and Society, 980-1420* (Chicago: University of Chicago Press, 1981). A good study of the cathedral as an expression of medieval life.

4. Erickson, Carolly, *The Medieval Vision* (New York: Oxford University Press, 1976). A nice, readable study of medieval ideas about the universe, Man and the social order.

Medieval Culture

5. Heer, F., *The Medieval World* (London: Weidenfeld and Nicolson, 1962). A good synthesis by a leading scholar in medieval intellectual history.

6. Herlihy, David., *Medieval Households* (Cambridge, Mass: Harvard University Press, 1985). New and important study of the development of family unity.

7. Keen, Maurice., *Chivalry* (New Haven: Yale University Press, 1984). A new study of the importance of chivalric ideals.

8. Male, Emile, *The Gothic Image* (New York: Harper, 1958). A lively study of medieval art.

9. Power, Eileen., *Medieval Women* (New York: Cambridge University Press, 1975). Nice sketches of several classes of women.

10. Southern, R. W., *Medieval Humanism and Other Studies* (Oxford: B. Blackwell, 1970). Argues that the humanism of the Renaissance had medieval roots.

11. Ward, B., *Miracles and the Medieval Mind* (Philadelphia: University of Pennsylvania Press, 1987). An important scholarly book.

DANTE ALIGHIERI from the DIVINE COMEDY

Dante (1265-1321) was born in Florence, a city torn by two political factions --- the Guelphs and the Ghibellines. The year after Dante's birth into a Guelph family, the Guelphs completely crushed the Ghibellines and stories of that epic struggle no doubt filled Dante's childhood. He was orphaned in his teens and received the normal education for a boy of his class. But he developed an early interest in the vernacular lyric and was encouraged in this by Guido Cavalcanti. He also developed a passion for Greek and Latin literature but this was difficult to pursue. The urbane, complex Latin of a Cicero is far different from the Latin then in use and Dante had no adequate teachers or texts to help him. In his <u>Convivio</u> or <u>Banquet</u>, he tells us how frustrating it was to go doggedly from one work to another, to read of a work and sometimes not even be able to get it, let alone learn how to read it.

In 1292, he wrote <u>La Vita Nuova</u> (<u>The New Life</u>) in Italian. It celebrated one of the most important influences in his life, Beatrice Portinari. In sonnets, prose passages and lyrics, he tells of meeting Beatrice when they were both about the age of nine and love was kindled. At the age of eighteen they met again, greetings were exchanged and he was plunged into grief when, through a misunderstanding, she disapproved of him. She died at the age of twenty-five but at the age of twenty-seven, he saw a vision of her.

In 1301, for political reasons, Dante was driven into exile. The <u>Comedy</u> was written while Dante was in exile. It is the story of an allegorical journey through Hell, Purgatory and Heaven beginning on Good Friday, 1300, and ending on Easter Sunday. Finding Dante in the "dark wood" of error, Beatrice, representing Human Love, intercedes with God who then sends the Roman poet Virgil to guide Dante through Hell and Purgatory. It is Beatrice herself who guides him through Heaven to Divine Love

Medieval Culture

itself. Virgil represents Human Reason and Dante's choice was not at all arbitrary. As we have already seen, Virgil's _Fourth Eclogue_ (see Chapter 4) had appeared to be a prophesy of Christ's coming and the _Aeneid_, especially Book VI which tells of Aeneas' own journey into the underworld, was a special inspiration to Dante.

The _Comedy_ consists of 100 _cantos_. There are 33 _cantos_ for each major section plus the introductory canto in the _Inferno_. The entire poem is written in _terza rima_ (aba, bcb, cdc, etc.) and each of the three realms is subdivided into nine regions. The multiples of three (notice the parallel with the encounters with Beatrice in the _Vita Nuova_) symbolize the Trinity and occur over and over again. As with a Gothic cathedral or Aquinas' _Summa_, Dante starts with the tangible, the earthly to mount step by step to God. It is the things of earth, Beatrice and Virgil, Human Love and Reason which lead Dante to God.

The following extracts are from the _Inferno_. The first describes the vestibule of Hell and the second describes the very pit where Satan stands frozen in a lake of ice.

I AM THE WAY INTO THE CITY OF WOE.
I AM THE WAY TO A FORSAKEN PEOPLE.
I AM THE WAY INTO ETERNAL SORROW.

SACRED JUSTICE MOVED MY ARCHITECT.
I WAS RAISED HERE BY DIVINE OMNIPOTENCE,
PRIMORDIAL LOVE AND ULTIMATE INTELLECT.

ONLY THOSE ELEMENTS TIME CANNOT WEAR
WERE MADE BEFORE ME, AND BEYOND TIME
STAND. ABANDON ALL HOPE YE WHO ENTER HERE.

These mysteries I read cut into stone
above a gate. And turning I said: "Master,
what is the meaning of this harsh inscription?"

And he then as initiate to novice:
"Here must you put by all division of spirit
and gather your soul against all cowardice.

This is the place I told you to expect.
Here you shall pass among the fallen people,
souls who have lost the good of intellect."

So saying, he put forth his hand to me,
and with a gentle and encouraging smile
he led me through the gate of mystery.

Here sighs and cries and wails coiled and recoiled
on the starless air, spilling my soul to tears.
A confusion of tongues and monstrous accents toiled

in pain and anger. Voices hoarse and shrill
and sounds of blows, all intermingled, raised
tumult and pandemonium that still

whirls on the air forever dirty with it
as if a whirlwind sucked at sand.
And I, holding my head in horror, cried: "Sweet Spirit,

what souls are these who run through this black haze?"
And he to me: "These are the nearly soulless
whose lives concluded neither blame nor praise.

They are mixed here with that despicable corps
of angels who were neither for God nor Satan,
but only for themselves. The High Creator

scourged them from Heaven for its perfect beauty,
and Hell will not receive them since the wicked
might feel some glory over them." And I:

"Master, what gnaws at them so hideously
their lamentation stuns the very air?"
"They have no hope of death," he answered me,

"and in their blind and unattaining state
their miserable lives have sunk so low
that they must envy every other fate.

No word of them survives their living season.
Mercy and Justice deny them even a name.
Let us not speak of them: look, and pass on."

* * * * * * *

These wretches never born and never dead
ran naked in a swarm of wasps and hornets
that goaded them the more the more they fled,

and made their faces stream with bloody gouts
of pus and tears that dribbled to their feet
to be swallowed there by loathsome worms and maggots.

Then looking onward I made out a throng
assembled on the beach of a wide river,
whereupon I turned to him: "Master, I long

to know what souls these are, and what strange usage
makes them as eager to cross as they seem to be
in this infected light." At which the Sage:

"All this shall be made known to you when we stand
on the joyless beach of Acheron." And I
cast down my eyes, sensing a reprimand

in what he said, and so walked at his side
in silence and ashamed until we came
through the dead cavern to that sunless tide.

There, steering toward us in an ancient ferry
came an old man with a white bush of hair,
bellowing: "Woe to you depraved souls! Bury

here and forever all hope of Paradise:
I come to lead you to the other shore,
into eternal dark, into fire and ice.

And you who are living yet, I say begone
from these who are dead." But when he saw me stand
against his violence he began again:

"By other windings and by other steerage
shall you cross to that other shore. Not here! Not here!
A lighter craft than mine must give you passage."

And my Guide to him: "Charon, bite back your spleen:
this has been willed where what is willed must be,
and is not yours to ask what it may mean."

The steersman of that marsh of ruined souls,
who wore a wheel of flame around each eye,
stifled the rage that shook his woolly jowls.

But those unmanned and naked spirits there
turned pale with fear and their teeth began to chatter
at sound of his crude bellow. In despair

they blasphemed God, their parents, their time on earth,
the race of Adam, and the day and the hour
and the place and the seed and the womb that gave them birth.

But all together they drew to that grim shore
where all must come who lose the fear of God.
Weeping and cursing they come for evermore,

and demon Charon with eyes like burning coals
herds them in, and with a whistling oar
flails on the stragglers to his wake of souls.

As leaves in autumn loosen and stream down
until the branch stands bare above its tatters
spread on the rustling ground, so one by one

the evil seed of Adam in its Fall
cast themselves, at his signal, from the shore
and streamed away like birds who hear their call.

So they are gone over that shadowy water,
and always before they reach the other shore
a new noise stirs on this, and new throngs gather.

"My son," the courteous Master said to me,
"all who die in the shadow of God's wrath
converge to this from every clime and country.

And all pass over eagerly, for here
Divine Justice transforms and spurs them so
their dread turns wish: they yearn for what they fear.

No soul in Grace comes ever to this crossing;
therefore if Charon rages at your presence
you will understand the reason for his cursing."

* * * * * * *

The Emperor of the Universe of Pain
jutted his upper chest above the ice;
and I am closer in size to the great mountain

the Titans make around the central pit,
than they to his arms. Now, starting from this part,
imagine the whole that corresponds to it!

If he was once as beautiful as now
he is hideous, and still turned on his Maker,
well may he be the source of every woe!

With what a sense of awe I saw his head
towering above me! for it had three faces:
one was in front, and it was fiery red;

the other two, as weirdly wonderful,
merged with it from the middle of each shoulder
to the point where all converged at the top of the skull;

the right was something between white and bile;
the left was about the color that one finds
on those who live along the banks of the Nile.

Under each head two wings rose terribly,
their span proportioned to so gross a bird:
I never saw such sails upon the sea.

They were not feathers--their texture and their form
were like a bat's wings--and he beat them so
that three winds blew from him in one great storm:

it is these winds that freeze all Cocytus.
He wept from his six eyes, and down three chins
the tears ran mixed with bloody froth and pus.

In every mouth he worked a broken sinner
between his rake-like teeth. Thus he kept three
in eternal pain at his eternal dinner.

For the one in front the biting seemed to play
no part at all compared to the ripping: at times
the whole skin of his back was flayed away.

"That soul that suffers most," explained my Guide,"
is Judas Iscariot, he who kicks his legs
on the fiery chin and has his head inside.

Of the other two, who have their heads thrust forward,
the one who dangles down from the black face
is Brutus: note how he writhes without a word.

And there, with the huge and sinewy arms, is the soul
of Cassius.--But the night is coming on
and we must go, for we have seen the whole."

John Ciardi, trans., <u>Dante. The Inferno</u> (New York: Mentor Books, 1954), 42-46, 284-285.

Study Questions

1. From the inscription on the gate of Hell, can you guess what is the worst punishment in Hell?

2. What kind of souls are in the vestibule? Why?

3. Besides the loss of God, what other loss do the damned suffer? Would a brilliant chemist in Hell be able to remember the formula for water? Why not?

Medieval Culture

4. Who is Charon? What does he look like? What is Acheron?

5. How do the souls of the damned behave? Can one end up in Hell by chance? Explain.

6. What does Satan look like? What is he doing? To whom? Identify these three sinners. Satan does not speak to Virgil and Dante. Why can't he?

7. How does the view of Satan and the bottom of Hell differ from the usual view? In Dante's allegory, why can there be neither heat (fire) nor light at the bottom of Hell?

From ROMANCE OF THE ROSE

The *Romance of the Rose* is perhaps the greatest monument to courtly love. It was begun by Guillaume de Lorris about 1237, left incomplete and picked up again by Jean de Meun around 1277. The story is simple. The Lover falls in love with the Lady, she initially encourages him and then is overcome with modesty (shame) and tries to block his advances. Love eventually overcomes her. The jealous husband, suspecting otherwise, however, discovers the affair and brutally punishes his wife. Courtly love was always completely irresistible and secretive because the lady was usually another man's wife. Her chastity and fidelity to the marriage vows would keep any thought of carnality or lust from entering into the relationship. And if the lovers ever were able to marry, the marriage was completely redundant.

In this excerpt, Reason chides the Lover. "Thy heart was carnal," she argues, "purer flame/Burnt not within thee." And the Lover answers thus:

The Lover

Thus Reason spent her words in air,
For Love had ta'en effectual care
That I should nought of profit draw
From all her wise and sober saw,
Though strict attention had I given
To every word, as though from Heaven
Her message came. But Love so held
My heart in bond, that he compelled
Me, as his thrall and liege confessed,
To shape my thought as pleased him best,
Keeping my heart beneath his wing,
While, as with shovel, did he fling

From out my head each sapient word
That I from Reason's mouth had heard
Fall, and e'en fast as in one ear
Words entered, so did they appear
From out the other, insomuch
That nowise did her sermon touch
My spirit but to raise my ire.
Then cried I: "Is it your desire,
Madam, that I should feel despite
'Gainst all my neighbours? Shall I 'quite
The world with hate because the
God Of Love hath laid on me the rod
Of pain and dole? I then should live
In mortal sin that ne'er forgive
Would God; and I should be forsooth
(If I should count your words for truth)
Worse than a heathen. Either hate
Or love must be to me the gate
Of life. I have small lust to try
The former, until finally I find that
Love has thrust me forth,
And proved his promises not worth
One penny. Counsel strict you gave
That I, all hastily, should save
Myself from Love's employ, or be
Accounted mad; but eloquently
Discoursed you of a love beside
The love I'm bound to, which you chide
So sharply. That's a love, meseems,
So pure as men but meet in dreams,
Where all is fair, and nought is wrong.
I humbly beg thee to prolong
Thy wise discourse, and you may deem
Me fool if I give not extreme
Attent thereto, and hear you out,
For you will teach me thus past doubt
The various forms oof love, and show
The loves my spirit fain would know." Reason.

"Good friend, no wiser than a daw
Art thou, who scarce above a straw
Esteem'st my sage discourse; yet fain
Thou seem'st to be that I amain

Should further speak of love. Good will
Have I to tech thee, hoping still,
Though doubtful if'tis worth the while,

    Love doth the soul of man beguile
In many ways, besides that blind,
Tormenting madness of the mind
'Neath which thou sufferest: God permit
That thou mayst free thy heart from it.

    One precious kind of love men know
As friendship, where two spirits grow
Together, and no difference make
(For love of God and virtue's sake)
Of thought, or speech, or worldly good,
But live in a sweetest brotherhood,
With earnest purpose to fulfil
Thereby God's high behest and will.

F. S. Ellis, trans., Guillaume de Lorris and Jean de Meun, *The Romance of the Rose* (London: J. M. Dent and Co., 1900), I, 165-168.

Study Questions

1. *Why can't the Lover profit from Reason's warnings?*

2. *What has the God of Love done to him?*

3. *What is the love "so pure as me but meet in dreams"?*

4. *According to Reason, what are the effects of love? What kind of love does she approve of?*

TROUBADOUR LYRICS

Troubadour poetry flourished in Provence in southern France and was associated with courtly love and the glorification of women

Troubadour's Song

Fair to me is April, bearing
    Winds that o'er me softly blow, -
Nightingales their music airing
    While the stars serenely glow;
        All the birds as they have power,
            While the dews of morning wait,
        Sing of joy in sky or bower,
            Each consorting with his mate.

And as all the world is wearing
    New delight while new leaves grow,
'Twould be vain to try forswearing
    Love which makes my joys o'erflow;
        Both by habit and by dower
            Gladness is my rightful state,
        And when clouds no longer lower
            Quick my heart throws off its weight.

Helen were not worth comparing,
    Gardens no such beauty show;
Teeth of pearl, -the truth declaring,
    Blooming cheeks, a neck of snow,
        Tresses like a golden shower,
            Courtly charms, for baseness, hate, -
        God who made her thus o'ertower
            All the rest, her way make straight!

Kindness may she do me, sparing
    Courtship long and favor slow,
Give a kiss to cheer my daring -
    More, if more I earn, bestow;
        Then the path where pleasures flower
            We shall tread nor slow nor late,
        Ah, such hopes my heart o'erpower
            When her charms I contemplate.

            * * * * * * *

Troubadour's Creed

As treasures buried in the earth
Possess no longer any worth,
I likewise count good sense quite vain
If one conceal it in his brain....
Whoe'er considers life with care
Will always find, -so I declare,
One thing enjoined by wisdom's rod:
To please at once the world and God....

One is not wise, as wise I deem,
Unless he oft can make it seem
That he is pleased with what annoys
And bored by what he most enjoys;
And who this maxim e'er applies, -
I' faith I count him truly wise....

A life of baseness and ill-fame
Destroys the body, soils the name,
And sends the rebel soul to dwell
Forever in the fires of hell...
No man of worth, it seems to me,
Should wish to live except it be
For joy and fame, since only these
Give life a flavor that can please....

James Harvey Robinson, *Readings in European History*, 2 vols. (Needham Heights, Massachusetts: Silver, Burdett, and Ginn, Inc., 1904), I, 435-436.

Medieval Culture

Study Questions

"Troubadour's Song"

1. What season of the year is it? What are the birds doing? What does this activity suggest to the troubadour?

2. What two things does the troubadour not even bother comparing his girl friend to?

3. What does she look like? What does he ask God to do for her?

4. What does he hope she will do for him? Does he want a long courtship or a quick one?

"Troubadour's Creed"

1. What does he think of "treasures buried in the earth" and good sense?

2. What is wisdom?

3. What two things should a man live for?

GEOFFREY CHAUCER from
CANTERBURY TALES

Born into a family of prosperous wine merchants, Chaucer (1340-1400) entered royal service and became a squire to King Edward III. He undertook a number of diplomatic missions for the king, at least two of which brought him to Italy at a time when the writings of Dante, Petrarch and Boccaccio were becoming popular. The latter two were laying the intellectual foundations for the Renaissance but Chaucer would remain very much a medieval man. Chaucer was a highly placed civil servant and thus constantly busy. He was never the leisured "man of letters" who could devote all his time to writing.

He was well read. He knew French fluently and was familiar with the allegories and dream visions popular at the time. He knew Italian literature and was familiar with both classical and ecclesiastical Latin.

His learning, however, pales in comparison with his impressive command of the English language and his incredible skill in observing and drawing character. People who have never heard of the Canterbury Tales know the story of the vain rooster, Chanticleer, and when we think of religious hypocrites it is often a character like Chaucer's pardoner that comes to mind. And the wife of Bath, deaf as a post, gap-toothed, sensuous and outrageously dressed would make a modern feminist look meek. And as children, our idea of medieval knights probably came from Chaucer's gentle, utterly courteous knight.

The frame of the Canterbury Tales is this: thirty pilgrims, including Chaucer, meet at the Tabard Inn at Southwark intending to journey together to visit the shrine of St. Thomas à Becket at Canterbury. They are from all walks of society and they agree that each will tell two stories going to Canterbury and two on the return. The "Prologue" which contains a description of each pilgrim is a remarkable cross-section of medieval people.

Medieval Culture

Yet each pilgrim is more than a mere type. Each emerges as a distinct, varied, completely real individual.

The following is Chaucer's description of the Prioress. Chaucer knew the <u>Romance of the Rose</u> --- he had translated it. We see here what could happen to the ideals of courtesy of the <u>Romance</u> when they crossed the Channel.

Prioress

There also was a Nun, a Prioress,
Who, in her way of smiling very simple and coy.
Her greatest oath was only 'By St Loy!'
And she was known as Madam Eglantyne.
And well she sang the services divine
Intoning through her nose, as was most seemly,
And she spoke daintily in French, extremely,
After the school of Stratford-atte-Bowe;
French in the Paris style she did not know.
At meat her manners were well taught withal;
No morsel from her lips did she let fall,
Nor dipped her fingers in the sauce too deep;
But she could carry a morsel up and keep
The smallest drop from falling on her breast,
For courtliness she had a special zest,
And she would wipe her upper lip so clean
That not a trace of grease was to be seen
Upon the cup when she had drunk; to eat,
She reached a hand sedately for the meat.
She certainly was very entertaining,
Pleasant and friendly in her ways, and straining
To counterfeit a courtly kind of grace,
A stately bearing fitting to her place,
And to seem dignified in all her dealings.
As for her sympathies and tender feelings,
She was so charitably solicitous
She used to weep if she but saw a mouse
Caught in a trap, if it were dead or bleeding.
And she had little dogs she would be feeding
With roasted flesh, or milk, or fine white bread.

And bitterly she wept if one were dead
Or someone took a stick and made it smart;
She was all sentiment and tender heart.
Her veil was gathered in a seemly way,
Her nose was elegant, her eyes glass-grey;
Her mouth was very small, but soft and red,
Her forehead, certainly, was fair of spread,
Almost a span across the brows, I own;
She was indeed by no means undergrown.
Her cloak, I noticed, had a graceful charm.
She wore a coral trinket on her arm,
A set of beads, the gaudies tricked in green,
Whence hung a golden brooch of brightest sheen
On which there first was graven a crowned A,
And lower, *Amor vincit omnia.*

Chaucer: *The Canterbury Tales*, translated by Neville Coghill (Penguin Classics, 1951, 1958, 1960, 1975, 1977), copyright (c) Neville Coghill, 1951, 1958, 1960, 1975, 1977, edited by E. V. Rieu (Baltimore: Penguin Books, 1963), 20-21.

Study Questions

1. *What is the Prioress' name? What does she look like? What is she wearing? What does "Amor vincit omnia" mean?*

2. *How good was her French? Why would she insist on speaking it with an English accent?*

3. *How many lines are given to a description of her table manners? Why do you think so much space is given to that?*

4. *Describe her "moral sense."*

5. *What is "courtliness" to her?*

Medieval Culture

6. *Is she a "good" nun? Explain. Is she a "bad" person?*

7. *Compare "courtesy" here with the courtesy you're accustomed to.*

CUCKOO'S SONG

Happily, we possess the melody for this gay little song. The spontaneous, buoyant joy of the peasant at the first signs of spring is infectious.

Sumer is icumen[1] in:
   Lhude[2] sing cuccu!
Groweth sed[3], and bloweth med[4],
   And springeth the wude nu[5].
      Sing cuccu!

Awe[6] bleteth after lomb;
   Lhouth after calve cu[7];
Bulluc sterteth[8], bucke verteth[9],
   Murie sing cuccu!

Cuccu, cuccu, well[10] singes thu, cuccu:
   Ne swike[11] thu naver nu.
Sing cuccu, nu, sing cuccu!
   Sing cucu, sing cuuc, nu!

[1] A-coming

[2] Loud

[3] Seed

[4] Blossemeth meadow

[5] Now

[6] Ewe

[7] Cow

[8] Springs up

[9] Breaks wind

[10] Pleasingly

[11] Cease

Grebanier, Bernard, Middlebrook, Samuel, Thompson, Stith, and Watt, William, eds., *English Literature and Its Backgrounds* Shorter edition (New York: Dryden Press, 1950), 65.

Study Question

1. List the signs of spring the peasant sings of here. It is sometimes said that a real love of Nature did not happen in Western Europe until the Renaissance. Does this little song confirm that idea?

DIES IRAE (DAY OF WRATH)

The Church's liturgy occasionally includes a "Sequence" between the Epistle and the Gospel. This "Sequence" is taken from the "Mass for the Dead."

Sequence

That day of wrath, that dreadful day,
Shall heaven and earth in ashes lay,
As David[1] and the Sybil[2] say.

What horror must invade the mind
When the approaching Judge shall find
And sift the deeds of all mankind!

The mighty trumpet's wondrous tone
Shall rend each tomb's sepulchral stone
And summon all before the Throne.

Now death and nature with surprise
Behold the trembling sinners rise
To meet the Judge's searching eyes.

Then shall with universal dread
The Book of Consciences be read
To judge the lives of all the dead.

For now before the Judge severe
All hidden things must plain appear;
No crime can pass unpunished here.

---

[1] King David of ancient Israel.
[2] In Roman mythology, the Sibyls were able to see into the future.

O what shall I, so guilty, plead?
And who for me will intercede?
When even Saints shall comfort need?

O King of dreadful majesty!
Grace and mercy You grant free;
As Fount of Kindness, save thou me!

Recall, dear Jesus, for my sake
You did our suffering nature take,
Then do not now my soul forsake!

In weariness You sought for me,
And suffering upon the tree!
Let not in vain such labor be.

O Judge of justice, hear, I pray,
For pity take my sins away
Before the dreadful reckoning day.

Your gracious face, O Lord, I seek;
Deep shame and grief are on my cheek;
In sighs and tears my sorrows speak.

You Who did Mary's guilt unbind,
And mercy for the robber[3] find,
Have filled with hope my anxious mind.

How worthless are my prayers, I know,
Yet, Lord, forbid that I should go
Into the fires of endless woe.

Divorced from the accursed band,
O make me with Your sheep to stand,
A child of grace, at Your right Hand.

When the doomed no more can flee
From the flames of misery
With the chosen call me.

---

[3] Jesus forgave the good thief who was crucified with Him when he asked to be remembered in Christ's kingdom.

Before You, humbled, Lord, I lie,
My heart like ashes, crushed and dry,
Assist me when I die.

Full of tears and full of dread
Is that day that wakes the dead,
Calling all, with solemn blast
To be judged for all their past.

Lord, have mercy, Jesus blest,
Grant them all Your Light and Rest. Amen.

Reverend Hugo H. Hoever, S. O. Cist., ed., *Saint Joseph Daily Missal* (New York: Catholic Book Publishing Co., 1957), 1243-1245.

Study Questions

1. *What is the view of God and his judgment in the first seven stanzas?*

2. *What feeling is expressed thereafter? What is the sinner's only hope?*

3. *What are the two or three strongest sentiments expressed? Describe the overall perception of God expressed here.*

4. *Compare this with the prayer of St. Francis; with St. Jerome's vision; with the opening prayer of the Quran.*

MIRACLES OF THE VIRGIN

Mary "cults" appeared in the later Middle Ages. Stories were told of how she appeared to people and miracles attributed to her became a part of the spiritual milieu of the period. Knights would fight for her, devotions of all kinds developed and St. Dominic claimed to have been given the Rosary by Mary herself to help in the fight against Albigensian heretics. The stories below are about a woman who is not only the Queen of Heaven but the Mother of sinners as well.

I

A certain woman of simple and upright life used to worship the Holy Mary, Mother of God, often strewing flowers and herbs before her image.

Now it chanced that the woman's only son was taken prisoner. And the mother weeping for him would not be comforted, and prayed with all her heart to the Blessed Virgin Mary for her son's deliverance. But seeing it was all in vain, she entered the church and thus addressed the image of the Blessed Virgin, "O Blessed Virgin Mary, often have I asked thee for the deliverance of my son and thou hast not heard me. Therefore, as my son was taken from me, so will I take away thine and will put him in durance as hostage for mine."

And taking the image of the Child from the bosom of Mary, she went home, wrapped him up in a clean cloth, and shut him up carefully in a chest. And, behold, the following night the Blessed Mary appeared to the captive youth bidding him to go forth and said to him: "Tell your mother to give me my Son." And he coming to his mother, described how he had been set free. But she with great rejoicing carried back the image of Jesus to Mary and gave her thanks.

II

In a certain convent of nuns many years ago there lived a virgin named Beatrice under vow of chastity. Devout in soul and a zealous servant of the Mother of God, she counted it her greatest joy to offer up her prayers to her in secret and, when she was made custodian, her devotion increased with her greater freedom. A certain cleric, seeing and desiring her, began to use enticements. When she scorned his wanton talk, he became so much the more eager, and the old serpent hotly tempted her, so that her heart could no longer endure the fires of passion, but going to the altar of the Blessed Virgin Mary, who was the patron saint there, she said: "Lady, I have served thee as faithfully as I could; behold I resign to thee thy keys. I can no longer withstand the temptations of the flesh." Placing the keys on the altar she went in secret after the cleric, and he, after dishonouring her, within a few days deserted her. And she having no means of living and being shamed to return to the cloister, became a harlot.

Having lived publicly for many years in this wickedness, one day she came in her secular dress to the gate of the convent, and said to the gatekeeper: "Do you know one Beatrice, formerly the custodian of this convent?" And he replied: "Yes, she is a very worthy lady, holy and without reproach from her childhood, who has lived in this convent to this day."

She, hearing these words, but not weighing their meaning, was about to go away, when the Mother of Mercy appeared to her in the form of a woman and said: "For fifteen years I have filled your office in your absence. Return now to your home and do penance, for no one knows of your departure." The Mother of God had actually in her shape and dress taken her place as guardian. At once she returned, and as long as she lived gave thanks to the Virgin Mary, and in confession made known to her confessor all that had happened to her.

III

A certain man lived carnally with another woman, his wife being aware of it. She finding it hard to endure this, made complaint in the church of St. Mary, praying to be avenged on her who had taken away her husband. St. Mary, appearing to her, said, "How can I bring harm upon her, for each day she bends her knee a hundred times to me?" But the woman in much vexation said: "Why will you not avenge me? I will make my complaint to your Son."

She went out of the church muttering those words. But the adulteress met her, and when she inquired what she was saying, the other replied: "I was complaining about you to the Virgin Mary, and she replied that she would do you no harm because every day you made a hundred genuflexions to her, and it is for that I am murmuring. But I hope that her Son will avenge me." Hearing that, the adulteress at once threw herself at her feet begging her pardon and faithfully promising never again to commit sin with her husband.

James Bruce Ross and Mary Martin McLaughlin, *The Portable Medieval Reader*, (New York: Viking Press, 1949), 527-529.

Study Questions

1. What kind of women are involved in all three stories?

2. How does Mary treat Beatrice's sin of adultery? Why is she so lenient?

3. The woman in the first story is, to say the least, a little presumptuous. How does Mary treat that? Why?